WORDSWO
OF WORLD

General Editor

CHEKHOV: PLAYS

Anton Chekhov

Plays

❖

Translated, with an introductory essay,
by Elisaveta Fen

with an introduction by
A. D. P. Briggs

WORDSWORTH CLASSICS
OF WORLD LITERATURE

In loving memory of
MICHAEL TRAYLER
the founder of Wordsworth Editions

I

For customers interested in other titles from
Wordsworth Editions visit out website at
www.wordsworth-editions.com

For our latest list and a full mail order service contact
Bibliophile Books, 5 Thomas Road, London E14 7BN
Tel: +44 0207 515 9222
Fax: +44 0207 538 4115
e-mail: orders@bibliophilebooks.com

This edition published 2007 by Wordsworth Editions Limited
8B East Street, Ware, Hertfordshire SG12 9HJ

ISBN 978 1 84022 617 1

Typeset in Great Britain by Chrissie Madden
Printed and bound by Clays Ltd, St Ives plc

CONTENTS

We Abide together
Reply, moving, philosophical

INTRODUCTION

The atmosphere of Chekhov's plays is laden with gloom, but it is a darkness of the last hour before the dawn begins.

MAURICE BARING

Chekhov at home and abroad

There is a significant difference between the reputation enjoyed by Anton Chekhov in his homeland and the way we see him in the west. Look him up in an English biographical dictionary and you will find him described as a 'Russian dramatist and short-story writer'.[1] The same description can be seen in a Companion to English Literature, a Reference Guide to Russian Literature,[2] and elsewhere. But that phrase would be unlikely to appear in Russia, where they define him less specifically as a 'great writer', and if you pressed them they would undoubtedly claim that his highest achievement was not in drama but in fiction.[3] As a leading Chekhov specialist puts it, 'In the West Chekhov's reputation as the founder of modern drama is unassailable . . . But in Russia it is almost universally agreed that his achievement in the short-story is still greater.'[4] So, when concentrating on the plays, we ought not to forget the other side of this man's literary activity, prose fiction. In fact, those four hundred stories – Chekhov never wrote a novel – may be indispensable. The same critic goes on to inform us that, 'The key to understanding his plays has always been his stories.' What could he mean by that?

1 *Chambers Biographical Dictionary*, Harrap, Edinburgh, 1997, 383.
2 *Oxford Companion to English Literature*, London, 1985, 189. *Reference Guide to Russian Literature*, Fitzroy Dearborn, London 1998, 213.
3 An English edition of Chekhov's *The Island: a Journey to Sakhalin*, Century, London, 1987 describes the author first as a 'celebrated playwright' and then as an 'acclaimed writer'; the first reference was written by an English editor, the second by a native Russian, Irina Ratushinskaya.
4 Donald Rayfield, *The Chekhov Omnibus: Selected Stories*, Everyman, Dent, London, 1994, xvii.

Chekhov began as a writer of humorous sketches, stories and jokes, some of which were published, under various pseudonyms such as 'Doctor with no Patients'. His first collections, *Motley Tales* (1886) and *In the Twilight* (1887), sold rather well, and encouraged him in his aspirations to become a professional writer. He was noticed, and taken up by people that mattered in publishing. As he rose to the beginnings of fame he began to write fewer stories, but the ones he did write were longer and their artistic quality gradually improved. At the same time he became attracted to the stage, and wrote his first plays, once again feeling his way from short pieces through to full-length dramas. But it would be wrong to think of Chekhov's career as consisting of two distinct stages. It is true that his best stories were written between 1888 (*The Steppe*) and 1899 (*The Lady with the Lapdog*), whereas his four mature dramas belong to the period from 1896 (*The Seagull*) to 1904 (*The Cherry Orchard*). Nevertheless, the two professions, of story-writer and playwright, ran in double-harness for many years. His play *Ivanov* was written as early as 1887 (when he was 27), and the negligible *Platonov* was completed several years before that; conversely, he was still writing stories as late as 1902–3. Thus the stories and the plays are chronologically interwoven more closely than is sometimes remembered.

Two story-tellers

There is more to it than that. As far as this writer is concerned the two genres are also intimately connected in themes, attitudes, atmosphere and artistic method. To begin with the latter, both the stories and the plays of Chekhov break new ground, and in similar ways. This can be illustrated first of all by comparing his stories with those of his French contemporary, Guy de Maupassant (1850–93). The Frenchman wrote no-nonsense tales with a strong story-line that often included sensational events and a sting-in-the-tail ending. For instance, in *The Necklace* a woman who has lost a borrowed necklace replaces it by taking out a huge loan, only to discover at the end of her life that the original was a paste imitation. Chekhov's stories depend less on plot and incident, being stronger in the depiction of character and the evocation of atmosphere.

Two stories written by the two writers at the same time on the same subject illustrate the difference. Chekhov's *The Dowry* (or, more properly, *The Trousseau*) (*Pridanoye*) (1883) and Maupassant's *The Dowry* (*La Dot*) (1884) form an interesting comparison. In the Russian story the narrator comes across a weird family with a pathetically unmarriageable young girl being helped by her mother to build up a trousseau for a wedding that is clearly never going to happen; sure enough, she dies without ever calling on it. Nothing actually happens in the story, but the reader will be fascinated by sheer atmosphere and portraiture, and left with an abiding impression of pathos as unrealistic expectations crumble until the grave closes them over. At the same time the story, and every scene in it, conveys a sense of the ridiculous; at the end you are not sure whether what you have been reading should be described as comic or tragic. All in all, something painful yet sadly amusing has been said about the unfairness and unhappiness of human existence. This is Chekhov's intention, method and hallmark.

Faced with a similar subject, Maupassant treats it quite differently. His heroine, using her substantial dowry to catch a promising husband, enjoys conjugal pleasures with him for a few days until, on their honeymoon, the groom suddenly abandons her on a bus and makes off with the dowry in cash. This tale of the unexpected is eventful, even sensational, full of entertainment and mordant humour.[5] Thus Maupassant follows the traditional rules of storytelling, and they serve him well. He also has what a French critic has described as the three great qualities of a French writer: clarity, more clarity and yet more clarity. A born raconteur, he delivers his anecdote at a fast pace, lucidly defining the characters, keeping the interest going, and providing enjoyable suspense and rich entertainment, all of which culminates in a satisfying (for us) *coup de théâtre*. Maupassant stands at the head of a line that will lead through Saki, Jack London and Somerset Maugham to Roald Dahl. Chekhov, by contrast, anticipates poetic or less determinate writers such as Katherine Mansfield, Kafka, Nabokov and Beckett, though his gentle pessimism contains only a hint of the bleakness and angst of the twentieth century. (These remarks are not meant

5 For a full discussion of these two stories see A. D. P. Briggs, 'Two Different Dowries: Chekhov's *Pridanoye* and Maupassant's *La Dot*', *Scottish Slavonic Revue*, 3, Autumn 1984, 65–77.

to be judgemental; we need all of these excellent writers to cater for different moods and occasions).

Another way of looking at this would be to say that, in the realm of painting, the two writers seem to exchange nationalities: Maupassant resembles the Russian narrative-realist Repin, whereas Chekhov's outlines create blurred impressions like those of Monet. There is even an analogy with modern scientific thinking, which has ranged reductionist scientific materialism against a belief in fuzzy thinking and chaos theory. Chekhov, of course, is on the fuzzy and chaotic side. A large proportion of his stories, including the longer, more mature pieces, are as indecisive as *The Trousseau*. Even a famous story like *The Lady with a Lapdog*, which has relatively strong narrative interest, concludes with deliberate open-endedness. Two devoted but separated lovers, unhappy with their married partners, know they cannot live without each other. But how can their situation be resolved? Maupassant would have known one way or the other, and the outcome, positive or negative, would have made a good yarn with a satisfying ending. Chekhov makes no move in this direction. Nothing is settled by the concluding words of his story: ' . . . they both knew only too well that the end was a long way off, and they were only at the start of the really complicated and difficult part.' As always, this author's interest is in people rather than events, in situations rather than resolutions, and in suggestions rather than analysis. Beyond that, the lasting impression is one of deep sympathy on the author's part for ordinary people who find happiness so elusive.

Chekhov the dramatist

As with the stories, so with the plays of Anton Chekhov. They too broke the rules of the day, and betrayed expectations. They too rely more on atmosphere, character and nuances of psychology than on incident and sensation. They too deliver no visceral thrills, but instead depict plain people living poor-quality lives, dogged by frustration and disappointment as they watch time and opportunity slipping away. Most important of all, they give no hint as to whether we should weep or laugh at the pathetically inadequate personalities, behaviour and conversations of the people on stage. As in *The Trousseau*, you have to abandon any idea of categorisation into comedy or tragedy. Consider, for instance, the opening words of *The Seagull* (1896). Chekhov's dialogue is so unexceptional (because its everyday language is so unliterary) that his lines cannot be described as memorable or quotable, but these words have become famous. Asked why she always goes about dressed in black, Masha replies, 'I'm in mourning for my life.' This is a strange way for any play to begin, especially one that describes itself as a 'comedy'. What can she mean?

Our first reaction is likely to be one of humour constrained by nervous uncertainty. Surely she must be making some kind of a joke. But perhaps not; maybe she is suicidally unhappy. How are we to tell? The play could go either way. And indeed, a director will have to decide in advance on a particular tone, playing down the humour and bringing out the pessimism, or vice versa, because he will not get decisive clues from the author. He can go a long way in either direction. There is a lot of humour in Chekhov; his literary career began with comedy, and he always insisted that his plays should not be enacted in a spirit of exaggerated melancholy, let alone tragedy. (This was the source of many an argument between him and Stanislavsky, the director of the Moscow Art Theatre.) On the other hand, all things considered, there does seem to be much ineradicable sadness in these plays. They may lack the cruelty and agony that can purge us of our poisons through catharsis, but when you have watched a Chekhov play, or if you know them well enough to look back on all four of the masterpieces, you are not likely to feel a lift of the spirit from recollecting the experience. Prince Dimitry Mirsky, the doyen of Russian literary criticism, sums up the dark side of this writer. While admitting that Chekhov's place as a classic is unchallenged — who is accepted as 'one of the ten best' — he goes on to assert that 'Even more consistently than in his stories, the dominant note of Chekhov's plays is one of gloom, depression and hopelessness.'[6]

A fuller discussion of Chekhov's life and art is contained in the accompanying introduction written by Elisaveta Fen at the time of her translations, which, incidentally, were used in several TV presentations of Chekhov, have survived the passing of the years and retain great value in terms of their accuracy and well-judged English.

6 D. S. Mirsky, *A History of Russian Literature*, New York, 1960, 364–7.

Chekhov's place in the Russian theatre

Chekhov the dramatist has had no successful imitators, so in placing him in the Russian theatre we have to look back at his predecessors. At first, it seems that there isn't much to look at, since great credit is given to Chekhov as an innovator. A publisher speaks for many when he writes as follows on the cover of a recent re-translation of Chekhov's plays: 'As a playwright he was subversive, even revolutionary, breaking away from the prevailing fashions of contemporary theatre to create an exhilarating new form of drama.'[7]

Three Russian dramatists are sometimes mentioned as important predecessors, Gogol, Ostrovsky and Turgenev. Of these the first is remote from Chekhov in years, ideas and form, and although the second is more important in this context, he hardly counts as a profoundly important influence. Ivan Turgenev does, however, and here we run into an unusual problem. On the face of it, Chekhov never read Turgenev's plays until it was too late for him to have absorbed any influence from them. Two American specialists, editing Chekhov's correspondence, claim that three of his letters 'demonstrate beyond any doubt that he simply did not know Turgenev as a dramatist until [the end of March 1903].'[8] By that time four years had passed since the first performance of *Uncle Vanya*, which is the play most directly related to Turgenev, and seven since the probable date of its completion.

This is odd, because Turgenev's play *A Month in the Country* is strikingly similar to Chekhov's main four plays, in method, atmosphere and ideas. The correspondences are so obvious that they have often been noticed (though never fully explored). A London theatre critic put it this way: 'A playgoer coming blind to *A Month in the Country* might think that he'd chanced on a piece by some highly gifted disciple of Chekhov . . . the setting, the atmosphere and personnel are distinctly Chekhovian . . . Even the way the drama is structured.'[9] Another complains that Chekhov's

---

7 Anton Chekhov, *Plays*, Penguin Classics, 2002, rear cover.
8 M. H. Heim (in collaboration with Simon Karlinsky), *Letters of Anton Chekhov*, London, 1973, 449.
9 Paul Taylor, writing in *The Independent,* 31 March 1994, 27.

disavowal of Turgenev is a 'perverse, unfilial judgement', which he finds distasteful since *A Month in the Country* 'has pre-echoes galore of the plays Chekhov was going to write . . . The tone is proto-Chekhovian too.'[10]

Academic critics fall into two categories: those who disclaim any influence at all (despite clear evidence), and those who take some kind of influence for granted, but without spelling it out.

Perhaps the strongest evidence of a connection between these two plays can be seen in the complex arrangement of characters and their relationships. In both of them the system is as follows. One of the central figures is an attractive and intelligent young woman in her late twenties (Turgenev's Natalya, 29, and Chekhov's Yelena, 27), married to an older man who is more preoccupied with his work than with his wife. (In both plays this man is attended by a doting dowager (Islayev's mother, Serebryakov's mother-in-law), who thinks he can do no wrong.) Each woman has a devoted admirer (Rakitin and Vanya, both of them maladjusted, unsuccessful bachelors, in love with another man's wife) whom she does not love, but whose attentions are welcome if only because of the husband's neglect. She falls in love with a third man (Belyayev, Astrov), but this innocent breaker of hearts is loved in turn from another quarter, by a young girl on brink of womanhood (Vera, Sonya) who is held in a particular bond by the first woman. The older and younger women become, in effect, rivals in love. For this to be plausible it is better for them not to be mother and daughter since that would involve too large an age-gap; thus it is arranged that Vera should be the ward of Natalya, and Sonya the step-daughter of Yelena. In both cases the age-gap is about the same, ten or a dozen years, so that all four women are well within the bounds of possible sexual attractiveness. From these relationships flow all the erotic interest of the two plays.

Are not these similarities too many and too close to be coincidental? In both *A Month in the Country* and *Uncle Vanya* no fewer than six of the characters (five of them central ones) build a complex series of relationships never seen before or since on stage. The correspondences are close, they ramify with intriguing

10 Benedict Nightingale, *The Times*, 31 March 1994.

symmetry and they are not traditional ones. On the contrary, there is not a clichéd personality or relationship in sight.

And if this is not enough, consider what happens in the middle of each play, in most of Act Three in *A Month in the Country* (which has five acts) and the overlap between Acts Two and Three in *Uncle Vanya,* (which has four). Here the experienced older woman takes charge of gathering events by seizing the initiative in two different interviews, one with the younger ingénue and a second with the man that this girl loves. Establishing that the girl is truly in love, she undertakes to discover whether there is any hope of reciprocation. In the event she ruins any outside possibility for the youngster by insensitive handling of the second interview and an irrepressible urge to press her own case rather than that of the protégée for whom she is responsible. Although clearly swept along by passion, each of the elder women is fully aware of what she is doing. Both playwrights give the older heroine a long soliloquy (itself an unusual device in modern theatre) in which she has time to contemplate the implications of all that is happening – and yet she still goes on.

There is much else in these two plays that suggests a degree of borrowing on Chekhov's part – the country-house setting, the atmosphere of the place, the weather, the arrivals and departures, the emphasis on the characters' ages and inactivity, and the passage of time, a scene of intrusion when people are caught kissing, and so on, right down to interpolated songs, very similar stage directions and the use of pauses and silences.[11] The whole range of what we consider typical of Chekhov's theatre, in subject-matter, character, events, mood and manner, seems to have been anticipated by Ivan Turgenev. Incidentally, it is no wonder that *A Month in the Country* was misunderstood in 1850. He had stumbled across what we now know as 'psychological drama', in which mood and thought speak louder than action, and the public was nowhere near ready for it. Even half a century later, when Chekhov adopted the same style, he too had the greatest difficulty in persuading audiences and critics that this was valid and meaningful theatre.

11 For a full discussion of this question, with further examples, see A. D. P. Briggs, 'Two Months in the Country: Chekhov's Unacknowledged Debt to Turgenev,' *New Zealand Slavonic Journal*, 1994, 17–32.

No-one would accuse Chekhov of plagiarism, though he is certainly being disingenuous when he claims not to have read *A Month in the Country* before 1903. We have no idea of the extent to which he did borrow from Turgenev, perhaps even subconsciously, and there is no evidence to suggest deliberate copying. In any case the plays have ended up noticeably different. In *Uncle Vanya* Chekhov has added Serebryakov, and all the action that derives from him; he also explores several different themes, whereas Turgenev is interested only on love and its effect on people's lives. The former writer is also much more openly humorous. But it does seem important to set the historical record straight, and this will involve a degree of diminution for Chekhov, who turns out not to have been quite so revolutionary as has often been claimed.

A world reputation

Nevertheless, Chekhov has deservedly triumphed on the world stage, and especially in England, where he has become accepted almost as part of our own culture. He is scarcely ever off the professional stage. His ambiguity has become increasingly relevant and interesting as the universe itself has been revealed as puzzlingly ambiguous. His apparent indecisiveness is now seen as deliberate depiction of how things are. The ordinariness of his characters and their speech have made this dramatist a favourite even on the amateur boards; to put him on, you do not need virtuoso thespians with sonorous voices and generous gestures, but sensible citizens who can speak well. Chekhov's plays also offer a good spread of roles roughly equal in importance, for everyone to have a go.

In his curious mixture of the tragic and the comic, Chekhov has resolved the conflict arising in the twentieth century between existentialist agony on the one hand and reckless hedonism on the other. His plays certainly remind us that living a human life is a difficult business for everyone, not just for the downtrodden and underprivileged, but they are delicately poised between the positive and the negative in their overall implications. For every Prince Mirsky, who reads into them nothing but gloom, depression and hopelessness, there is a Maurice Baring (see epigraph), who can see the light of a new dawn breaking through

Chekhov's clouds of darkness. And even Mirsky himself, while noting Chekhov's limitations and disliking his gloominess, was forced to admit that, 'The Cherry Orchard has been described as the best play since Shakespeare, and Three Sisters as the best play in the world.' [12]

A. D. P. BRIGGS
Senior Research Fellow, University of Bristol
Professor Emeritus, University of Birmingham

---

12 Mirsky, op. cit., 364.

TRANSLATOR'S INTRODUCTORY ESSAY

An ordinary story

Just as Chekhov's plays appear to be quietly undramatic on first reading, so does the story of his life impress one at first as a very ordinary story. The background from which the writer's personality emerges on to the stage of life is drab, almost sordid. He was born into the family of a small shopkeeper, in a small provincial town about which in later years he could only say that it was 'dirty and dull, with deserted streets and a lazy, ignorant population'. The name of the town was Taganrog, and it was situated on the Azov Sea, near the borders of Northern Caucasus.

Anton was the third child of Pavel and Yevgeniya Chekhov, and had two elder brothers, Alexander and Nikolay. He was baptised on 27 January, 1860, ten days after he was born. Later, a sister and two more brothers followed. The Chekhovs must have found it difficult to make both ends meet, with the family of six children and the father's preference for the arts, which made him neglect his business. Pavel Chekhov had undoubted artistic gifts: he taught himself to play the violin and became quite a competent painter of holy images. Unfortunately, the artistic propensities of the father became his children's scourge, and not only because by neglecting his business he subjected them to perhaps unnecessary physical privations. His passion for religious music prompted him to train his sons to sing in church before they were old enough to go to school (which in Russia was not usually started before the age of 8 or 9). The Chekhov children had to get up before dawn and trail to church in all weathers. 'As my brothers and I sang a trio in church, people gazed at us admiringly and appeared to envy our parents, but we children felt like small convicts doing a term of hard labour,' wrote Anton in 1892.

Their upbringing was harsh. In later life Chekhov wrote with bitterness: 'I could never forgive my father for having whipped me when I was quite small.' Scenes of churlish behaviour on Pavel Chekhov's part towards his wife left another painful and bitter memory to which Anton refers in his letter to his brother Alexander in 1889. 'I want you to remember that despotism and lies destroyed your mother's youth. Despotism and lies so spoiled our childhood, that it frightens and sickens me to think of it even now. Remember the horror and disgust we used to feel when Father, at dinner time, would make a row and call Mother a fool because the soup happened to be too salt for his taste . . . Despotism is thrice criminal.'

From such early impressions might have arisen the intense loathing of the petty-bourgeois domestic routine which inspires the subject-matter of many of Chekhov's short stories, and is often expressed by characters in his plays. 'People here,' says Andrey Prozorov in *Three Sisters*, 'do nothing but eat, drink, and sleep . . . and just to introduce a bit of variety into their lives, so as to avoid getting completely stupid with boredom, they indulge in their disgusting gossip, and vodka, and gambling, and in law-suits. The wives deceive their husbands, and the husbands lie to their wives, and pretend they don't see anything or hear anything. And all this overwhelming vulgarity and pettiness crushes the children and puts out any spark they might have in them, so that they, too, become miserable, half-dead creatures, just like one another and just like their parents.'

Whatever effects Chekhov's early upbringing may have had on his character, it certainly did not crush him or put out the 'spark' he had in him. All his biographers speak of his cheerfulness and vitality, his enormous capacity for work, his wide human sympathies, and the love of practical jokes which distinguished him in early youth as well as in maturer years. Already as a boy he showed the courage and the sense of humour which did not leave him even on his deathbed. One of the few pleasures attainable for the Chekhov children was a yearly summer trip to a large estate where their paternal grandfather was a bailiff. This old 'protagonist of serfdom', as Chekhov described him in a letter to his wife, was himself a former serf and quite a remarkable character. Some years before the emancipation of peasant-serfs in 1861, Yegor Chekhov bought from his owner, Chertkov, his own freedom, as well as the freedom of his sons, one of whom was Anton's father. The fact that he was able to pay his landlord a sum of three and a half thousand roubles, which he must have saved while still a serf, indicates that he was a man of unusual ability and perseverance. Most likely, he had been even then working as a bailiff and was valued as such. This position of authority over his own kind could be achieved and retained in those days only at the cost of a certain harshness of character, which is implied in Chekhov's phrase describing him.

The Chekhov children had the run of the estate when they stayed with their grandfather, and loved it; the only thing they were strictly forbidden to do was to pick fruit from the landlord's orchards. No doubt a sound thrashing would have been the punishment if they had dared to disobey. Yet Chekhov's younger brother, Ivan, tells of an occasion when Anton made a bet with him that he would pick an apple before the very eyes of his redoubtable Grandpa. He told Ivan to place himself under an apple tree, then took a flying leap over his back and picked an apple in mid-air with his grandfather looking on. The old man, disarmed by his grandson's resourcefulness, merely laughed and sucked away at his pipe.

Whatever the drawbacks of provincial existence under the Tsarist regime in the latter half of the nineteenth century, schooling was not expensive, and Pavel Chekhov, despite his straitened circumstances, was able to send all his sons to a secondary school. Anton was a hard-working scholar, but conditions at home were not favourable to study, and he had to spend two extra years at the 'Gymnasia', because he failed to work up to standard in his second and fifth years at school. At the age of 14, simultaneously with his school studies, Anton was learning tailoring, but this experiment was not very successful and lasted only a year. When Anton was 16, his father went bankrupt and had to leave Taganrog secretly, taking his wife and young children with him. His two elder sons were already in Moscow, Alexander studying at the University, and Nikolay at the Arts' School. The family joined them there, leaving Anton to finish his schooling at Taganrog.

Significantly enough, this period during which Anton was left more or less to fend for himself and partly earn his living by coaching younger schoolboys proved to be his 'blossoming-out' period. His school work improved rapidly and he also became the editor of the school magazine, called *The Stutterer*, to which he contributed humorous sketches, and which met with the approval of his brother Alexander, then a budding journalist. *The Stutterer* was evidently a successor of an earlier school magazine in which Anton had taken part at the age of 13.

How rapidly his character was developing and his ideals of conduct were being formed appears from his letter to his younger brother, Mikhail, written when Anton was 16. He reproached Mikhail for signing himself as 'your insignificant small brother', 'I don't like this description of yourself. You can profess your insignificance before God, Beauty, Nature, but before men you must assert your human dignity. I assume you are an honest man, not a scoundrel. Well then, respect the honest man in yourself and remember that no honest man can be called "insignificant".'

An ideal of character

Ten years later, in a letter to his brother Nikolay, this ideal of conduct is developed into something like a code of behaviour worthy of a 'well brought-up' man.

> Your trouble is that you were very badly brought-up. People who are well brought-up usually keep to the following rules of conduct. They have respect for Man, and for that reason are always tolerant, gentle, courteous and cooperative. They never make trouble about trifles . . . They feel compassion not only for beggars or cats . . . They respect other people's property, and so pay their debts . . . They do not pose, but behave in public just as they do at home, and they do not show off before their inferiors. They are not garrulous and do not inflict their confidences on people who have not asked for them . . . They do not humble themselves in order to arouse sympathy . . . They cultivate their aesthetic taste. They strive as far as possible to restrain and ennoble the sexual instinct . . .
>
> What one needs is constant work, day and night, incessant reading, study and exercise of will. Every hour is precious . . .

This was not mere gratuitous preaching, but a living creed in accordance with which he lived his life.

An ideal of character so admirably uncompromising could hardly be attained without a struggle, but of such inner struggles we learn only indirectly, through one or two phrases in Chekhov's letters.

In 1889, to Suvorin, the editor of *The New Times*, and a personal friend for many years:

> Write a story about a young man, the son of a former serf, and a small shopkeeper by profession, who sang in the church choir; who, as a schoolboy, was brought up to show reverence for the officials, to kiss the hands of priests, to bow before the opinions of others, to be thankful for every slice of bread he ate. Write a story about this youth, who has been flogged many a time, who had no overshoes to put on in winter as he trudged through the snow to give his coaching lessons; who fought other boys; who tortured animals; who liked having meals at his wealthy relatives' house; who played a part before God and men for no reason at all, perhaps for no other reason but the awareness of his personal insignificance. Describe how this young man gradually, bit by bit, squeezed the slavish self out of his system, and how he awoke one fine morning feeling that real human blood was flowing through his veins, instead of the blood of slaves.

And to his wife in 1903, a year before his death, in answer to some remarks she had made, praising his character:

> I must tell you that I am really harsh by disposition, that I am quick-tempered, etc., etc. But I have formed the habit of controlling my impulses, for no decent person should relinquish his hold on himself. God alone knows what I used to do in the old days!

This exacting attitude towards himself never left him. He made himself into his own 'animal trainer'; and it was just this reason – the need for self-discipline – that he gave to explain his apparently sudden decision to leave Petersburg in 1890, the year which saw his accession to fame, and to undertake the difficult and dangerous trip to Sakhalin. 'I must be my own animal trainer. The journey means a good six months of uninterrupted physical and mental exertion, but I must do it because I'm a southerner and am apt to grow lazy; I must train myself.' And in another context: 'I despise laziness just as I despise weakness and sluggishness of the emotions.'

It is interesting to speculate about the influences which shaped Anton's character. His mother was apparently an intelligent and warm–hearted person, who did all she could for her children, sacrificing her own comforts and striving to alleviate the effects of their father's harshness. Anton had often said about his family that 'we', the children, 'inherit our souls from Mother and our gifts from Father'. He himself was a great believer in the powerful effects of upbringing. His brother Mikhail tells us that Anton often proclaimed his conviction that upbringing mattered more than heredity, that by the right kind of upbringing even the worst hereditary traits could be overcome. Yet he might have found himself at a loss to explain by what mysterious interplay of heredity and environment the Chekhov parents produced several children who differed so greatly among themselves. Alexander, who became a journalist, led a dissipated life and frittered away his gift; Nikolay, a talented painter, drank heavily and died young in consumption; Ivan and Mikhail did not distinguish themselves in any way; while Anton became a remarkable writer and an admirable person.

There is no evidence to show that there had been any strong, beneficial influence in his life when he was a schoolboy. No elder friend or teacher is known to have inspired him with the ideals for which he strove in his personal and public life. The only friend of his early years whom his biographers mention is the school doctor who treated him during a long illness at the age of 15. They ascribe to this friendship Chekhov's decision to take up medicine as a profession.

Moscow, medicine and a *ménage à trois*

In August 1879 Anton came to live with his family in Moscow and entered the Medical Faculty of the Moscow University. He himself explained his choice by saying that he had only 'the vaguest notion about university faculties', and 'did not remember what sort of considerations made him choose medicine', but added that he 'never regretted his choice'.

It is significant that, simultaneously with his entrance to the university, he took over the responsibilities of the head of the family. His father at that time had an inferior post as a salesman at a Moscow stores where he often spent the night; his elder brother,

Alexander, was living away from home; his next brother, Nikolay, was a weak character, unable to assume responsibility. Anton became the principal bread-winner and authority in the home, issuing moral precepts to his younger brothers and sister: 'You mustn't lie. You must be fair,' and so forth. The time he could spare from his studies was spent in writing sketches and short stories for literary weeklies and the money thus earned supported the whole family.

It is known that during the four years of his studentship he worked extremely hard. The year 1883 especially is marked by a large increase in literary production which amounted to 120 short stories written chiefly for a humorous weekly magazine called *The Splinters*. The editor, Leykin, had a gift for discovering young talents and securing regular contributions from them for his magazine. During the years 1882–5, Chekhov remained his regular contributor, supplying stories, sketches, and articles, which had to be short and humorous.

Much of the material he turned out in those years was undoubtedly of rather inferior quality, and Chekhov himself had no illusions about it. He wrote fast, he wrote for money; it is doubtful whether in these years writing meant anything more to him than just a means of earning his living. 'I've scratched off a mangy little sketch,' 'I've spun off a tale' – such are the expressions in which he talks of his literary work.

A Russian writer said once that there were two contrasting types of Russian character. One was gay, carefree, over-confident, boastful, a character which 'treats the sea as if it were knee-deep', as a Russian saying puts it. The other was quiet, unassuming, conscientious, and above all modest, with an instinctive dislike for all forms of self-advertisement and self-glorification. These traits cut across all distinctions of social and economic status, they were to be found in all classes of Russian society. Chekhov appears to have combined the gaiety of the first type with all the qualities of the second. Sometimes from the way he speaks about himself one could almost suspect him of suffering from inferiority feelings.

Behind me there are mountains of mistakes, tons of paper covered with writing, an Academy prize and a life of sudden success, like Potemkin's,[1] yet in spite of all this, I don't believe there is a single line I've written that has real literary value. I long to hide somewhere for five years or so and do a piece of painstaking, serious work. I must study, learn everything from the beginning, for as a writer I am completely ignorant.

This was written in 1889, which was the happiest year of his entire career as a writer.

Whether we call it 'inferiority complex' or 'divine discontent', this attitude remained characteristic of Chekhov until the end of his life. It was not until the year 1886 that he began to take his writing seriously. From that year dates his letter to the writer, Grigorovich, in which he says: 'Up to the present I took an extremely frivolous attitude towards my literary work. I was careless, slapdash . . . ' The recognition by the literary men of Petersburg whom he admired and whose opinion he respected gradually effected this change of attitude, which was reflected in the falling-off of his productivity. In 1885 he published 129 short stories and sketches; in 1886, 112; in 1887, 66; in 1888 only 12. Yet he spent more time on writing them in 1888 than he did in each of the preceding years. At the same time he worked as a general practitioner in Moscow, regarding this branch of his activities as at least of equal importance with his literary work. 'I feel somehow more alert and more pleased with myself when I know that I have two occupations, and not one . . . Medicine is my legal spouse, while literature is my mistress. When I get tired of one, I go and sleep with the other . . . '

This *ménage-à-trois* was not quite as harmonious as this remark suggests: there was a certain amount of rivalry in which the 'mistress' usually won the day. As years went by, literary work absorbed more and more of Chekhov's energy and time, but now and again he returned to medicine, especially during epidemics when there was a shortage of doctors. During one such spell of medical activity he managed to treat a thousand patients within a few months. Most of his practice was in Moscow, or in the country around Moscow, in the villages within easy reach of a small estate which he acquired in 1892 and where he spent several summers.

1 A court favourite of Empress Catherine II.

The Soviet biographers of Chekhov are hard put to it to explain his complete lack of participation in the political activities of the years 1880–1900. The years he spent at the university were the time of great revolutionary ferment: not a few of his friends must have paid with their freedom for belonging to secret political organisations. Yet there is not the slightest hint in any of his writings of Chekhov taking an interest in such activities, let alone sharing them. His serious thinking appears to have been on social not on political lines, although much of the social criticism implicit in his writings can be regarded as an indictment of the contemporary political system.

Nor was he an apologist or accuser of any one class of Russian society; if he exposes the ineffectiveness, the eccentricity, the childishness of the gentry in the characters of Ranevskaya, Gayev, and others in *The Cherry Orchard*, he is no less objective in his representation of the self-righteous young doctor belonging to the lower middle class, with his envious hatred of upper-middle-class habits and manners, in his play *Ivanov*.

Writing for the stage

Chekhov had tried his hand at writing plays when still at school. His first play, *The Fatherless*, written in 1877 when Chekhov was 17, was condemned as 'utterly false' by his elder brother Alexander, whose opinion Anton valued greatly, and was never published in its original form. Not until some eight years later did Chekhov attempt to write for the stage again. His theme in this case was an adaptation of his short story *Autumn* and the play a one-act entitled *On the High Road*. Like *The Fatherless*, it was neither published nor performed in Chekhov's lifetime.

During the years 1887–90 he began to give more and more time to writing plays. The plays of that period fall into two groups: the five one-act humorous sketches [2] which Chekhov called 'vaudevilles', and the two four-act serious plays, *Ivanov* and *The Wood Demon*.

The first of the vaudevilles, *The Swan Song*, was a dramatic version of another of his short stories – *Kalkhas*. It is a very short scene – Chekhov boasted of having written it in an hour and five minutes – and it presents the reminiscences of an old comic actor

2 *The Bear* and *The Proposal* are included in the present volume.

who has fallen asleep in the theatre after a drinking party, and wakes up in a mood of sentimental self-pity. The other four sketches are farcical. They are *The Bear, The Proposal, An Unwilling Martyr*, and *The Wedding*. With these must be included a one-act play written in 1891, *A Jubilee*.

Chekhov always tended to speak of his writing in a semi-apologetic, self-deprecatory way. It is true that he began writing on the advice of his brother Alexander, chiefly in order to add to the inadequate income of his family, and that a great many of his early humorous sketches were miniature pot-boilers. He took the same attitude towards his one-act plays as he did towards his short stories. Thus he wrote of *The Bear*: 'I've managed to write a stupid vaudeville which, owing to the fact that it is stupid, is enjoying surprising success', and he described *The Proposal* as 'a scabby little vaudeville which I've scratched out for the provinces'.

However, as frequently happens, audiences were enthusiastic about the work which the author himself regarded with scorn. They laughed so much when they saw *The Bear* acted that Chekhov, who was present at the performance, described them as being 'in the seventh heaven of delight'. His father, a severe and critical task-master during Anton's childhood, returned from one of these performances full of admiration and told him: 'What a wonderful thing you've written, Anton!' Financially, too, the vaudevilles proved quite profitable, and in the lean year 1889 Chekhov wrote to his friend Pleshcheyev: 'I live on the charity of my *Bear*.'

Whatever his feelings about these plays may have been at the time, there is no doubt that through writing them Chekhov learned a great deal about dramatic technique and that it served him well when he began to write full-length plays.

His first four-act play, *Ivanov*, was begun on the suggestion of Korsh, the owner of a theatre in Moscow, who expected Chekhov to write an uproarious comedy. Chekhov wrote *Ivanov* in ten days, and was hoping to make a thousand roubles (about £100)[3] out of it. It was first performed at the Korsh Theatre in 1887.

At the time *Ivanov* was written Chekhov had very definite notions of what dramatic art ought to be. He told his friends that the theatre should 'show life and men as they are, and not as they

3 Perhaps about £2,000 in today's money.

would look if you put them on stilts'. 'Let the things that happen on the stage be as complex and yet just as simple as they are in life. For instance, people are having a meal at the table, just having a meal, but at the same time their happiness is being created, or their lives are being smashed up.'

He was no longer indifferent to the way in which his plays were presented to the public and wanted to have *Ivanov* acted according to his own ideas. However, he found it well-nigh impossible to convey his ideas to the actors. 'The actors do not understand, talk nonsense, don't take parts they should,' he wrote to his brother Alexander. The painful situation was somewhat relieved by his capacity to treat it humorously. Chekhov's description of the first night of *Ivanov*, in a letter to his brother Alexander, might have come out of one of his own short stories. 'I'll describe it all in order,' he wrote.

Act I. I am behind the scenes in a tiny box like a prisoner's cell. Our family are trembling in a box on the pit-tier. Against all expectation, I am cool and feel no excitement. The actors are excited and tense, and cross themselves. The curtain goes up. Enter the actor *bénéficiare*. He is at once presented with a bouquet, and as he doesn't know his part, I do not recognise his first remarks as my own. Kiselyovsky, on whom I placed great hopes, doesn't say a single phrase correctly. Literally, *not a single one*. He speaks his own. In spite of this and of the producer's blunders, the first act is a great success. Many calls.

Act II. A crowd of people on the stage. Visitors. The actors don't know their parts, they make a mess of the scene, talk nonsense. Every word cuts me like a knife in my back. But – O Muse! – this act also is a success. All the actors are called; I, too, am called twice. I am congratulated on the success.

The letter ends on a note of disappointment: 'On the whole I feel fatigued and annoyed. Disgusted – although the play had a solid success.' The excitement caused by *Ivanov* soon died down and left Chekhov with very mixed feelings, almost wishing that he had never written the play.

Chekhov was not a complacent writer – on the contrary, self-doubt constantly beset him. As soon as he saw a play of his on the stage, he felt the urge to make alterations, so that the final version of *Ivanov* was very different from that given at the Korsh Theatre. It was accepted for production by the Alexandrinsky Theatre in Petersburg and the first performance took place on 31 January 1889. This was quite a triumph for Chekhov. The play was widely and favourably reviewed and he began to feel that his work was not altogether wasted.

Yet the success of *Ivanov* with the audiences and critics of that day may have been due just to those features of the play which Chekhov was to condemn and discard in favour of a new technique so soon afterwards. In fact, during the year 1889 he was working on *The Wood Demon*, a play in which he dispensed with most of the generally accepted theatrical devices. In December of that year *The Wood Demon* was ready and was produced by a Moscow theatre. It was a failure. The critics accused Chekhov of merely reproducing on the stage a slice of life which did not even have the interest of being original or exciting. Chekhov withdrew the play and refused to have it printed or produced until it emerged some eight years later, very much altered, under the new title of *Uncle Vanya*.

The Seagull

Five years, a trip to Sakhalin, and a tour of Western Europe were interposed between the writing and production of *The Wood Demon* and Chekhov's next play *The Seagull*. By that time his material position had improved sufficiently for him to acquire a small estate near Moscow, and it was there, at Melikhovo, that he settled to work on *The Seagull* in the autumn of 1895. Self-criticism and doubt beset him as usual, and in a letter to his friend Suvorin, written in October 1895, he described it as a 'comedy with three female parts, six male parts, four acts, a landscape (a view of the lake), much talk about literature and five tons of love'. In November of the same year he announced its completion to the same correspondent in the following terms: 'Well, I have now finished the play. I began it *forte* and finished it *pianissimo*, against all the rules of dramatic art. It came out like a story. I am more dissatisfied than satisfied with it, and, reading over my newborn piece, I become once more convinced that I am not a playwright at all.'

His own feelings and ideas about 'the rules of dramatic art' prevalent in his time have clearly found a partial expression in the words he put into the mouth of one of the characters in *The Seagull* – the budding playwright, Treplyov. He says to his uncle, Sorin: 'In my opinion the theatre of today is in a rut, and full of prejudices and conventions . . . When I watch these great and talented people, these high priests of a sacred art, depicting the way people eat, drink, make love, walk about and wear their clothes; when I hear them trying to squeeze a moral out of the tritest words and emptiest scenes . . . when I am presented with a thousand variations of the same old thing, the same thing again and again – well, I just have to escape, I run away . . .' And further: 'We need new art forms . . . and if they aren't available we might just as well have nothing at all . . .'

Yet with an almost uncanny objectivity and a capacity for self-parody so much his own, Chekhov provided in the same act of *The Seagull* an example of this 'new art' in the pretentious, almost ludicrous, scene with which Treplyov's own play begins. Nina's speech, starting with the words: 'The men, the lions, the eagles, the partridges, the antlered deer, the geese, the spiders, the silent fishes of the deep', was in fact misunderstood by the audience at the first performance of *The Seagull*. They missed its humorous intention, took it to be genuine Chekhov and expressed their disapproval without restraint.

This first production – by the Alexandrinsky Theatre in Petersburg – took place in October 1896. The date of production was fixed at very short notice at the request of the leading actress who wanted the principal part – that of Arkadina – for her benefit performance. There was time for only nine rehearsals. Chekhov managed to be present at most of them, and he tried to convey his ideas to the actors by telling them that 'Everything must be simple . . . completely simple . . .' and that 'The main thing is not to be theatrical.' Needless to say, this did not go down too well with the actors of the 'old school', and in a letter Chekhov wrote at that time to his sister Marya he remarked that 'So far *The Seagull* is going in a tiresome way.'

A circumstance which had nothing to do with the play itself played a decisive part in its vicissitudes. The actress who had asked for the play to be produced at short notice, and who usually acted broad comedy parts, had to be left out of the cast at the last moment. There was no time to notify the public, and her admirers, who filled the theatre after having paid the high prices charged on benefit nights, were disgusted to find her name absent from the programme. The trouble started near the beginning of the play when Nina's monologue was greeted with jeers and derisive guffaws. As the play proceeded the uproar increased, and when in the third act Treplyov appeared with his head bandaged, laughter, hissing, and catcalls became so loud that the actors could hardly hear themselves speak.

Chekhov did not see this display. He left the theatre after the second act and, in his agony of mind, walked the streets of Petersburg until two o'clock in the morning. His friend Suvorin was waiting for him at his hotel, but Chekhov asked him not to put on the light. 'I don't want to see anyone,' he remarked, 'and I only want to say one thing: Let people call me a — fool if I ever write anything else for the stage.' To another friend – Nemirovich-Danchenko – he wrote from Melikhovo in November: 'Yes, my Seagull was a huge failure. The theatre breathed malice, the air was compressed with hatred, and in accordance with the law of physics, I was thrown out of Petersburg like a bomb.' And to Koni, a famous lawyer who wrote to console him: 'After the performance people assured me that I had depicted mere idiots, that my play was scenically clumsy, that it was silly, unintelligible, and even senseless, and so on, and so forth. You can imagine my state of mind – it was a failure such as I had never dreamed of! I felt humiliated and vexed, and I left Petersburg full of doubts of all kinds.'

He wrote to the management of the Alexandrinsky Theatre asking that The Seagull should be taken off. His request was disregarded. The second performance was quite well received and two further performances were equally encouraging. But ill-luck seemed to be pursuing Chekhov with regard to this play, for just as it seemed to be gaining ground, the management decided to remove it from their repertoire.

The failure of The Seagull rankled with Chekhov for several years. His confidence in his ability to write plays was so severely shaken that he even tended to dismiss the favourable comments on that play as mere attempts to console him. It was only with great reluctance that he allowed it to be published in Russian

Thought, one of the 'fat' literary journals of the time, in December of the same year.

If Chekhov was engaged on play-writing during the two years that followed the failure of *The Seagull*, he made no mention of it in his letters. The illness which had remained concealed from him and his family probably for some years suddenly revealed itself by a haemorrhage in the lung, and was diagnosed as tuberculosis. Chekhov spent several months at a clinic near Moscow, and in September went to the south of France, where he stayed through the winter. He returned to Russia in May 1898.

It was a momentous year – for Chekhov, both as a dramatist and a private individual, and for the history of Russian dramatic art. The Moscow Art Theatre came into being. Its creation was the work of two men about the same age as Chekhov, the actor-producer Stanislavsky and the writer Nemirovich-Danchenko. Nemirovich-Danchenko and Chekhov had known one another for some years; Stanislavsky had never met him, but the ideas which the three men held about dramatic art in general and the needs of the Russian theatre in particular had a great deal in common. Like Chekhov, Nemirovich-Danchenko and Stanislavsky abhorred the over-theatrical style of acting which was turning the drama into a dead art. They wanted the acting to be natural and sincere, and every production to be a unity, a conscientious and imaginative work of art. They were against the tradition which concentrated the limelight on a few stars while leaving most of the other participants in the shadow. They planned to achieve their effects by frequent, careful rehearsals and devoted team work, directed by a benevolent despot – the producer.

Most of these ideas were Chekhov's own, but so diffident was he concerning the qualities of his own plays, so sensitive to the possible repetition of failure, that it took Nemirovich-Danchenko some time to persuade him to let the Art Theatre produce *The Seagull*.

Nemirovich-Danchenko had to use persuasion with his co-director as well, for Stanislavsky was not entirely convinced of the qualities of the play, while Danchenko regarded the failure of *The Seagull* as one more proof of the inadequacy of the existing theatre and was eager to demonstrate that a fresh and intelligent approach could make a success of it. On his insistence the play was included in the repertoire of the Art Theatre, and was to follow on the production of several other plays, by Alexey Tolstoy, Shakespeare, and Hauptmann.

The Seagull was given twenty-six rehearsals, and Chekhov managed to attend one of them before he left for Yalta, where he was to spend the winter. Like many shy people, he produced a first impression which was not only unfavourable, but quite inconsistent with his real character. Stanislavsky remarked that he struck him as 'arrogant and insincere', owing to the way he had of throwing back his head when speaking to people. Nor was he of much help to the actors who, when they asked him how a certain part should be acted, received the reply: 'As well as possible'.

An event of deep personal significance which took place at the same time was Chekhov's first meeting with the actress Olga Knipper, who took the part of Irina in Tolstoy's play *Tsar Fyodor Ivanovich*. He wrote to Suvorin in October from his retirement in Yalta: 'Before I left Moscow I was at the rehearsal of *Fyodor Ivanovich*. I was pleasantly impressed by the intelligent and fine tone . . . there was real art on the stage. Irina in my opinion is superb. Her voice, noble bearing, and sincerity are so good that it brought a lump to my throat . . . If I remained in Moscow I should fall in love with that Irina.'

As fate would have it, the play about which both Stanislavsky and Chekhov himself felt so doubtful was to act as a linchpin in the destinies of the Art Theatre. The success of *Tsar Fyodor* – its first production – with the Moscow audiences was followed by the failure of *The Merchant of Venice*, then by another blow – the banning of Hauptmann's play *Hannele* on religious grounds. Thus the performance of *The Seagull* acquired an importance out of all proportion to the producers' original intention. Its success or failure could mean success or failure for the theatre as a whole. Everything combined to make the experience an extremely tense one for all concerned. This was increased by the intervention of Chekhov's sister Marya, who wrote to the management imploring them to cancel the performance, for she feared that its failure might have a serious effect on her brother's health. Nemirovich-Danchenko took the responsibility of refusing her request.

Stanislavsky described what happened at the first performance. At the end of the first act the curtain came down in dead silence and the horrified actors stood still looking at one another. Olga Knipper had difficulty in repressing her sobs. Suddenly the applause broke out with such force that there could be no doubt of the effect the play had on the audience. When the curtain went up again the actors were too overcome to bow. The rest of the play went off extremely well, and on the demand of the audience a telegram was sent to Chekhov at Yalta assuring him of a great success.

The situation was thus suddenly and wonderfully transformed. It now seemed that Russian audiences were capable of appreciating both the new kind of play and the new technique of presenting it. The Moscow Art Theatre recognised its debt to Chekhov's genius and the decisive role *The Seagull* had played in its destinies, by adopting a seagull as its permanent emblem. In subsequent years the theatre became the chief exponent of Chekhov's dramatic art, and a firm and affectionate friendship developed between the members of its company and the author. It is evident from Chekhov's letters that he returned their devotion and that his appreciation of the Art Theatre's role in Russian life was spontaneous and far-seeing. He wrote to Nemirovich-Danchenko from Yalta in November 1899: 'In your letter there is a tremulous, hardly audible note, like that of an old bell. It is where you write of how the details of theatrical life harass you. Oh, do not get tired, do not cool off! The Art Theatre will provide the best pages of the history – when it is written – of the modern Russian theatre. Your theatre should be your pride, and it is the only theatre I love, although I have not yet been there.'

Uncle Vanya and Three Sisters

It was not until 1900, when the directors of the Art Theatre organized a tour of the Crimea, that Chekhov had an opportunity of seeing his plays performed as Moscow audiences had seen them in 1898 and 1899. Meanwhile Stanislavsky and Nemirovich-Danchenko were eager to follow up the success of *The Seagull* by the performance of another play by Chekhov. Such a play was already in existence – *The Wood Demon*, re-written by Chekhov at some time during the intervening period and re-named *Uncle Vanya*. It had been published in a collection of his plays which appeared in 1897, and was taken up by some provincial theatres where it seemed to have enjoyed great success. Nemirovich-Danchenko pressed Chekhov for the release of the play to the Art Theatre in the spring of 1899. Chekhov then had to reveal that the play had been already promised to the Maly Theatre in Moscow.

He felt unhappy about disappointing his friends, and took the first opportunity to withdraw *Uncle Vanya* when the management of the Maly Theatre suggested some considerable alterations. The play went into rehearsal with the Art Theatre company at once and was acted before the Moscow audience for the first time on 26 October 1899. Chekhov did not know this was taking place until he was awakened by a telephone call in the middle of the night at his home in Yalta, and received the first of a series of congratulatory telegrams.

However, *Uncle Vanya* did not repeat the exceptional triumph of *The Seagull* in the previous year. The reviews in the papers were mostly unfavourable, and Olga Knipper sent a self-accusatory letter to Chekhov, blaming herself for having acted badly in the part of Yelena. Chekhov, on the other hand, took the matter calmly. He wrote back, consoling her and pointing out that the company had been spoiled by too many spectacular successes and must learn to be satisfied with the more modest ones.

Uncle Vanya had certainly not been a failure, but its reception showed that Russian audiences were not as ripe for the new drama as Chekhov and the management of the Art Theatre had hoped on the evidence of *The Seagull*'s success. Nemirovich-Danchenko afterwards wrote that the broad public did not immediately understand Chekhov's maturer plays, *Uncle Vanya*, *Three Sisters*, and *The Cherry Orchard*. They achieved full recognition only with their second season, and they have remained established ever since.

After the production of *Uncle Vanya* everyone urged Chekhov to write a play specially for the Art Theatre. He replied that he could do nothing until he had seen a proper performance of his existing plays. As he was forbidden to visit Moscow during the theatre season on account of his health, the directors of the Art Theatre decided to bring the theatre to him. The company's tour of the Crimea was a triumphant success. Performances of Chekhov's two plays were given at Sebastopol and Yalta. The author, Maxim Gorky, and Ivan Bunin were present, Chekhov being preoccupied chiefly with remaining invisible to the audience. The company was afterwards entertained at Chekhov's villa in Yalta, where Olga Knipper acted as an additional hostess with his mother and sister, thus confirming the rumour of the growing friendship between Chekhov and herself.

After the Art Theatre returned to Moscow Chekhov settled to writing *Three Sisters*. His failing health, an increasing number of callers, and probably the more stringent demands he made on himself as a dramatist combined to make this task more arduous than anything he had done before. He wrote to his sister in September 1900: 'It is very difficult to write *Three Sisters*, more difficult than the former plays. But – well, perhaps something will come out of it, if not this season then the next.'

Yet in November he was already able to let the actress Komisarzhevskaya know that he had finished the play. '*The Three Sisters* is ready, but its future, at any rate its immediate future, is wrapped in the darkness of uncertainty. The play turned out to be dreary, long, and awkward; I say awkward because it has, for instance, four heroines and a spirit more gloomy than gloom itself, as the saying goes.'

By that time Chekhov's name as a dramatist was so well known in Russia as to make the writing of the play a piquant item of news. The hostile press in Moscow made fun of it by pretending to publish telegrams announcing its progress in the following manner: 'First act written', 'Half second act sketched out', and so on. Ignoring the prohibitions of his doctors, Chekhov brought the play to Moscow himself and took a more than usually active part in supervising its rehearsals. He had heard that the military circles of the city had been alarmed by the rumour that he intended to satirise them, and so he instructed the actors to act the officers in *Three Sisters* as 'simple, charming and good-natured people, without any theatrico-military erectness of carriage, raising of shoulders, bluffness, and so on.'

Chekhov was not present at the first performance; he left for Nice, where he spent the whole of January maintaining contact with the producers by post. The play was given for the first time on 31 January 1901, again without the spectacular success of *The Seagull*. It established itself gradually, like *Uncle Vanya* before, and *The Cherry Orchard* after it.

The Cherry Orchard

Since 1898 Chekhov had been living in Yalta, in the Crimea, and was not allowed to travel to Moscow on account of his health. It was then that he had met Olga Knipper, one of the actresses of the Art Theatre, who later became his wife. In the spring of 1900, still in exile in his 'warm Siberia', as he designated the Crimea, he had the excitement of seeing the whole theatre arrive at Yalta to give performances for his benefit. His old cheerfulness returned, and with it a hope for improvement in health. He proposed to Olga Knipper and was accepted. They were married in May 1901.

It was a happy marriage, despite the strain of frequent separations and the disappointment of not having children. Olga was devoted to her work at the Art Theatre, while Chekhov, for reasons of health, was unable to live in Moscow. She became pregnant in the second year of their marriage, but miscarried and was very ill for some months. Chekhov's concern for her health and many sleepless nights he spent at her bedside made serious inroads on his own failing health. He found the writing of plays a more and more protracted business, and his last, *The Cherry Orchard*, was very slow in taking shape. His letters indicate that he had a new play in mind as early as 1901 when he told Olga: 'The next play I write for the Art Theatre will definitely be funny, very funny – at least in intention.' In January 1902 he mentioned his play to Olga again, but it was still 'a faint glimmering in the brain'. By the end of the year the subject was sufficiently thought out for him to mention the title, *The Cherry Orchard*, and he had some conception of what the characters were going to be. One of them was to be 'a stupid woman', a comic part which he intended for his wife. There was to be another comic role for Stanislavsky. These were probably the first conceptions of the characters of Varya and Lopahin respectively. The actual writing of the play was spread over the months of March to October 1903, and the commentary on its progress provided by Chekhov's correspondence is especially full. The play was altered and re-copied several times, but there was one point on which Chekhov remained consistent – it was 'not a drama but a comedy: in places almost a farce'.

Despite the mild climate and, for those days, expert medical care, the progress of his illness could not be arrested, and in 1903, when he was working on *The Cherry Orchard*, Chekhov was a very sick man. He wrote to Nemirovich-Danchenko: 'I write about four lines a day, and even that costs me an intolerably painful effort.'

The first performance of *The Cherry Orchard*, awaited so impatiently by the Moscow audiences and the company of the Art Theatre, was planned for 17 January 1904, Chekhov's birthday, and the twenty-fifth anniversary of his literary career. Chekhov attended its rehearsals in December and January, for his new medical adviser insisted on his spending winter near Moscow. For the first time the differences between the producers and the author in the interpretation of the play took an acute form when Chekhov insisted that it should be treated as 'a light comedy', while Stanislavsky and Nemirovich-Danchenko wanted to present it as 'a serious drama of Russian life'.

A great celebration was planned for the first night; most of Chekhov's friends and many prominent people were present. There was a general dismay when it was discovered some way through the first act that Chekhov was not in the theatre. It was not merely ill-health that kept him away: he suffered agonies of embarrassment on all such ceremonial occasions, even when the recipients of honours were other people. His friends had to use most forceful persuasion to induce him to face the audience that night.

The great celebration turned out to be a poignant experience for everyone present. Emaciated and exhausted, Chekhov no sooner took his position on the stage than he was seized with a fit of uncontrollable coughing. The audience called out to him to sit down: 'A chair for Anton Pavlovich!' but he remained on his feet. The applause which greeted him left him in no doubt as to the warmth of their feeling for him. After many speeches and presentations, Nemirovich-Danchenko concluded the ceremony by the tribute from his colleagues: 'Our theatre,' he told Chekhov, 'is so much indebted to your talent, to your tender heart and pure soul, that you have every right to say "This is my theatre".'

Two days later Chekhov wrote to Batyushkov: 'At the first performance of *The Cherry Orchard* I was feted so lavishly, so warmly, and above all so unexpectedly, that I have not yet re-covered from it.'

There was more truth in this remark than he had meant to imply, for he was never to recover. After two months at Yalta, he passed through Moscow on the way to Badenweiler in Germany, where he died on the night of 1–2 July 1904.

Career of a dramatist

It is characteristic of Chekhov that a few hours before he died he sat up in bed, making up a humorous story at which his wife was able to laugh wholeheartedly. Neither of them realised how near was his end until he awoke the same night, feeling very ill, and asked her to send for the doctor. Chekhov said to him: 'I am dying.' The doctor ordered ice to be put on his heart. 'You don't need to put ice on an empty heart,' said Chekhov. The doctor then gave him champagne. Chekhov sat up, smiled, and said to his wife: 'It's long since I last drank champagne!' He emptied his glass, leaned back, and died – without a long-drawn-out agony and apparently without pain.

There could hardly be anyone in the Russia of those days – a land full of revolutionary ferment – who resembled a revolutionary less than Chekhov, with his diffident, self-effacing gentleness, his lack of dogmatism, and the lively sense of humour with which he regarded himself as well as people and life in general. Yet his development as a dramatist made a break with tradition so complete that he can be said to have caused a revolution in the art of the theatre.

It has been pointed out by someone that revolution is not the opposite of evolution, as is generally assumed, but is the evolutionary process which at first remains concealed and then is so greatly accelerated that it appears sudden and explosive. This is certainly true of Chekhov's development as a dramatist. His early play *The Fatherless* was entirely in the dominant tradition of the day. It apparently aimed at strong melodramatic effects and included two unsuccessful attempts at murder, one successful murder – of the hero – an attempt of the heroine to throw herself under a train, and a succession of hysterical love scenes. His next full-length play, *Ivanov*, contained a considerable admixture of melodrama and a number of harrowing scenes between Ivanov and the two women who were in love with him. In that play

Chekhov plucks too hard at the spectator's heart-strings. He himself confessed that he deliberately contrived each act of *Ivanov* so as to end it with a situation of suspense, or, as he put it, to give his audience 'a sock on the jaw'. Two of the chief characters die a tragic death, and the play ends with a highly melodramatic scene of 'exposure' and the suicide of the hero on his wedding morning. Chekhov, however, insisted that there were no real 'heroes' in the play, in the sense commonly understood, and that he had conducted the play on the whole 'quietly and peacefully'.

In *The Wood Demon* he attempted to dispense completely with such old-fashioned devices, but was still not very sure of himself and was somewhat surprised at the results of his efforts. In a letter to Suvorin, in May 1889, he remarks: 'The play is awfully strange, and I wonder that such strange things should come from my pen.' And later in the same month, writing to the same correspondent: 'The play turned out tedious, somewhat like a mosaic, yet it gives me the impression of a real work.'

There are indications in his letters of that period that Chekhov was hoping for a success with *The Wood Demon* greater than he had had with *Ivanov*, and that the failure of the play shook his confidence and deterred him from continuing with the experiment which he felt was long overdue. It is generally agreed, however, that *The Wood Demon* was not a good play: Chekhov was not yet in command of his new technique. He was much more successful with *The Seagull* seven years later.

It has since become a commonplace to describe Chekhov's approach to drama by the word 'realistic'. He has said himself that he wanted to depict 'real life' as it is lived by ordinary people. 'A play should be written in which people arrive, go away, have dinner, talk about the weather, and play cards. Life must be exactly as it is, and people as they are – not on stilts . . . Let everything on the stage be just as complicated, and at the same time just as simple as it is in life.'

The means by which he achieved this lifelike effect have been described as 'untheatrical'. In the plays of his mature period he avoids exciting, dramatic situations; the most important events in the lives of his characters are communicated indirectly, as if in passing. For instance, in *The Seagull* Nina's eventful career, including her love affair with Trigorin, is mentioned almost casually in conversation between two men, one of whom – Treplyov – is deeply in love with her. The characters usually converse in an inconsequent, illogical way as most people do in everyday life. Stock situations and stock characters are carefully excluded, while ordinary trivial happenings are given poignancy and significance by the suggestion of a contrast between the apparent simplicity of things and the underlying complexity of feeling and situation. The individuality of each character is brought out at once by the remarks they seem to drop casually.

Nevertheless, in Chekhov's own opinion he had not quite managed to do without the old 'tricks of the trade' in *The Seagull*, for there is a painful love and jealousy scene in it, between Arkadina and Trigorin, and an attempt at suicide by Treplyov, followed by his successful suicide. There is thus the famous 'revolver shot' which represented to Chekhov a compromise with tradition, and with which, on his admission, he found it so difficult to dispense.

Uncle Vanya constitutes a step forward in so far as the application of the new technique is concerned. Although he was still unable to do without the revolver shot, the shot fired in the third act of *Uncle Vanya* does not kill anyone. True, suicide is talked about, but is not even attempted. The love scene between Astrov and Yelena is more restrained and brief than that between Arkadina and Trigorin.

In *Three Sisters* the poignancy of lifelong frustration, of unrequited love, of soul-destroying marriage, of partings without a hope of reunion, is conveyed with touches so light that only consummate acting can communicate it to the audience. There are perhaps few scenes so moving in the whole modern drama as the one between Tuzenbakh and Irina before his duel, when they utterly fail to put into words the anxiety and longing which torment them. But the revolver shot is still fired – and again it kills.

Finally, in *The Cherry Orchard* Chekhov relied for his effects entirely on creating an atmosphere, and he succeeded in dispensing with the revolver shot. But his intention to make it into a 'light comedy' cannot be regarded as fulfilled. Intelligent audiences may laugh at Gayev's mannerisms, Charlotta's tricks, and the persistent attempts of the penniless landowner Simeonov-Pishchik to borrow money, but it is doubtful whether they could regard these characters as merely 'funny'. They are pathetic in their essential loneliness and their efforts to keep their heads above water. All the people in this play arouse our compassion, even the strongest of them – Anya – who at the age of 17 has to be maternal to her mother and whose youthful enthusiasm for the bright distant future is not likely, we know, to survive contact with cold grey reality.

Chekhov biographers have been puzzled by the apparent discrepancy between the dominant mood of his plays and the dramatist's own character. All his friends spoke of him as an invariably gay, light-hearted companion who enjoyed and apparently loved life. Yet his plays and the majority of his short stories, despite their flashes of humour, impress one as infinitely sad, full as they are of frustration, disappointed hopes, and unfulfilled longings. Russian life, as he paints it, often strikes one as utterly depressing; the characters he draws may be lovable, but there is little in them to admire or to imitate. How could the dramatist combine this vision of Russian life with an apparently inexhaustible good humour and cheerfulness?

Chekhov himself perhaps answers this question best through the mouth of the character who resembles him most. He was the least autobiographical of Russian writers and drew no portrait of himself in his works, as Turgenev, Lermontov, Leo Tolstoy, and even Pushkin had done. Yet now and again he made his characters express his most cherished hopes and desires, or his very intimate confessions. Doctor Astrov in *Uncle Vanya* says about himself: 'I love life, but our kind of life, the provincial, dreary Russian life, I just can't bear; I despise it with all my heart.' In every one of his plays there is a character who talks of the bright future ahead, not for himself but for future generations: Vershinin in *Three Sisters*, Trofimov and Anya in *The Cherry Orchard*, Sonya in *Uncle Vanya*. The generation to which Chekhov belonged lived on the eve of a tremendous social upheaval. Prophetically, it knew that it was going to be sacrificed, and it sought to discover the meaning of this holocaust in the hope of happiness for 'those who come after us'.

The social significance of Chekhov's dramatic art is a vast theme, beyond the scope of this introduction. What did he intend in presenting these characters and these situations? Why did he believe it was necessary 'to depict life as it is and people as they are'? Had he a moral lesson to teach? Where lay his own sympathies? These are the questions to which it is still possible to give varied and even contradictory answers. Chekhov himself does not help us much in this respect: in his letters he sometimes describes his characters, but he never pronounces judgement on them. His own manner of creative writing is so objective that it provides material for interpretation which might accord with almost any political, social, or moral theory. Perhaps, like Treplyov in *The Seagull*, he simply believed that 'new art forms' were needed, and so he proceeded to give us these new forms to the best of his remarkable ability. Perhaps in his aversion from everything stilted, affected, and pretentious he just created out of the sincerity and directness of his − very Russian − character. Perhaps his natural tolerance, his saving sense of humour, and deep sympathy with human beings moved him to show that people − however misguided, silly, and ineffectual − are still lovable. Perhaps he believed that even the rogues, like Misha in *Ivanov*, and the successful businessmen, like Lopakhin in *The Cherry Orchard*, deserved our compassion.

He was, after all, the least dogmatic of writers and one of the most human of men.

ELISAVETA FEN
London, January 1959

FURTHER READING

Michael Henry Heim, translator, in collaboration with Simon Karlinsky, *Anton Chekhov's Life and Thought: Selected Letters and Commentary*, Berkeley, University of California Press, 1975.

Beverly Hahn, *Chekhov: a Study of the Major Stories and Plays*, Cambridge University Press, 1977.

Richard Peace, *Chekhov: a Study of the Four Major Plays*, New Haven, Yale University Press, 1983.

Patrick Miles, editor and translator, *Chekhov on the British Stage, 1903–1987*, Cambridge University Press, 1993.

Donald Rayfield, *Catastrophe and Comedy*, New York, Twayne, 1994.

Gordon McVay, *Three Sisters*, London, Bristol Classical Press, 1995.

Donald Rayfield, *Chekhov's 'Uncle Vanya' and 'The Wood Demon'*, London, Bristol Classical Press, 1995.

Donald Rayfield, *Anton Chekhov: a Life*, London, Harper Collins, 1997.

Lawrence Senelick, *The Chekhov Theatre: a Century of the Plays in Performance*, Cambridge University Press, 1997.

Donald Rayfield, *Understanding Chekhov*, London, Bristol Classical Press, 1998.

IVANOV

A Drama in Four Acts

Characters in the Play

IVANOV, Nikolay Alexeyevich (Kolya, Nicolàs, Nikolasha), Permanent Member of the County Council

ANNA PETROVNA (Anya, Anyuta), his wife, before her marriage and baptism called Sarah Abramson

SHABELSKY, Matvey Semyonych, Count, Ivanov's maternal uncle

LEBEDEV, Pavel Kerylych (Pasha), Chairman of the County Council

ZINAÏDA SAVISHNA (Zyuzyushka), his wife

SASHA (Alexandra Pavlovna, Shura, Shurochka, Sanechka), their daughter, aged 20

LVOV, Yevgeniy Konstantinovich, a young doctor

BABAKINA, Marfa Yegorovna (Marfusha), the young widow of a landowner, daughter of a rich merchant

KOSYKH, Dmitriy Nekitych, Excise officer

BORKIN, Mikhail Mikhailovich (Misha, Michel), a distant relative of Ivanov and steward of his estate

AVDOTYA NAZAROVNA, an old woman of no definite occupation

YEGORUSHKA, a dependent of the Lyebedevs

FIRST GUEST

SECOND GUEST

THIRD GUEST

FOURTH GUEST

PYOTR, Ivanov's manservant

GAVRILA, Lebedev's manservant

VISITORS of both sexes

The action takes place in one of the provinces of Central Russia.

ACT ONE

The garden in IVANOV's *estate. On the left, the front of the house with a terrace. One window is open. In front of the terrace a wide semicircular space from which, centre and right, avenues lead into the more distant parts of the garden. On the right, garden seats and tables. A lamp on one of the tables is lit. The evening is drawing in. As the curtain rises, the sound of a 'cello and piano duet being practised can be heard coming from indoors.*

IVANOV *is sitting at the table, reading a book.* BORKIN, *wearing shooting boots and carrying a gun, appears at the far end of the garden; he is rather drunk. On seeing* IVANOV, *he approaches him on tip-toe and, when quite near, aims the gun at his face.*

IVANOV [*sees* BORKIN, *starts and jumps up*]. Misha, my God! what are . . . You frightened me . . . I'm upset enough as it is, and now you, with your stupid tricks . . . [*sits down*] You frightened me, and of course you're only too pleased . . .

BORKIN [*laughs heartily*]. There, there! I'm sorry, I'm sorry. [*sits down beside him*] I won't do it again, honestly I won't. [*takes off his peaked cap*] It's hot. You won't believe me, old chap, but I've covered fifteen miles in less than three hours . . . I'm worn out . . . Just feel my heart, see how it's thumping.

IVANOV [*continues reading*]. All right, later on . . .

BORKIN. No, feel it now. [*takes* IVANOV's *hand and puts it to his chest*] Do you hear? Tum-tum-tum-tum-tum. That means I've got heart disease. I might die suddenly at any moment. Tell me, will you be sorry if I die?

IVANOV. I'm reading . . . later on . . .

BORKIN. No, seriously, will you be sorry if I die suddenly? Nikolay Alexeyevich, will you be sorry if I die?

IVANOV. Don't pester me!

BORKIN. Tell me, my friend, will you be sorry?

IVANOV. I'm sorry that you smell of vodka. It's disgusting, Misha.

BORKIN [*laughs*]. Do I really smell? Surprising . . . Not that there's really anything surprising about it. At Plesniki I happened to meet the examining judge, and I must admit we both knocked back about eight glasses. Drinking is very harmful, generally speaking. Tell me, it is harmful, isn't it? Eh? Isn't it?

IVANOV. This is positively unbearable . . . I wish you'd understand how maddening it is . . .

BORKIN. Well, well . . . I'm sorry, I'm sorry! Bless your heart! Stay there, don't get up. [*gets up and walks off*] What amazing people, you're not even allowed to talk to them. [*returns*] Oh, yes. I'd almost forgotten . . . Please let me have eighty-two roubles.

IVANOV. Why eighty-two roubles?

BORKIN. I must pay the workmen tomorrow.

IVANOV. I haven't got it.

BORKIN. Thanks very much! [*mimics him*] I haven't got it! . . . Can't you see that the workmen have got to be paid? Haven't they?

IVANOV. I don't know. I haven't got anything today. Wait till the first of the month, then I'll be getting my salary.

BORKIN. Oh, what's the use of discussing things with people like you? . . . The workmen won't come for their money on the first of the month, they'll come tomorrow morning!

IVANOV. Well, what can I do about it now? What's the good of going on nagging and pestering me? And where did you get this abominable habit of plaguing me just when I'm busy reading or writing, or . . .

BORKIN. What I want to know is: are the workmen to be paid, or aren't they? Oh, what's the use of talking to you! . . . [*waves his hand*] Call themselves landowners, the devil take them! Rationalised farming! A thousand acres of land – and not a farthing in your pocket. It's like owning a wine-cellar without a corkscrew! . . . See if I don't sell the troika* tomorrow. I will! I sold the oats before they were harvested, and you see if I don't go and sell the rye tomorrow, too. [*walks up and down the stage*] You needn't think I'm going to stand on ceremony about it – or do you? Well, I shan't, I'm not that sort of man.

---

* A team of three carriage horses.

The same; SHABELSKY *(offstage) and* ANNA PETROVNA. SHABELSKY'S *voice is heard through the window: 'It's quite impossible to play with you . . . You've no more ear than a stuffed fish, and your touch is revolting!'*

ANNA PETROVNA [*appears at the open window*]. Who was it talking here just now? Was it you, Misha? Why arc you stamping about like that?

BORKIN. Anyone who had to deal with your *cher Nicolàs* would stamp about!

ANNA PETROVNA. I say, Misha, will you have some hay brought to the croquet lawn?

BORKIN [*waves his hand*]. Leave me alone, please.

ANNA PETROVNA. Tut-tut, what a tone of voice! . . . That tone of voice doesn't suit you at all. If you want women to like you, you must never be angry or high and mighty with them. [*to her husband*] Nikolay, let's go and do somersaults in the hay!

IVANOV. It's bad for you to stand at the open window, Anyuta. Go in, please. [*shouts*] Uncle, will you shut the window?

[*the window is shut*]

BORKIN. Another thing, don't forget that in two days' time Lebedev will have to be paid the interest.

IVANOV. I know. I shall be at Lebedev's today and I'll ask him to wait . . . [*looks at his watch*]

BORKIN. When will you be going to him?

IVANOV. Quite soon.

BORKIN [*eagerly*]. Wait a minute! . . . isn't it Shurochka's birthday today? . . . Dear, dear, dear . . . And I'd almost forgotten! What a memory, eh? [*skips about*] I'll be off, I'll be off . . . [*chants*] I'll be off. I'm going to have a swim, and chew some paper and take a few drops of methylated spirit to get rid of the smell of this vodka – and then I'll be ready to start the day all over again. My dear Nikolay Alexeyevich, what a fellow you are! Always nervy and depressed, and moaning about yourself – and yet, you know, you and I could do great things together. Heaven knows, I'd be prepared to do anything for your sake. How would you like me to marry Marfusha Babakina? I'd give you half the dowry – no, not half – you could have it all!

IVANOV. I should stop talking nonsense if I were you.

BORKIN. No, I mean it seriously. Would you like me to marry

Marfusha? We'll share the dowry . . . But why am I talking to you like this? You don't understand, do you? [*mimics him*] 'I should stop talking nonsense!' You're a good man and an intelligent man, but you haven't got that touch of – you know what I mean – you haven't got any drive. If only you could take a good smack at something, enough to make the sparks fly, I mean . . . You're a neurotic, a weakling. If you were a normal man, you'd be making a million a year. Take me, for instance. If I had two thousand three hundred roubles now, I'd have twenty thousand in a fortnight. You don't believe me? You think that's nonsense, too? Well, it's not. You give me the two thousand three hundred roubles, and in a week I'll show you twenty thousand. On the other side of the river, just opposite us, Ovsianov is selling a strip of land for two thousand three hundred roubles. If we buy that strip, both the banks will be ours. And if both the banks are ours, then – you see what I mean? – we'd have the right to dam the river, d'you see? That's so, isn't it? Then we'll start building a mill, and as soon as we announce that we want to make a dam, everybody living down the river will raise a hubbub. All right, we'll say, *kommen Sie hierher*, if you don't want the dam, you must pay. You see what I'm driving at? The Zarev factory will give us five thousand, Korolkov – three thousand, the monastery – five thousand . . .

IVANOV. That's all sharp practice, Misha. If you don't want to quarrel with me, keep it to yourself.

BORKIN [*sitting down at the table*]. Of course! . . . I knew it! You don't do anything yourself, and you won't let me do anything.

The same, SHABELSKY *and* LVOV

SHABELSKY [*coming out of the house with* LVOV]. Doctors are just the same as lawyers; the only difference is that lawyers merely rob you, whereas doctors rob you and kill you, too. I'm not speaking of present company. [*sits down on one of the seats*] Charlatans, exploiters. Perhaps in some Paradise you might come across an exception to the general rule, but . . . in the course of a lifetime I've spent about twenty thousand on medical treatment and I've not met a single doctor who didn't seem to me an obvious swindler.

BORKIN [*to* IVANOV]. Yes, you do nothing yourself, and you don't let me do anything either. That's why we haven't any money.

SHABELSKY. As I say, I'm not speaking of present company. Possibly there may be exceptions, but anyway . . . [*yawns*]

IVANOV [*closing his book*]. Well, what have you got to say, Doctor?

LVOV [*glancing back at the window*]. The same as I said in the morning: she must leave for the Crimea immediately. [*walks up and down the stage*]

SHABELSKY [*bursts out laughing*]. To the Crimea! . . . Why aren't we doctors, Misha, both of us? It's so simple. Some woman or other, say Madame Angot or Ophelia, starts sneezing or coughing out of sheer boredom . . . So you take a sheet of paper and write out a prescription based on the most scientific principles: to begin with – a young doctor, then a trip to the Crimea, and when she gets to the Crimea – a handsome Tartar guide . . .

IVANOV [*to the Count*]. Oh, will you stop drivelling? . . . [*to* LVOV] To go to the Crimea you need money. But even suppose I do find the money – she still flatly refuses to go.

LVOV. Yes, I know she does.

[*pause*]

BORKIN. Listen, Doctor, is Anna Petrovna really so seriously ill that she must go to the Crimea?

LVOV [*glances back at the window*]. Yes, she's got tuberculosis.

BORKIN. Hm! . . . that's not so good . . . For a long time I've thought from the look on her face that she wouldn't last long.

LVOV. But . . . please speak more quietly . . . they can hear you in the house.

[*pause*]

BORKIN [*sighs*]. Such is life . . . It's like a flower that blossoms gaily in a meadow: along comes a goat, eats it up, and – it's all over . . .

SHABELSKY. All this is just nonsense, nonsense, nonsense! . . . [*yawns*] Nonsense and pretence.

[*pause*]

BORKIN. Well, gentlemen, I've been trying yet once again to teach Nikolay Alexeyevich how to make money. I've given him a marvellous idea, but, as usual, the seed fell on barren ground. You can't teach him anything. Just look at him – sour, depressed, gloomy, miserable . . .

SHABELSKY [*rises and stretches himself*]. You're so clever, you make plans for everybody and teach everybody what they ought to do – but you've never taught me anything, never once! . . . Come on, clever, show me the way to get on!

BORKIN [*rises*]. There are scores of ways of getting on. If I were in your place, I'd have twenty thousand roubles in a week's time. [*walks off*]

SHABELSKY [*following him*]. What's that? Show me how, then.

BORKIN. There's nothing to show. It's very simple. [*returns*] Nikolay Alexeyevich, give me a rouble!

[IVANOV *silently gives him the money*]

BORKIN. *Merci*. [*to the Count*] You've still got plenty of trumps in your hand.

SHABELSKY [*following him*]. Well, what are they?

BORKIN. If I were in your place, I'd have thirty thousand in a week, if not more. [BORKIN and COUNT go out]

IVANOV [*after a pause*]. Useless people, useless talk, having to answer stupid questions . . . Doctor, all this has tired me to the point of making me ill. I've become so irritable, bad-tempered, rude and petty-minded that I don't recognise myself. Every day I have a headache, I can't sleep, there are noises in my ears. And there's simply nowhere where I can get any peace . . . simply nowhere . . .

LVOV. I must have a serious talk with you, Nikolay Alexeyevich.

IVANOV. Very well.

LVOV. It's about Anna Petrovna. [*sits down*] She hasn't agreed to go to the Crimea, but she would go with you.

IVANOV [*after a moment's thought*]. It would need a lot of money for both of us to go. Besides, I shan't be given a long leave. I've already had leave once this year.

LVOV. All right, let's accept that. The next point is this. The most effective medicine for tuberculosis is absolute rest. But your wife never gets any rest, not even for a minute. She's worrying continually about her relationship with you. Forgive me, I'm upset about it and I must speak frankly. Your conduct's killing her. [*pause*] Nikolay Alexeyevich, I wish you'd let me think better of you! . . .

IVANOV. All that is true, I know . . . I suppose I'm dreadfully to blame, but my mind is so confused . . . I feel in the grip of a kind of indolence, I can't understand myself. I don't understand myself or other people. [*glances at the window*] Someone may hear us, let's take a stroll.

[*they rise*]

My friend, I would like to tell you the whole story from the beginning, but it's so long and complicated that I could hardly hope to finish it before the morning.

[*they start walking off*]

Anyuta is a remarkable, an extraordinary woman. She changed her religion for my sake, left her father and mother, gave up her money, and if I'd asked for a hundred more sacrifices, she would have made them without blinking an eyelid. As for me – well, there's nothing remarkable about me, and I've sacrificed nothing. However, it's a long story . . . The gist of the matter, my dear Doctor, is that . . . [*hesitates*] that, to put it briefly, I was passionately in love with her when I got married and I swore I'd love her for ever, but . . . Well, five years have passed, and she still loves me, but I . . . [*makes a helpless gesture with his hands*] Here you are, telling me that she's soon going to die, and I don't feel any love or pity but just a sort of indifference and lassitude . . . To anyone looking at me it must seem dreadful; I don't understand myself what's happening to me . . .

[*they walk off down the avenue*]

Enter SHABELSKY *and later* ANNA PETROVNA.

SHABELSKY [*laughs loudly as he comes in*]. Upon my word, he's not a fraud, after all, he's a thinker, a brilliant fellow! They ought to put up a monument in his honour. He's a combination of every variety of up-to-date rottenness: lawyer, doctor, official, accountant. [*sits down on the bottom step of the terrace*] Apparently he never finished off a proper course of study anywhere – which only goes to prove that he would have been a perfect genius of a scoundrel if only he could have acquired some culture and a liberal education! 'You could have twenty thousand in a week,' he tells me. 'You still have an ace of trumps in your hand,' he says, 'your title of Count.' [*laughs uproariously*] 'Any girl with a dowry would marry you.' . . .

[ANNA PETROVNA *opens the window and looks down*]

SHABELSKY. 'Would you like me to arrange a match between you

and Marfusha?' he says. Who is this Marfusha, anyway? Oh, of
course, it's that woman Balabalkina . . . Babakalkina . . . the one
that looks like a washerwoman.

ANNA PETROVNA. Is that you, Count?

SHABELSKY. Who's that?

[ANNA PETROVNA *laughs*]

SHABELSKY [*with a mock Jewish accent*]. What are you laughing at?

ANNA PETROVNA. I was thinking of something you said . . .
Something you said at dinner, do you remember? A repentant
thief, a horse . . . How did it go?

SHABELSKY. A baptised Jew, a repentant thief and a horse that's
been ill and got over it – they're all worth the same in the end.

ANNA PETROVNA [*laughs*]. You can't even make a simple joke without bitterness. You're a malicious person. [*seriously*] Joking apart,
Count, you really are very bitter and spiteful, you know. Living
with you is so depressing and upsetting. You're always complaining and grumbling; according to you everyone is some sort
of a cad or a scoundrel. Tell me frankly, Count, have you ever
said a good word for anybody?

SHABELSKY. What sort of a cross-examination is this?

ANNA PETROVNA. We've been living in the same house for five
years now, and I've never once heard you speak of other people
calmly, without bitterness or sneers. What harm have they
done you? Do you really think you're better than everybody
else?

SHABELSKY. I don't think that at all. I'm just as much of a cad and a
scoundrel as anybody else. *Mauvais ton*, an old washout, that's
me. I'm always running myself down. Who am I? What am I?
For a while I was rich and free and happy, but now. . . . I'm just
a parasite, a hanger-on, a futile buffoon. I show my indignation
and contempt for them, and they laugh at me; I laugh, and they
shake their heads sadly and say: 'The old man's off his chump.'
But most often they don't hear me at all, or notice me . . .

ANNA PETROVNA [*quietly*]. It's screeching again . . .

SHABELSKY. What's screeching?

ANNA PETROVNA. The owl. It screeches every night.

SHABELSKY. Let it screech. Things can't get any worse than they
are already. [*stretches himself*] Ah, my dear Sarah, if only I'd won
a hundred thousand or so – I'd have shown you something to

make you sit up! You wouldn't have seen me again. I'd have run away from this hole, away from all your blessed charity, and my feet wouldn't have trod this dust again till the Last Judgement.

ANNA PETROVNA. And what would you have done if you'd won the money?

SHABELSKY [*after a moment's thought*]. First of all, I'd have gone to Moscow and listened to the gipsy choir. Then . . . then I'd have made a dash for Paris. I'd have rented a flat there and gone to the Russian church regularly . . .

ANNA PETROVNA. And what else?

SHABELSKY. I'd have spent days sitting by my wife's grave, thinking. I'd have sat by her grave till I died. You see, my wife is buried in Paris.

[*pause*]

ANNA PETROVNA. How terribly depressing! Shall we play another duet, or what?

SHABELSKY. Very well. Will you get the music ready?

[ANNA PETROVNA *moves away from the window*]

SHABELSKY, IVANOV *and* LVOV

IVANOV [*comes down the avenue with* LVOV]. You only qualified last year, my dear boy, you're young and full of energy, while I'm thirty-five. I'm entitled to offer you advice. Don't marry a Jewess, or a neurotic, or a blue-stocking, but choose someone ordinary and undistinguished, someone who doesn't sparkle, who doesn't make a lot of unnecessary noise. And, generally speaking, my friend, build your whole life according to an ordinary, commonplace pattern. The more flat and monotonous the background, the better. Don't try to battle with the multitude single-handed, don't go fighting with windmills, don't try to ram down walls with your head . . . And for Heaven's sake avoid all this rationalised farming, and new-fangled education for peasants, and passionate speech-making . . . Shut yourself up in your shell and do your small job, the job God gave you . . . It's more human and honest and healthy. As for my own life – how tiring it's been! Ah, how tiring! So many mistakes, faults, inconsistencies! [*seeing the Count, with irritation*] You're always hanging around, uncle, you never give me a chance to talk to anyone alone!

SHABELSKY [*in a tearful voice*]. I might as well go and drown myself! There's no place for me anywhere! [*jumps up and goes into the house*]

IVANOV [*shouts after him*]. I'm sorry, I'm sorry! [*to* LVOV] Why did I hurt his feelings like that? Really, I'm positively overwrought. I must do something about myself. I must . . .

LVOV [*agitated*]. Nikolay Alexeyevich, I've heard you out, and . . . and – forgive me – but I want to speak frankly, without beating about the bush. In the way you talk, in the very tone of your voice, to say nothing about what you say, there's so much heartless egoism, such cold inhumanity . . . Here there's someone near to you, dying just because she's near to you; her very days are numbered, and yet it's possible for you not to feel any affection for her at all, to walk about, to give advice, to show off . . . I can't express it very well, I'm not clever at talking, but . . . Really, you revolt me!

IVANOV. Perhaps, perhaps . . . You can see better from outside. Maybe you can see through me. Probably I am very much to blame. [*listens*] It sounds as if the horses are ready. I must go and change. [*walks towards the house, then stops*] You don't like me, Doctor, and you don't conceal it. That does you credit . . . [*enters the house*]

LVOV [*alone*]. I could curse myself . . . I missed the chance again! I didn't speak to him as I ought to have done . . . I can't talk to him calmly. I've only got to open my mouth and say one word, and something here [*points at his chest*] begins to suffocate me and turns over inside me, and my tongue seems to stick to my palate. How I hate this Tartuffe, this pompous impostor! I hate him with all my heart . . . There he is, going out! . . . His unhappy wife's only pleasure in life is having him near her; he's the breath of life to her; she implores him to spend at least one evening with her, but he . . . he can't! He finds his home too suffocating, there's not enough scope here! Just one evening at home and he'd have to shoot himself for sheer boredom! Poor fellow . . . he needs plenty of scope to think up some new bit of dirty work, I know . . . Oh, I know why you go to visit these Lebedev people every evening! I know!

LVOV, IVANOV, *wearing his hat and coat,* SHABELSKY *and*
ANNA PETROVNA

SHABELSKY [*coming out of the house with* IVANOV *and* ANNA PETROVNA].
Really, *Nicolàs,* this is simply barbarous! You go out every night,
and we're left here alone. We have to go to bed at eight o'clock
from sheer boredom. It's a hideous existence, it's simply not life
at all. How is it that you can go out, and we're not allowed to?
Why?

ANNA PETROVNA. Leave him alone, Count! Let him go, let him . . .

IVANOV [*to his wife*]. But where could you go, with your illness?
You're ill, you're not allowed to go outside after sunset. Ask the
doctor here. You're not a child, Anyuta, you must be reasonable . . . [*to the Count*] And why should you want to go there?

SHABELSKY. I'd go to the devil, to Hell itself, if only I could get
away from here! I'm bored. I've gone stupid with boredom!
Everybody's tired of me. You leave me at home to keep her
from getting bored, but I've almost nagged her to death!

ANNA PETROVNA. Leave him alone, Count, do. Let him go if he
finds it amusing there.

IVANOV. Anya, why that tone of voice? You know I'm not going
there for amusement. I must see them about that promissory
note.

ANNA PETROVNA. I don't know why you should want to try to
justify yourself. Go along. Who's trying to stop you?

IVANOV. Let's not nag at one another. It's really so unnecessary.

SHABELSKY [*in a tearful voice*]. *Nicolàs,* my dear boy, do please take
me along with you! It might be amusing to see all those nitwits
and bad eggs. You know I haven't been out since Easter.

IVANOV [*irritated*]. All right then, come along! How tired I am of
you all!

SHABELSKY. Yes? Well, *merci, merci!* . . . [*takes his arm gaily and leads
him aside*] May I wear your straw hat?

IVANOV. Yes, but hurry up, please.

[*the* COUNT *runs into the house*]

How tired I am of you all! However . . . Lord! what am I saying?
I know, it's positively outrageous the way I'm talking to you,
Anya. It's never happened like this to me before. Well, goodbye,
Anya, I'll be back by one o'clock.

ANNA PETROVNA. Kolya, dear, do stay at home!

IVANOV [*agitated*]. My darling, my own, my poor unhappy girl, I do
implore you not to try to stop me going out in the evenings. I
know it's cruel and selfish of me, but you must allow me to be
selfish. I find it so unbearably oppressive at home. As soon as the
sun goes down, a sort of anguish begins to torment me. And what
anguish it is! Don't ask me why. I don't know myself. Honestly, I
don't know. I'm depressed here, but when I go to the Lyebedevs',
it's even worse there. I come home, and I'm still depressed, and
so it goes on all night . . . I feel quite desperate . . .

ANNA PETROVNA. Kolya . . . but . . . why don't you stay at home?
Let's talk, as we used to . . . Let's have supper together, then
read . . . We've practised lots of duets for you, the old misery
and I . . . [*puts her arms round him*] Do stay! . . .

[*pause*]

I don't understand you. This has been going on for a whole year.
Why have you changed?

IVANOV. I don't know, I don't know . . .

ANNA PETROVNA. And why don't you want me to go out with you
in the evenings?

IVANOV. Oh, well, I suppose I might as well tell you if you really
want me to. It's a bit cruel to say it, but it's better if I do. When
I feel so tormented by this mental pain, I . . . I begin not to love
you. Then I run away from you, too. I have to get away from
home, that's all.

ANNA PETROVNA. Mental pain? I understand, I understand . . .
Listen, Kolya! Why don't you try to sing and laugh and get
angry, as you used to? Stay at home, and let's have a laugh and a
drink together, and your depression will be gone in a minute.
Would you like me to sing something? Or shall we go and sit
in your study, in the dark, like we used to, and you can tell
me about your depression . . . Your eyes look so tormented! I'll
look into them and cry, and we'll both feel better for it . . .
[*laughs and weeps*] Or − can't we? How does the song go,
Kolya? 'The flowers return in the spring but not the joy.' . . .
No? Well, go, go . . .

IVANOV. Pray for me, Anya! [*starts off, then stops and thinks*] No, I
can't! [*goes out*]

ANNA PETROVNA. Go! . . . [*sits down at the table*]

LVOV [*walking about the stage*]. Anna Petrovna, you must make it a
  rule: as soon as it strikes six o'clock, you must go indoors and
  stay in until the morning. The evening damp is bad for you.

ANNA PETROVNA. Yours to command, sir.

LVOV. Why 'yours to command'? I'm quite serious.

ANNA PETROVNA. But I don't want to be serious. [*coughs*]

LVOV. You see – you're coughing already.

LVOV, ANNA PETROVNA *and* SHABELSKY

SHABELSKY [*comes out of the house wearing a hat and an overcoat*].
  Where's Nikolay? Are the horses ready? [*walks quickly up to* ANNA
  PETROVNA *and kisses her hand*] Good night, my charmer! [*makes a
  grimace*] Gewalt!* 'Shcuse me, please! [*goes out quickly*]

LVOV. What a clown!
           [*pause; the distant sound of an accordion is heard*]

ANNA PETROVNA. How depressing! . . . You see, the coachmen and
  the cooks are having a dance, while I . . . I'm left alone . . .
  Yevgeniy Konstantinovich, what are you walking about for?
  Come here, sit down! . . .

LVOV. I can't sit still.
                         [*pause*]

ANNA PETROVNA. They're playing the 'Starling' in the kitchen.
  [*sings*] 'Starling, starling, where have you been? Drinking vodka
  down on the green.' . . .
                         [*pause*]
  Doctor, have you got a father and mother?

LVOV. My father's dead, but my mother's alive.

ANNA PETROVNA. Don't you miss having your mother living with
  you?

LVOV. I have no time to miss anybody.

ANNA PETROVNA [*laughs*]. 'The flowers return in the spring, but not
  the joy.' . . . Who told me that? I wish I had a better memory!
  I think Nikolay himself must have told me. [*listens*] The owl's
  screeching again!

LVOV. Well, let it screech!

ANNA PETROVNA. You know, Doctor, I'm beginning to think that
  Fate's cheated me. Lots of people who are probably no better

---

* A Jewish exclamation, meaning 'shouts', 'uproar'.

than me are happy, and yet they don't pay anything for their happiness. But I've paid for everything, absolutely for everything! . . . And how dearly! Why should I have to pay such terribly high interest? My dear friend, you're always so considerate with me, so delicate, so afraid to tell me the truth – but do you think I don't know what my illness is? I know perfectly well. However, it's boring to talk about that . . . [with a Jewish accent] 'Shcuse me, please! Can you tell funny stories?

LVOV. No, I can't.

ANNA PETROVNA. Nikolay can . . . And now, you know, I'm beginning to feel surprised at the unfairness of people: why don't they respond to love with love, why must they pay back truth with falsehood? Tell me, how much longer are my father and mother going to go on hating me? They live about fifty miles away from here, but I can feel their hatred day and night, even in my sleep. And what am I to make of Nikolay's depression? He says it's only in the evenings he doesn't love me, when he feels depressed. I understand that, and I think it's probably true, but suppose he's stopped loving me altogether? Of course, that's impossible but – if he has? No, no, I mustn't even think about it. [sings] 'Starling, starling, where have you been?' [starts] What frightening thoughts I have! You haven't a family of your own, Doctor, and there are lots of things you can't understand . . .

LVOV. You are surprised . . . [sits down beside her] No, it's I that am surprised – surprised at you! Explain this to me, please – how did it happen that you, an intelligent, honourable, in a way almost a saintly woman, allowed yourself to be so impudently deceived, to be dragged into this mire? Why are you here? What have you got in common with that cold, heartless . . . but let's leave your husband out of it – what have you in common with these futile, vulgar people? Oh, my God, oh Lord! . . . That eternally grumbling, mouldy old lunatic Count – and that scoundrel, that outrageous impostor Misha with his disgusting face! Well, explain it to me, what are you here for? How did you get here?

ANNA PETROVNA [laughs]. He used to talk just like that . . . Exactly like that . . . But he's got bigger eyes than you, and when he began to talk with passion about anything, they used to glow like burning coals . . . Go on talking . . .

LVOV [*gets up and waves his hand*]. What's the use of my talking? Please go indoors.

ANNA PETROVNA. You're saying all sorts of things about Nikolay. How can you know him? Is it really possible to get to know a man in six months? He's a remarkable man, Doctor, and I'm sorry you didn't know him two or three years ago. He's depressed now, he doesn't talk, he doesn't do anything, but in the past . . . How fascinating he was! I fell in love with him at first sight. [*laughs*] I just looked at him, and – bang went the mouse-trap! He said: Come with me . . . I cut all my connexions, you know, just like cutting off dead leaves with a pair of scissors – and I went . . .

[*pause*]

But now it's different . . . Now he goes off to the Lyebedevs to amuse himself with other women, and I . . . sit in the garden and listen to the owl screeching . . .

[*a watchman can be heard knocking*]*

Doctor, have you any brothers?

LVOV. No, I haven't.

[ANNA PETROVNA *sobs*]

LVOV. Well, what is it now? What's the matter?

ANNA PETROVNA. I can't, Doctor, I'm going there . . .

LVOV. Where do you mean?

ANNA PETROVNA. To where he is . . . I'm going . . . Will you order the horses? [*runs into the house*]

LVOV. I absolutely refuse to treat anybody in these conditions! It's not merely that they don't pay me a farthing, but they upset me, too. No, I've finished. Enough of it! [*goes into the house*]

CURTAIN

* In former days it was usual for a man to go round an estate, striking a wooden board with a stick to frighten away potential thieves.

ACT TWO

A reception room in the Lyebedevs' house; doors left, right and centre, the last leading into the garden. Expensive antique furniture. Chandeliers, candlesticks and pictures, all under dust covers.

ZINAÏDA SAVISHNA, KOSYKH, AVDOTYA NAZAROVNA, YEGORUSHKA, GAVRILA, BABAKINA. *Girls and elderly ladies, visitors in the house. A maid.*

ZINAÏDA SAVISHNA *is on a sofa; on either side of her sit elderly ladies in armchairs; the young people sit on chairs. In the background, by the door leading into the garden, several guests are playing cards; among them are* KOSYKH, AVDOTYA NAZAROVNA *and* YEGORUSHKA. GAVRILA *stands by the door on the right; the maid hands round a tray of sweets and pastries. Throughout the act, the guests pass in and out from the garden and through the door on the right.* BABAKINA *enters through the door on the right and walks up to* ZINAÏDA SAVISHNA.

ZINAÏDA SAVISHNA [*joyfully*]. Darling, Marfa Yegorovna!
BABAKINA. How are you, Zinaïda Savishna? Congratulations on your daughter's birthday!
               [*they embrace*]
  God grant that . . .
ZINAÏDA SAVISHNA. Thank you, darling, I'm so glad to . . . And how are you?
BABAKINA. Thank you, very well. [*sits down on the sofa beside her*] Good evening, you young people! . . .
             [*the guests rise and bow*]
FIRST GUEST [*laughing*]. 'Young people' . . . as if you were so old yourself!
BABAKINA [*with a sigh*]. I feel out of place among young people.
FIRST GUEST [*laughs deferentially*]. Good gracious, why . . . You may be a widow, but you can outshine any girl you like.
        [GAVRILA *serves* BABAKINA *with tea*]

ZINAÏDA SAVISHNA [*to* GAVRILA]. Really, Gavrila, why do you serve the tea like that? Why don't you bring some preserve? Some gooseberry, or something? . . .

BABAKINA. Please don't trouble, thank you so much . . .

[*pause*]

FIRST GUEST. Did you come by Mushkino, Marfa Yegorovna?

BABAKINA. No, through Zaimeshche. The road's better that way.

FIRST GUEST. Yes, of course.

KOSYKH. Two spades.

YEGORUSHKA. Pass.

AVDOTYA NAZAROVNA. Pass.

BABAKINA. Lottery tickets are going up fast again, Zinaïda Savishna, my dear. Can you imagine it: tickets for the first draw are two hundred and seventy already, and for the second they're nearly two hundred and fifty. It's never happened before . . .

ZINAÏDA SAVISHNA [*with a sigh*]. The people with a lot of tickets are in luck.

BABAKINA. Well, hardly, my dear. Even though their price is high, they aren't really a profitable investment. The insurance alone is enough to ruin you.

ZINAÏDA SAVISHNA. Maybe, my dear, but all the same one keeps on hoping. [*sighs*] God is merciful . . .

THIRD GUEST. In my view, ladies, it isn't profitable to have capital at all at the present time. Gild-edged securities bring in very little, and speculation is extremely risky. As I see it, ladies, anyone with capital at the present time is in a more tricky position than people who . . .

BABAKINA [*sighs*]. That's quite true!

[*the* FIRST GUEST *yawns*]

BABAKINA. You think it well-mannered to yawn in the presence of ladies?

FIRST GUEST. I beg your pardon, I didn't mean to . . .

[ZINAÏDA SAVISHNA *gets up and goes out through the door on the right; a long silence follows*]

YEGORUSHKA. Two diamonds.

AVDOTYA NAZAROVNA. Pass.

KOSYKH. Pass.

BABAKINA [*aside*]. Oh Lord, how boring all this is! Enough to kill you!

The same, ZINAÏDA SAVISHNA *and* LEBEDEV

ZINAÏDA SAVISHNA [*coming out of the door on the right with* LEBEDEV, *in a subdued voice*]. What's the idea – sitting out there by yourself? What a prima donna you are! Sit in here with the guests! [*she takes her former seat*]

LEBEDEV [*yawns*]. Oh, what a life, for our sins! [*seeing* BABAKINA] Goodness gracious, there's our little ray of sunshine, our little lollipop! . . . [*greets her*] How are you, my sweetheart?

BABAKINA. Thank you, very well.

LEBEDEV. Thank God for that! Thank God! [*sits down in an armchair*] Well, well . . . Gavrila!

[GAVRILA *serves him with a small glass of vodka and a glass of water; he drinks the vodka first, then the water*]

FIRST GUEST. Good health to you! . . .

LEBEDEV. Health, indeed! I'm thankful to manage to keep alive. [*to his wife*] Where's our little one, Zyuzyushka?

KOSYKH [*tearfully*]. Now just tell me, how is it we didn't get a single trick? [*jumps up*] Why the devil did we lose?

AVDOTYA NAZAROVNA [*also jumps up, angrily*]. I'll tell you why, my dear man – if you don't know how to play, don't join in the game. What business have you to go into somebody else's suit? So you held back your ace and got left with it!

[*both run forward from behind the table*]

KOSYKH [*tearfully*]. Just listen, my friends . . . I was holding the ace, king, queen, knave and eight down in diamonds, ace of spades and one, you understand, just one little heart . . . and she, Heaven forgive her, couldn't go a small slam! I declared no trumps . . .

AVDOTYA NAZAROVNA [*interrupting*]. I was the one who went no trumps! You bid two no trumps . . .

KOSYKH. That's preposterous! . . . Just let me . . . You had . . . I had . . . you had . . . [*to* LEBEDEV] Now, you be the judge, Pavel Kerylych! I had the ace, king, queen, knave and eight down in diamonds . . .

LEBEDEV [*stopping his ears*]. Leave me alone . . . please, please . . . leave off . . .

AVDOTYA NAZAROVNA [*shouts*]. It was I who said no trumps!

KOSYKH [*fiercely*]. I'll be damned if I ever sit down to play with that old trout again! [*goes rapidly out into the garden*]

AVDOTYA NAZAROVNA. Ugh! He makes my blood boil! Trout! Trout yourself!

BABAKINA. Well, you're not so sweet-tempered yourself, Grandma!

AVDOTYA NAZAROVNA [*seeing* BABAKINA, *throws up her hands*]. If that's not my precious Marfa Yegorovna! . . . She's here all the time and I'm such a blind old hen that I didn't see her . . . My little darling! [*kisses her shoulder and sits down beside her*] What a joy this is! Now let me look at you, my precious! It can't do any harm to look at you — I haven't got an evil eye!

LEBEDEV. There she goes! . . . You'd do better to find her a husband.

AVDOTYA NAZAROVNA. Just see if I don't! Before I'm dead and buried, I'll have her and Sanechka married, I'll be hanged if I don't. Before I'm dead and buried, I say . . . [*sighs*] But where are you to find them nowadays, these husbands? Here they are, our future husbands, all sitting around, huddled up like a lot of wet cockerels! . . .

THIRD GUEST. Not a very suitable comparison. In my view, if modern young men prefer a bachelor existence, it's social conditions that are responsible for that, so to speak . . .

LEBEDEV. There, there, please don't philosophise! I don't like it.

The same and SASHA

SASHA [*comes in and walks up to her father*]. Such marvellous weather we're having, yet here you're all sitting in a stuffy room!

ZINAÏDA SAVISHNA. Sashenka, don't you see that Marfa Yegorovna's here?

SASHA. I'm sorry. [*goes up to* BABAKINA *and greets her*]

BABAKINA. How stand-offish you're getting, Sanechka . . . You haven't been to see me once lately.

[*they embrace*]

Congratulations, darling! . . .

SASHA. Thank you. [*sits down beside her father*]

LEBEDEV. Yes, Avdotya Nazarovna, it's a difficult business getting husbands nowadays. And not only husbands — you can't even get a decent best man. Modern young men, if I may say so without offence, seem to me to be insipid, like food that's overdone.

God help them! . . . You can't dance, or talk, or drink with them properly.

AVDOTYA NAZAROVNA. They're all past-masters at drinking – as long as you give them something to drink.

LEBEDEV. There isn't much in mere drinking – even a horse can drink . . . No, you must drink intelligently! In my days a young man would swot at his studies the whole day long, but as soon as the evening came round, off he'd go straight to the first brightly-lit place he could find, and dance like a top until morning . . . He'd dance and flirt with the ladies, and all that . . . [gives himself a flick on the throat] And he'd tell stories and philosophise until his tongue nearly dropped off . . . But the modern young men . . . [waves his hand] I can't understand them. No good to man or beast. In the whole district there's only one decent fellow, but he's married [sighs], and it seems that he's beginning to run wild, too . . .

BABAKINA. Who's that?

LEBEDEV. Nikolasha Ivanov.

BABAKINA. Yes, he's a nice man [with a grimace] – only he's so unhappy.

ZINAÏDA SAVISHNA. You're right there, darling. Well, how could he be happy? [sighs] What a mistake he made, poor man! He married a Jewess, and, of course, the poor fellow calculated that her parents would give away a fortune with her, but it turned out to be quite the reverse . . . From the day she changed her religion, her father and mother simply haven't recognised her, in fact, they've put their parental curse on her. So he didn't get a farthing, after all. He's regretting it now, but it's too late.

SASHA. Mamma, it's not true.

BABAKINA [with animation]. But how isn't it true, Shurochka? You know that everybody knows it. If he didn't count on that, why should he have married a Jewess? Aren't there enough Russian girls? He just made a mistake, darling, he made a mistake! . . . [eagerly] And, good Lord! doesn't she get it in the neck from him now! It's quite laughable! Sometimes he comes home from somewhere or other, and goes straight to her and says, 'Your father and mother have swindled me! Get out of my house!' But where can she go to? Her father and mother won't take her back; she might do a servant girl's job, but she hasn't been trained to work. So he torments and torments her until the Count takes her side. If it weren't for the Count, he'd soon send her to her grave . . .

AVDOTYA NAZAROVNA. And sometimes he locks her up in a cellar and tells her to eat garlic. 'Come on, you so-and-so, swallow it,' he says. So she goes on eating it until it blows her out terribly . . .

[*laughter*]

SASHA. Papa, but this is all lies!

LEBEDEV. Well, what does it matter? Let them talk rubbish as much as they like. [*shouts*] Gavrila!

[GAVRILA *serves him with vodka and water*]

ZINAÏDA SAVISHNA. So that's how it is the poor man's ruined, darling. His financial affairs are in a very bad way. If Borkin weren't looking after his estate, he and his Jewess wouldn't have anything to eat. [*sighs*] As for us, darling, I can't tell you how we've suffered on his account. God alone knows how we've suffered! Would you believe it, my dear? – he's had nine thousand owing to us for the last three years!

BABAKINA [*horrified*]. Nine thousand!

ZINAÏDA SAVISHNA. Yes . . . it was my dear husband Pashenka who arranged to lend him money. He can't tell a man you can lend money to from a man you can't. I'm not complaining about the capital – God be with it! but I wish he'd pay the interest regularly.

SASHA [*passionately*]. Mamma, you've told us all this a thousand times already!

ZINAÏDA SAVISHNA. What's it got to do with you? Why are you defending him?

SASHA [*rising*]. But how have you the heart to say all that about a man who hasn't done you any harm? Tell me, what harm has he done you?

THIRD GUEST. If I may say so, Alexandra Pavlovna, I respect Nikolay Alexeyevich, and I've always felt it an honour to know him – though, speaking *entre nous*, he does seem to me to be an adventurer.

SASHA. If that's how you feel, I congratulate you.

THIRD GUEST. Just as a proof of what I was saying I'll tell you something that was passed on to me by his *attaché*, or, if you like, his *chicherone* Borkin. Two years ago when there was a cattle epidemic, he bought a lot of cows, insured them . . .

ZINAÏDA SAVISHNA. Yes, yes, yes! I remember that. I've been told about it, too.

THIRD GUEST. He insured them, and, do you know, then he infected them with the plague and got the insurance money.

SASHA. Oh, but all this is sheer nonsense! Utter rubbish! No-one ever dreamed of buying cattle or infecting cattle! Borkin invented the idea himself and went boasting about it everywhere. When Ivanov found it out, Borkin had to beg his forgiveness for a whole fortnight afterwards. Ivanov's only fault is weakness of character, so that he hasn't the heart to turn that Borkin out. And then he trusts people too much! He's had everything stolen and plundered from him; anyone who felt inclined could make money out of his generosity.

LEBEDEV. Shura, don't get so heated about it. That's enough.

SASHA. But why do they talk such nonsense? And how boring it all is! Ivanov, Ivanov, Ivanov — there's no other topic of conversation. [*goes towards the door, then returns*] I'm simply astonished! [*to the young guests*] I'm simply astonished at your patience. Aren't you bored to be sitting here like this? The very air is stiff with boredom! Well, say something, try to entertain the young ladies, do something! If you've nothing else to talk about except Ivanov, can't you laugh, or sing, or dance, or something? . . .

LEBEDEV [*laughing*]. That's right, tell them off! Tell them off properly!

SASHA. Listen then, just do me this favour. If you don't want to dance, or sing, or laugh, if all that bores you, then just for once in your life, as an exception, I mean, do try to make a tremendous effort and think of something witty and brilliant to say, something to amuse us. It doesn't matter if it's rude and impertinent, so long as it's funny and novel. Or if you could all *do* something, something quite small, hardly noticeable, but something a bit original and daring, so that we young ladies could look at you and say 'Oh', admiringly, for once in our lives! You do want to be popular with us, don't you? . . . Then why don't you try to make us admire you? Oh, you gentlemen! You're a poor lot, a poor lot, all of you — it's enough to make a cat weep, just to look at you! I've told you a thousand times, and I'll go on telling you, too — you're a poor lot!

The same, IVANOV *and* SHABELSKY

SHABELSKY [*comes in with* IVANOV *through the door on the right*]. Who's making a speech here? You, Shurochka? [*laughs loudly and shakes hands with her*] Congratulations on your birthday, my dear, may you live long and never be born again.

ZINAÏDA SAVISHNA [*joyfully*]. Nikolay Alexeyevich, Count!

LEBEDEV. Well! Who do I see . . . Count! [*goes to meet him*]

SHABELSKY [*seeing* ZINAÏDA *and* BABAKINA *and stretching his arms towards them*]. Two bankers on one sofa! . . . Beautiful to behold! [*greets them; to* ZINAÏDA] How d'you do, Zyuzyushka? [*to* BABAKINA] How d'you do, my precious?

ZINAÏDA SAVISHNA. I'm so glad to see you. You're such a rare visitor here, Count. [*shouts*] Gavrila, bring some tea! Do sit down, please. [*gets up and goes out through the door on the right, then returns immediately, looking extremely preoccupied*]

[SASHA *takes her former seat.* IVANOV *greets everybody in silence.*]

LEBEDEV [*to* SHABELSKY]. Where have you come from? What's brought you here? This really is a surprise. [*embraces him*] Count, you're a wretch, you know! Decent people don't behave the way you do. [*leads him to the front of the stage by his arm*] Why don't you ever come to see us? Angry, or what?

SHABELSKY. But how can I come to see you? Riding a broomstick? I haven't got any horses of my own, and Nikolay won't bring me with him. He tells me to stay at home with Sarah, so that she won't feel lonely. Send your horses to fetch me, then I'll come to see you . . .

LEBEDEV [*waves his hand*]. No fear! Zyuzyushka would sooner die than lend her horses. My dear fellow, my good old friend, don't you know that you're nearer and dearer to me than anybody else? You and I are the only ones left now out of all the old cronies! 'In you I love my former griefs, And the days of my ruined youth.' . . . Joking apart, I do feel I could almost weep. [*embraces the Count*]

SHABELSKY. Let me go, do! You smell like a wine cellar . . .

LEBEDEV. My dear fellow, you can't imagine how I miss my friends! Sometimes I could hang myself with boredom. [*quietly*] Zyuzyushka has driven all the decent people away with her moneylending, so that now we only have Zulus, as you

see . . . all these Dudkins and Budkins . . . Now, have some
tea . . .

[GAVRILA *serves Count with tea*]

ZINAÏDA SAVISHNA [*preoccupied, to* GAVRILA] Really, why will you
serve tea in this way? Why don't you bring some preserves?
Gooseberry, or something?

SHABELSKY [*laughing loudly, to* IVANOV]. Well, what did I tell you? [*to*
LEBEDEV] I had a bet with him on the way that when we arrived,
Zyuzyushka would immediately offer us gooseberry preserve.

ZINAÏDA SAVISHNA. You enjoy laughing at people, Count, just as
you used to.

LEBEDEV. They've made about twenty barrels of it, so what can
you do with it?

SHABELSKY [*sits down beside the table*]. You're still making money,
Zyuzyushka? I suppose you've got a million or so by now, eh?

ZINAÏDA SAVISHNA [*with a sigh*]. To an outsider we may appear to
be richer than anybody else, but where do they think the money
comes from? It's only talk.

SHABELSKY. Rather! We know! We know what a poor hand you
are at the game . . . [*to* LEBEDEV] Pasha, tell me on your honour,
have you saved a million?

LEBEDEV. I don't know. You ask Zyuzyushka.

SHABELSKY [*to* BABAKINA]. And our plump little pigeon here will soon
have a million, too! She gets prettier and plumper every hour, let
alone every day . . . That's what a lot of money does to a woman!

BABAKINA. Thank you very much, your Excellency, but I don't
like all this mockery.

SHABELSKY. But, my dear little banker, do you call this mockery?
It's simply a cry from the heart, I'm moved to speech by excess
of feeling. Really, I love you and Zyuzyushka beyond words.
[*gaily*] It's sheer rapture! . . . It's ecstasy! I can't look at either of
you unmoved . . .

ZINAÏDA SAVISHNA. You're just as you used to be. [*to* YEGORUSHKA]
Yegorushka, blow out the candles. What's the point of keeping
them alight if you're not playing?

[YEGORUSHKA *starts, then blows out the candles and sits down*]

[*to* IVANOV] How's your wife keeping, Nikolay Alexeyevich?

IVANOV. Not at all well. Today the doctor told me definitely that
she has T.B. . . .

ZINAÏDA SAVISHNA. Really? What a pity! . . . [*sighs*] And we all are so fond of her . . .

SHABELSKY. Nonsense, nonsense, nonsense! . . . She hasn't got T.B. at all, it's just a doctor's quackery, nothing but a trick. Aesculapius wants to come to the house, so he invents T.B. A good thing that the husband's not jealous!

[IVANOV *makes an impatient movement*]

As for Sarah herself, I don't trust a single word or action of hers. All my life I've never trusted doctors, or lawyers, or women. Nonsense, nonsense, quackery and tricks!

LEBEDEV. You are an astonishing fellow, Matvey! You've adopted a sort of misanthropic pose and carry it about with you like a child with a new toy. You're a man like any other, but as soon as you start talking, anyone would think you'd got a frog in your throat, or perpetual catarrh.

SHABELSKY. Well, you wouldn't expect me to embrace all these impostors and cads, would you?

LEBEDEV. But where do you see these impostors and cads?

SHABELSKY. Well, present company excepted, of course, but . . .

LEBEDEV. There's your 'but' . . . All this is just a pose.

SHABELSKY. A pose? . . . You're lucky not to have a philosophy of life of any kind.

LEBEDEV. What's my philosophy of life? I just sit about and wait for the moment when I can kick the bucket. That's my philosophy of life. You and I, brother, are past the age when one thinks of philosophies of life. [*shouts*] Gavrila!

SHABELSKY. You've had enough of Gavrila already. Just look at the colour of your nose!

LEBEDEV. Never mind, my dear fellow. I'm not getting married today.

ZINAÏDA SAVISHNA. Doctor Lvov hasn't been to see us for a long time. He's quite forgotten us.

SASHA. He's my pet aversion. A paragon of honesty! He can't ask for a glass of water, or light a cigarette without letting you know how wonderfully honest he is. Walking or talking, it's written all over his forehead: 'I'm an honest man!' He bores me.

SHABELSKY. He's a narrow-minded, bigoted leech! [*mimics*] 'Make way for honest labour!' He lays down the law at every step, like a parrot, and he's got it into his head that he really is another

Dobrolyubov.* Anyone who doesn't lay down the law is a cad. His opinions are quite astonishing in their profundity. If a peasant is prosperous and lives like a human being, it means he's a cad and a profiteer. If I wear a velvet jacket and have a manservant to help me to dress – I'm a cad and a serf-owner. He's so honest, so wonderfully honest, that he's bursting with it. He's all on edge with it. I'm almost afraid of him. Really, I am . . . I feel at any moment he may, out of a sense of duty, punch me in the face or call me a cad.

IVANOV. I find him terribly tiring, but all the same I like him. He's very sincere.

SHABELSKY. And what sincerity! Last night he came up to me, and, *à propos* of nothing, said, 'You are profoundly repugnant to me, Count.' Thank you very much! And all this isn't just naïveté, it's done with a purpose: his voice trembles, his eyes burn, his knees shake . . . The devil take his pig-headed sincerity! Why, I may be repulsive and vile to him, that's natural in a way . . . I'm conscious of it myself, but why need he say so to my face? I'm a worthless man, but when all's said and done, I have got grey hair . . . This futile, ruthless honesty!

LEBEDEV. Now, now, now! Surely, you've been young yourself, you ought to understand.

SHABELSKY. Yes, I've been young and foolish, and I've fancied myself as another Chatsky,† too, exposing the cads and impostors, but never in all my life have I called thieves thieves to their face, or talked about a rope in the house of a condemned man. I was properly brought up. But your fat-headed leech would think he was on top of the world, grappling with his life's problem, if only Fate would give him an opportunity, in the name of principles and human ideals, to swipe me publicly in the face.

LEBEDEV. All young men have their little foibles. I had an uncle once, a follower of Hegel . . . he would fill up his house with guests, and, after a drink or two he'd get up on a chair and begin: 'You are ignoramuses! You're the power of darkness! The dawn of a new life . . .' etc., etc., etc. And so he'd go on lecturing them . . .

* A Russian literary critic of the nineteenth century, well known for his radical views.
† The hero of a famous comedy by Griboyedov, *The Mischief of Being Clever*.

SASHA. And what did the guests do?

LEBEDEV. Nothing. They just listened and went on drinking. However, once I challenged him to a duel . . . my own uncle. It happened because of Lord Bacon. As far as I remember – God help my poor memory – I was sitting just as Matvey is sitting now, and my uncle, with poor Gerasim Nilovich, was just about where Nikolasha is standing . . . Well, Gerasim Nilovich asked a question . . . [*enter* BORKIN]

The same and BORKIN. *He comes skipping and singing into the room through the door on the right. He is smartly dressed and carries a parcel. There is a hum of welcome.*

YOUNG LADIES. Mikhail Mikhailovich!

LEBEDEV. Michel Michelich! I can hear him . . .

SHABELSKY. The life of the party!

BORKIN. Here I am! [*runs up to* SASHA] Most noble signorina, may I congratulate the universe on the birth of so noble a flower as yourself? . . . As a testimony of my admiration, may I present you [*hands her the parcel*] with these fireworks and Roman candles of my own manufacture? May they brighten the night just as you brighten the gloom of this dark realm. [*bows theatrically*]

SASHA. Thank you.

LEBEDEV [*laughing loudly, to* IVANOV] Why don't you turn out this Judas?

BORKIN [*to* LEBEDEV]. Pavel Kerylich, my respects! . . . [*to* IVANOV] My patron . . . [*sings*] *Nicolàs voilà*, hidy-ho! [*goes round greeting everybody*] The most estimable Zinaïda Savishna . . . The divine Marfa Yegorovna . . . The most worthy Avdotya Nazarovna . . . His Excellency the Count . . .

SHABELSKY [*laughing loudly*]. The life of the party! . . . As soon as he comes, the atmosphere gets brighter. D'you notice it?

BORKIN. Ugh, I'm tired. I've said 'how d'you do' to everybody, haven't I? Well, what's the news, gentlemen? Isn't there something special, something with a strong smell? . . . [*earnestly, to* ZINAÏDA SAVISHNA] Just listen to this, Mamma dear . . . As I was on my way here . . . [*to* GAVRILA] Gavrila, bring me some tea, but no gooseberry preserve! [*to* ZINAÏDA SAVISHNA.] As I was on my way here, I saw some peasants stripping the bark off your willow

bushes by the river. Why don't you lease out those willow
bushes?

LEBEDEV [*to* IVANOV]. Why don't you turn out this Judas?

ZINAÏDA SAVISHNA [*alarmed*]. But that's quite true! It never entered
my head!

BORKIN [*moving his arms as if doing physical exercises*]. I can't manage
without exercise . . . Now, Mamma dear, isn't there some game
we could play? Marfa Yegorovna, I'm in such high fettle . . . I
feel quite exalted! [*sings*] 'Again I stand before you.' . . .

ZINAÏDA SAVISHNA. Do let's arrange something, please – everybody's feeling bored.

BORKIN. Really, gentlemen, why are you all so downcast? You sit
there like a lot of jurymen in court! Let's arrange something!
What would you like? Forfeits, a game of catch, dancing or
fireworks? . . .

YOUNG LADIES [*clapping*]. Fireworks, fireworks! [*they run into the
garden*]

SASHA [*to* IVANOV]. Why are you looking so sad today?

IVANOV. I've got a headache, Shurochka – besides, I'm depressed.

SASHA. Come to the drawing-room.

[*they go out through the door on the right; all the others go out into
the garden except* ZINAÏDA SAVISHNA *and* LEBEDEV]

ZINAÏDA SAVISHNA. That's what I like – there's a young man for
you. He hasn't been here a minute and he's cheered up everybody already. [*turns down the large lamp*] While they're in the
garden there's no point in burning good candles. [*blows out the
candles*]

LEBEDEV [*following her*]. Zyuzyushka, we ought to offer our visitors
some refreshments. . . .

ZINAÏDA SAVISHNA. There! Look at all these candles . . . no wonder
people think we're rich. [*blows them out*]

LEBEDEV [*following her*]. Zyuzyushka, why don't you give these
people something to eat? . . . They're young, they must be
hungry by now, poor things . . . Zyuzyushka. . . .

ZINAÏDA SAVISHNA. The Count hasn't finished his glass. What a
waste of sugar! . . . [*goes out through the door on the left*]

LEBEDEV. Pshaw! . . . [*goes out into the garden*]

IVANOV *and* SASHA

SASHA [*entering with* IVANOV *through the door on the right*]. Everyone's
gone into the garden.

IVANOV. That's how things are, Shurochka. In the past I used to
think a great deal and work a great deal, yet I never felt tired.
Nowadays, I do nothing and think about nothing, but I feel
exhausted in mind and body. My conscience worries me day
and night, I feel I'm deeply at fault, yet how exactly I am at fault
I can't make out. And in addition to that, there's my wife's
illness, the lack of money, the constant nagging, the scandal-
mongering, the futile talk, the stupid Borkin . . . My own home
has become odious to me, and living there is worse than torture.
I tell you frankly, Shurochka, even the company of my wife
who loves me has become unbearable to me. You're an old
friend, and you won't mind my frankness. I've come here to
you now just to amuse myself, but I feel bored even here, and
I'm longing to go home again. Forgive me, please, I'll go back
quietly now.

SASHA. Nikolay Alexeyevich, I understand your trouble. Your
mis-fortune is that you're lonely. You need someone with you
whom you could love, someone who would understand you.
Only love can regenerate you.

IVANOV. Can it indeed, Shurochka! It would be the last straw if
an old wash-out like me started a new love affair! God preserve
me from any such misfortune! No, my little clever-head, it
isn't a love affair that I need. I tell you, before God I tell
you, I can bear anything: anxiety, mental depression, financial
ruin, the loss of my wife, premature old age and loneliness,
but I just can't bear the contempt I feel for myself. I'm dying
of shame at the thought that I, a healthy, strong man, have
somehow got transformed into a sort of Hamlet, or Manfred,
or one of those 'superfluous' people, the devil knows which!
There are some pitiable people who are flattered when you
call them Hamlets or 'superfluous', but to me it's a disgrace!
It stirs up my pride, a feeling of shame oppresses me, and I
suffer. . . .

SASHA [*jokingly, through tears*]. Nikolay Alexeyevich, let us run
away to America.

IVANOV. I feel too lazy to walk to that door, and you talk of America! . . .

[*they go towards the garden exit*]

Really, Shura, you must find it terribly difficult living here. When I look at the sort of people who surround you, I feel quite afraid. Whom could you marry here? The only hope is for some passing lieutenant or student to take you away. . . .

ZINAÏDA SAVISHNA *enters through the door on the left with a jar of preserves.*

IVANOV. Excuse me, Shurochka, I'll catch you up . . .

[SASHA *goes out into the garden*]

IVANOV. Zinaïda Savishna, I have a request to make . . .

ZINAÏDA SAVISHNA. What is it, Nikolay Alexeyevich?

IVANOV [*hesitates*]. The fact is, you see, that my promissory note is due for payment the day after tomorrow. You would oblige me greatly by deferring it, or by allowing me to add the interest to the capital. I have no money at all at present . . .

ZINAÏDA SAVISHNA [*alarmed*]. But, Nikolay Alexeyevich, how could I? What sort of arrangement would it be? No, no, please don't suggest it. For God's sake, don't torment an unfortunate woman! . . .

IVANOV. I'm sorry, I'm sorry . . . [*goes out into the garden*]

ZINAÏDA SAVISHNA. Ugh, my goodness, how he frightened me! . . . I'm trembling all over . . . all over . . . [*goes out through the door on the right*]

KOSYKH *enters through the door on the left and walks across the stage.*

KOSYKH. I was holding ace, king, queen, jack, eight down in diamonds, ace of spades and one . . . one little heart, and she, devil take her, couldn't go a small slam . . . [*goes out*]

AVDOTYA NAZAROVNA *and the* FIRST GUEST

AVDOTYA NAZAROVNA [*enters with the* FIRST GUEST *from the garden*]. I'd like to tear her to pieces, the old miser . . . tear her to pieces, I would. It's really no joke – here I am – I've been in this house since five o'clock, and she hasn't offered me a bit of stale herring! What a house! What a household! . . .

FIRST GUEST. I'm so bored, I could almost run and smash my head against the wall! What people, God forgive them! I feel I could start howling like a wolf and biting people from sheer boredom and hunger!

AVDOTYA NAZAROVNA. I'd like to tear her to pieces, God forgive me!

FIRST GUEST. I think I'll have a drink, and be off! Not even the brides you offered to find me would keep me here. How the devil can a fellow think of love when he hasn't had a single glass of anything since dinner?

AVDOTYA NAZAROVNA. Shall we go and look, or what? . . .

FIRST GUEST. Sh-sh! Quietly! I think there's some Schnapps in the sideboard in the dining-room. We'll tackle Yegorushka. Sh-sh!
[*they go out through the door on the left*]

ANNA PETROVNA *and* LVOV *enter through the door on the right.*

ANNA PETROVNA. Never mind, they'll be glad to see us. No one's in here. I suppose they're in the garden.

LVOV. I wish you'd tell me why you've brought me here, to this vultures' nest? This is no place for either of us. Honest people can't breathe in this atmosphere!

ANNA PETROVNA. Now just listen to me, Mister Honest! It isn't good manners to take a lady out and talk about nothing but your own honesty all the time! It may be honest, but it's also boring, to say the least. Never talk to women about your virtues. Let them discover them on their own. When my Nikolay was like you, he only sang songs and told quaint stories when he was with women, yet they all knew what sort of man he was.

LVOV. Ah, don't talk to me about your Nikolay, I know all about him!

ANNA PETROVNA. You're a good man, Doctor, but you don't understand anything. Let's go into the garden. He never used to say, 'I'm honest. I suffocate in this atmosphere!' He never talked about 'vultures' and 'this owls' nest' and 'these crocodiles'. He left the menagerie alone, but when he felt indignant about something, all he'd say was, 'Oh, how unfair I've been today!' or 'Anyuta, I'm sorry for that man!' That's how it was with him, but you . . .
[*they go out*]

AVDOTYA NAZAROVNA *and* FIRST GUEST

FIRST GUEST [*entering through the door on the left*]. If there isn't any in the dining-room, there must be some in the pantry or somewhere. We ought to find Yegorushka. Let's go through the drawing-room.

[*they go out through the door on the right*]

BABAKINA, BORKIN *and* SHABELSKY

BABAKINA *and* BORKIN *run in from the garden, laughing;* SHABELSKY *trots in after them, also laughing and rubbing his hands.*

BABAKINA. Oh, how boring it is! [*laughs loudly*] How boring! They all just walk about or sit as stiffly as if they'd all swallowed pokers. My very bones are numb with boredom. [*jumps about*] I must stretch my legs!

[BORKIN *seizes her by the waist and kisses her cheek*]

SHABELSKY [*laughs and snaps his fingers*]. Well, I'll be damned! [*grunts*] In a way. . . .

BABAKINA. Let go, keep your hands off me, you shameless man! Or God knows what the Count here will be thinking! Leave me alone!

BORKIN. My soul's delight, my heart's desire! [*kisses her*] Lend me two thousand three hundred roubles!

BABAKINA. No, no, no . . . It's all very well, but when it comes to money . . . thank you very much . . . No, no, no! . . . Please let go of my hands! . . .

SHABELSKY [*trotting round them*]. Little pompon! She has her attractive points. . . .

BORKIN [*seriously*]. Well, that's enough of that. Let's talk business. Let us discuss things straightforwardly, in a business-like way. Answer me honestly, without evasions or beating about the bush – just yes or no. Listen! [*points at the Count*] He needs money, at least three thousand a year. You need a husband. Do you want to be a Countess?

SHABELSKY [*laughing loudly*]. What an amazing cynic!

BORKIN. Do you want to be a Countess? Yes or no?

BABAKINA [*agitated*]. You're making it all up, Misha, really . . . Besides, such things aren't done like this, in such a rush. . . . If the Count wants to, he can talk about it himself, and . . . and anyway I don't know how it can . . . so suddenly, I mean, all at once . . .

BORKIN. Now, now do stop putting it on! . . . It's a business matter . . . Yes, or no?

SHABELSKY [*laughing and rubbing his hands*]. Well, I must say . . . The devil take it, I'd better arrange this scandalous business for myself, eh? Little precious . . . [*kisses* BABAKINA'S *cheek*] Charmer! . . . You little duck! . . .

BABAKINA. Stop, stop a moment, you've quite upset me . . . Go away, go! . . . No, don't go yet! . . .

BORKIN. Quickly! Yes, or no? We've no time to waste . . .

BABAKINA. What do you say to this, Count? Come and stay at my house for a day or two . . . We have a gay time there, it's not like this place. Come tomorrow. [*to* BORKIN] You were joking, weren't you?

BORKIN [*angrily*]. Now who'd want to joke about serious matters like this?

BABAKINA. Stop, stop a moment . . . Oh, I feel quite faint! I feel faint! A Countess . . . I'm going to faint . . . I'm going to fall down . . .

[BORKIN *and the* COUNT, *laughing, take her by the arms and kiss her on the cheeks as they lead her out through the door on the right*]

IVANOV, SASHA *later;* ANNA PETROVNA

IVANOV *and* SASHA *run in from the garden.*

IVANOV [*clutching his head in despair*]. It can't be! Please don't, Shurochka, don't . . . Oh, it mustn't be!

SASHA [*with abandon*]. I love you madly . . . You're all my joy, without you my life has no meaning – no happiness! To me – you're everything. . . .

IVANOV. But why, why? My God, I don't understand anything . . . Shurochka, please don't go on like this!

SASHA. When I was a child you were the only joy in my life. I loved you, I loved you body and soul, more than I loved myself, and now . . . Oh, I love you, Nikolay Alexeyevich . . . I'll go anywhere with you, to the other end of the world, even beyond the grave . . . only for Heaven's sake, do let's go soon, otherwise I'll suffocate. . . .

IVANOV [*bursts into happy laughter*]. What is all this? Can it mean beginning life all over again, from the beginning? Can it, Shurochka? Oh, my happiness! . . . [*draws her to himself*] My youth, my freshness!

ANNA PETROVNA [*enters from the gardens and, seeing her husband and* SASHA, *stops as if rooted to the spot*]

IVANOV. It means — to live again? Yes? Work again?

> [*they kiss; after kissing,* IVANOV *and* SASHA *look round and see* ANNA PETROVNA]

IVANOV [*horrified*]. Sarah!

CURTAIN

ACT THREE

IVANOV'S *study. A desk, on which papers, books, official envelopes, knick-knacks and revolvers are lying in disorder; beside the papers a lamp, a bottle of water, a plate with salt herring, slices of bread and cucumbers. On the walls are maps of the locality, pictures, shotguns, pistols, sickles, riding-whips, etc. It is midday.*

SHABELSKY, LEBEDEV, BORKIN *and* PYOTR

[SHABELSKY *and* LEBEDEV *are sitting by the desk.* BORKIN *is astride a chair in the middle of the stage.* PYOTR *is standing by the door*]

LEBEDEV. France has a clear-cut and definite policy . . . The French know what they want. They just want to rip the guts out of the sausage-makers, and that's all. But Germany's playing quite a different tune, my friend. Germany has plenty of irons in the fire besides France . . .

SHABELSKY. Nonsense! In my view, the Germans are cowards, and so are the French . . . They shake their fists at one another but they keep their other hands in their pockets. Believe me, the matter won't go beyond gestures. They won't fight.

BORKIN. And what I say is, why should they? What's the use of all these armaments and congresses and all the expense? You know what I'd do? I'd collect all the dogs in the country, inject them with a good dose of Pasteur's poison, then let them loose at the enemy's country. All my enemies would be mad in a month.

LEBEDEV [*laughing*]. His head's small to look at, but what great ideas it contains – millions of them, like fish in the sea.

SHABELSKY. Quite a virtuoso!

LEBEDEV. God bless you, Michel Michelich, anyway, you make us laugh! [*stops laughing*] Well, gentlemen, we talk and talk, but what about some vodka? *Repetatur.* [*fills three glasses*] Our good health!

[*they drink and eat*]

Salt herring makes a good snack, better than anything I know.

SHABELSKY. Well, no, I don't think so, cucumber's better . . .
Scientists have been puzzling their brains since the world began,
but they've never thought up anything nicer than a salt cucumber. [*to* PYOTR] Pyotr, go and fetch some more cucumbers,
and tell them to bake us four pasties with some onions. And see
they are hot.

[PYOTR *goes out*]

LEBEDEV. Caviare goes well with vodka, too. Only you must
know how to serve it. You must use intelligence . . . Take a
quarter of pressed caviare, two heads of green onion, some
olive oil, mix it all up and then, you know . . . just a little lemon
juice on top . . . It's enough to bowl you over! The smell alone
makes you dizzy!

BORKIN. Another nice snack after vodka is fried gudgeon. Only
you must know how to fry them. First you clean them, then roll
them in crumbs and fry until they're brown, so that they crackle
as you eat them . . . Crackle-crackle-crackle . . .

SHABELSKY. Yesterday Babakina had a nice hors-d'œuvre – white
mushrooms.

LEBEDEV. Ah, lovely!

SHABELSKY. Only they were prepared in a special way. You know,
with onion and bay leaf and all sorts of spices. When they took
the lid off the saucepan, the steam, the fragrance that came out!
It was a real joy!

LEBEDEV. Now then! *Repetatur*, gentlemen!

[*they drink*]

Our good health . . . [*looks at his watch*] It doesn't look as if I'd see
Nikolasha today. It's time for me to be going.

You say you've had mushrooms at Babakina's, but in my house
there's not a sign of a mushroom yet. Tell me, Count, why the
devil do you go to Marfutka's so often?

SHABELSKY [*pointing at* BORKIN *with a movement of his head*]. It's
him – he wants me to marry her . . .

LEBEDEV. Marry? How old are you?

SHABELSKY. I'm sixty-two.

LEBEDEV. Just the right age to get married. And Marfutka is just the
right woman for you.

BORKIN. Marfutka's not the point, it's Marfutka's money . . .

LEBEDEV. Is that what you want – Marfutka's money? Perhaps you'd like the moon, too?

BORKIN. You won't talk about the moon when you see this fellow marry and fill his pockets. You'll be licking your lips with envy then.

SHABELSKY. He's serious, you know. Our great genius here is quite certain that I'm going to take his advice and get married.

BORKIN. Well, aren't I right then? Isn't it definite any more?

SHABELSKY. What? You must be mad! When was it definite? . . . Pshaw! . . .

BORKIN. Thank you very much! I'm very grateful to you. Does this mean you're going to let me down? Now you say you will marry her, now you say you won't . . . the devil alone knows which. Yet you gave me your word of honour! So you won't marry her, then?

SHABELSKY [shrugs his shoulders]. He's really serious . . . What an amazing fellow!

BORKIN [indignantly]. In that case, what did you get an honest woman excited for? Now she's mad to be a Countess, she can't sleep or eat . . . Is that the sort of thing to joke about? Is it honourable? . . .

SHABELSKY [snaps his fingers]. All right then – supposing I do do this ignominious thing? Eh? Just to spite them! I'll go and do it. My word of honour, I will. That'll be quite a joke!

Enter LVOV.

LEBEDEV. Aesculapius – our most humble respects . . . [he shakes LVOV's *hand and sings*] 'Doctor, little father, save me, pray, I'm scared to death of my dying day.' . . .

LVOV. Hasn't Nikolay Alexeyevich come back yet?

LEBEDEV. No, I've been waiting for him for more than an hour myself.

[LVOV *paces the stage impatiently*]

Tell me, old man, how's Anna Petrovna?

LVOV. She's bad.

LEBEDEV [sighs]. May I go and say 'good morning' to her?

LVOV. No, please don't. I think she's asleep.

[*pause*]

LEBEDEV. A nice, likeable woman . . . [sighs] When she fainted on Shurochka's birthday round at our house, I happened to glance at her face – and I knew then she wouldn't live long, poor thing. I can't understand why she fainted then. I ran into the room, and there she was on the floor, quite pale, with Nikolasha kneeling beside her. He was pale, too, and Shurochka was there, crying. After that Shurochka and I just went about for a whole week as if we were in a daze.

SHABELSKY [to LVOV]. Tell me, most talented priest of Science, who's the great scientist that discovered that frequent visits from a young physician are beneficial to ladies suffering from chest complaints? It's a great discovery! A very great discovery indeed! Should one class it as allopathy or homoeopathy?

[LVOV makes as if to answer him, then with a contemptuous gesture goes out]

SHABELSKY. What a withering glance!

LEBEDEV. What's gnawing at you, Count? Why did you try to hurt him?

SHABELSKY [with irritation]. Well, why does he tell lies, then? T.B., there's no hope, she's going to die . . . He's lying, I say! I can't stand that.

LEBEDEV. But why do you think he's lying?

SHABELSKY [gets up and walks to and fro]. I can't conceive how a living being can suddenly die for no reason at all! Let's drop the subject!

KOSYKH runs in, out of breath.

KOSYKH. Is Nikolay Alexeyevich at home? How d'you do? [quickly shakes hands all round] Is he at home?

BORKIN. He is not.

KOSYKH [sits down, then jumps up]. In that case, I'll get along. [drinks a glass of vodka and quickly eats a snack] I must go. Business . . . I'm quite worn out . . . Can hardly stand on my feet . . .

LEBEDEV. Where have you come from?

KOSYKH. Barabanov. We played vint all night, and we've only just finished. I lost all I had on me . . . That Barabanov plays like a trooper. [tearfully] Just listen to this: I was holding hearts all the time . . . [he addresses BORKIN, who retreats from him abruptly] He goes diamonds, I go hearts again, he goes diamonds . . . Well, I don't get a trick. [*to* LEBEDEV] We play four clubs. I hold ace, queen, six in my hand, ace and ten, three of spades . . .

LEBEDEV [*stops his ears*]. Spare me, for Christ's sake, spare me!

KOSYKH [*to the* COUNT]. You do understand – ace, queen, six in clubs, ace, ten, three of spades . . .

SHABELSKY [*pushing him away*]. Go away, I don't want to listen . . .

KOSYKH. And all at once – bad luck! My ace of spades taken in the first round! . . .

SHABELSKY [*snatching up a revolver from the desk*]. Go away, or I'll shoot! . . .

KOSYKH [*waving his hand*]. What the devil . . . Can't I even talk to anybody? It's like living in Australia: no common interests, no social life . . . Everyone living on their own . . . However, I'd better go . . . it's time. [*snatches up his cap*] Time's precious. [*shakes hands with* LEBEDEV] Pass! . . .

[*laughter*]

KOSYKH *goes out and collides with* AVDOTYA NAZAROVNA
in the doorway.

AVDOTYA NAZAROVNA [*gives a shriek*]. Curse you, you nearly knocked me off my feet!

ALL TOGETHER. Ah-ah! Here she is again!

AVDOTYA NAZAROVNA. Oh, there you are! and I've been looking all over the house for you. How d'you do, my charming people, good appetite to you! [*shakes hands*]

LEBEDEV. What are you doing here?

AVDOTYA NAZAROVNA. I'm on business, my friend . . . [*to the* COUNT] It concerns you, your Excellency. [*bows*] The lady told me to give you her regards and inquire after your health . . . And she also commanded – the pretty little darling – she commanded me to tell you that if you don't come to see her this evening, she'll cry her pretty eyes out. 'Take him aside and whisper it secretly into his ear', that's what the little darling said. But why secretly? You're all friends here. Anyway, we're not stealing chickens; this is a genuine love match, and we're arranging it according to law and with mutual consent . . . I never touch drink, old sinner that I am, but just for this once I'll have one!

LEBEDEV. So shall I. [*pours it out*] You know, old girl, you do wear

well! I've known you as an elderly woman for the last thirty
years . . .

AVDOTYA NAZAROVNA. Well, I've lost count of my age. I've
buried two husbands, and I'd have married a third, but no one
would have me without a dowry. I've had about eight children.
[*takes her glass*] Well, we've begun a good job, may God help us
to finish it. They'd live happily together, and we'd be able
to look at them and rejoice. We'd offer them good advice
and wish them love and happiness . . . [*drinks*] This vodka's
strong!

SHABELSKY [*laughing loudly, to* LEBEDEV]. The curious thing is, you
know, that they seriously think that I . . . Amazing! [*rises*] But
what if I really decided to go through with this ignominious
thing? Eh, Pasha? Just out of spite . . . there, you old dog, knock
it back! Pasha, eh?

LEBEDEV. You're talking nonsense, Count. Your business is to
prepare to kick the bucket, brother – and mine, too. As for
Marfutka's money, you've missed your chance there, long ago.
Our time's over.

SHABELSKY. Yes, I'll do it! My word of honour, I will!

Enter IVANOV *and* LVOV.

LVOV. I want you to give me just five minutes.

LEBEDEV. Nikolasha! [*goes to meet* IVANOV *and embraces him*] How
are you, my friend? I've been waiting for you a whole hour.

AVDOTYA NAZAROVNA [*bows*]. How d'you do, sir?

IVANOV [*bitterly*]. So you've turned my study into a public bar
again! I've asked you all a thousand times not to do this . . .
[*walks up to the table*] There, you've spilled vodka over my
papers . . . crumbs . . . cucumbers . . . It's disgusting, you know!

LEBEDEV. My fault, Nikolasha, my fault . . . Forgive me. I must
have a talk with you, my friend, about a very serious matter.

BORKIN. And I, too.

LVOV. Nikolay Alexeyevich, may I have a word with you?

IVANOV [*points at* LEBEDEV]. He wants me too. Will you wait? I'll
see you afterwards . . . [*to* LEBEDEV] What is it you want?

LEBEDEV. Gentlemen, I want to speak to him privately. Please . . .

[*the* COUNT *goes out with* AVDOTYA NAZAROVNA,
BORKIN *follows, then* LVOV]

IVANOV. Pasha, you can drink as much as you like, it's your weakness, but I do entreat you not to make a drunkard of my uncle. He never used to drink before. It's bad for him.

LEBEDEV [*alarmed*]. My dear fellow, I didn't know . . . I didn't even notice . . .

IVANOV. If that silly old baby dies – God forbid! – it is I who'd feel bad about it, not you . . . What is it you want?

[*pause*]

LEBEDEV. You see, my dear friend . . . I don't know how to begin, to make it seem less shocking . . . Nikolasha, I'm ashamed, I know I'm blushing, and my tongue's sticking in my throat, but, my dear fellow, do try to put yourself in my place. Please understand that I'm just a subordinate, a slave, a mere doormat. Do forgive me . . .

IVANOV. What is it?

LEBEDEV. My wife's sent me . . . Do me a favour, be a good friend, please pay her the interest! You'd hardly believe it, she's almost nagged me to death. She keeps on going for me. Settle up with her, for God's sake!

IVANOV. Pasha, you know that I haven't any money at present.

LEBEDEV. I know, I know, but what am I to do? She won't wait. If she presents your promissory note, how will Shurochka and I ever be able to look you in the face?

IVANOV. I'm ashamed myself, Pasha, I wish I could sink into the earth, but . . . but where can I get money from? Tell me: where? The only thing is to wait until the autumn, when I sell the corn.

LEBEDEV [*shouts*]. She doesn't want to wait!

[*pause*]

IVANOV. Your position is awkward and unpleasant, but mine is far worse. [*walks up and down, thinking*] I can't think of anything . . . I've nothing to sell . . .

LEBEDEV. Why don't you go and ask Millbach? You know he owes you sixteen thousand.

[IVANOV *hopelessly waves his hand*]

I'll tell you what, Nikolasha . . . I know you'll be angry, but . . . do a favour to an old drunkard! As one friend to another . . . Do consider me as a friend . . . We've both been to the university, and liberals, too . . . Community of ideas and interests . . . We both studied at Moscow University . . . *Alma Mater* . . . [*he takes out his wallet*] Here, I've got some special money, not a soul at home knows about it. Take it as a loan . . . [*takes out the money and puts it on the table*] Drop your pride and take it as from one friend to another . . . I'd accept it from you, my word of honour I would . . .

[*pause*]

There it is, on the table: one thousand one hundred. You go and see her today and give it her yourself. Say, 'There, Zinaïda Savishna, and may it choke you!' Mind, though, don't give a hint that you borrowed it from me – God help you! Or I'll get it in the neck from Madam Gooseberry Preserve! [*stares into* IVANOV's *face*] There, there, don't! [*quickly picks up the money from the table and puts it in his pocket*] Please, don't! I was joking . . . Forgive me, for Christ's sake!

[*pause*]

You're fed up with it all?

[IVANOV *waves his hand*]

Yes, it's a bad business . . . [*sighs*] You're going through a bad patch, a sad time. You know, my friend, a man is like a samovar. He isn't always put away quietly on a shelf, every now and again he gets some live charcoal pushed into him: psh . . . psh! . . . Of course, that's a rotten comparison, but I can't think of anything cleverer . . . [*sighs*] Misfortune hardens the soul. I don't pity you, Nikolasha, you'll land on your feet, things will come right, but I feel hurt and angry, my friend, when I hear what other people . . . Tell me, where does all this gossip come from? The sort of thing that's being said about you all over the district – it's almost enough to make the public prosecutor's assistant drop in on you . . . You're said to be a murderer, a blood-sucker, a robber. . . .

IVANOV. All that's nonsense, I don't care . . . but I've got a headache.

LEBEDEV. It's all because you think too much.

IVANOV. I'm not thinking anything.

LEBEDEV. Anyway, Nikolasha, don't take any notice of all that, just you come to see us. Shurochka is fond of you, she understands and appreciates you. She's a good, honest girl, Nikolasha. She doesn't take after her father or mother, perhaps it was a passing stranger! Sometimes I look at her, my friend, and I can hardly believe that a drunkard with a red nose like mine could own such a treasure. Just come along and discuss something clever with her and – it'll cheer you up. She's loyal and sincere. . . .

[pause]

IVANOV. Pasha, my dear friend, leave me alone. . . .

LEBEDEV. I understand, I understand . . . [hurriedly looks at his watch] I understand. [embraces IVANOV] Goodbye. I've got to get to a consecration service at a school they're opening. [walks to the door, then stops] She's intelligent . . . Yesterday Shurochka and I began to talk about gossip. [laughs] And she fired off an aphorism: 'Papa,' she said, 'the glow-worms only shine so that the birds can find them easier at night, and good men only shine so that gossip and rumour can prey on them.' What do you think of that? Quite a genius! George Sand! . . .

IVANOV. Pasha! [stops him] What's the matter with me?

LEBEDEV. I've been wanting to ask you that question myself, but I felt too shy to do it. I don't know, my friend. Sometimes it seems to me that bad luck has got you down, but on the other hand I know that you're not that sort, that you . . . You'd not be defeated by misfortune. It must be something else, Nikolasha, but what it is – I can't make out.

IVANOV. I can't grasp it myself . . . It seems to me, or . . . anyway, it's not that!

[pause]

What I wanted to say is this. I used to have a workman, a fellow called Semyon, you must remember him. Once, during the threshing, he wanted to show his strength off before the girls, so he hoisted two sacks of rye on to his back, and strained himself. He died soon after. Well, it seems to me that I've strained myself, too. The high school, then the university, then farming, schools for peasant children, all sorts of plans and projects . . . I had different ideas from all the other people, I married differently, I took risks, I threw my money about right and left, I got too excited, as you know . . . I've been happier and I've suffered more than anyone in the district. Those have been my sacks, Pasha . . . I hoisted a load on my back, but my back gave way. At twenty we're all heroes, we undertake anything, we can do anything, but at thirty we're tired already and good for nothing. Tell me, how do you explain the way one gets so tired?

However, perhaps it isn't that . . . Not that, not that! . . . Go
now, Pasha, God bless you, you must be tired of me.

LEBEDEV [*eagerly*]. D'you know what? It's your surroundings that
are killing you.

IVANOV. That's silly, Pasha . . . and stale, too. Be off with you!

LEBEDEV. True enough, it is silly. Now I see it myself. I'm going,
I'm going! . . . [*goes out*]

IVANOV *alone.*

IVANOV. I'm a rotten, pitiful, contemptible creature. You need to
be a wretched, worn-out drunkard, like Pasha, to be able to love
and respect me still. Oh, God, how I despise myself! I hate my
voice, my footsteps, my hands, these clothes, my thoughts. Isn't
it ridiculous, isn't it infuriating? It's hardly a year since I was
tough and healthy, in good spirits, too, energetic, enthusiastic . . .
since I worked with my own hands, and could talk so well that
even the commonest louts were moved to tears . . . since I could
weep when I saw grief, and feel indignation when I met with
wickedness. I knew what inspiration was then, I knew the
charm and poetry of those quiet nights when you sit at your
desk working from sunset till dawn, or just sit and muse, and
dream. I had faith then, I could look into the future as if it
were my own mother's eyes . . . And now, oh, my God! I'm
tired, I've no faith, I idle away my days and nights. I can't
make my brain, or my hands, or my feet do what I want them to.
The estate goes to ruin, the forests are groaning under the axe.
[*weeps*] My land looks at me as an orphan looks at a stranger. I
expect nothing, I regret nothing, but my soul trembles with fear
at the thought of tomorrow . . . And this business with Sarah! I
swore I'd love her for ever, said how happy we'd be, I painted a
picture of a future life such as she'd never dreamed of! She
believed me. During all these five years I've just seen her wasting
away under a burden of self-sacrifice, exhausting herself in her
struggle with her conscience, yet – God knows – with never a
glance or a word of reproach to me . . . And what happens then?
I fall out of love with her . . . How? Why? What for? I can't
understand it. Now she's ill and suffering, she's going to die . . .
and I . . . I run away from her pale face, her sunken chest, her

imploring eyes like the mean coward I am . . . I'm ashamed, ashamed! . . .

[*pause*]

Sasha, a mere child, is touched by my troubles. She says she's in love with me – me, almost an old man – and I get drunk with it, I forget everything else in the world, like someone fascinated by music, and I start shouting: 'A new life! Happiness!' But the next day I don't believe in the new life or the new happiness any more than I believe in ghosts . . . What is it that's the matter with me then? What is this precipice that I seem to be pushing myself over? Where does all this weakness come from? What's happened to my nerves? If my poor wife upsets my vanity, or the servants annoy me, or my gun doesn't go off, I immediately get boorish and bad-tempered, quite unlike myself . . .

[*pause*]

I don't understand it, I don't, I don't! . . . I feel like putting a bullet into my head! . . .

LVOV *comes in.*

LVOV. I must talk things over with you, Nikolay Alexeyevich.

IVANOV. If we both keep talking things over day after day, Doctor, it will be more than human strength can stand.

LVOV. Will you hear me out?

IVANOV. I hear you out every day, but I still can't make out what it really is you want from me.

LVOV. I've said it clearly enough, and only someone completely heartless could fail to understand me.

IVANOV. My wife is about to die – I know that; I'm irreparably guilty as far as she's concerned – I know that, too; you are an honest, sincere man – I know it! What else do you want to say?

LVOV. I feel indignant when I see human cruelty! A woman is dying. She has a father and a mother whom she loves and whom she would like to see before she dies; they are perfectly well aware that she's going to die soon and that she still loves them, but – the damnable cruelty of it! – they still go on cursing her, as if they wanted to astound everybody by their own religious strength of mind. You, the man for whom she's sacrificed everything – her own home, her peace of mind – you go off every day quite openly and with the most obvious intentions to visit those Lebedev people!

IVANOV. Oh, I haven't been there for a fortnight . . .

LVOV [*without listening to him*]. With people like you, you have to speak plainly, without beating about the bush, but if you don't want to listen to me, don't . . . I'm used to calling a spade a spade. You want her to die, so as to be free for new adventures; all right, then, but couldn't you wait? If you let her die naturally, without hammering away at her all the time with your beastly cynicism, do you think you'd lose the Lebedev girl and her dowry? What of it? In a year's time, or maybe in two years, you'd succeed in turning some young girl's head and in getting hold of her dowry, just as you would now – you wonderful Tartuffe . . . So what are you in such a hurry for? Why is it so essential that your wife should die now, and not in a month, or a year? . . .

IVANOV. You're torturing me . . . You're a poor sort of doctor if you imagine that a man can go on controlling himself indefinitely. It's costing me a terrific effort not to answer back your insults.

LVOV. Oh, enough of that! Whom are you trying to fool? Drop this pretence!

IVANOV. Try to think clearly, if you're so clever: you seem to imagine it's the simplest thing in the world to understand me. Don't you? I married Anya in order to get a fat dowry . . . I wasn't given the dowry, I lost the trick, so now I'm kicking the life out of her, so that I can marry someone else and get another dowry . . . Is that right? How simple and uncomplicated! A man is such a simple, uncomplicated machine . . . No, Doctor, we all have too many wheels, and screws, and valves inside of us to be judged by first impressions or by a few external traits. I don't understand you, you don't understand me, and we don't understand ourselves. It's possible to be an excellent physician – and at the same time not to know anything about people. Admit that I'm right – and don't be so sure of yourself.

LVOV. But do you really think that you're so deep and I'm so lacking in intelligence that I can't distinguish between wickedness and honesty?

IVANOV. It's obvious that you and I will never agree about these things. For the last time I ask you . . . and please answer me without beating about the bush: what exactly do you want from me? What are you driving at? [*with irritation*] And, anyway, with whom have I the honour to be talking: with the counsel for the prosecution, or with my wife's doctor?

LVOV. I'm a doctor, and as a doctor, I demand that you behave differently . . . Your conduct is killing Anna Petrovna.

IVANOV. But what am I to do? What? If you understand me better than I understand myself, then answer me straight: what am I to do?

LVOV. At least, don't do what you do so openly.

IVANOV. Oh, my God! Do you really understand yourself? [*drinks water*] Leave me. I'm at fault a thousand times. I'll answer for it before God . . . but no one has given you the right to torture me every day like this.

LVOV. And who's given you the right to offend against my idea of what's right! You've worn me out and poisoned my mind. Until I happened to come into this district, I used to be able to accept the existence of people who were stupid and mad and capable of being carried away by their feelings, but I never believed that there were actually criminal people who deliberately and consciously directed their activities towards evil ends . . . I used to respect and love human beings, but when I saw you . . .

IVANOV. I've already heard all about that!

LVOV. You have, have you?

LVOV *catches sight of* SASHA *who has just come in; she is wearing a riding habit.*

LVOV. Well, now I hope we understand each other perfectly! [*shrugs his shoulders and walks out*]

IVANOV [*alarmed*]. Sasha – you here?

SASHA. Yes, I'm here! How are you? Weren't you expecting me? Why haven't you been to see us for so long?

IVANOV. Shura, for God's sake, this is rash of you! This might have a dreadful effect on my wife.

SASHA. She won't see me. I came in through the back door. I'll go in a minute. I'm worried: are you well? Why haven't you been to see us for so long?

IVANOV. My wife is upset with me as it is, she's almost dying, and you come here! Shura, Shura, this is thoughtless and unfeeling of you!

SASHA. But what was I to do? You haven't been to see us for a fortnight, you never answered my letters. I've been worn out with worry. I imagined you here, suffering unbearably, ill, dead . . . I haven't slept a single night in peace. I'll go in a minute . . . But do tell me at least: are you well?

IVANOV. No, I've worn myself out, and other people are torment- ing me continually . . . I just can't bear it any longer. And now you! How unhealthy all this is, how unnatural! Shura, I'm so much to blame, so much! . . .

SASHA. How you do like saying frightening, gloomy things! You to blame? You? To blame? Well, tell me what for, then?

IVANOV. I don't know, I don't know . . .

SASHA. That's not an answer. A sinner must know how he's sinned. Have you been forging banknotes, or what?

IVANOV. That's not funny.

SASHA. Are you to blame because you've stopped loving your wife? Well, maybe, but a man isn't master of his feelings; you didn't want to stop loving her. Are you to blame because she saw me telling you I loved you? No, you didn't want her to see it . . .

IVANOV [interrupting]. Go on, go on . . . Fallen in love, fallen out of love, not master of my feelings – what commonplaces these are . . . trite phrases which just don't help . . .

SASHA. It's tiring, talking to you. [looks at the pictures on the walls] How well that dog's painted! Was it done from life?

IVANOV. Yes, from life. And this love affair of ours is all just some- thing commonplace and trite: 'He lost heart and lost his grip on things. She appeared, cheerful and strong in spirit, and held out a helping hand.' It's beautiful, but it's only like what happens in novels. In real life you don't . . .

SASHA. In real life it's just the same.

IVANOV. I can see you've a very deep understanding of life! My whining inspires you with a sort of reverent awe, you seem to think that you've got hold of a second Hamlet in me . . . but in my opinion this neurotic state of mine and all the symptoms that go with it are just something to laugh at, and nothing else! People ought to laugh till their sides split at all my affectations, but you – what a wonderful fuss you make! You want to save me, to do something heroic! . . . Oh, how angry I am with myself today! I feel this state of tension I'm in today will come to a crisis. Either I shall break something, or . . .

SASHA. That's it, that's it, that's just what you need. Do break something, smash something, or start shouting . . . You're angry with me, it was stupid of me to come here. All right, then, show your indignation, shout at me, stamp your feet. Well? Start being angry . . .

[pause]

Well?

IVANOV. Funny child!

SASHA. Splendid! We actually seem to have smiled! Now do me a favour and deign to smile again!

IVANOV [laughs]. I've noticed when you start trying to save me and drive some sense into me, the expression on your face gets quite naïve, and the pupils of your eyes get bigger, as if you were staring at a comet, or something. Just a minute, your shoulder's covered with dust . . . [brushes the dust off her shoulder with his hand] A man who's naïve is a fool. But you women somehow contrive to be naïve in such a way that it's charming and natural, and comforting . . . and not as silly as it appears to be . . . And then there's another queer thing about you. As long as a man is healthy, and strong, and cheerful, you don't take any notice of him, but as soon as he starts slithering downhill and playing the poor Lazarus, you hang yourself round his neck. Is it really worse to be the wife of a strong, courageous man than a nurse to some tearful failure?

SASHA. It is worse.

IVANOV. But why? [laughs loudly] It's lucky Darwin didn't hear you say that, or he would have told you what's what. You're spoiling the human race. Thanks to people like you, we shall soon only have slobberers and neurotics born into the world.

SASHA. There are a lot of things men don't understand. Every girl is more attracted by a man who's a failure than by one who's a success, because what she wants is active love . . . Do you understand that? Active love. Men are taken up with their work and so love has to take a back seat with them. To have a talk with his wife, to take a stroll with her in the garden, to pass time pleasantly with her, to weep a little on her grave – that's all. But for us – love is life. I love you, and that means that I dream about how I'd cure you of your depression, how I'd follow you to the end of the world . . . If you went up a mountain, I'd follow you, if you fell over a precipice, I'd follow you . . . For instance, it would be sheer happiness for me to copy out your papers all night long, or watch over you all night so that no one woke you up, or just walk with you for miles, a hundred miles! . . . I remember once you came to our house about three years ago at harvest time, and you were all covered in dust and tired out, and you asked for a drink of water. I went to get you a glass, but you were lying on the sofa, sound asleep, when I came back with it. You slept the best part of the day in our house, and I stood outside the door all the time and guarded it, so that no one should come in. And I was so happy! The greater the effort, the greater the love . . . I mean one feels it more strongly.

IVANOV. Active love . . . Hm . . . It's infatuation, girlish muddle-headedness . . . or, perhaps, that's the way it ought to be . . . [shrugs his shoulders] God knows! [gaily] Shura, on my word of honour, I really am a decent fellow! You can judge for yourself: I know I've always been one for talking, but at least I've never in my life accused women of being depraved, or said: 'That woman's on the downward path!' I've merely been grateful, and nothing else. Nothing else! My sweet little girl, how good you are, and how entertaining, too! And what a ridiculous fool I am! I go about upsetting honest people, playing the poor Lazarus day in, day out. [laughs] Boo-hoo! . . . [walks quickly to one side] But do please go away, Sasha! We've been forgetting ourselves . . .

SASHA. Yes, it's time I went. Goodbye! I'm afraid your honest doctor may tell Anna Petrovna about my being here – just out of a sense of duty. Now listen to me: go to your wife now and stay with her, keep staying with her . . . If it's necessary to stay a year – then stay a year. If you have to stay ten years – stay ten years. Do your duty. Experience the grief of it, ask her forgiveness, weep – all that's just as it should be. But the main thing is – don't forget your work!

IVANOV. I've got this sensation again – as if I'd eaten an enormous meal of toadstools. Again!

SASHA. Well, God bless you, Nikolay! You needn't think about me at all! If you send me a line in about a fortnight – I'll be grateful for that. As for me, I'll write to you . . .

BORKIN *pokes his head through the door.*

BORKIN. Nikolay Alexeyevich, may I come in? [*seeing* SASHA] I beg your pardon, I didn't notice . . . [*comes in*] Bonjour! [*bows*]

SASHA [*embarrassed*]. How d'you do?

BORKIN. You've grown plumper and prettier.

SASHA [*to* IVANOV]. Well, I'll be going now, Nikolay Alexeyevich. I'll go. [*goes out*]

BORKIN. What a wonderful vision! I came on a prosaic matter, but found poetry . . . [*sings*] 'You came into my sight as the bird flies to the light.' . . .

[IVANOV *paces backward and forward in agitation*]

BORKIN [*sits down*]. You know, Nicolàs, she's got something, some-thing the others haven't got. Isn't that so? Something special, phantasmagoric . . . [*sighs*] As a matter of fact, she's the wealthiest match in the whole district, but her Mamma's such a Tartar that no one wants to hook up with her. After she's dead Shurochka will get everything, but until she dies she'll only give her ten thousand or so, and perhaps a few old crocks, and she'll expect gratitude even for that. [*rummages through his pockets*] Have a smoke – *de-los-majoros*. Would you like one? [*offers his cigarette case*] They're good . . . Quite smokeable.

IVANOV [*walks up to* BORKIN, *almost speechless with rage*]. Get out this minute and never dare cross my threshold again! This very minute!

[BORKIN *half-rises and drops a cigar*]

IVANOV. Out this very minute!

BORKIN. Nicolàs, what does this mean? Why are you angry?

IVANOV. Why? And where did you get those cigars? And do you think I don't know where you take the old man every day and what for?

BORKIN [*shrugs his shoulders*]. What do you want to worry about that for?

IVANOV. Cad that you are! You're giving me a bad name all over the district with your vile scheming. We've nothing in common, and I want you to leave my house now, this very minute! [*paces backwards and forwards*]

BORKIN. I know you're saying all this because you're irritated about something, and for that reason I don't feel angry with you.

You may insult me as much as you like . . . [*picks up the cigar*] As for this melancholia of yours, it's time you dropped all that. You're not a schoolboy . . .

IVANOV. What did I tell you? [*trembling*] Are you playing the fool with me?

Enter ANNA PETROVNA.

BORKIN. Well, now Anna Petrovna's come . . . I'll go. [*goes out*]
[IVANOV *stops beside his desk and stands with his head down*]

ANNA PETROVNA [*after a pause*]. Why was she here just now?
[*pause*]
Oh, so that's what you are! Now I understand you. At last I see what sort of a man you are. Dishonourable, base . . . Do you remember how you came and lied to me and said you loved me? I believed you and I left my father and mother, I gave up my religion and I followed you . . . It was lies you told me about goodness and truth, about your high-minded plans, and I believed every word . . .

IVANOV. Anyuta, I have never lied to you . . .

ANNA PETROVNA. I've lived with you five years, I've been wretched and I've fallen ill, but I've loved you and never left you for a minute . . . You've been my idol . . . And what now? All that time you were just deceiving me brazenly . . .

IVANOV. Anyuta, don't tell untruths. I made mistakes, that's true, but I've never lied once in my life . . . You daren't reproach me with that . . .

ANNA PETROVNA. Everything's clear now. You married me thinking that my parents would forgive me and give me money . . . You thought that . . .

IVANOV. Oh, my God! Anyuta, why must you try my patience like this? . . . [*weeps*]

ANNA PETROVNA. Be quiet! When you saw that there wouldn't be any money, you started a new game . . . Now I remember everything, now I understand. [*weeps*] You've never loved me, or been faithful to me . . . Never! . . .

IVANOV. Sarah, that is a lie! . . . Say what you like, but don't insult me by lying to me . . .

ANNA PETROVNA. Dishonourable and base . . . You owe money to Lebedev, and now to avoid paying your debt you're trying to turn his daughter's head, to deceive her just as you've deceived me. Isn't that true?

IVANOV [*suffocating*]. Stop, for God's sake! I can't answer for myself like this! I feel absolutely suffocated with rage, and I . . . I might say something insulting to you . . .

ANNA PETROVNA. You've always deceived me scandalously, and not me alone . . . You've blamed all your wicked acts on Borkin, but now I know who was guilty . . .

IVANOV. Sarah, stop this, go away, or I'll lose control and say something! I can hardly stop myself saying something horrible and insulting . . . [*shouts*] Be quiet, Jewess! . . .

ANNA PETROVNA. I won't be quiet . . . You've deceived me too long for me to stay silent now . . .

IVANOV. So you won't be silent? [*struggles with himself*] For God's sake . . .

ANNA PETROVNA. Now go and deceive Lebedev . . .

IVANOV. Then you might just as well know that you . . . will die soon. The doctor told me that you'll die soon . . .

ANNA PETROVNA [*sits down, her voice failing her*]. When did he say that?

[*pause*]

IVANOV [*clutching his head with his hands*]. How wicked I am! God, how wicked! [*sobs*]

CURTAIN

About a year passes between the Third and Fourth Acts.

ACT FOUR

One of the drawing-rooms at the Lyebedevs' house. In the centre of the stage there is an arch, separating the drawing-room from the ballroom; there are doors right and left. Antique bronze, family portraits. Everything is ready for a reception. There is an upright piano with a violin on top of it and a cello beside it. During the whole of the Act visitors pass to and fro through the ballroom. They are in evening dress.

LVOV [*comes in, looks at his watch*]. It's gone four. I suppose the blessing will begin in a minute. The blessing, and then off to the wedding. So here's the triumph of virtue and righteousness. He didn't succeed in robbing Sarah, so he sent her to her grave, and now he's found another one! He'll play the honest man with this one, too, until he's robbed her, and after he's robbed her, he'll send her to the same place that poor Sarah's lying in now. It's the old money-grubbing story.

[*pause*]

So now he's in his seventh heaven, and he's going to live nicely to a ripe old age, and then die with a clear conscience . . . But no, you won't, I'll show you up! When I tear off your damned mask, and everyone knows what sort of a cur you are, you'll be chucked down from your seventh heaven head first into such a pit that all the devils in Hell won't be able to get you out of it! I'm an honest man; it's my duty to come forward and open their eyes. I'll do my duty, and then, tomorrow – I'll get out of this accursed district! [*muses*] But what am I to do? Explain everything to Lebedev – waste of breath! Challenge Ivanov to a duel? Start a row? Oh, my God, I feel as nervous as a schoolboy, and I've completely lost the power to think things out. What am I to do? A duel?

KOSYKH *comes in.*

KOSYKH [*gleefully to* LVOV]. Yesterday I went a small slam in clubs, but got a grand slam. This fellow Barabanov spoiled the whole game for me again. We play. I go no trumps, he passes. Two no trumps, he passes. I go two diamonds . . . three clubs . . . and would you believe it? – I bid slam, but he doesn't show his ace. If the idiot had only shown his ace, I should have declared grand slam in no trumps . . .

LVOV. Excuse me, I don't play cards, and so can't share your feelings. Is the blessing to be soon?

KOSYKH. It must be soon. They're trying to bring Zyuzyushka round. She's sobbing her heart out . . . so upset to lose the dowry.

LVOV. But not her daughter?

KOSYKH. No, it's the dowry. She's annoyed, too. As he's marrying her daughter, it means he won't pay his debt. You can't very well produce your son-in-law's promissory note as evidence.

BABAKINA, *overdressed, walks across the stage past* LVOV *and* KOSYKH *in an affectedly pompous manner.* KOSYKH *bursts out laughing, his hand over his mouth.*

BABAKINA [*looks round*]. Stupid!

[KOSYKH *touches her waist with his finger and laughs loudly*]

BABAKINA. The oaf! [*goes out*]

KOSYKH [*laughing loudly*]. That woman's gone quite off her chump! Until she began wanting to be an Excellency, she was a woman like any other, but now you simply can't go near her. [*mimics her*] The oaf!

LVOV [*agitated*]. Listen, tell me honestly, what's your opinion of Ivanov?

KOSYKH. He's no good. Plays cards like a cobbler. Just think, last year, about Easter time we sat down to play: I, the Count, Borkin and Ivanov. I dealt . . .

LVOV [*interrupting him*]. Is he a good man?

KOSYKH. What, Ivanov? A clever scoundrel! A cunning fellow! He knows all the tricks of the trade. He and the Count are birds of a feather. They'll manage to sniff out anything that's easy to pinch. He missed the mark with the Jewess, so now he's nosing his way into Zyuzyushka's money bags. I'll bet you — and you can call me what you like if I'm wrong — that in a year's time he'll send Zyuzyushka begging in the streets. He'll be the ruin of Zyuzyushka, and the Count will be the ruin of Babakina. They'll grab the money and then go on living happily ever after, just getting richer and richer. Doctor, why are you so pale today? You look like nothing on earth.

LVOV. Nothing, nothing's the matter. I drank a bit too much yesterday.

LEBEDEV *comes in with* SASHA.

LEBEDEV. We'll have a talk here. [*to* LVOV *and* KOSYKH] Go into the ballroom, boys, and join the young ladies. We want to talk privately here.

KOSYKH [*snaps his fingers in admiration as he passes* SASHA]. What a picture! A queen of trumps!

LEBEDEV. Out you go, caveman, pass along!

[LVOV *and* KOSYKH *go out*]

Sit down, Shurochka, that's it . . . [*sits down and glances round*] Now just listen to me attentively and with proper respect. The fact is that your mother's ordered me to give you a message . . . Is that clear? I'm not speaking in my own name, but on orders from your mother.

SASHA. Be quick about it, Papa!

LEBEDEV. Fifteen thousand roubles in silver have been made over to you as a dowry. So see there isn't any argument about it later. Wait a moment, be quiet! That's only the blossom, the fruit will come afterwards. Fifteen thousand are made over to you, but as Nikolay Alexeyevich owes your mother nine thousand, a deduction is being made from your dowry . . . Then, in addition, besides that . . .

SASHA. Why are you telling me all this?

LEBEDEV. Your mother's orders.

SASHA. Leave me alone! If you had the slightest respect for me and yourself, you wouldn't allow yourself to talk to me like this. I don't want your dowry. I haven't asked for it, and I'm not asking for it!

LEBEDEV. What are you coming down on me for? The rats in Gogol's play at least smelt the thing first and then ran away —

but you go for me without even sniffing at my offer, you independent creature!

SASHA. Leave me alone, don't insult me with your petty sums and calculations!

LEBEDEV [*flying into a temper*]. Pshaw! You'll finish by making me stick a knife into myself, or cutting somebody's throat, you and your mother! One sets up a hullabaloo all day long, nagging and pestering me, and counting her farthings, while the other's so clever and humane and emancipated that she can't understand her own father, devil take it! I insult her! Can't you see that before I came here to insult you, I was being hanged, drawn and quartered in there? [*points at the door*] She can't understand! You've made me dizzy, I'm losing my senses . . . I'll go! [*goes to the door, then stops*] I don't like it . . . I dislike everything about it!

SASHA. What is it you dislike?

LEBEDEV. I dislike everything! Everything!

SASHA. What do you mean by everything?

LEBEDEV. Do you expect me to sit down in front of you and tell you all about it? I don't like anything, and I don't want to see your wedding! [*approaches* SASHA *and continues affectionately*] Do please forgive me, Shurochka . . . perhaps your marriage is clever and honest and high-minded, and all according to the best principles, but there's something wrong about it, it's not the real thing! It isn't like other marriages. You're young and fresh, clean as a pane of glass, good-looking, too, while he – he's a widower, and he's knocked about a lot, and worn-out. I can't understand him, either, God help him! [*kisses his daughter*] Shurochka, forgive me, but there's something not quite right. People are talking too much. First that Sarah woman died at his house, then for some reason or other he suddenly decided to marry you . . . [*with animation*] However, I'm just an old woman, an old woman. I've turned womanish, like an old maid. Don't listen to me. Don't listen to anybody, only listen to yourself.

SASHA. Papa, I've been feeling myself that something's wrong . . . Not quite as it should be, not, not as it should be. If you only knew how oppressed I feel! Unbearably! I feel embarrassed and afraid to confess it. Dear Papa, do say something to cheer me up, for God's sake . . . tell me what to do!

LEBEDEV. What's that? What are you saying?

SASHA. I'm more afraid than I've ever been! [*looks round*] I feel as though I don't understand him and never shall understand him. During the whole time I've been engaged to him, he's never once smiled, never once looked me straight in the eyes. All the time complaining, repenting about something, hinting at some guilt or other, trembling . . . I'm tired of it. There are even moments when it seems to me that I . . . that I don't love him as much as I should. And when he comes to see us, or talks to me, I begin to feel bored. What does it all mean, Papa dear? I'm afraid!

LEBEDEV. My darling, my only child, listen to your old father! Give him up!

SASHA [*alarmed*]. Don't, don't!

LEBEDEV. I mean it, Shurochka! There'll be a row, all the neighbours will wag their tongues like a lot of church-bells, but it's surely better to live through a row than to ruin your whole life.

SASHA. Don't say that, don't, Papa! I don't want to listen. One must just struggle against all these gloomy thoughts. He's a good, unhappy, misunderstood man; I will love him, learn to understand him, put him on his feet again. I'll fulfil my task. That's settled!

LEBEDEV. That's not fulfilling a task, that's just madness!

SASHA. That's enough. I've confessed something to you which I didn't even want to confess to myself. Don't tell anybody. Let's forget it.

LEBEDEV. I don't understand anything. Either I've got dull with old age, or you've all got too clever, but I'll eat my hat before I understand anything about it.

SHABELSKY *comes in.*

SHABELSKY. The devil take everybody, including myself! It's revolting!

LEBEDEV. What is it?

SHABELSKY. No, I mean it seriously; I'm going to have to do something so mean and base that everyone will be disgusted, including myself. But, whatever the cost, I'll do it. My word of honour! I've told Borkin to announce my engagement today. [*laughs*] Everyone's rotten, so I'll be rotten, too.

LEBEDEV. I'm tired of you! Listen, Matvey, if you go on talking like that, it'll end by your being taken to the loony-bin, excuse the expression.

SHABELSKY. And how's the loony-bin worse than anywhere else? Do me a favour and take me there now. Yes, please do! Everyone's so low and small-minded and dull-witted, and I'm vile even to myself, I don't believe a single word I say . . .

LEBEDEV. I'll tell you what to do, my friend. Put some tallow into your mouth, light it up and breathe fire at people. Or better still, take your hat and go home. There's a wedding on here, everyone's enjoying themselves, and you go about croaking like a crow. Yes, I mean it . . .

[SHABELSKY *leans on the piano and sobs*]

LEBEDEV. Good Heavens! . . . Matvey! . . . Count! . . . What's the matter with you? Matiusha, my dear chap . . . my dearest fellow . . . Did I hurt you? You must forgive me, old fool that I am . . . Forgive an old drunkard . . . Have a drink of water . . .

SHABELSKY. I don't want it. [*raises his head*]

LEBEDEV. Why are you crying?

SHABELSKY. It's nothing . . . just nothing . . .

LEBEDEV. No, Matiusha, don't tell lies . . . Now, why? What's the cause of it?

SHABELSKY. I happened to see this 'cello just now, and . . . that made me think of the little Jewess! . . .

LEBEDEV. Eh! what a time to think of her! May she rest in peace, poor soul, but this isn't the time to think of her . . .

SHABELSKY. We used to play duets together . . . A wonderful, excellent woman! . . .

[SASHA *sobs*]

LEBEDEV. What, now you? . . . Do leave off! Oh, Lord, now they're both howling, while I . . . I . . . Why don't you go somewhere else where the guests won't see you? . . .

SHABELSKY. Pasha, when the sun shines you can feel cheerful even in a cemetery. And when there's hope, you can be happy even in old age. But I haven't got a ray of hope, not a single ray!

LEBEDEV. Yes, it's true, you are in a pretty bad way . . . You haven't got any children, or money, or work . . . However, what can you do about it? [*to* SASHA] But why are you crying?

SHABELSKY. Pasha, let me have some money. I'll settle with you in the next world. I'll go to Paris and have a look at my wife's grave.

I've given away a lot in my life. I've given away half my fortune, so I've a right to ask. Besides, I'm asking it of a friend . . .

LEBEDEV [*bewildered*]. My dear fellow, I haven't got a farthing! However, all right, all right! That is, I don't promise, but you understand . . . of course, of course! [*aside*] They've worn me out!

BABAKINA *comes in.*

BABAKINA. And where's my cavalier, now? Count, how dare you leave me alone? Oo-oo, you naughty man! [*strikes the* COUNT *on the hand with her fan*]

SHABELSKY [*with revulsion*]. Leave me alone! I hate you!

BABAKINA [*taken aback*]. What? Eh? . . .

SHABELSKY. Get away!

BABAKINA [*falls into an armchair*]. Oh! [*weeps*]

ZINAÏDA SAVISHNA [*comes in, weeping*]. Someone's just arrived . . . I think it's the best man. It's time for the blessing . . . [*sobs*]

SASHA [*imploringly*]. Mamma! . . .

LEBEDEV. There now, everyone's blubbering now. A quartet! Do stop spreading all this wet weather around! Matvey! . . . Marfa Yegorovna! . . . If you go on, I . . . I'll start crying, too . . . [*cries*] Oh, Lord!

ZINAÏDA SAVISHNA. If you don't want your mother, if you're not an obedient daughter . . . well, have your own way . . . I'll give you my blessing . . .

IVANOV *comes in, wearing a tail-coat and gloves.*

LEBEDEV. This is the last straw. What is it?

SASHA. What are you here for?

IVANOV. Forgive me, ladies and gentlemen . . . please allow me to have a word with Sasha alone.

LEBEDEV. It's not right to come to see your bride just before the wedding! You ought to be going to the church!

IVANOV. Pasha, please . . .

    [LEBEDEV *shrugs his shoulders, then he,* ZINAÏDA SAVISHNA,
                the COUNT *and* BABAKINA *go out*]

SASHA [*sternly*]. What do you want?

IVANOV. I'm boiling over with anger, but I'll speak coolly. Listen. Just now, as I was dressing for the wedding, I glanced at myself in a mirror, and I saw . . . grey hair on my temples. Shura, let us drop it! We must stop this senseless comedy while it's still not too late . . . You're young and pure, you have your life before you, while I . . .

SASHA. All this isn't new, I've heard it a thousand times, and I'm tired of it! Go to the church, and don't keep people waiting!

IVANOV. I'll go home in a minute, and then you tell your people that there won't be a wedding. Explain to them somehow. It's time we came to our senses. I've acted Hamlet and you've acted a high-minded young woman – but we can't go on like that.

SASHA [*flushing*]. What are you talking like this for? I'm not listening.

IVANOV. But I'm speaking, and I'll go on speaking.

SASHA. What have you come for? Your whining's becoming a sheer mockery.

IVANOV. No, I'm not whining any more. A mockery! Yes, I'm mocking you! And if I could mock myself a thousand times more bitterly and make the whole world jeer at me, I'd do that, too! I caught sight of myself in the mirror – and it was like a shell exploding inside my conscience. I laughed at myself and I nearly went out of my mind with shame. [*laughs*] Melancholy! Noble anguish! Inexplicable grief! Only one thing's lacking – I ought to write poetry. Whining and playing the poor Lazarus and making everyone miserable with your anguish – no, no, no! To realise that your life's energy has gone for ever, that you've got rusty and outlived your time, that you've given way to cowardice and got stuck up to your neck in a disgusting bog of melancholy – and all that when you can see the sun shining and even the ants dragging their burdens manfully and feeling pleased with themselves – no, no, no! To have some people take you for a charlatan and others feel sorry for you and stretch out a helping hand to you, and others – this is worst of all – others listen to your sighs with awe and look at you as though you were a second Mahomed about to reveal a new religion at any moment . . . No, thank God, I still have some pride and conscience left! As I was coming here, I laughed at myself, and it seemed that the birds were laughing at me, and the trees, too . . .

SASHA. This isn't anger, it's madness!

IVANOV. You think so? No, I'm not mad. Now I see things in their true light, and my thoughts are as clear as your conscience is. We love each other, but our wedding won't take place! I'm entitled to rave and groan as much as I like, but I've no right to ruin other people! I poisoned the last year of my wife's life with my whining. Since we've been engaged, you've forgotten how to smile and you've grown five years older. Then your father – everything used to be clear and simple to him, but thanks to me he doesn't understand people any more. It doesn't matter whether I go to a meeting, or to a shooting party, or to visit someone – wherever I go, I produce boredom and dejection and discontent. Stop, don't interrupt me! I'm being rude and fierce about it, but you must forgive me, the bitterness of it is choking me, and I can't speak any differently. I've never meant to lie, I've never deliberately spoken ill of life, but I've developed into a grumbler and I curse it against my will, without noticing it myself – I blame fate, I complain, and everyone who listens to me is infected with a sort of disgust towards life, and begins to curse it, too. And what an attitude! As if I were doing Nature a favour by being alive! Oh, the devil take me!

SASHA. Just a minute! From what you've just been saying it follows that you're tired of all your whining and it's time to begin a new life! That's excellent! . . .

IVANOV. I see nothing excellent in it. What new life is there? I'm ruined irretrievably! It's time we both understood that. A new life!

SASHA. Nikolay, pull yourself together! Where's the proof that you're ruined? What's all this cynicism about? No, I don't want to talk, or listen . . . Go to the church!

IVANOV. I'm ruined!

SASHA. Don't shout like that, the guests will hear!

IVANOV. If an intelligent, educated, healthy man starts playing the poor Lazarus without any obvious cause, if he starts rolling downhill, he'll go on rolling without stopping, and there's no salvation for him! Well, where is my salvation? Where? I can't drink – wine gives me a headache; I can't write bad poetry, I can't enjoy spiritual idleness and see it as something noble and lofty. Idleness is idleness, weakness is weakness – I don't know any other names for them. I'm ruined, ruined – that's beyond any argument! [glances around] We may be interrupted here. Listen, if you really love me, you must help me. Now, this very minute, you must give me up! Now, quickly! . . .

SASHA. Oh, Nikolay, if you knew how tired you make me! You've worn my spirit down! You're a kind, intelligent man – ask yourself: is it fair to set me these problems? Every day there is some problem, each one harder than the last . . . I wanted active love, but this is martyred love!

IVANOV. When you're my wife the problems will be more complicated still, so you'd better give me up now! I wish you'd understand: you're not moved by love, but just the stubbornness of your own honesty. You set yourself a goal – to resurrect the man in me, to save me at whatever cost – and the idea of doing a great deed gratified you. Now you're ready to withdraw, but there's a false emotion preventing you. I wish you'd understand!

SASHA. What a queer, crazy logic! How can I give you up? How? You haven't got a mother, or a sister, or a friend . . . You're ruined, your estate's been pilfered away, everyone slanders you . . .

IVANOV. I was a fool to come here. I should have done what I wanted to . . .

Enter LEBEDEV.

SASHA [*runs towards her father*]. Papa, for God's sake help me; he's come bursting in here like a lunatic, and he's tormenting the life out of me! He says I must give him up because he doesn't want to ruin me. Tell him I don't want his magnanimity! I know what I'm doing.

LEBEDEV. I don't understand anything about it . . . What magnanimity?

IVANOV. There'll be no wedding.

SASHA. There will be a wedding! Papa, tell him that there will be a wedding!

LEBEDEV. Wait, wait! Why don't you want the wedding to take place?

IVANOV. I've explained to her why, but she doesn't want to understand.

LEBEDEV. No, not to her, explain it to me, and explain it so that I can understand it. Oh, Nikolay Alexeyevich, may God be your judge! You've brought so much fog into our lives that I feel as if I were living in a chamber of horrors. I look on and I don't understand anything . . . It's simply dreadful . . . Well, what do you expect me to do, what do you want an old man to do about it? Shall I challenge you to a duel, or what?

IVANOV. There's no need for any duel. All that's needed is for you to have a head on your shoulders and to understand plain language.

SASHA [*paces the stage in agitation*]. This is dreadful, dreadful! He's just like a child!

LEBEDEV. There's nothing for it but just shrug your shoulders, that's all. Listen to me, Nikolay! You think you're acting intelligently, subtly, according to all the rules of psychology – but I think this is all a scandal and disaster. Now hear an old man out for the last time. This is all I want to tell you: just calm your mind down! Look at things simply, as everybody else does! In this world everything is simple. The ceiling is white, the boots are black, sugar is sweet. You love Sasha, she loves you. If you love her – stay with her, if you don't love her – go, we won't bear you any malice. It's really as simple as that! You're both healthy, intelligent and clean-living, and you're well fed and clothed, thank God . . . What else do you want? You've no money? That doesn't really matter. Happiness doesn't depend on money . . . Of course, I understand . . . your estate's mortgaged, you haven't any money to pay the interest, but I – I'm her father, I understand . . . Mother can do as she likes, God be with her; if she won't give you any money, she needn't. Shurka says she doesn't need a dowry. Principles, Schopenhauer . . . All that's nonsense . . . I've got my special ten thousand in the bank. [*looks round*] Not a soul knows about it in the house . . . It's Granny's. That'll be for you both . . . You can take it, only promise me one thing – give Matvey a thousand or two . . .

[*visitors begin to assemble in the ballroom*]

IVANOV. Pasha, this is all useless talk. I'm acting according to my conscience.

SASHA. And I'm acting according to mine. You can say what you like, I won't release you. I'll go and call Mamma. [*goes out*]

LEBEDEV. I don't understand anything . . .

IVANOV. Listen, my poor old fellow . . . I won't try to explain to you what sort of a person I am – whether I'm honest or base, healthy or mentally sick. You wouldn't grasp it. I used to be young, eager, sincere and intelligent. I used to love, hate and believe in my own way, differently from other people; I used to work like ten men, and hope like ten men, too; I fought windmills, I tried to ram down walls with my head . . . Without realising my strength or weakness, without reasoning, without knowing anything about life, I took up a burden which promptly tore my muscles and broke my back; I went all out to spend myself, I got drunk, I got excited, I worked madly, I did everything without moderation. Well, what else could I do? There are so few of us, there's so much work to be done, so much! God, how much! And now how cruelly life, the life which I fought against, is avenging itself on me. I've worn myself out. At thirty-five I feel like a man after a drunken bout, I'm old already, I've put on an old man's dressing-gown. I go about with a heavy head, with a lazy soul, tired and broken, without faith, without love, without aim; I wander about among my friends like a shadow, and I don't know who I am, or why I live, or what I want. Already it seems to me that love is silly, that caresses and endearments are sugary nonsense, that there isn't any meaning in work, that song and impassioned words are trivial and old-fashioned. And wherever I go, I bring misery, blank boredom, discontent, disgust with life . . . I'm ruined, hopelessly ruined! Before you stands a man tired at thirty-five, disenchanted, crushed by his trivial efforts – burning with shame and jeering at his own weakness . . . Oh, how my pride revolts. I feel suffocated with anger! [*swaying slightly*] You see how I've worn myself out. I can't stand straight . . . I've gone weak. Where's Matvey? Tell him to take me home.

VOICES IN THE BALLROOM. The best man's arrived!

SHABELSKY *comes in.*

SHABELSKY. Here I am. In a shabby old tail-coat, not even my own . . . and no gloves . . . and so, of course, they all sneer, and leer, and start making stupid jokes . . . Disgusting, small-minded creatures!

BORKIN [*comes in quickly, carrying a bouquet; he wears a tailcoat and the best-man's buttonhole*]. Ugh! Where is he? [*to* IVANOV] They've been waiting all this time for you in church, and you're still here, talking philosophy. What a comical person you are! You really are a joke! Don't you know you're not supposed to drive with the bride? You're supposed to go separately, with me, and then

I have to come from the church to fetch the bride. Can't you even understand that? Honestly, you're a joke!

LVOV [*comes in, to* IVANOV]. Oh, you're here? [*loudly*] Nikolay Alexeyevich Ivanov, I want to tell you publicly that you're a cad!

IVANOV [*coldly*]. Thank you very much.

[*general astonishment*]

BORKIN [*to* LVOV]. Sir, this is contemptible conduct! I challenge you to a duel!

LVOV. Monsieur Borkin, I regard it as a humiliation to have to speak to you, let alone fight you. As for Monsieur Ivanov, he can have satisfaction from me whenever he wishes.

SHABELSKY. Then, sir, I'll fight you!

SASHA [*to* LVOV]. What did you do it for? What did you insult him for? My friends, please make him tell me what he did it for!

LVOV. Alexandra Pavlovna, I didn't insult him without reason. I came here as an honest man in order to open your eyes to the truth, and I beg you to hear me out.

SASHA. Well, what do you want to say? That you're an honest man? All the world knows that! I'd rather you told me whether you understand yourself, or whether you don't. You just came in here now and hurled a shocking insult at him which nearly killed me — you did that as an honest man; before that you'd been pursuing him like a shadow and interfering with his life, and, of course, you did that too in the certainty that you were fulfilling your duty, that you were an honest man. You meddled with his private life, you slandered and ran him down whenever you could; you bombarded me and all my friends with anonymous letters — and all the time you were doing it you thought of yourself as an honest man. Yes, Doctor, you thought it was honest not even to spare his sick wife, to keep on worrying her with your suspicions. And whatever you may do in the future — acts of violence, or cruelty, or meanness — you'll still think yourself an extraordinarily honest and high-minded person!

IVANOV [*laughing*]. This isn't a wedding, it's a parliament! Bravo, bravo! . . .

SASHA [*to* LVOV]. So just think that over: do you understand yourself, or don't you? Stupid, heartless creatures! [*takes* IVANOV's *hand*] Let us go from here, Nikolay! Father, come!

IVANOV. Go? Where to? Just wait a moment, I'll put an end to all this! I can feel youth waking up in me – the old Ivanov speaks again! [*takes out a revolver*]

SASHA [*shrieks*]. I know what he's going to do! Nikolay, for God's sake!

IVANOV. I've been going downhill long enough, now I'm going to stop! There's a limit to everything! Stand away! Thank you, Sasha!

SASHA [*shrieks*]. Nikolay, for God's sake! Stop him!

IVANOV. Leave me alone! [*runs aside and shoots himself*]

CURTAIN

THE SEAGULL

A Comedy in Four Acts

Characters in the Play

ARKADINA, Irina Nikolayevna (Madame Treplyova by marriage), an actress

TREPLYOV, Konstantin Gavrilovich (Kostya), her son, a young man

SORIN, Pyotr Nikolayevich (Petrusha), her brother

ZARECHNAYA, Nina Mikhailovna, a young girl, the daughter of a wealthy landowner

SHAMRAYEV, Ilya Afanasyevich, a retired lieutenant of the Army, Sorin's bailiff

POLINA ANDREYEVNA, his wife

MASHA (Marya Ilyinichna), his daughter

TRIGORIN, Boris Alexeyevich, a writer

DORN, Yevgeniy Sergeyevich, a doctor

MEDVEDENKO, Semyon Semyonovich, a schoolmaster

YAKOV, a workman

A CHEF

A HOUSEMAID

The action takes place in Sorin's house and garden. Between the Third and the Fourth Acts there is an interval of two years.

ACT ONE

The park on SORIN's *estate. A wide avenue leads towards a lake in the background. A rough stage erected for an amateur theatrical performance has been built across the avenue and conceals the view of the lake. There are bushes close to the stage, right and left, and in the foreground a few chairs and a small table.*

The sun has just gone down. YAKOV *and some other men are working on the stage behind the curtain; they can be heard hammering and coughing.* MASHA *and* MEDVEDENKO, *returning from a walk, enter from the left.*

MEDVEDENKO. Why do you always wear black?

MASHA. I am in mourning for my life. I'm unhappy.

MEDVEDENKO. But why? [*meditatively*] I can't understand it. You're in good health. Your father isn't rich, but he's comfortably off. My life is much harder than yours. I only get twenty-three roubles a month, and from that my superannuation is deducted. Yet I don't wear mourning.

MASHA. It isn't money that matters. Even a pauper can be happy.

MEDVEDENKO. Yes, in theory he can, but in practice it works out like this: there's myself, my mother, two sisters, and a small brother, and there's my salary, twenty-three roubles in all. We all have to eat and drink, haven't we? And then what about tea and sugar? What about tobacco? You've got to scrape and save . . .

MASHA [*glancing back at the stage*]. They'll be starting the show soon.

MEDVEDENKO. Yes. Zarechnaya is going to act, and the play is by Konstantin Gavrilovich. They are in love with one another, and today their souls will be merged in an attempt to create a single work of art. But your soul and mine have no points of contact. I love you. I can't stay at home because of my longing for you, and I walk six miles here and six miles back every day, but I get nothing from you except indifference. Oh, it's quite

understandable. I haven't any money, we are a large family . . .
Who would want to marry a man who hasn't even got enough
to eat?

MASHA. Nonsense. [*takes snuff*] I feel touched by your love, but I
can't return it, that's all. [*holds out the snuff box*] Have some snuff.

MEDVEDENKO. I don't feel like it now.

[*pause*]

MASHA. It's close. There'll be a thunderstorm tonight, I think.
You're always philosophising, or else talking about money. You
believe there is no greater misfortune than poverty, but in my
opinion it's a thousand times better to go about in rags and be
a beggar than . . . However, that's something you wouldn't
understand . . .

SORIN *and* TREPLYOV *enter from the right.*

SORIN [*leaning on a walking stick*]. Somehow country life doesn't suit
me, my boy. It's obvious that I never shall get accustomed to it.
Last night I went to bed at ten, and this morning I woke up at
nine, feeling as though my brain was sticking to the inside of my
skull from sleeping too long. [*laughs*] Then after dinner I fell
asleep again by mistake, and now I feel sort of jaded, as if I'd had
a nightmare . . .

TREPLYOV. You're right, you ought to live in town. [*seeing* MASHA
and MEDVEDENKO] I say, you two, we'll be calling you as soon as
we begin, but you shouldn't be here now. Please go away.

SORIN [*to* MASHA]. Marya Ilyinichna, I wish you'd ask your father
to have the dog let off his chain. It keeps howling. My sister was
kept awake again all night.

MASHA. Why don't you speak to my father yourself? I won't.
Please excuse me. [*to* MEDVEDENKO] Come, let's go.

MEDVEDENKO. You will send someone to tell us when you're
going to begin, won't you?

[MASHA *and* MEDVEDENKO *go out*]

SORIN. That means that the dog will be howling all night again.
The strange thing is that I've never really lived in the country in
the way I wanted to. I used to take a month's leave and come
down here to have a rest, and all that sort of thing . . . But as
soon as I got here, people started to plague me with all sorts of
rubbish, and within a day I'd feel like running away again.

[*laughs*] I was always pleased to leave this place . . . But there you are, I'm retired now, I've got nowhere to go. I've got to live here now, whether I want to or not . . .

YAKOV [*appears from behind the curtain*]. We're going to have a swim, Konstantin Gavrilovich.

TREPLYOV. Very well then, but you must be sure to be back in your places in ten minutes' time. [*looking at his watch*] We're going to start soon.

YAKOV. Yes, sir. [*goes out*]

TREPLYOV [*looking over the stage*]. There's a theatre for you! Just the curtain and the two wings and beyond it − open space. No scenery. You have an unimpeded view of the lake and the horizon. We'll raise the curtain at half past nine when the moon comes up.

SORIN. Splendid!

TREPLYOV. But if Zarechnaya is late, the whole effect will be lost, of course. It's time she was here now. Her father and stepmother always keep watch on her, and it's as hard for her to break out of the house as it would be if it were a prison. [*adjusting his uncle's tie*] Your hair and beard are all in a tangle. Oughtn't you to have them cut, or trimmed, or something? . . .

SORIN [*combing his hair*]. That's the tragedy of my life. My appearance . . . even in my young days I looked as if I were a secret drinker, and all that sort of thing. The women never loved me. [*sits down*] Why is my sister so out of humour today?

TREPLYOV. Why? She's bored. [*sits down beside him*] Jealous, too. She's got a down on me anyway, and she's got a down on this show and on my play because Zarechnaya − and not she − is acting in it. She hasn't read my play, but she hates it all the same.

SORIN [*laughing*]. Well, really! What an idea!

TREPLYOV. It makes her angry to think that it won't be she, but Zarechnaya, who's going to make a success of it on this tiny stage! [*glancing at his watch*] A psychological oddity − that's my mother. Oh, there is no doubt about her being very gifted and intelligent: she's capable of weeping bitterly over a book, of reciting the whole of Nekrasov by heart, of nursing the sick with the patience of an angel. But just try and give a word of praise to Duse! Oh-ho-ho! You mustn't praise anybody but her, you mustn't write about anybody but her, you must acclaim her and go into raptures over her wonderful acting in *The Lady with the Camellias*, or *The Fumes of Life*. But we can't offer her such intoxicating praise here in the country, so she feels bored and out of humour, and we all seem like enemies, we are all to blame. And then she's superstitious – she's afraid of having three candles alight, she's afraid of the number thirteen. And she's close-fisted, too. She has seventy thousand in the bank, in Odessa – that I know for certain. But you try to borrow money from her, and she'll just burst into tears.

SORIN. You've somehow got it into your head that your mother doesn't like your play, and so you're upset, and so on . . . Calm yourself, your mother adores you.

TREPLYOV [*pulling off the petals of a flower, one by one*]. She loves me . . . she loves me not . . . she loves me – loves me not . . . loves me – loves me not. [*laughing*] You see, my mother doesn't love me. And why should she indeed? She wants to live, to have love affairs, to wear light-coloured blouses, and here I am, twenty-five years old already. I'm always reminding her that she isn't young any longer. When I'm not about she's thirty-two, but when I'm with her, she's forty-three, and she hates me for it. Moreover, she knows that I have no use for the theatre. She loves the theatre, she imagines that she's serving humanity, whereas in my opinion the theatre of today is in a rut, and full of prejudices and conventions. When I see the curtain rise on a room with three walls, when I watch these great and talented people, these high priests of a sacred art depicting the way people eat, drink, make love, walk about and wear their clothes, in the artificial light of the stage; when I hear them trying to squeeze a moral out of the tritest words and emptiest scenes – some petty little moral that's easy to understand and suitable for use in the home; when I'm presented with a thousand variations of the same old thing, the same thing again and again – well, I just have to escape, I run away as Maupassant ran away from the Eiffel Tower which so oppressed him with its vulgarity.

SORIN. We can't do without the theatre.

TREPLYOV. We need new art forms. New forms are wanted, and if they aren't available, we might as well have nothing at all. I'm fond of my mother, very fond of her, but she leads such a fatuous life, for ever fussing around with this novelist of hers, her name always being bandied about in the papers. I find it all so fatiguing. And sometimes I simply regret, like the ordinary selfish mortal I am, that I have a famous actress for a mother, and I find myself imagining that if she were an ordinary woman I should have been happier. Uncle, can you imagine a sillier, a more hopeless situation? Often she'd have a room full of visitors, all famous people, writers and actors, and there I'd be among them, alone – a nonentity, tolerated only because I was her son. Who am I? What am I? I left the University in my third year, owing to 'circumstances over which we have no control', as the editors sometimes say. I have no special gifts, not a penny of my own, and in my passport I'm described as a member of the lower middle class, born in Kiev. Well, my father was a member of the petty bourgeoisie, as you know – although he was a well-known actor too – and his native town was Kiev. So when all these artists and writers who were gathered together in my mother's drawing-room deigned to pay a little attention to me, I used to feel that they were sizing me up as they looked at me standing there in all my insignificance; I read their thoughts, and I suffered with the humiliation of it all.

SORIN. By the way, you might tell me, what sort of a person is this writer? He's hard to understand. Always so silent.

TREPLYOV. He's intelligent, unaffected, a bit on the melancholy side, I think. Really a very decent fellow. He's still a long way off forty, but he's famous already, and he's had his fill of the good things of life . . . As for his writing . . . well, how shall I put it? It's very clever and charming, but . . . if you've been reading Tolstoy, or Zola, you don't feel like reading Trigorin afterwards.

SORIN. I must admit I am fond of writers, my boy. You know, years ago there were just two things I wanted passionately. One was to get married and the other was to be a novelist. I haven't managed to pull it off either way. Yes, even to be a minor writer must be rather nice, when all is said and done . . .

TREPLYOV [listening]. I can hear footsteps. [throws his arms round his uncle] I can't live without her . . . The very sound of her footsteps is beautiful . . . I feel insanely happy . . .

[quickly walking to meet NINA ZARECHNAYA, who comes in]
You . . . enchanting being . . . my dream . . .

NINA [agitated]. I'm not late . . . Surely I'm not late . . .

TREPLYOV [*kissing her hands*]. No, no, no . . .

NINA. I've been worrying the whole day, I've been feeling so afraid! I was afraid father wouldn't let me come . . . but he's just gone out with my stepmother. The sky was red, the moon was coming up, and I kept hurrying the horse, urging it on and on. [*laughs*] I'm glad, all the same! [*shakes* SORIN *warmly by the hand*]

SORIN [*laughing*]. Your dear little eyes look as if they'd been crying. He-he! That isn't as it should be, you know.

NINA. It's nothing . . . Look, how out of breath I am! I'll have to leave in half an hour, we must hurry. I can't I can't, don't try to keep me, for Heaven's sake! My father doesn't know I've come.

TREPLYOV. It's time to begin, as a matter of fact. We must go and call everybody.

SORIN. I'll go and call them, and all that sort of thing. I'll go at once. [*walks left, singing 'The Two Grenadiers', then glances back*] I remember I once burst into song like this and the Assistant Public Prosecutor said to me: 'I say, your Excellency, that's a powerful voice you've got.' Then he thought a bit and added: 'And an offensive one too.' [*laughs and goes out*]

NINA. My father and stepmother won't let me come here. They say this place is Bohemian . . . they're afraid of my going on the stage. And I am drawn to this place, to this lake, as if I were a seagull.

TREPLYOV. We are alone.

NINA. I believe there's someone there.

TREPLYOV. There isn't anybody. [*they kiss*]

NINA. What sort of a tree is this?

TREPLYOV. An elm.

NINA. Why is it so dark?

TREPLYOV. It's late, everything's turning dark now. Don't go early, I implore you.

NINA. I can't stay.

TREPLYOV. And what if I followed you home, Nina? I would stay in the garden all night, watching your window.

NINA. You can't do that, the watchman would notice you. And Tresor isn't used to you yet. He'd bark.

TREPLYOV. I love you.

NINA. Sh-sh!

TREPLYOV [*hearing footsteps*]. Who's there? Is it you, Yakov?

YAKOV [*behind the stage*]. Yes, sir.

TREPLYOV. Take up your positions. It's time to begin. Is the moon coming up?

YAKOV. Yes, sir.

TREPLYOV. Have you got the methylated spirit? Have you got the sulphur? There must be a smell of sulphur directly the red eyes are seen. [*to* NINA] You can go now, everything is ready for you there. Are you nervous?

NINA. Yes, very. Your mother – she's all right, I'm not afraid of her. But there's Trigorin . . . I'm so afraid and ashamed of acting in front of him . . . a famous writer . . . Is he young?

TREPLYOV. Yes.

NINA. What marvellous stories he's written!

TREPLYOV [*coldly*]. I don't know about that. I haven't read them.

NINA. It's difficult to act in your play. There are no real living characters in it.

TREPLYOV. Living characters! We don't have to depict life as it is, or as it ought to be, but as we see it in our dreams.

NINA. But there's hardly any action in your play, there are only speeches. And then I do think there ought to be love in a play.

[*both go behind the stage*]

POLINA ANDREYEVNA *and* DORN *come in.*

POLINA. It's getting damp out here. Please do go back and put on your goloshes.

DORN. I feel hot.

POLINA. You don't take care of yourself. It's just sheer obstinacy. You're a doctor, and you know perfectly well that the damp air is bad for you, but you just want to cause me pain and anxiety. Yesterday you stayed outside on the terrace the whole evening on purpose . . .

DORN [*hums*]. 'Say not your youth was ruined' . . .

POLINA. You were so absorbed in your conversation with Irina Nikolayevna . . . you simply weren't aware of the cold. Now own up, you do find her attractive . . .

DORN. I'm fifty-five.

POLINA. That's nothing. A man's not old at that age. You've kept your good looks and you're still attractive to women.

DORN. Well, what am I to do about it?

POLINA. You're so anxious to prostrate yourselves before an actress. Every single one of you!

DORN [*hums*]. 'Again I stand before you' . . . It's in the nature of things for people to admire artists and treat them differently from . . . well, let us say, tradesmen. It's a sort of idealism.

POLINA. Women always used to be falling in love with you and throwing themselves at you. Was that idealism, too?

DORN [*shrugging his shoulders*]. Well, what of it? There was a lot that was good in the feelings these women had for me. What they mostly loved in me was my skill as a doctor. Ten or fifteen years ago, you remember, I was the only good obstetrician in the whole district. Besides, I've always been straight.

POLINA [*seizing him by the hand*]. You dear man!

DORN. Sh-sh! They're coming.

Enter ARKADINA *on* SORIN's *arm, accompanied by* TRIGORIN, SHAMRAYEV, MEDVEDENKO *and* MASHA.

SHAMRAYEV. I remember I saw her play marvellously at the Poltava Fair in '73! A sheer delight! Marvellous acting! [*to* ARKADINA] I wonder if you happen to know where Chadin – Pavel Semyonich Chadin, the comedian – is at present? He was quite inimitable in the part of Raspliuyev, better than Sadovsky himself. I'm willing to swear he was, my dear lady! But where is he now?

ARKADINA. You're always inquiring about some old fossil or other. How should I know? [*sits down*]

SHAMRAYEV [*with a sigh*]. Pashka Chadin! We don't have men like him nowadays! The theatre is in a decline, Irina Nikolayevna. We used to have massive oak trees, now we see nothing but stumps.

DORN. It's true enough, there aren't so many outstandingly gifted people nowadays – on the other hand, the average actor is much more competent.

SHAMRAYEV. I can't agree at all with you there. However, it's a matter of taste. *De gustibus aut bene, aut nihil.*

TREPLYOV *enters from behind the stage.*

ARKADINA [*to her son*]. When is it going to start, my dear?

TREPLYOV. In a minute. Please have patience.

ARKADINA [*reciting from* Hamlet].

> Oh, Hamlet, speak no more!
> Thou turn'st mine eyes into my very soul;
> And there I see such black and grained spots
> As will not leave their tint.

TREPLYOV [*from* Hamlet].

> And let me wring thy heart, for so I shall,
> If it be made of penetrable stuff.

[*a horn is sounded behind the stage*]

Ladies and gentlemen, we are about to begin! Attention please! [*a pause*] I'll start now. [*taps with a stick and recites in a loud voice*] O venerable shades of ancient days, you who float over this lake at night, lull us to sleep and bring us dreams of things as they will be two hundred thousand years from now.

SORIN. Two hundred thousand years from now there will be just nothing.

TREPLYOV. Well then, let them show us that nothing!

ARKADINA. Yes, let them. We are asleep already.

> *The curtain rises, revealing the view of the lake, with the moon above the horizon and its reflection in the water.* NINA ZARECHNAYA, *in white, is sitting on a rock.*

NINA. The men, the lions, the eagles, the partridges, the antlered deer, the geese, the spiders, the silent fishes of the deep, starfishes and creatures unseen to the eye – in short, all living things, all living things, having completed their mournful cycle, have been snuffed out. For thousands of years the earth has borne no living thing, and this poor moon now lights its lamp in vain. The cranes no longer wake in the meadows with a cry, no longer are May beetles heard humming in the groves of lime trees. It is cold, cold, cold . . . It is deserted, deserted, deserted . . . It is terrifying, terrifying, terrifying . . .

[*pause*]

All living bodies have turned to dust and the Eternal Matter has transformed them into stones, into water, into clouds, while their souls have all been merged into one. This common soul of the world is I – I . . . The souls of Alexander the Great, of Caesar, of Shakespeare, of Napoleon, and of the basest leech are contained in me! In me the consciousness of men is merged with the instincts of the animals; I remember all, all, all, and live every single life anew in my own being!

[*will-o'-the-wisps appear*]

ARKADINA [*in a low voice*]. This suggests the Decadent school.

TREPLYOV [*imploringly and reproachfully*]. Mamma!

NINA. I am lonely. Once in a hundred years I open my lips to speak, and then my voice rings dismally through this void unheard by anybody . . . And you too, pale spirits, hear me not. The stagnant marsh gives birth to you before dawn, and you wander until day breaks – without thought, without will, without a quiver of life. The Devil, father of the Eternal Matter, fearing lest life reappear in you, has created in you, as also in the rocks and water, a perpetual flux of atoms, so that you are constantly changing. The spirit alone remains constant and un-changeable in the whole universe.

[*pause*]

Like a prisoner cast into a deep and empty well, I know not where I am, or what awaits me here. All I know is that I am destined to struggle with the Devil, and in cruel and stubborn battle to conquer the principle of material force, after which matter and spirit will merge in beautiful harmony and the Kingdom of Cosmic Will will come into being. But this will only happen after a long succession of millennia during which time the moon, bright Sirius, and this earth will all have been gradually turned to dust. Until then horror, horror . . .

[*pause; two red spots appear over the lake*]

And now my powerful enemy, the Devil, is approaching. I see his terrifying, blood-red eyes . . .

ARKADINA. There's a smell of sulphur. Is that right?

TREPLYOV. Yes.

ARKADINA [*laughing*]. Ah! it's quite a good effect!

TREPLYOV. Mamma!

NINA. He is bored without Man . . .

POLINA [*to* DORN]. You've taken off your hat. Put it on before you catch cold.

ARKADINA. The Doctor's taken his hat off to the Devil, the father of Eternal Matter.

TREPLYOV [*flaring up, loudly*]. The play's over! Enough of it! Curtain!

ARKADINA. But why get cross about it?

TREPLYOV. That's enough! Curtain! Let down the curtain! [*stamping his foot*] Curtain!

[*the curtain drops*]

I apologise! I overlooked the fact that only a select few are permitted to write plays and act on the stage. I've encroached on the preserves of a monopoly! To me . . . I mean, I . . . [*tries to continue, then makes a resigned gesture and goes out to the left*]

ARKADINA. What is the matter with him?

SORIN. Irina, my dear, you shouldn't hurt a young man's self-esteem like this!

ARKADINA. But what have I said to him?

SORIN. You've offended him.

ARKADINA. He told us himself that it was going to be a joke, and I treated it as a joke.

SORIN. All the same . . .

ARKADINA. And now it turns out he's written a great work of art! Just think of that! So it wasn't for a joke that he got up this show and perfumed the air with sulphur, but in order to teach us something. He wanted to show us how we ought to write plays and what plays we should act in. Really, this is becoming tedious! These perpetual jibes at my expense, these pin-pricks – anyone would get tired of them, surely you'll grant me that! He's a conceited, difficult boy!

SORIN. He wanted to give you pleasure.

ARKADINA. Did he? Even so, he didn't choose an ordinary play, but had to make us listen to these decadent ravings. I'm even prepared to listen to mad ravings for the sake of a joke, but here we have pretensions to new creative forms, to a new era in art. To my way of thinking, there are no new forms in this stuff at all, just a display of bad temper.

TRIGORIN. Everyone writes what he wants to and as he is able to.

ARKADINA. Let him write what he wants to and as he is able to, if only he leaves me out of it.

DORN. Jupiter! You are angry, therefore . . .

ARKADINA. I'm not Jupiter, I'm a woman. [*lights a cigarette*] And I'm not angry, I'm merely irritated that a young man should spend his time in such a tiresome way. I had no wish to offend him.

MEDVEDENKO. There's no ground for making a distinction between spirit and matter, because spirit might consist of a combination of material atoms. [*with animation to* TRIGORIN] But you know, someone ought to write a play describing how our sort of people live – I mean we teachers – and get it produced somewhere. It's a hard life, a very hard life!

ARKADINA. That's not a bad idea. But don't let us talk about plays now, or atoms either. It's such a nice evening. Can you hear? There's someone singing.

[*all listen*]

How nice it is!

POLINA. It's on the other side of the lake.

[*pause*]

ARKADINA [*to* TRIGORIN]. Sit down here, beside me. Ten or fifteen years ago you could always hear music and singing on this lake – almost every night. There are six country houses around the lake. I remember such laughter, and noise, and shooting – and love affairs, love affairs all the time . . . And the *jeune premier* and idol of all those houses was . . . allow me to introduce him – [nods towards DORN] Doctor Yevgeniy Sergeich. He's fascinating still, but in those days he was irresistible . . . But my conscience is starting to torment me. Why did I hurt my poor boy's feelings? I'm so worried. [*loudly*] Kostya! Kostya, dear!

MASHA. I'll go and look for him.

ARKADINA. Please do, my dear!

MASHA [*walks to the left*]. Ah-oo! Konstantin Gavrilovich! Ah-oo! [*goes off*]

NINA *comes out from behind the stage.*

NINA. Apparently we aren't going to continue, so I may as well come out. Good evening! [*kisses* ARKADINA *and* POLINA]

SORIN. Bravo! Bravo!

ARKADINA. Bravo! Bravo! We did admire you. You know, with your looks and your lovely voice, you really ought not to stay in the country! It's a sin. I'm sure you have a gift for acting. Listen to me! You must go on the stage!

NINA. Oh, it's my one dream! [*sighs*] But it'll never come true.

ARKADINA. Who knows? Here now, let me introduce you – Mr Trigorin, Boris Alexandrovich Trigorin.

NINA. Oh, I'm so glad . . . [*overcome with embarrassment*] I always read everything you . . .

ARKADINA [*making her sit down beside them*]. Don't be shy, my dear. He's a famous man, but he has a simple soul. You see, he's shy himself.

DORN. I think the curtain might be raised now. This place gives me a sort of eerie feeling.

SHAMRAYEV [*loudly*]. Yakov, pull the curtain up, will you!
[*the curtain goes up*]

NINA [*to* TRIGORIN]. It was a strange play, wasn't it?

TRIGORIN. I didn't understand it at all. But I watched it with pleasure, all the same. You acted with such sincerity. And the scenery was beautiful.
[*pause*]
There must be a lot of fish in this lake.

NINA. Yes.

TRIGORIN. I'm very fond of fishing. As far as I'm concerned, there's no greater pleasure than to sit on the bank of a river in the late afternoon and watch the float . . .

NINA. I should have thought that for anyone who'd experienced the joy of doing creative work no other pleasure could exist.

ARKADINA [*laughing*]. You mustn't talk like that. When anyone talks high-flown language to him, he hasn't the least idea what to say.

SHAMRAYEV. I remember hearing the great Silva sing low C one night at the Moscow Opera. As it happened, a bass from our parish church choir was sitting in the gallery. Suddenly – imagine our utter amazement – we heard 'Bravo, Silva!' from the gallery . . . but a whole octave lower . . . Like this. [*in a deep bass*] Bravo, Silva! And after that – dead silence. You could hear a pin drop.
[*pause*]

DORN. The angel of silence has flown over us!

NINA. It's time for me to be going. Goodbye.

ARKADINA. Where are you off to? Why so early? We won't let you go.

NINA. My father is expecting me.

ARKADINA. What a man, really! . . . [*they embrace*] Well, if it can't be helped . . . We're sorry, very sorry to let you go.

NINA. I wish you knew how hard it is for me to go.

ARKADINA. Someone ought to see you home, my little one.

NINA [*frightened*]. Oh no, no!

SORIN [*to* NINA, *imploringly*]. Do stay!

NINA. I can't, Pyotr Nikolayevich.

SORIN. Stay just for an hour, that's all. Why must you, really? . . .

NINA [*after a moment's thought, tearfully*]. It's impossible. [*shakes hands with him and goes off quickly*]

ARKADINA. She's an unfortunate girl, really. They say her mother left all her enormous fortune to her husband, every penny of it, and now this girl has nothing, as her father has already made a will in favour of his second wife. It's really scandalous.

DORN. Yes, her charming father is a regular swine, to give him his due.

SORIN [*rubbing his hands to warm them*]. Let us go too, friends. The air is getting damp. My legs are hurting.

ARKADINA. Your legs! They might as well be made of wood – you can hardly walk on them. Come along, you poor old man! [*takes his arm*]

SHAMRAYEV [*offering his arm to his wife*]. Madame?

SORIN. I can hear that dog howling again. [*to* SHAMRAYEV] Ilya Afanasiyevich, I wish you'd be good enough to tell them to let it off the chain.

SHAMRAYEV. It isn't possible, Pyotr Nikolayevich. I'm afraid of thieves breaking into the barn – I've got millet there. [*to* MED-VEDENKO, *who is walking beside him*] Yes, lower by a whole octave: 'Bravo, Silva!' And he wasn't a proper singer either – just a fellow in the church choir.

MEDVEDENKO. And what sort of pay does a fellow in the choir get?
[*all go out except* DORN]

DORN [*alone*]. I don't know, maybe I don't understand anything, maybe I've gone off my head, but I did like that play. There is something in it. When that child was holding forth about loneliness, and later when the devil's red eyes appeared, I was so moved that my hands were shaking. It was fresh, unaffected . . . Ah! I think he's coming along now. I feel like telling him a lot of nice things about it.

TREPLYOV [*enters*]. They've all gone already!

DORN. I'm here.

TREPLYOV. Mashenka has been looking for me all over the park. Insufferable creature!

DORN. Konstantin Gavrilovich, I liked your play exceedingly. It's a bit strange and, of course, I didn't hear the end, and yet it made a deep impression on me. You've got talent and you must carry on.

[TREPLYOV *shakes his hand warmly and embraces him impulsively*] Tut-tut! How strung up you are! Tears in your eyes! . . . What I mean to say is this. You took your subject from the realm of abstract ideas. That was as it should be, because a work of art must without fail convey some great idea. Only things conceived in high seriousness can be beautiful. How pale you are!

TREPLYOV. So you're telling me to carry on?

DORN. Yes. But you must depict only what is significant and permanent. You know, I've lived a varied life, I've chosen my pleasures with discrimination. I'm satisfied. But if it had ever been my lot to experience the exaltation an artist feels at the moment of creative achievement, I believe I should have come to despise this material body of mine and all that goes with it, and my soul would have taken wings and soared into the heights.

TREPLYOV. Forgive me, where's Zarechnaya?

DORN. There's one more thing. A work of art must express a clear, definite idea. You must know what you are aiming at when you write, for if you follow the enchanted path of literature without a definite goal in mind, you'll lose your way and your talent will ruin you.

TREPLYOV [*impatiently*]. Where is Zarechnaya?

DORN. She's gone home.

TREPLYOV [*in despair*]. What shall I do? I want to see her . . . I've got to see her . . . I'm going . . .

Enter MASHA.

DORN [*to* TREPLYOV]. Do be a little calmer, my friend.

TREPLYOV. But I'm going all the same. I must go.

MASHA. Please, Konstantin Gavrilovich, come indoors. Your mamma is waiting for you. She's worried.

TREPLYOV. Tell her I've gone away. And I beg you – all of you – leave me alone! Leave me alone! Don't follow me about.

DORN. But . . . but, my dear boy . . . you shouldn't . . . That's not right.

TREPLYOV [*tearfully*]. Goodbye, Doctor. Thank you . . . [*goes out*]

DORN [*with a sigh*]. Youth will have its own way! Youth! . . .

MASHA. When people can't think of anything else to say, they say: youth! youth! . . . [*takes snuff*]

DORN [*takes the snuff box from her and flings it into the bushes*]. Disgusting!

[*a pause*]

I think I can hear music in the house. We ought to go in.

MASHA. Wait a moment.

DORN. What is it?

MASHA. There's something I want to tell you again . . . I feel like talking . . . [*agitated*] I'm not really fond of my father, but I've a soft spot in my heart for you. For some reason I feel a sort of deep affinity with you . . . You must help me. Help me, or I'll do something stupid, something that'll make a mockery of my life and mess it up . . . I can't go on like this . . .

DORN. But what is it? How am I to help you?

MASHA. I'm so unhappy. Nobody, nobody knows how unhappy I am! [*leaning her head against his breast, softly*] I love Konstantin.

DORN. How distraught they all are! How distraught! And what a quantity of love about! . . . It's the magic lake! [*tenderly*] But what can I do, my child? Tell me, what can I do? What?

CURTAIN

ACT TWO

A croquet lawn and flower beds. In the background on the right a house with a large terrace. On the left, a view of the lake with bright sunlight reflected in the water. It is midday and hot. On one side of the croquet lawn ARKADINA, DORN, *and* MASHA *are sitting on a garden seat in the shade of an old lime tree.* DORN *has an open book on his lap.*

ARKADINA [*to* MASHA]. Come, let us get up.
           [*both get up*]
  Stand by my side. You are twenty-two, and I'm nearly twice that. Yevgeniy Sergeyevich, which of us looks the younger?
DORN. You, of course.
ARKADINA. There you are! And why is it? Because I work, I care about things, I'm always on the go, while you stay in the same place all the time, you don't really live . . . And I have a rule – never to wonder about the future! I never think of old age, or of death. What is to be, will be.
MASHA. And I feel as though I'd been born long, long ago, and I'm trailing my life behind me like a dress with an endless train . . . And often I don't feel like going on with life at all. Of course, that's all nonsense. One ought to shake oneself and throw it all off.
DORN [*hums quietly*]. 'Tell her, my flowers' . . .
ARKADINA. And one more thing – I am as particular about myself as an Englishman. Yes, my dear, I keep myself in hand, as they say – I'm always properly dressed and have my hair done just *comme il faut*. Do you think I'd permit myself to come out of the house, even into the garden like this, in a dressing-gown or with my hair untidy? Never. That's why it is I've kept so young-looking – because I've never been a slattern or let myself go, as some women do . . . [*walks up and down the lawn, her hands on her hips*] There! you see? I'm as brisk as a bird. Fit to take the part of a fifteen-year-old girl!

DORN. Well, I may as well go on. [*picks up the book*] We'd just come to the corn merchant and the rats . . .

ARKADINA. Yes, the rats. Go on reading. [*sits down*] No, give it to me, I'll read. It's my turn. [*takes the book and looks for the place*] The rats . . . Here it is. [*reads*] 'And it goes without saying that it is as dangerous for society people to pamper and encourage writers of novels, as it is for corn merchants to breed rats in their granaries. And yet novelists are very much sought after. Thus, when a woman has chosen a writer whom she wishes to capture, she lays siege to him with the aid of compliments, flattery and favours.' Well, that may be true of the French, but there's nothing like that with us. We don't plan ahead. Over here, a woman is usually head over heels in love with a writer long before she decides to capture him, don't you see? To go no further afield, take Trigorin and myself . . .

> SORIN *enters leaning on his stick with* NINA *walking beside him. They are followed by* MEDVEDENKO, *who wheels an empty bath-chair.*

SORIN [*fondly, as to a child*]. Indeed? So we're quite delighted, are we? We're feeling cheerful today, after all? [*to his sister*] We're delighted! Our father and step-mother have gone off to Tver, and we are free now for three whole days.

NINA [*sits down beside* ARKADINA *and embraces her*]. I'm so happy! Now I belong to you.

SORIN [*sits down in his bath-chair*]. She's looking very pretty today.

ARKADINA. Prettily dressed and interesting-looking . . . That's a good girl . . . [*kisses her*] But we mustn't praise her too much or it may bring bad luck. Where's Boris Alexeyevich?

NINA. He's down by the bathing-shed – fishing.

ARKADINA. Surprising he doesn't get bored with it!

> [*prepares to go on reading*]

NINA. What is that?

ARKADINA. Maupassant's *Sur l'eau*, my dear. [*reads a few lines to herself*] Oh, well, the next bit isn't interesting, or true either. [*closes the book*] I'm worried. Tell me, what is the matter with my son? Why is he so sullen and depressed? He spends day after day on the lake and I hardly ever see him.

MASHA. His heart is troubled. [*to* NINA, *timidly*] Please, will you read us something from his play?

NINA [*shrugging her shoulders*]. Would you like me to? It's so uninteresting!

MASHA [*restraining her enthusiasm*]. When he reads himself, his eyes blaze and his face turns pale. He has a beautiful sad voice and the bearing of a poet.

[SORIN *is heard snoring*]

DORN. Good-night!

ARKADINA. Petrusha!

SORIN. Eh?

ARKADINA. Are you asleep?

SORIN. Not in the least.

[*a pause*]

ARKADINA. You're not taking any medical treatment, my friend. It's not wise, you know.

SORIN. I'd be glad to have some treatment, but the doctor here doesn't want me to.

DORN. Treatment! At sixty!

SORIN. Even at sixty one wants to go on living.

DORN [*tartly*]. Oh, all right then, take some valerian drops.

ARKADINA. I believe it would do him good to go and stay at a spa.

DORN. Well, he might go . . . Or he might not.

ARKADINA. What is one to make of that?

DORN. There's nothing to make of it. It's perfectly clear.

[*a pause*]

MEDVEDENKO. Pyotr Nikolayevich ought to give up smoking.

SORIN. Nonsense.

DORN. No, it isn't nonsense. Wine and tobacco deprive you of your individuality. After a cigar or a glass of vodka you're no longer just Pyotr Nikolayevich, but Pyotr Nikolayevich plus somebody else; your 'I' becomes blurred, and you begin to think of yourself as if you were someone quite different – as 'he'.

SORIN [*laughing*]. It's all very well for you to talk. You've had a good life, but what about me? I've served in the Department of Justice for twenty-eight years, but I haven't really lived, I haven't really experienced anything yet – so obviously I feel very much like going on living. You're satisfied and you don't care any more, so you're inclined to be philosophical – but I want to live. That's why I drink sherry at dinner and smoke cigars, and all that . . . And there it is . . .

DORN. Life has to be taken seriously, but when it comes to taking cures at sixty and regretting that you didn't get enough enjoyment out of life when you were young – all that, forgive me, is just futile.

MASHA [*getting up*]. It must be about lunch time. [*walking languidly and with an effort*] My leg's gone to sleep. [*goes out*]

DORN. She'll go and have a couple of drinks before lunch.

SORIN. She's not happy in her personal affairs, poor girl.

DORN. Rubbish, your Excellency!

SORIN. You talk like a man who's had his fill of experience.

ARKADINA. Oh, what could be more boring than this cloying country boredom! So hot, so still, nobody doing anything, everybody talking like a philosopher . . . It's nice to be here with you, my friends, it's pleasant to listen to you, but . . . how much better to be sitting alone in a hotel room learning a part!

NINA [*enthusiastically*]. How true! I do understand you!

SORIN. It's better in town, of course. You sit in your study, your footman doesn't let anyone in unannounced, you have a telephone . . . There are cabs in the streets, and all that sort of thing . . .

DORN [*hums*]. 'Tell her, my flowers' . . .

SHAMRAYEV *comes in, followed by* POLINA ANDREYEVNA.

SHAMRAYEV. Here they are! Good morning to you! [*kisses* ARKADINA's *hand, then* NINA's] So glad to see you looking so well. [*to* ARKADINA] My wife tells me that you're thinking of going to town with her today. Is that right?

ARKADINA. Yes, we are thinking of going.

SHAMRAYEV. Hm! That's splendid. But – my dear lady, how do you propose to travel? We're carting the rye today, and all the men are busy. What horses are you going to have, may I ask?

ARKADINA. What horses? How am I to know what horses?

SORIN. But we have carriage horses.

SHAMRAYEV [*agitated*]. Carriage horses? Where am I to get collars for carriage horses? Where am I to get collars? It amazes me! It is really beyond my understanding! My dear lady! Forgive me, I have the greatest admiration for your talent, I'm prepared to give ten years of my life for you – but I can't let you have the horses.

ARKADINA. But if I have to go? How very odd!

SHAMRAYEV. My dear lady! You don't realise what farming means.

ARKADINA [*flaring up*]. The old, old story! All right, then, I'm leaving for Moscow this very day. Please have the horses hired for me in the village, or I'll walk to the station.

SHAMRAYEV [*flaring up*]. In that case, I'm giving up my post. You can look for another bailiff. [*goes out*]

ARKADINA. Every summer it's like this, every summer they insult me here. I won't set my foot in this place again! [*goes out to the left, in the direction of the bathing-shed which is off-stage; a moment later she is seen entering the house, followed by* TRIGORIN, *who is carrying fishing-rods and a pail*]

SORIN [*flaring up*]. This is pure insolence! It's the limit! I'm sick and tired of it, once and for all! Bring all the horses here this minute!

NINA [*to* POLINA ANDREYEVNA]. To refuse Irina Nikolayevna, the famous actress! Surely, any wish of hers, even a mere whim, is more important than your farming? It's simply incredible.

POLINA [*in despair*]. But what can I do? Put yourself in my position, what can I do?

SORIN [*to* NINA]. Let us go along to my sister. We'll all try to persuade her not to go away, eh? [*looking in the direction in which* SHAMRAYEV *has gone*] Insufferable fellow! Tyrant!

NINA [*preventing him from rising*]. Sit still, sit still . . . We'll take you along . . .

　　　　[*she and* MEDVEDENKO *push the bath-chair*]

Oh, how dreadful all this is!

SORIN. Yes, yes, it is dreadful. But he won't leave, I'll speak to him presently.

　　　[*they go out;* DORN *and* POLINA ANDREYEVNA *are left alone*]

DORN. People are tiresome. Speaking candidly, your husband ought to be simply chucked out of here. But the end of it all will be that this old woman, Pyotr Nikolayevich, and his sister will go and apologise to him. You'll see.

POLINA. He's even sent the carriage horses to work in the fields. And misunderstandings like this happen every day. If you only knew how it upsets me! It makes me ill; you see I'm shaking . . . I can't bear his ill-manners. [*entreating him*] Yevgeniy, my dear, dear man, won't you take me to live with you? . . . Our time's passing; we're no longer young . . . and I wish we could stop concealing things and lying, now we're so near the end of our lives . . .

DORN. I'm fifty-five; it's too late for me to change my way of life.

POLINA. I know, you refuse me because there are other women with whom you are intimate. You can't take them all to live with you. I understand. Forgive me . . . you're tired of me.

NINA *appears near the house; she is picking flowers.*

DORN. No, not really.

POLINA. I'm so tormented by jealousy. Of course, you're a doctor, you can't avoid women. I understand . . .

DORN [*to* NINA, *who comes up*]. Well, how are things now?

NINA. Irina Nikolayevna's crying and Pyotr Nikolayevich has got an attack of asthma.

DORN [*getting up*]. I'd better go and give them some valerian drops . . .

NINA [*giving him the flowers*]. For you!

DORN. *Merci bien!* [*goes towards the house*]

POLINA [*going with him*]. What pretty flowers! [*near the house, in a low voice*] Give me those flowers! [*he gives them to her and she tears them to pieces and throws them aside. Both go into the house*]

NINA [*alone*]. How strange it is to see a famous actress crying . . . and for such a trifling reason! And isn't it strange, too? Here we have a famous author, a favourite with the public – they write about him in all the papers – they sell pictures of him everywhere, his works are translated into foreign languages – and he spends the whole day fishing and is quite delighted if he catches a couple of gudgeon. I used to think that famous people were proud and inaccessible and that they despised the crowd; I thought that the glory and lustre of their names enabled them, as it were, to revenge themselves on people who put high birth and wealth above everything else. But here they are, crying, fishing, playing cards, laughing and getting angry like anyone else.

TREPLYOV *enters, hatless, carrying a gun and a dead seagull.*

TREPLYOV. Are you alone here?

NINA. Yes, alone.

[TREPLYOV *lays the seagull at her feet*]

NINA. What does this mean?

TREPLYOV. I was despicable enough to kill this seagull to-day. I'm laying it at your feet.

NINA. What is the matter with you? [*picks up the seagull and looks at it*]

TREPLYOV [*after a pause*]. Soon I shall kill myself in the same way.

NINA. This is not like you at all!

TREPLYOV. True – but it's only since you've not been like yourself. You've changed towards me, you look at me coldly, my presence seems to embarrass you.

NINA. You've grown so irritable lately, and most of the time you've been talking unintelligibly, in a sort of symbolic way. And now this seagull here is apparently another symbol, but – you must forgive me – I don't understand it . . . [*puts the seagull on the seat*] I'm too simple-minded to understand you.

TREPLYOV. It started that evening when my play was such a stupid fiasco. Women don't forgive failure. I burnt it all, down to the last scrap. If you only knew how unhappy I am! Your growing coldness towards me is frightening, it's incredible! . . . It is as if I woke one day and saw this lake suddenly drying up, or draining away into the ground. You said just now that you're too simple-minded to understand me. Oh, tell me – what is there to understand? My play wasn't liked, you despise my kind of inspiration, and now you think I'm commonplace and insignificant, just like all the rest . . . [*stamping his foot*] How well I understand it! I do indeed! It feels as though a nail has been knocked into my brain. Damnation take it – and my pride, too, which is sucking my life blood, sucking it like a snake . . . [*seeing* TRIGORIN, *who comes in reading a book*] But here comes the real genius, stepping out like Hamlet himself, and with a book, too. [*mimics*] 'Words, words, words.' . . . The sun hasn't come near you yet, but you're smiling already and your eyes are melting in its rays. I won't inconvenience you further . . . [*goes out quickly*]

TRIGORIN [*making notes in his book*]. Takes snuff and drinks vodka. Always dresses in black. A schoolmaster in love with her . . .

NINA. Good morning, Boris Alexeyevich!

TRIGORIN. Good morning. It turns out that we may have to leave here today, rather unexpectedly. It doesn't seem very likely that we shall meet again. Girls don't often come my way, I mean girls who are young and interesting to meet. I've forgotten what it feels like to be eighteen or nineteen, indeed I can't imagine it at all clearly. That's why the girls in my novels and stories are usually so artificial. I wish I could exchange places with you, even if only for an hour, just to find out what your thoughts are, and what kind of a pretty little thing you are in a general sort of way.

NINA. And I would like to be in your place for a while.

TRIGORIN. Whatever for?

NINA. So that I could know what it feels like to be a famous, gifted writer. How does one experience fame? What sort of feeling does it give you to be famous?

TRIGORIN. What sort of feeling? Perhaps none. I've never thought about it. [*after a moment's thought*] It's one or the other: either you exaggerate the extent of my fame, or it is something not felt at all.

NINA. But what if you read about yourself in the papers?

TRIGORIN. When they praise me I am pleased, and when they attack me I feel out of humour for a couple of days.

NINA. What a wonderful world you live in! How I envy you – if only you knew! . . . How different people's destinies are! Some just drag out their obscure, tedious existences, all very much like one another, and all unhappy. And there are others – like you for instance, one in a million – who are given an interesting life, a life that is radiant and full of significance. You are fortunate!

TRIGORIN. I? [*shrugs his shoulders*] Hm! You talk about fame and happiness, and this radiant and interesting life, but to me all these fine words of yours – you must forgive me – are just like so many delicious sweets which I never eat. You are very young and very kind.

NINA. Your life is beautiful.

TRIGORIN. But what is there beautiful about it? [*looking at his watch*] I must go and do some writing presently. Forgive me, I haven't much time to spare . . . [*laughs*] You've stepped on my favourite corn, as the saying goes, and here I am getting excited and a little bit angry, too. All the same, let's talk. Let's talk about my radiant and beautiful life. Well, where shall we begin? [*after a moment's thought*] You know what it is to have a fixed idea, for instance when a man keeps on thinking about the same thing day and night, about . . . let us say, the moon. Well, I, too, have a kind of moon of my own. I'm obsessed day and night by one thought: I must write, I must write, I just must . . . For some reason, as soon

as I've finished one novel, I feel I must start writing another,
then another, then another . . . I write in a rush, without
stopping, and can't do anything else. What is there radiant or
beautiful in that, I ask you? Oh, it's a fatuous life! Here I am with
you, I'm quite worked up, and yet not for a single moment do I
forget that there's an unfinished novel waiting for me. I look
over there and I see a cloud shaped like a grand piano . . .
At once I think I must put it into some story or other – the fact
that a cloud looking like a grand piano has floated by. There's
the scent of heliotrope in the air. I make a mental note: 'sickly
scent . . . flower – the colour of a widow's dress . . . mention
when describing a summer evening.' . . . I snatch at every
word and sentence I utter, and every word you utter, too, and
hurriedly lock them up in my literary pantry – in case they might
come in useful! When I finish a piece of work, I dash off to the
theatre, or go off on a fishing trip, and that's the time when I
ought to relax and forget myself – but no! Something that feels
like a heavy cast-iron ball begins to revolve in my brain – a new
subject for a novel! So immediately I drag myself back to my
desk again, and I have to push on with my writing once more,
to keep on writing and writing . . . And it's like that always,
always . . . and I can't get any rest away from myself. I feel as
though I'm devouring my own life, that for the sake of the
honey I give to all and sundry I'm despoiling my best flowers
of their pollen, that I'm plucking the flowers themselves and
trampling on their roots. Am I out of my mind? Do you think
my relatives and friends treat me like a sane person? 'What are
you jotting down now? What surprises have you in store for us?'
It's the same thing over and over again, until I begin to imagine
that this attentiveness on the part of my friends, all this praise and
admiration, is just a sham, that they are trying to deceive me just
as if I were insane. Sometimes I feel afraid of them stealing
up on me from behind, seizing me and carrying me off, like
Poprishchin,* to a lunatic asylum. As for the years when I was
starting – my younger, better years – in those days my writing
used to be one continuous torment. A minor writer, especially if
he hasn't had much luck, sees himself as clumsy, awkward, and

* The principal character in the story *The Diary of a Madman*, by N. V.
Gogol.

unwanted. He gets nervous and overwrought, and feels irresistibly drawn towards people connected with literature, or art, but then he just wanders among them unrecognised and unnoticed, unable to look them straight and courageously in the eye, like a passionate gambler who hasn't any money. I could not see my readers, but for some reason I always imagined them as unfriendly and sceptical. I was afraid of the public, it terrified me, and whenever a new play of mine was produced, I always felt that the dark-haired people in the audience were hostile to it, and the fair-haired ones coldly indifferent. Oh, how dreadful it all was! What a torment!

NINA. But even so, don't you have moments of happiness and exaltation – moments when you feel inspired, when your creative work is actually in progress?

TRIGORIN. Yes, while I'm writing I enjoy it. I enjoy reading proofs, too, but . . . as soon as the thing comes out in print I can no longer bear it. I immediately see that it's not what I intended, that it's a mistake, that it oughtn't to have been written at all, and I feel angry and depressed . . . [laughing] And then the public reads it and says: 'Yes, it's charming, so cleverly done . . . Charming, but a far cry from Tolstoy.' . . . Or 'A very fine piece of work, but Turgenev's *Fathers and Children* is a better book.' And so it will go on till my dying day – everything will be charming and clever – and nothing more. And when I die, my friends as they pass by my grave, will say: 'Here lies Trigorin. He was a good writer, but not as good as Turgenev.'

NINA. You must forgive me, but I refuse to try to understand you. You've simply been spoiled by success.

TRIGORIN. What success? I've never liked myself. I dislike myself as a writer. But the worst of it is that I live in a sort of haze, and I often don't understand what I'm writing. I love this water here, the trees, the sky. I have a feeling for nature, it arouses a sort of passion in me, an irresistible desire to write. But you see, I'm not a mere landscape painter, I'm also a citizen of my country; I love it, I love its people. As an author, I feel I'm in duty bound to write about the people, their sufferings, their future – and about science, the rights of man, and so on, and so forth. And I write about everything in a great hurry while I'm being prodded and urged on from all sides and people keep getting cross with me, so that I dash about from one side to the other like a fox badgered by the hounds. I see science and society forging ahead, while I drop further and further behind, like a peasant who's just missed his train, and in the end I feel that all I can do is to paint landscapes, and that everything else I write is a sham — false to the very core.

NINA. You've been working too hard. You haven't the time or the inclination to recognise your own importance. You may be dissatisfied with yourself, but to others you are a great and wonderful person! If I were a writer like you, I should give my whole life to the ordinary people, realising at the same time that their happiness lay in striving to rise to my level — and then they'd have harnessed themselves to my chariot.

TRIGORIN. Chariot, indeed! . . . Am I an Agamemnon, or what?

[*both smile*]

NINA. For the sake of being happy like that — of being a writer or an actress — I would put up with unfriendliness from my family, with poverty and disappointment, with living in a garret and having nothing to eat but rye bread. I would gladly suffer dissatisfaction with myself in the knowledge of my own imperfections, but in return I would demand fame . . . real, resounding fame . . . [*covering her face with her hands*] My head's going round! Ugh!

ARKADINA'S VOICE [*from the house*] Boris Alexeyevich!

TRIGORIN. They're calling me . . . To pack, I suppose. But I don't feel like leaving. [*looks round at the lake*] What a heavenly sight! How lovely it is!

NINA. Do you see a house with a garden on the other side?

TRIGORIN. Yes.

NINA. It belonged to my mother when she was alive. I was born there. I've spent all my life beside this lake and I know every tiny island on it.

TRIGORIN. It's a beautiful place! [*noticing the seagull*] But what is this?

NINA. A seagull. Konstantin Gavrilovich killed it.

TRIGORIN. What a beautiful bird! Really, I don't feel like going away. Why don't you persuade Irina Nikolayevna to stay? [*writes in his notebook*]

NINA. What are you writing?

TRIGORIN. Just making a few notes . . . An idea suddenly came into my head. A subject for a short story: a young girl, like you, has lived beside a lake from childhood. She loves the lake as a seagull does, and she's happy and free as a seagull. But a man chances to come along, sees her, and having nothing better to do, destroys her, just like this seagull here.

A pause; ARKADINA *appears in the window.*

ARKADINA. Boris Alexeyevich, where are you?
TRIGORIN. I'm coming! [*goes, then looks back at* NINA; *to* ARKADINA *at the window*] What is it?
ARKADINA. We're staying.
                    [TRIGORIN *goes into the house*]
NINA [*advances to the footlights; after a few moments' meditation*]. It's a dream!

CURTAIN

ACT THREE

The dining-room in SORIN's *house. Doors right and left. A sideboard and a medicine cupboard. In the middle of the room a table. A trunk and some cardboard hat boxes indicate preparations for departure.* TRIGORIN *is having his breakfast while* MASHA *stands beside the table.*

MASHA. I'm telling you all this because you're a writer. You can make use of it if you like. I tell you honestly – if he had wounded himself badly, I wouldn't have lived another minute. But I've got courage all the same. I just decided I'd tear this love of mine out of my heart, tear it out by the roots.

TRIGORIN. But how?

MASHA. I'm getting married. To Medvedenko.

TRIGORIN. You mean the schoolmaster?

MASHA. Yes.

TRIGORIN. I don't see the point of it.

MASHA. What is the point of love without hope, of waiting whole years for something . . . one doesn't know what . . . But when I'm married there'll be no time for love, new cares will drive out all the old ones . . . And anyway, it'll be a change, you know. Shall we have another?

TRIGORIN. Do you think we ought to?

MASHA. Oh, come! [*fills two glasses*] Don't look at me like that. Women drink more often than you imagine. A few drink openly as I do, but most drink in secret. Yes. And it's always vodka or cognac. [*clinks glasses with him*] Here's good luck! You're a genuine, sincere man – I'm sorry to be parting from you. [*they drink*]

TRIGORIN. I don't feel like going away myself.

MASHA. Why don't you ask her to stay?

TRIGORIN. No, she won't stay now. Her son is behaving very tactlessly. First he shoots himself, and now they say he's going to challenge me to a duel. Whatever for? He sulks and snorts, and preaches new forms of art . . . But there's room enough for all, for new and old alike. Why does he have to push and shove?

MASHA. There's jealousy, too. However, it's not my affair.

A pause; YAKOV *passes from left to right carrying a suitcase.*
NINA *comes in and stands by the window.*

MASHA. My schoolmaster is not particularly clever, but he's kind-hearted and poor, and he's very fond of me. I'm sorry for him. I'm sorry for his old mother, too. Well, let me wish you all the best. Don't think badly of me. [*shakes his hand warmly*] I'm very grateful to you for your friendly interest . . . Do send me your books and be sure to autograph them. Only don't write: 'To the highly respected' and all that, but just put 'To Marya, who doesn't know where she belongs and has no object in life'. Goodbye! [*goes out*]

NINA [*holding out her hand towards* TRIGORIN, *with her fist clenched*]. Odd or even?

TRIGORIN. Even.

NINA [*with a sigh*]. That means 'no'. I've only got one pea in my hand. I was trying to tell my fortune – whether to go on the stage or not. If only someone would give me advice!

TRIGORIN. One can't give advice about that.

[*a pause*]

NINA. We are going to part now and . . . perhaps we shall not meet again. Will you take this little medallion to remember me by? I had your initials engraved on it . . . and on the other side the title of a book of yours – *Days and Nights.*

TRIGORIN. How exquisite! [*kisses the medallion*] A charming gift!

NINA. Think of me sometimes.

TRIGORIN. I will indeed. I shall think of you as you were on that sunny day – do you remember? – a week ago, when you were wearing that light-coloured dress . . . we talked . . . there was a white seagull lying on the seat.

NINA [*pensively*]. Yes, a seagull . . .

[*a pause*]

We can't go on talking, someone's coming. Let me have two minutes with you before you go, I implore you . . .

[*goes out on left*]

At the same time ARKADINA *and* SORIN *come in, the latter wearing a frock-coat with the star of an order on it. They are followed by* YAKOV, *who is looking after the packing.*

ARKADINA. Better stay at home, my friend. Are you really up to running round visiting people, with your rheumatism? [*to* TRIGORIN] Who was it just went out? Nina?

TRIGORIN. Yes.

ARKADINA. I'm sorry we've disturbed you . . . [*sits down*] I believe I've packed everything. I'm worn out.

TRIGORIN [*reading the inscription on the medallion*]. *Days and Nights,* page 121, lines 11 and 12.

YAKOV [*clearing the table*]. Am I to pack your fishing rods too, sir?

TRIGORIN. Yes, I shall be wanting them again. But you can give the books away.

YAKOV. Yes, sir.

TRIGORIN [*to himself*]. Page 121, lines 11 and 12. What can they be? [*to* ARKADINA] Are there any of my books in the house?

ARKADINA. Yes, in my brother's study, in the corner bookcase.

TRIGORIN. Page 121 . . . [*goes out*]

ARKADINA. Really, Petrusha, you'd better stay at home.

SORIN. You are going away – I shall find it hard to stay at home without you.

ARKADINA. But what is there to do in town?

SORIN. Nothing special, but all the same . . . [*laughs*] There'll be the laying of the foundation stone of the County Hall, and all that sort of thing . . . I feel I'd like to shake myself out of this stagnant existence, if only for an hour or two. I've been lying about too long, like some old cigarette holder, or something. I've ordered the horses for one o'clock, so that we shall be starting at the same time.

ARKADINA [*after a pause*]. You must go on living here, don't let yourself get bored and avoid catching cold. Watch over my son. Take care of him. Give him good advice.

[*a pause*]

Here I am going away, and I shan't even know why Konstantin tried to shoot himself. I believe jealousy was the chief reason, and the sooner I take Trigorin away from here, the better.

SORIN. How shall I say it? . . . There were other reasons, too. It's not to be wondered at, really — a young man, intelligent, living in the country, in the wilds . . . with no money, no position, no future. No occupation whatsoever. Ashamed and afraid of his idleness. I am extremely fond of him, and he's attached to me too, but all the same, he does feel in a way that he doesn't belong here, that he's a cadger, living on charity. It's not to be wondered at — he's got pride.

ARKADINA. He's a great anxiety to me! [*pondering*] Ought he to get some sort of job? . . .

SORIN [*begins to whistle, then speaks irresolutely*]. I think quite the best thing would be if you were to . . . give him a little money. In the first place, he ought to have proper clothes, and all that sort of thing. Just look at him, he's been wearing the same wretched jacket for the last three years, and he's got no overcoat . . . [*laughs*] And it wouldn't do the boy any harm to have a little fun . . . to go abroad, or something . . . It wouldn't cost much.

ARKADINA. All the same . . . I might manage the suit, perhaps, but as for going abroad . . . No, just at the moment I can't even manage the suit. [*resolutely*] I haven't got the money.

[*SORIN laughs*]

ARKADINA. No!

SORIN [*begins to whistle*]. Quite so. Forgive me, my dear, don't be annoyed. I believe you . . . You're a generous, noble-hearted woman.

ARKADINA [*tearfully*]. I have no money!

SORIN. Naturally, if I had any money I would give it him myself, but I've got nothing, not a penny. [*laughs*] My bailiff takes all my pension and spends it on farming — on the cattle and the bees — and my money is all wasted. The bees die, the cows die, and I'm never allowed to use the horses . . .

ARKADINA. Well, I do have some money, but after all, I'm an actress: my dress-bill alone is enough to ruin me.

SORIN. You're a dear, kind-hearted woman . . . I respect you . . . Yes . . . There's something the matter with me again . . . [*sways*] I feel dizzy. [*holds on to the table*] I feel faint and all that sort of thing.

ARKADINA [*alarmed*]. Petrusha! [*trying to support him*] Petrusha, my dear! . . . [*calling*] Help! Help! . . .

TREPLYOV, *with a bandage round his head,*
and MEDVEDENKO *come in.*

ARKADINA. He's feeling faint!

SORIN. It's nothing, nothing . . . [*smiles and drinks some water*] It's passed off already . . . and all that sort of . . .

TREPLYOV [*to his mother*]. Don't get alarmed, mamma, it's not serious. Uncle often has these attacks nowadays. [*to his uncle*] You ought to lie down for a while, uncle.

SORIN. Yes, for a while . . . But I'll go to town all the same. I'll lie down for a bit, then go . . . That's definite . . . [*goes out leaning on his stick*]

MEDVEDENKO [*supporting him by the arm*]. Here's a riddle for you: in the morning on four legs, at noon on two, in the evening on three . . .

SORIN [*laughing*]. Quite so. And at night on its back. I can walk on my own, thank you . . .

MEDVEDENKO. Come, come, don't stand on ceremony. [*goes out with* SORIN]

ARKADINA. How he scared me!

TREPLYOV. It doesn't do his health any good living in the country. He gets depressed. Suppose you suddenly felt generous, mamma, and lent him a couple of thousand? Then he could spend a whole year in town.

ARKADINA. I have no money. I'm an actress, not a banker.

[*a pause*]

TREPLYOV. Mamma, will you change my bandage for me? You do it so well.

ARKADINA [*takes some iodine and a box of bandages out of the medicine cupboard*]. The doctor's late.

TREPLYOV. He promised to be here by ten o'clock, and it's midday already.

ARKADINA. Sit down. [*takes the bandage off his head*] You look as if you're wearing a turban. Yesterday there was some stranger in the kitchen asking what nationality you were. But your wound is almost healed. There's only a tiny bit still open. [*kisses him on the head*] You won't play about with a gun again when I'm away, will you?

TREPLYOV. No, mamma. That was a moment of mad despair, when

I had no control over myself. It won't happen again. [*kisses her hands*] You've got magic hands. I remember ever so long ago, when you were still playing in the state-aided theatres – I was quite young then – there was a fight in our courtyard. One of the tenants, a washerwoman, was badly hurt. Do you remember? She was taken off unconscious . . . and you went to see her several times and took medicine to her, and bathed her children in a tub. Don't you remember?

ARKADINA. No. [*puts on a fresh bandage*]

TREPLYOV. Two ballet dancers lived in the same house as we did then . . . They used to come and have coffee with you . . .

ARKADINA. That I do remember.

TREPLYOV. They were so religious.

[*a pause*]

Just lately, these last few days, I've felt that I loved you as tenderly and uncritically as I did when I was a child. I have no-one left but you now. Only why, why did you let yourself fall under the influence of that man?

ARKADINA. You don't understand him, Konstantin. He's such an honourable man . . .

TREPLYOV. And yet, when he was told I was going to challenge him, his honour didn't prevent him from behaving like a coward. He's leaving. Ignominious flight!

ARKADINA. What nonsense! I asked him to go myself.

TREPLYOV. A most honourable man, indeed! Here we are on the point of quarrelling about him, while at this very moment he may be laughing at us in the garden, or the drawing-room . . . bringing out Nina's potentialities, trying to convince her finally that he's a genius.

ARKADINA. You take a delight in saying these unpleasant things. I admire him, so please don't speak ill of him in my presence.

TREPLYOV. Well, I don't admire him. You want me to think he's a genius too, but you must forgive me – I can't lie. His books make me sick.

ARKADINA. That's envy. Mediocre people trying to make unjustifiable claims about themselves have to run down people with real talent. Poor comfort, I must say!

TREPLYOV [*ironically*]. Real talent! [*wrathfully*] I have more talent than the lot of you if it comes to that! [*tearing the bandage off his head*] It's conventional, hidebound people like you who have grabbed the best places in the arts today, who regard as genuine and legitimate only what you do yourselves. Everything else you have to smother and suppress! I refuse to accept you at your own valuation! I refuse to accept you or him!

ARKADINA. You're decadent!

TREPLYOV. Take yourself off to your lovely theatre and go on acting in your futile, miserable plays!

ARKADINA. I've never acted in futile, miserable plays! Let me alone! You're incapable of writing even a couple of miserable scenes! You're just a little upstart from Kiev! A cadger!

TREPLYOV. You miser!

ARKADINA. You beggar!

[TREPLYOV *sits down and weeps quietly*]

ARKADINA. Nonentity! [*walks up and down in agitation, then stops*] Don't cry . . . You mustn't cry! . . . [*weeps*] You mustn't . . . [*kisses his forehead, then his cheeks and his head*] My darling child, forgive me . . . Forgive your wicked mother. Forgive an unhappy woman.

TREPLYOV [*embraces her*]. If only you knew! I've lost everything. She doesn't love me, and I can't write any more . . . all my hopes are gone.

ARKADINA. Don't despair . . . Everything will come right. He'll be leaving soon, and she'll love you again. [*wipes away his tears*] That's enough. We've made it up now.

TREPLYOV [*kissing her hands*]. Yes, mamma.

ARKADINA [*tenderly*]. Make it up with him, too. There's no need for a duel . . . Is there, now?

TREPLYOV. Very well . . . Only, mamma, don't make me see him. It's painful for me . . . it's too much for my strength . . .

TRIGORIN *comes in.*

There . . . I'm going . . . [*quickly puts away the dressings in the cupboard*] The doctor will do the bandaging now . . .

TRIGORIN [*looking through the book*]. Page 121 . . . lines 11 and 12. Here it is . . . [*reads*] 'If ever you need my life, come and take it.'

[TREPLYOV *picks up the bandage from the floor and goes out*]

ARKADINA [*glancing at her watch*]. The horses will soon be here.

TRIGORIN [*to himself*]. 'If ever you need my life, come and take it.'

ARKADINA. You've got all your things packed, I hope?

TRIGORIN [*impatiently*]. Yes, yes . . . [*musing*] Why does it seem so sad to me, this cry from a pure soul – why does it wring my heart so agonisingly? . . . 'If ever you need my life, come and take it.' [*to* ARKADINA] Let us stay one more day!

[ARKADINA *shakes her head*]

Do let us stay!

ARKADINA. Darling, I know what's holding you here. But do control yourself. You've become a little intoxicated, try to sober down.

TRIGORIN. You must try to be sober, too – and sensible and reasonable. Do try to see all this like a true friend, I implore you . . . [*presses her hand*] You are capable of sacrifice . . . Be a friend to me, release me . . .

ARKADINA [*in great agitation*]. Has she fascinated you as much as that?

TRIGORIN. I'm drawn to her! Perhaps it is just what I need.

ARKADINA. The love of a provincial girl? Oh, how little you know yourself!

TRIGORIN. Sometimes people go to sleep on their feet, and that's just the state I'm in as I talk to you – all the time I feel as if I were asleep and dreaming of her. I'm possessed by sweet and wonderful dreams . . . Let me go . . .

ARKADINA [*trembling*]. No, no . . . I'm just an ordinary woman, you mustn't talk to me like that . . . Don't torment me, Boris . . . I'm frightened . . .

TRIGORIN. You could be extraordinary, if you chose. Young love, enchanting, poetical – love that carries you off into a world of dreams – it's the only thing that can bring happiness on this earth! I've never yet known a love like that . . . In my youth I never had time, I was always hanging around on editors' doorsteps, struggling with poverty . . . And now it is here – it has come, it is beckoning to me . . . What's the sense in running away from it?

ARKADINA [*angrily*]. You're out of your mind!

TRIGORIN. And why not?

ARKADINA. You've all been conspiring to torment me today! [*weeps*]

TRIGORIN [*clasping his head with his hands*]. She doesn't understand! She doesn't want to understand!

ARKADINA. Am I really so old and ugly that you can talk to me about other women without embarrassment? [*embraces and kisses him*] Oh, you must have gone mad! My beautiful, my wonderful . . . You – the last page of my life! [*kneels before him*] My joy, my pride, my happiness! . . . [*embraces his knees*] If you leave me even for a single hour I shall never survive it, I shall go out of my mind – my wonderful, magnificent man, my master . . .

TRIGORIN. Someone might come in. [*helps her to her feet*]

ARKADINA. Let them, I'm not ashamed of my love for you. [*kisses his hands*] My darling reckless boy, you may want to behave as if you were mad, but I won't let you, I won't let you . . . [*laughs*] You're mine . . . mine . . . This forehead is mine, and these eyes, and this beautiful silky hair is mine, too . . . All of you is mine. You're so gifted, so clever – you're the best of all the modern writers, the only hope of Russia . . . You have such sincerity, simplicity, freshness, stimulating humour . . . With a stroke of your pen you can convey the whole essence of a character or a landscape; people in your books are so alive. It is impossible to read your work and not be delighted by it. Do you think this is just hero-worship? You think I'm flattering you? Come, look into my eyes . . . look . . . Do I look like a liar? There! you see – I alone know how to appreciate you, I'm the one person who tells you the truth, my darling, my wonderful man . . . Will you come? Yes? You'll not leave me? . . .

TRIGORIN. I have no will of my own . . . I've never had a will of my own. Sluggish, flabby, always submissive – how can any woman like that sort of thing? Take me, carry me off, but don't let me ever move a step away from you . . .

ARKADINA [*to herself*]. Now he's mine! [*affecting an easy manner as if nothing had happened*] But, of course, you can stay if you want to. I'll go myself, and you can come on afterwards, a week later. After all, why should you hurry?

TRIGORIN. No, we may as well go together.

ARKADINA. Just as you like. Let's go together then . . .

[*a pause;* TRIGORIN *writes in his notebook*]

ARKADINA. What is it?

TRIGORIN. I heard a good phrase this morning – 'The Maiden's Forest' . . . Might come in useful. [*stretches*] So we are going? More railway carriages, stations, refreshment bars, veal cutlets, conversations . . .

SHAMRAYEV [*coming in*]. I have come to inform you that the horses are ready — I am sorry to say. It's time, my dear lady, we were off to the station: the train comes in at five minutes past two. You will do me that little favour, won't you, Irina Nikolay-evna? You won't forget to inquire where the actor Suzdaltsev is now? Is he alive? Is he well? We used to stand each other drinks years ago . . . He used to be quite inimitable in *The Mail Robbery* . . . I remember at that time there was a tragedian Izmailov who always played with him at Elizavetgrad . . . He was a remarkable personality too . . . Don't be in a hurry, my dear lady, you needn't start for another five minutes. Once they were playing as conspirators in a melodrama, and when they were suddenly discovered they had to say: 'We're caught in a trap.' But Izmailov said 'We're taught in a cap'. [*laughs loudly*] 'Taught in a cap!'

> *While he is speaking,* YAKOV *fusses with the suitcases; a maid brings* ARKADINA's *hat, coat, umbrella, and gloves, and everyone helps her to put them on. The chef looks in through the door at left, and after some hesitation enters.* POLINA ANDREYEVNA, *then* SORIN *and* MEDVEDENKO *also come in.*

POLINA [*with a small basket in her hand*]. Here are some plums for your journey . . . very sweet. You might feel like having something refreshing.

ARKADINA. You are very kind, Polina Andreyevna.

POLINA. Goodbye, my dear! If there has been anything that wasn't quite as you like it, please forgive us. [*weeps*]

ARKADINA [*embracing her*]. Everything was all right, everything! Only you shouldn't cry!

POLINA. Our days are passing!

ARKADINA. There's nothing we can do about it.

> SORIN, *wearing an overcoat with a shoulder cape and a hat, and carrying a cane, comes in from the door at left. He speaks as he walks across the room.*

SORIN. It's time to go, sister. Don't let us be late for the train after all . . . I'm going to get into the carriage. [*goes out*]

MEDVEDENKO. I'll walk to the station . . . to see you off. I'll be there in no time. [*goes out*]

ARKADINA. Goodbye, my dears . . . If all goes well, we'll meet
again next summer . . .
    [*the maid, the chef, and* YAKOV *kiss her hand*]
Don't forget me. [*gives the chef a rouble*] Here's a rouble between
you three.

THE CHEF. Thank you kindly, madam. Good journey to you!
We're most grateful for your kindness.

YAKOV. God-speed to you!

SHAMRAYEV. Perhaps you'll write to us — it would make us so
happy! Goodbye, Boris Alexeyevich.

ARKADINA. Where is Konstantin? Tell him that I'm leaving. We
must say goodbye. Think kindly of me. [*to* YAKOV] I gave a
rouble to the chef. It's between the three of you.
    [*All go out at right. The stage is empty. There is the noise off-stage
    of people being seen off. The maid returns to fetch the basket of plums
    from the table and goes out again.*]

TRIGORIN [*returning*]. I've forgotten my cane. I believe it's out
there, on the terrace. [*walks towards the door at left and meets* NINA,
who comes in] It's you! We're going . . .

NINA. I felt sure that we should see each other again. [*excitedly*]
Boris Alexeyevich, I've decided irrevocably, the die is cast —
I'm going on the stage. I shall be gone from here tomorrow,
I'm leaving my father, leaving everything, I'm beginning a new
life . . . I'm going to Moscow . . . like you. We shall see each
other there.

TRIGORIN [*glancing behind him*]. Stay at the Slaviansky Bazaar. Let
me know at once . . . at Molchanovka, Grokholsky House . . . I
must hurry . . .
    [*a pause*]

NINA. One minute more . . .

TRIGORIN [*in an undertone*]. You are so beautiful . . . Oh, how
happy I am to think that we shall be seeing each other soon!
    [*she leans her head on his breast*]
I shall see these wonderful eyes again, this indescribably beautiful, tender smile . . . these sweet features, the expression of
angelic purity! My darling . . . [*a prolonged kiss*]

CURTAIN

Between the Third and the Fourth Acts there is an interval of two years.

ACT FOUR

A drawing-room in SORIN's *house, converted into a study by* KONSTAN-TIN TREPLYOV. *Doors right and left leading to other rooms. In the centre, a french window opening on to the terrace. There is a writing desk in the corner on the right and an ottoman by the door on the left; also a bookcase and the usual drawing-room furniture. Books are lying on the window-sills and on chairs. It is evening. The room is dimly lit by a shaded table-lamp. There is the noise of wind in the trees and the chimneys.*

A watchman is heard tapping.* Enter MEDVEDENKO *and* MASHA.

MASHA [*calling*]. Konstantin Gavrilich! Konstantin Gavrilich! [*looking round*] No, there's no-one here. The old man keeps on asking: where's Kostya, where's Kostya . . . He just can't live without him . . .

MEDVEDENKO. He's afraid of being alone. [*listening*] What dreadful weather! It's been like this for nearly two days.

MASHA [*turning up the lamp*]. There are waves on the lake, enormous ones.

MEDVEDENKO. It's very dark outside. By the way, we might as well tell them to pull down that stage in the garden. It stands there naked and ugly like a skeleton, with the curtain flapping in the wind. You know, last night as I was walking past it, I thought I heard someone inside – crying.

MASHA. What next . . .

[*a pause*]

MEDVEDENKO. Let's go home, Masha.

MASHA [*shaking her head*]. No, I shall stay here for the night.

MEDVEDENKO [*imploringly*]. Masha, do let us go! The baby may be hungry.

MASHA. What nonsense! Matriona will feed him.

[*a pause*]

---

* In former days it was usual for a man to go round an estate, striking a wooden board with a stick to frighten away potential thieves.

MEDVEDENKO. I feel sorry for him. This is the third night he's been without his mother.

MASHA. How boring you've become! In the old days you did at least philosophise a bit now and again. Now all you talk about is baby and home, baby and home – I never hear anything else from you.

MEDVEDENKO. Do come along, Masha!

MASHA. You go by yourself.

MEDVEDENKO. Your father won't let me have a horse.

MASHA. Yes, he will. You go and ask him.

MEDVEDENKO. I suppose I might ask him . . . And you'll be coming home tomorrow then?

MASHA [takes snuff]. Well, yes . . . tomorrow. How you pester me!

Enter TREPLYOV *and* POLINA ANDREYEVNA. TREPLYOV *carries pillows and a blanket and* POLINA ANDREYEVNA *some sheets, which they put on the ottoman.* TREPLYOV *then goes to his desk and sits down.*

MASHA. What is this for, mamma?

POLINA. It's for Pyotr Nikolayevich. He wants his bed made in Kostya's room.

MASHA. Let me . . . [makes the bed]

POLINA [sighing]. Old people are like children . . . [walks over to the writing desk and, leaning on her elbow, looks at an open manuscript] [a pause]

MEDVEDENKO. Well, I'd better go. Goodbye, Masha. [kisses his wife's hand] Goodbye, mother. [tries to kiss his mother-in-law's hand]

POLINA [with irritation]. Go on with you! It's time you went if you are going.

MEDVEDENKO. Goodbye, Konstantin Gavrilich.

[TREPLYOV gives him his hand without speaking;
MEDVEDENKO goes out]

POLINA [looking at the manuscript]. Who would have thought that you would turn out to be a real writer, Kostya? But, thank God, here you are getting money from magazines for your work. [strokes his hair] You've grown so good-looking, too . . . Kostya, my dear, you're so kind, couldn't you be a little kinder to my Mashenka?

MASHA [making the bed]. Leave him alone, mamma.

POLINA [*to* TREPLYOV]. She's a nice girl, you know.

[*a pause*]

Give a woman a kind glance sometimes, Kostya, and she won't ask for more. I know that.

[TREPLYOV *gets up from his desk and goes out without speaking*]

MASHA. There! now you've made him angry. What's the point of pestering him?

POLINA. I feel so sorry for you, Mashenka!

MASHA. A lot of use that is to me!

POLINA. My heart's been aching for you. I see it all, you know – I understand it all.

MASHA. All this is just nonsense. Love without hope – it only happens in novels. It's really nothing. You've only got to keep a firm hold on yourself, to stop yourself hoping for . . . hoping for the tide to turn . . . If love sneaks into your heart the best thing to do is to chuck it out. My husband's been promised a transfer to another district. Once we get there, I'll forget it all . . . tear it out of my heart, roots and all.

[*a waltz with a melancholy tune is being played two rooms away*]

POLINA. That's Kostya playing. He must be feeling sad.

MASHA [*noiselessly takes two or three waltz turns*]. The most important thing, mamma, is not to have him constantly in front of me. Just let them give my Semyon his transfer, and you'll see, I'll forget it all in a month. The whole thing is just nonsense.

Door at left opens. DORN *and* MEDVEDENKO *wheel in* SORIN.

MEDVEDENKO. I've got six people at home now, and flour is two kopecks a pound.

DORN. Yes, you've got to scrape and save!

MEDVEDENKO. It's all very well for you to laugh. You've got more money than you know what to do with.

DORN. Money? My dear fellow, in thirty years of practice – and very worrying practice at that, for I was day and night at everyone's beck and call – in all those years I've only managed to save two thousand roubles, and I've just spent that on a holiday abroad. I've got positively nothing.

MASHA [*to her husband*]. So you haven't gone after all?

MEDVEDENKO [*apologetically*]. Well . . . how could I if they wouldn't let me have a horse?

MASHA [*bitterly, in an undertone*]. I just can't bear the sight of you!
[SORIN *is wheeled to the left side of the room;* POLINA, MASHA *and*
DORN *sit down beside him;* MEDVEDENKO, *looking depressed,*
stands a little apart from them]

DORN. What a lot of changes you've made, though! You've turned
this drawing-room into a study.

MASHA. Konstantin Gavrilych is more comfortable working here.
He can walk out into the garden whenever he likes, and he can
think there.

[*the watchman can be heard tapping*]

SORIN. Where's my sister?

DORN. She's gone to the station to meet Trigorin. She'll be back
soon.

SORIN. I must be dangerously ill, if you thought it necessary to send
for my sister. [*after a short silence*] Isn't it odd? I'm dangerously ill,
yet no-one gives me any medicine.

DORN. Well, what would you like to have? Valerian drops? Soda?
Quinine?

SORIN. There he goes again, the philosopher! Oh, how trying it all
is! [*jerks his head in the direction of the ottoman*] Has that been got
ready for me?

POLINA. Yes, Pyotr Nikolayevich, it's for you.

SORIN. Thank you.

DORN [*hums*]. 'The moon floats through the night sky . . .'

SORIN. You know, I'd like to give Kostya a subject for a novel. I'd
call it: 'The Man Who Wished'. '*L'homme qui a voulu.*' Long ago
in my young days I wanted to become a writer — and I didn't; I
wanted to be a fine speaker — and I spoke abominably [*mimicking
himself*] — 'and all that sort of thing, and all the rest of it, and so
on, and so forth' . . . When I tried to sum up my argument, I'd
go plodding on and on until I broke into perspiration . . . I
wanted to get married — and I didn't, I always wanted to live in
town — and here I am finishing my life in the country, and all
that sort of thing . . .

DORN. You wanted to become a civil councillor, and you did.

SORIN [*laughs*]. That was something I didn't strive for. It just
happened.

DORN. Fancy expressing dissatisfaction with life at the age of sixty-
two! It's a little indecent, you must admit.

SORIN. What a persistent fellow he is! Can't you understand anyone wanting to live?

DORN. That's just foolish. Every life must have an end – it's the law of nature.

SORIN. You talk like a man who's had his fill of experience. You've satisfied your hunger, and so life means nothing to you, you don't care about it. But when it comes to dying, you'll be afraid too.

DORN. The fear of death is an animal fear. You've got to suppress it. It's only religious people who consciously fear death – because they believe in a future life and are afraid they'll be punished for their sins. Your case is different – in the first place, you're not religious, and in the second – what sins have you committed? You've served in the Ministry of Justice for twenty-five years, that's all.

SORIN [*laughs*]. Twenty-eight . . .

Enter TREPLYOV, *who sits down on a low stool at* SORIN's *feet.*
MASHA *gazes at him continuously.*

DORN. We're preventing Konstantin Gavrilich from getting on with his work.

TREPLYOV. Oh no, it doesn't matter.

[*a pause*]

MEDVEDENKO. If I might ask you, Doctor, which city do you like best of all those you've seen abroad?

DORN. Genoa.

TREPLYOV. Why Genoa?

DORN. Because there's something very fine about the street crowds there. You go out of your hotel at night, and the whole street is packed with people. You just wander among them aimlessly, anywhere you like, up and down, you live with them, become part of the crowd spiritually, and you end by almost believing that a world-soul can really exist – something like the world-soul in your play, the one Nina Zarechnaya acted in some time back. By the way, where is Zarechnaya now? Do you know how she is?

TREPLYOV. I suppose she's all right.

DORN. Someone told me she's been leading a rather peculiar kind of life. What's been happening?

TREPLYOV. Well, Doctor, it's a long story.

DORN. Never mind, you can make it short.

[*a pause*]

TREPLYOV. She ran away from home and had an affair with Trigorin. You knew that, didn't you?

DORN. Yes, I did know.

TREPLYOV. She had a child. It died. Trigorin fell out of love with her and went back to his former attachments, as might have been expected. In fact he never gave them up, but in his spineless way he somehow managed to keep them all going. As far as I can make it out from what I've heard, Nina's personal life turned out a complete failure.

DORN. And what about the stage?

TREPLYOV. That was worse still, I believe. She started acting in a small theatre at some holiday place near Moscow, then went to the provinces. I never lost sight of her at that time, and wherever she went, I followed. She would always take on big parts, but she acted them crudely, without distinction – with false intonations and violent gestures. There were moments when she showed talent – as when she uttered a cry, or died on the stage – but they were only moments.

DORN. Then she has some talent, after all?

TREPLYOV. It's very hard to tell. I believe she has. I saw her, of course, but she refused to see me, and the servants wouldn't let me go up to her room at the hotel. I understood her state of mind and did not insist on seeing her.

[*a pause*]

What more can I tell you? Afterwards, when I got back home, I had letters from her, intelligent, warm, interesting letters . . . She did not complain, but I could feel that she was profoundly unhappy, every line was like an exposed, aching nerve . . . Her imagination seemed to be confused, too. She signed herself 'Seagull'. You remember, in Pushkin's play *The River Nymph* the miller says he's a raven. So in the same way she kept calling herself 'the seagull' in her letters. By the way, she is here now.

DORN. What do you mean – here?

TREPLYOV. I mean she's staying in the town, at a hotel. She's been there for four or five days. I did go to call on her, and Marya

Ilyinichna here went too, but she won't see anyone. Semyon
Semyonich insists that he saw her yesterday afternoon in the
fields, a mile or so from here.

MEDVEDENKO. Yes, I did see her. She was walking away from here,
towards the town. I bowed to her and asked why she didn't
come to see us. She said she would.

TREPLYOV. She won't come.

[a pause]

Her father and stepmother won't have anything to do with her.
They put men all round to make sure that she doesn't come near
the house. [goes with the doctor towards the writing desk] How easy it
is to be philosophical on paper, Doctor, and how difficult when
it comes to real life.

SORIN. She was a most charming girl.

DORN. What?

SORIN. She was a most charming girl, I said. Councillor Sorin was
actually in love with her for a time.

DORN. The old philanderer!

[off-stage SHAMRAYEV can be heard laughing]

POLINA. I think they've arrived from the station. . . .

TREPLYOV. Yes, I can hear mamma.

Enter ARKADINA and TRIGORIN, followed by SHAMRAYEV.

SHAMRAYEV [as he comes in]. We all of us get older, we wither away
like trees battered by the elements, but you, my dear lady, you're
still as young as ever . . . A light-coloured blouse, vivacious
manner . . . grace in all your movements . . .

ARKADINA. You want to bring me ill luck again, you tiresome man?

TRIGORIN [to SORIN]. How do you do, Pyotr Nikolayevich? So
you're still poorly? That's not so good! [seeing MASHA, happily]
Ah, Marya Ilyinichna!

MASHA. So you remember me? [shakes hands with him]

TRIGORIN. Married?

MASHA. A long time now.

TRIGORIN. Happy? [bows to DORN and MEDVEDENKO – who bow in
return – then hesitatingly approaches TREPLYOV] Irina Nikolayevna
has told me that you've forgotten the past, and aren't angry with
me any longer.

[TREPLYOV holds out his hand]

ARKADINA [*to her son*]. Look, Boris Alexeyevich has brought the magazine with your new story in it.

TREPLYOV [*taking the magazine, to* TRIGORIN]. Thank you, you're very kind.

TRIGORIN. Your admirers send their greetings to you . . . People in Petersburg and Moscow are very intrigued by you – always asking me what you are like, how old, and whether you're fair or dark. For some reason they all think that you're getting on in years. And no-one knows your real name – you always publish your work under a pseudonym, don't you? You're as mysterious as the Man in the Iron Mask.

TREPLYOV. Will you be stopping with us for a while?

TRIGORIN. No, I think I'll go back to Moscow tomorrow. I've got to, really. I'm in a hurry to finish a novel, and besides, I've promised to give them something for an anthology. In short, it's just the same as ever.

[*while they talk,* ARKADINA *and* POLINA *move a card table into the middle of the room and open it.* SHAMRAYEV *lights the candles and puts the chairs in place. A game of lotto is brought out of the cupboard*]

TRIGORIN. The weather isn't greeting me very kindly. There's a cruel wind. Tomorrow morning, if it drops, I'll go fishing on the lake. Besides, I want to have a look around the garden and see the place where your play was acted – you remember? I've a subject for a story, I only want to revive my memories of the scene where the action is supposed to take place.

MASHA [*to her father*]. Papa, do let Semyon have a horse! He must get home somehow.

SHAMRAYEV [*mimics her*]. A horse . . . must get home . . . [*sternly*] You saw the horses have just been to the station! How can I send them out again?

MASHA. But there are other horses . . . [*on seeing that her father says nothing, makes a gesture of discouragement*] Oh, you're hopeless . . .

MEDVEDENKO. I can walk, Masha. Really . . .

POLINA [*with a sigh*]. Walk in this weather! . . . [*sits down at the card table*] Please come along, ladies and gentlemen.

MEDVEDENKO. It's only four miles, after all . . . Goodbye . . . [*kisses his wife's hand*] Goodbye, mother.

[POLINA *reluctantly holds out her hand for him to kiss*]

I wouldn't have made any bother if it weren't for the baby . . .
[*bows to the company*] Goodbye . . . [*goes out guiltily*]

SHAMRAYEV. He can walk all right! He's not a general, after all!

POLINA [*tapping on the table*]. Do come along, please! Don't let's
waste time, they'll be calling us to supper soon.

[SHAMRAYEV, MASHA, *and* DORN *sit down at the table*]

ARKADINA [*to* TRIGORIN]. They always play lotto here when the
long autumn evenings come on. Look, this is the same old set of
lotto my mother used when she played with us children. Won't
you have a game with us before supper? [*sits down at the table with*
TRIGORIN] It's a dull game, but it's not so bad when you get used
to it. [*deals three cards to everyone*]

TREPLYOV [*turning over the pages of the magazine*]. He's read his own
story, but he hasn't even cut the pages of mine. [*puts the magazine
down on his desk and walks towards door at left. As he passes his
mother, he kisses her on the head.*]

ARKADINA. What about you, Kostya?

TREPLYOV. Please forgive me, I don't feel like it somehow . . . I'll
go for a stroll. [*goes out*]

ARKADINA. The stake is ten kopecks. Put it down for me, Doctor,
will you?

DORN. I will.

MASHA. Have you all put down your money? I'm starting. Twenty-
two!

ARKADINA. Yes.

MASHA. Three.

DORN. Right!

MASHA. Did you play three? Eight! Eighty-one! Ten!

SHAMRAYEV. Don't be in such a hurry!

ARKADINA. What a reception I had in Harkov! My goodness! It
makes my head go round even now!

MASHA. Thirty-four!

[*a waltz with a melancholy tune is being played off-stage*]

ARKADINA. The students gave me a regular ovation . . . Three
baskets of flowers, two garlands, and this as well . . . [*unfastens a
brooch on her throat and tosses it on to the table*]

SHAMRAYEV. Yes, that's really worth having . . .

MASHA. Fifty!

DORN. Just fifty?

ARKADINA. I had a wonderful dress on . . . I know how to dress, if I know anything at all.

POLINA. Kostya's playing the piano. He's depressed, poor boy.

SHAMRAYEV. They've been attacking him a lot in the papers.

MASHA. Seventy-seven!

ARKADINA. He needn't take any notice of that!

TRIGORIN. He's unlucky. He still can't manage to strike the right note somehow. There's something strange and vague about his writing, at times it even suggests the ravings of a sick man. And not a single living character!

MASHA. Eleven!

ARKADINA [*looking round at* SORIN]. Petrusha, are you bored?

[*a pause*]

He's asleep.

DORN. The councillor is asleep.

MASHA. Seven! Ninety!

TRIGORIN. If I lived in a place like this, beside a lake, do you suppose I should ever write anything? I should overcome this passion of mine and do nothing but fish.

MASHA. Twenty-eight!

TRIGORIN. Just to catch a perch, or a ruff — how delightful it is!

DORN. Well, I believe in Konstantin Gavrilich. He's got something! He certainly has! He thinks in images, his stories are vivid, full of colour, and personally I'm deeply moved by them. But it's a pity he doesn't set himself any definite goal. He makes an impression, that's all, but an impression alone doesn't take you very far. Irina Nikolayevna, are you glad that you've got a writer for a son?

ARKADINA. Can you imagine it? — I haven't read anything of his yet. There's never any time.

MASHA. Twenty-six!

TREPLYOV *comes in quietly and walks over to his desk.*

SHAMRAYEV [*to* TRIGORIN]. By the way, Boris Alexeyevich, we've still got something of yours down here.

TRIGORIN. What is it?

SHAMRAYEV. Konstantin Gavrilich shot a gull once, and you asked me to get it stuffed for you.

TRIGORIN. I don't remember. [*pondering*] No, I don't remember.

MASHA. Sixty-one! One!

TREPLYOV [*throws open the window and listens*]. How dark it is! I can't understand why I'm feeling so restless.

ARKADINA. Kostya, will you shut the window? There's a draught.

[TREPLYOV *shuts the window*]

MASHA. Eighty-cight!

TRIGORIN. The game is mine, my friends.

ARKADINA [*gaily*]. Bravo, bravo!

SHAMRAYEV. Well done!

ARKADINA. This man's a lucky fellow, always and everywhere! [*gets up*] But now let us go and have something to eat. Our famous man hasn't had a proper meal today. We'll go on with the game after supper. [*to her son*] Kostya, do leave your writing and come to supper.

TREPLYOV. I don't want any, mamma, I'm not hungry.

ARKADINA. Just as you like. [*wakes* SORIN] Petrusha, supper is ready! [*takes* SHAMRAYEV's *arm*] Let me tell you about the reception I had at Kharkov . . .

[POLINA ANDREYEVNA *blows out the candles on the table, then she and* DORN *wheel out* SORIN's *chair. Everyone goes out by door on left,* TREPLYOV *remains alone in the room sitting at his desk*]

TREPLYOV [*preparing to write, reads through what he has already written*]. I used to talk such a lot about new forms in art, and now I feel I'm slipping into a rut myself, little by little. [*reads*] 'The placard on the wall proclaimed . . . A pale face in its frame of dark hair . . .' Proclaimed . . . a frame of dark hair . . . This won't do at all! [*crosses out*] I'll start with the passage where the hero is woken by the noise of the rain. The rest will have to come out. The description of the moonlit evening is too long and rather precious. Trigorin has worked out his own methods – it comes easily to him . . . He would just mention the neck of a broken bottle glistening on the dam and the black shadow of a mill-wheel – and there you'd have a moonlit night. But I have to put in the tremulous light, the soft twinkling of the stars, and the distant sounds of a piano, dying away in the still, fragrant air . . . It's excruciating!

[*a pause*]

Yes, I'm becoming more and more convinced that it isn't a matter of old or new forms – one must write without thinking about forms, and just because it pours freely from one's soul.

[*there is a tap on the window nearest to his desk*]

What's that? [*looks through the window*] I can't see anything . . . [*opens the french window and looks out into the garden*] Someone ran down the steps. [*calls*] Who's there? [*goes out and is heard walking rapidly along the terrace, then returns half a minute later with* NINA ZARECHNAYA] Nina! Nina!

[NINA *leans her head against his breast and sobs quietly*]

TREPLYOV [*deeply moved*]. Nina! Nina! It's you . . . you . . . I seem to have had a presentiment, my heart's been aching terribly all day . . . [*takes off her cape and hat*] Oh, my sweet, my precious girl, she's come at last! Don't let us cry, don't!

NINA. There's someone here.

TREPLYOV. There isn't anyone.

NINA. Please lock the doors, or someone will come in.

TREPLYOV. No-one will come in.

NINA. I know Irina Nikolayevna is here. Lock the doors.

TREPLYOV [*locks the door on right, then crosses to the left*] There's no lock on this one. I'll put a chair against it. [*puts an armchair against the door*] Don't be afraid, no-one will come in.

NINA [*looks intently at his face*]. Let me look at you for a little while. [*looking round*] How warm, how nice it is here! . . . This used to be a drawing-room. Have I changed a lot?

TREPLYOV. Yes . . . You are thinner and your eyes have grown bigger. Nina, it's so strange to be seeing you! Why wouldn't you let me see you? Why haven't you come here before now? I know you've been in the town almost a week . . . I've been to your place every day, several times a day: I stood under your window like a beggar.

NINA. I was afraid that you might hate me. Every night I dream that you look at me and don't recognise me. If only you knew! Ever since I came I've been walking round here . . . beside the lake. I've been near this house many times, but I dared not come in. Let us sit down.

[*they sit down*]

Let us sit and talk, talk . . . It's nice here, warm and comfortable . . . Do you hear the wind? There's a passage in Turgenev: 'Fortunate is he who on such a night has a roof over him, who has a warm corner of his own.' I am a seagull . . . No, that's not it. [*rubs her forehead*] What was I saying? Yes . . . Turgenev . . . 'And Heaven help the homeless wayfarers' . . . Never mind . . . [*sobs*]

TREPLYOV. Nina, you're crying again! . . . Nina!

NINA. Never mind, it does me good . . . I haven't cried for two years. Yesterday, late in the evening I came into the garden to see whether our stage was still there. And it is still standing! I began to cry for the first time in two years, and it lifted the weight from my heart, and I felt more at ease. You see, I'm not crying now. [*takes his hand*] And so you've become a writer . . . You are a writer and I'm an actress. We've been drawn into the whirlpool, too. I used to live here joyously, like a child – I used to wake up in the morning and burst into song. I loved you and dreamed of fame . . . And now? Tomorrow morning early I have to go to Yelietz in a third-class carriage . . . with the peasants; and at Yelietz, upstart business men will pester me with their attentions. Life is coarse!

TREPLYOV. Why do you have to go to Yelietz?

NINA. I've accepted an engagement for the whole winter. It's time to go.

TREPLYOV. Nina, I used to curse you: I hated you, I tore up your letters and photographs, but all the time I knew that I was bound to you heart and soul, and for ever! It's not in my power to stop loving you, Nina. Ever since I lost you, ever since I began to get my work published, my life's been intolerable. I'm wretched . . . I feel as if my youth has been suddenly torn away from me, as if I've been inhabiting this world for ninety years. I call out your name, I kiss the ground where you've walked; wherever I look I seem to see your face, that sweet smile that used to shine on me in the best years of my life . . .

NINA [*bewildered*]. Why does he talk like this, why does he talk like this?

TREPLYOV. I am lonely. I've no-one's love to warm me, I feel as cold as if I were in a cellar – and everything I write turns out lifeless and bitter and gloomy. Stay here, Nina, I entreat you, or let me come with you!

[NINA *quickly puts on her hat and cape*]

TREPLYOV. Nina, why – for Heaven's sake, Nina . . .

[*looks at her as she puts on her clothes. A pause*]

NINA. The horses are waiting for me at the gate. Don't see me off, I'll go by myself . . . [*tearfully*] Give me some water.

TREPLYOV [*gives her water*]. Where are you going now?

NINA. To the town. [*a pause*] Irina Nikolayevna's here, isn't she?

TREPLYOV. Yes . . . My uncle had an attack on Thursday, so we telegraphed for her.

NINA. Why did you say you kissed the ground where I walked? Someone ought to kill me. [*droops over the table*] I am so tired. Oh, I wish I could rest . . . just rest! [*raising her head*] I'm a seagull . . . No, that's not it. I'm an actress. Oh, well! [*she hears* ARKADINA *and* TRIGORIN *laughing off-stage, listens, then runs to the door at left and looks through the keyhole*] So he is here, too! . . . [*returning to* TREPLYOV] Oh, well! . . . Never mind . . . Yes . . . He didn't believe in the theatre, he was always laughing at my dreams, and so gradually I ceased to believe, too, and lost heart . . . And then I was so preoccupied with love and jealousy, and a constant fear for my baby . . . I became petty and common, when I acted I did it stupidly . . . I didn't know what to do with my hands or how to stand on the stage, I couldn't control my voice . . . But you can't imagine what it feels like – when you know that you are acting abominably. I'm a seagull. No, that's not it again . . . Do you remember you shot a seagull? A man came along by chance, saw it and destroyed it, just to pass the time . . . A subject for a short story . . . That's not it. [*rubs her forehead*] What was I talking about? . . . Yes, about the stage. I'm not like that now . . . Now I am a real actress, I act with intense enjoyment, with enthusiasm; on the stage I am intoxicated and I feel that I am beautiful. But now, while I'm living here, I go for walks a lot . . . I keep walking and thinking . . . thinking and feeling that I am growing stronger in spirit with every day that passes . . . I think I now know, Kostya, that what matters in our work – whether you act on the stage or write stories – what really matters is not fame, or glamour, not the things I used to dream about – but knowing how to endure things. How to bear one's cross and have faith. I have faith now and I'm not suffering quite so much, and when I think of my vocation I'm not afraid of life.

TREPLYOV [*sadly*]. You have found your right path, you know which way you're going – but I'm still floating about in a chaotic world of dreams and images, without knowing what use it all is . . . I have no faith, and I don't know what my vocation is.

NINA [*listening*]. Sh-sh! . . . I'm going now. Goodbye. When I become a great actress, come and see me act. Promise? And now . . . [*presses his hand*] It's late. I can hardly stand up . . . I'm so tired and hungry . . .

TREPLYOV. Do stay, I'll give you some supper.

NINA. No, no . . . Don't see me off, I'll go by myself . . . My horses are not far off . . . So she brought him with her? Oh, well, it doesn't matter . . . When you see Trigorin don't tell him anything . . . I love him. I love him even more than before. A subject for a short story . . . Yes, I love him, I love him passionately, I love him desperately! How nice it all used to be, Kostya! Do you remember? How tranquil, warm, and joyous, and pure our life was, what feelings we had – like tender, exquisite flowers . . . Do you remember? . . . [*recites*] 'The men, the lions, the eagles, the partridges, the antlered deer, the geese, the spiders, the silent fishes of the deep, starfishes and creatures unseen to the eye – in short all living things, all living things, all living things, having completed their mournful cycle, have been snuffed out. For thousands of years the earth has borne no living creature, and this poor moon now lights its lamp in vain. The cranes no longer wake up in the meadows with a cry, the May bugs are no longer heard humming in the groves of lime trees.' . . . [*impulsively embraces* TREPLYOV *and runs out through the french window*]

TREPLYOV [*after a pause*]. It won't be very nice if someone meets her in the garden and tells mamma. It might upset mamma . . . [*he spends the next two minutes silently tearing up all his manuscripts and throwing them under the table, then unlocks the door at right and goes out*]

DORN [*trying to open the door at left*]. That's strange. The door seems to be locked . . . [*comes in and puts the armchair in its place*] Quite an obstacle race.

[*enter* ARKADINA *and* POLINA, *followed by* YAKOV *carrying drinks, then* MASHA, SHAMRAYEV *and* TRIGORIN]

ARKADINA. Put the red wine and the beer on the table here for Boris Alexeyevich. We'll drink as we play. Let us sit down, friends.

POLINA [*to* YAKOV]. Bring the tea in as well. [*lights the candles and sits down at the card table*]

SHAMRAYEV [*leads* TRIGORIN *to the cupboard*]. Here is the thing I was telling you about just now . . . [*takes the stuffed seagull out of the cupboard*]. This is what you ordered.

TRIGORIN [*looking at the seagull*]. I don't remember. [*musing*] No, I don't remember!

[*there is a sound of a shot off-stage on right; everyone starts*]

DORN. That's nothing. It must be something in my medicine chest that's gone off. Don't worry. [*goes out through door at right, returns in half a minute*] Just as I thought. A bottle of ether has burst. [*hums*] 'Again I stand before you, enchanted.' . . .

ARKADINA [*sitting down to the table*]. Ough, how it frightened me! It reminded me of how . . . [*covers her face with her hands*] Everything went dark for a moment.

DORN [*turning over the pages of a magazine, to* TRIGORIN]. There was an article here about two months ago . . . a letter from America, and I wanted to ask you . . . [*puts his arm round* TRIGORIN's *waist and leads him to the footlights*] Because I'm very much interested in this question . . . [*dropping his voice, in a lower tone*] Take Irina Nikolayevna away from here somehow. The fact is, Konstantin Gavrilovich has shot himself . . .

CURTAIN

UNCLE VANYA

Scenes from Country Life in Four Acts

Characters in the Play

SEREBRYAKOV, Alexandre Vladimirovich, a retired professor
YELENA ANDREYEVNA (Hélène Lenochka), his wife, aged 27
SONYA (Sofya Alexandrovna), his daughter by his first wife
VOYNITSKAYA, Marya Vasilyevna, widow of a Privy Councillor
   and mother of the professor's first wife
VOYNITSKY, Ivan Petrovich (Vanya), her son
ASTROV, Mikhail Lvovich, a doctor
TELEGIN, Ilya Ilyich (nicknamed 'Waffles'), a landowner reduced
   to poverty
MARINA, an old children's nurse
A WORKMAN

The action takes place on Serebryakov's estate.

ACT ONE

A garden. Part of a house with a terrace can be seen. There is a table laid for tea under an old poplar in the avenue. Garden seats and chairs; on one of them lies a guitar. Not far from the table there is a swing. It is between two and three o'clock in the afternoon. The sky is overcast.

MARINA, *a small, plump, slow-moving elderly woman, is sitting beside the samovar, knitting a stocking.* ASTROV *is pacing up and down the avenue near her.*

MARINA [*pours out a glass of tea*]. Here, drink it, dearie.

ASTROV [*reluctantly accepting the glass*]. I don't feel like it somehow.

MARINA. Perhaps you'd like a drop of vodka?

ASTROV. No. I don't drink vodka every day. It's too close, anyway. [*a pause*] By the way, Nanny, how many years is it we've known each other?

MARINA [*pondering*]. How many? The Lord help my memory . . . You came to live around here . . . well, when was it? . . . Sonechka's mother, Vera Petrovna, was still living then. You came to see us for two winters when she was alive . . . That means at least eleven years have gone by . . . [*after a moment's thought*] Maybe more . . .

ASTROV. Have I changed a lot since then?

MARINA. Yes, a lot. You were young and handsome then, but you've aged now. And you're not as good-looking as you were. There's another thing too – you take a drop of vodka now and again.

ASTROV. Yes . . . In ten years I've become a different man. And what's the cause of it? I've been working too hard, Nanny. I'm on my feet from morning till night – I never have any peace. At night as I lie under the blankets I feel afraid all the time that I may be dragged out to see a patient. During the whole time you and I have known each other I haven't had a single day free. How could I help ageing? Besides, the life itself is tedious, stupid, squalid . . . This sort of life drags you down. You're surrounded by queer people – they're a queer lot, all of them – and after you've lived with them for a year or two, you gradually become queer yourself, without noticing it. That's inevitable. [*twisting his long moustache*] Ugh, what a huge moustache I've grown . . . Silly moustache! I've become an eccentric, Nanny . . . I haven't grown stupid yet, thank God! My brains are still functioning all right, but my feelings are somewhat duller. I don't wish for anything, I don't feel I need anything, I don't love anybody. Except you perhaps – I believe I'm fond of you. [*kisses her on the head*] I had a Nanny like you when I was a child.

MARINA. Wouldn't you like something to eat?

ASTROV. No. You know, in the first week of Lent I went to Malitskoye, because of the epidemic – spotted typhus . . . In the houses you could hardly move for sick people . . . Dirt, stench, and smoke everywhere . . . and calves mixed up with the sick on the floor . . . Young pigs there as well. I struggled with it all day, hadn't a moment to sit down or to swallow a bit of food. But would they let me rest when I got home? No, they brought me a signalman from the railway. I laid him on the table to operate, and he went and died on me under the chloroform. And just when I least wanted it my feelings seemed to wake up again, and my conscience began to worry me as if I had killed him deliberately . . . I sat down, closed my eyes – just like this – and I started to think. I wondered whether the people who come after us in a hundred years' time, the people for whom we are now blasting a trail – would they remember us and speak kindly of us? No, Nanny, I'll wager they won't!

MARINA. If people won't remember, God will.

ASTROV. Thank you. You've put it well.

> VOYNITSKY *comes out of the house; he has had a sleep after*
> *lunch and looks dishevelled. He sits down on the garden*
> *seat and adjusts his smart tie.*

VOYNITSKY. Yes . . . [*a pause*] Yes . . .

ASTROV. Had a good sleep?

VOYNITSKY. Yes . . . very good. [*yawns*] Since the professor and his consort came to live here, our usual routine has been completely upset . . . Now I sleep at the wrong time, I eat the wrong kinds of food at dinner and lunch, I drink wine . . . it's all bad for my health! In the past I never had a free moment – Sonya and I used to work like Trojans . . . But now only Sonya works while I just sleep, eat, and drink . . . It's a bad business!

MARINA [*nods her head disapprovingly*]. Such goings-on! The professor gets up at midday, but the samovar is kept boiling the whole morning waiting for him. Before they came we always had dinner soon after twelve, like everybody else, but now they are here we have it after six in the evening. The professor spends the night reading and writing, and then suddenly, past one o'clock, the bell rings . . . My goodness, what is it? He wants some tea! So you've got to wake people up to heat the samovar . . . Such goings-on!

ASTROV. Are they going to stay here much longer?

VOYNITSKY [*whistles*]. A hundred years maybe! The professor's decided to settle here.

MARINA. You see, it's just the same now. The samovar's been on the table for two hours, and they've gone for a walk.

VOYNITSKY. They're coming, they're coming! Don't fuss!

Voices are heard. SEREBRYAKOV, YELENA ANDREYEVNA, SONYA *and* TELEGIN *approach from the farther part of the garden, returning from their walk.*

SEREBRYAKOV. It was beautiful, beautiful! . . . Wonderful scenery!

TELEGIN. Yes, Your Excellency, the views are remarkable.

SONYA. Tomorrow we'll go to the plantation, Papa. Would you like to?

VOYNITSKY. Tea's ready, my friends!

SEREBRYAKOV. My friends, will you be good enough to send my tea to my study? I've something more I must do today.

SONYA. I'm sure you will like it at the plantation.

[YELENA ANDREYEVNA, SEREBRYAKOV *and* SONYA *go into the house.* TELEGIN *goes to the table and sits down beside* MARINA]

VOYNITSKY. It's hot and close, but our great man of learning has got his overcoat and goloshes on, and he's carrying his umbrella and gloves.

ASTROV. He's obviously taking care of himself.

VOYNITSKY. But how lovely she is! How lovely! I've never seen a more beautiful woman in all my life.

TELEGIN. You know, Marina Timofyeevna, whether I'm driving through the fields, or taking a walk in a shady garden, or even just looking at this table — I feel inexpressibly happy! The weather is marvellous, the birds are singing, and we all live here in peace and harmony — what more do we need? [*taking the glass she hands him*] Thank you kindly . . .

VOYNITSKY [*dreamily*]. Her eyes . . . a wonderful woman!

ASTROV. Tell us something, Ivan Petrovich.

VOYNITSKY [*listlessly*]. What do you want me to tell you?

ASTROV. Isn't there anything new?

VOYNITSKY. Nothing at all. Everything's old. I'm just the same as I was — perhaps worse, because I've grown lazy: I don't do anything, I just grumble like some old fogy. As for my *Maman*, the old magpie still goes on chattering about the emancipation of women. With one eye she looks into her grave and with the other she studies her learned books looking for the dawn of a new life.

ASTROV. And the professor?

VOYNITSKY. And the professor, as usual, sits in his study writing from morning till dead of night. 'With furrowed brows and thought intense, we write and write our odes immense, but no praise ever comes our way for what we are, or what we say.' I feel sorry for the paper he writes on! It would be better if he wrote his autobiography! What a superb subject! A retired professor, don't you see? — a dull old stick, a sort of scholarly dried fish . . . Afflicted with gout, rheumatism, migraine . . . his liver swollen with jealousy and envy . . . This dried fish is living on his first wife's country estate, living there against his will, because he can't afford to live in town. He's forever complaining about his misfortunes, though as a matter of fact he's been extraordinarily lucky. [*becoming excited*] Just think how lucky! The son of a common sexton, trained as a priest, he somehow managed to get university qualifications and a professorship; later he became 'your Excellency' and the son-in-law of a senator, and so on, and so forth. However, all that's not the main thing. Just consider this. The man has been lecturing and writing about art for exactly twenty-five years, and yet he understands nothing whatever about art. For twenty-five years he has been chewing over other people's ideas about realism, naturalism and all that sort of nonsense; for twenty-five years he has been lecturing and writing about things that intelligent people have known all the time, and stupid people aren't interested in, anyway – in fact, for twenty-five years he's been just wasting time and energy. And yet, what an opinion of himself! What pretensions! Now he's retired, and not a living soul is aware of him: today he is completely unknown, and that simply means that for twenty-five years he's been occupying a place to which he wasn't in the least entitled. But just look at him – he struts around like a little tin god!

ASTROV. Come now, I believe you envy him.

VOYNITSKY. Yes, I do envy him! And what a success with women! No Don Juan ever experienced success as complete as his. My sister – his first wife – a beautiful, gentle creature, as pure as that blue sky, generous and noble-hearted, who had more admirers than he has ever had pupils, loved him as only innocent-hearted angels can love beings as pure and beautiful as themselves. My mother still adores him; he still inspires her with a feeling of reverent awe. His second wife – you've just seen her – she's intelligent and a beauty – married him when he was already an old man. She gave him her youth, beauty, freedom – her whole brilliant personality. Whatever for? Why?

ASTROV. Is she faithful to the professor?

VOYNITSKY. I am sorry to say she is.

ASTROV. But why should you be sorry?

VOYNITSKY. Because that sort of loyalty is false from beginning to end. There's plenty of rhetoric in it, but no logic. To be unfaithful to an old husband whom she couldn't bear would be immoral – but to do her utmost to stifle within her all her youth, her vitality, her capacity to feel – that is not immoral!

TELEGIN [*tearfully*]. Vanya, I don't like it when you say these things. Come, really! Anyone who can betray a wife or a husband is an unreliable person who might betray his own country, too!

VOYNITSKY [*with annoyance*]. You dry up, Waffles!

TELEGIN. Forgive me, Vanya. My wife ran away from me the day after our wedding with a man she loved – because of my unprepossessing appearance. But even after that I never failed in my duty towards her. I still love her; I'm faithful to her, I help her as much as I can, and I've spent all I possessed on educating the children she had by the man she loved. I've lost my happiness, but I've still got my pride. And what about her? Her youth is gone, her beauty has faded, as nature ordains that it must, the man she loved has died . . . What has she got left?

Enter SONYA *and* YELENA ANDREYEVNA; *shortly after* MARYA VASILYEVNA *enters with a book. She sits down and reads; tea is put before her; she drinks it without looking up.*

SONYA [*hurriedly to the nurse*]. Nanny, some peasants have come to the door. Please go and talk to them, and I'll see to the tea myself . . . [*pours out tea*]

[*the nurse goes out;* YELENA ANDREYEVNA *takes her tea and drinks it sitting on the swing*]

ASTROV [*to* YELENA ANDREYEVNA]. You know I've come to see your husband. You wrote and told me that he was very ill – rheumatism and something else – but I find that he's perfectly well.

YELENA. Last night he was depressed and complained of pains in his legs, but today he seems all right. . . .

ASTROV. And I've galloped twenty miles at breakneck speed to get here. Well, never mind, it's not the first time. At least I can stay with you till tomorrow and get as much sleep as I need – *quantum satis*.

SONYA. That's splendid. It's so rare for you to stay the night with us. I don't suppose you've had dinner?

ASTROV. No, I haven't.

SONYA. Then you'll dine with us. We have dinner soon after six nowadays. [*drinks her tea*] The tea's cold!

TELEGIN. There's been a big fall in the temperature of the samovar.

YELENA. Never mind, Ivan Ivanovich, we will drink it cold.

TELEGIN. Excuse me . . . My name's not Ivan Ivanovich, it's Ilya Ilyich . . . Ilya Ilyich Telegin, or as some people call me on account of my spotty face, Waffles. I'm Sonyechka's godfather and his Excellency, your husband, knows me very well. I'm now living here on your estate . . . You may have been so kind as to notice that I have dinner with you every day.

SONYA. Ilya Ilyich is our helper, our right-hand man. [*tenderly*] Let me pour you out some tea, godfather dear.

MARYA. Oh!

SONYA. What's the matter, Grandmamma?

MARYA. I forgot to tell Alexandre . . . I'm losing my memory . . . I had a letter today from Pavel Alexeyevich, from Kharkov . . . He sent us his new pamphlet . . .

ASTROV. Is it interesting?

MARYA. It's interesting, but somehow strange. He disproves the very thing he was maintaining seven years ago. That's dreadful!

VOYNITSKY. There's nothing dreadful in that. Drink your tea, *Maman*.

MARYA. But I want to talk!

VOYNITSKY. But we've been talking and talking, and reading pamphlets for the last fifty years! It's about time to stop.

MARYA. For some reason you don't like listening when I talk. Forgive my saying so, *Jean*, but you've changed so much in the last year or so that I positively don't recognise you . . . You used to be a man with definite convictions, an inspiring personality . . .

VOYNITSKY. Oh, yes! I used to be an inspiring personality who never inspired anybody! . . . [*a pause*] I used to be an inspiring personality! . . . You could hardly have made a more wounding joke! I'm forty-seven now. Up to a year ago I tried deliberately to pull the wool over my eyes – just as you do yourself with the aid of all your pedantic rubbish – so that I shouldn't see the realities of life . . . and I thought I was doing the right thing. But now – if you only knew! I lie awake, night after night, in sheer vexation and anger – that I let time slip by so stupidly during the years when I could have had all the things from which my age now cuts me off.

SONYA. Uncle Vanya, this is boring!

MARYA [*to* VOYNITSKY]. You seem to be blaming those former principles of yours for something or other . . . It isn't they but you who are to blame. You're forgetting that principles are nothing in themselves – just empty phrases . . . You ought to have done something that mattered.

VOYNITSKY. Something that mattered? It isn't everyone who's capable of being a non-stop writer like your Herr Professor.

MARYA. What do you mean by that?

SONYA [*imploringly*]. Grandmamma! Uncle Vanya! I entreat you!

VOYNITSKY. I'll be quiet. I'll hold my tongue . . . and apologise.

[a pause]

YELENA. What a lovely day! . . . Not too hot either . . .

VOYNITSKY. It would even be pleasant to hang oneself on a day like this . . .

[TELEGIN *tunes the guitar.* MARINA *walks to and fro near the house, calling the chickens*]

MARINA. Chook, chook, chook!

SONYA. Nanny, what did the peasants come for?

MARINA. The same as before – they are still going on about the waste land. Chook, chook, chook. . . .

SONYA. Which is it you're calling?

MARINA. The speckled one. She's gone off somewhere with her chicks . . . The crows might get them . . . [*walks away*]

[TELEGIN *plays a polka; all listen in silence*]

Enter a WORKMAN.

WORKMAN. Is the doctor here? [*to* ASTROV] Mikhail Lvovich, they've come for you, please.

ASTROV. Where from?

WORKMAN. From the factory.

ASTROV [*with annoyance*]. Many thanks! . . . Well, I'll have to go . . . [*looks around for his cap*] Hang it! What a nuisance!

SONYA. It really is annoying . . . Come back to dinner from the factory.

ASTROV. No, it'll be too late. How could I, anyway? . . . How could I? . . . [*to the* WORKMAN] My good fellow, you might get me a glass of vodka, or something.

[*the* WORKMAN *goes out*]

How could I, anyway? . . . How could I? [*finds his cap*] In a play by Ostrovsky there's a man with a big moustache but very little brain. That's me. Well, I'll bid you all goodbye. [*to* YELENA] If you ever cared to look me up – with Sofya Alexandrovna here – I'd be so pleased. I've a small estate, about ninety acres altogether, but if you're interested – there's a model orchard and nursery such as you won't find for hundreds of miles around. And next to my place there's a plantation belonging to the Government. The forester there is old and he often gets ill, so that in fact I'm in charge of everything.

YELENA. Yes, I've been told that you're very fond of forestry. Of course, you can do a lot of good that way, but doesn't it interfere with your real vocation? You are a doctor, after all.

ASTROV. Only God knows what our real vocation is.

YELENA. Is it interesting?

ASTROV. Yes, it's interesting work.

VOYNITSKY [*ironically*]. It must be.

YELENA [*to* ASTROV]. You're still a young man . . . you don't look more than . . . well, thirty-six or thirty-seven . . . I doubt whether you find it as interesting as you say. Nothing but trees and trees. I should think it must be monotonous.

SONYA. No, it's extremely interesting. Mikhail Lvovich puts down new plantations every year, and he's already been awarded a bronze medal and a diploma. He does his best to stop the old forests being laid waste. If you'd only listen to him, you'd understand what he means and agree with him. He says that forests add beauty to the country, that they teach men to appreciate beauty and induce lofty emotions. Forests make a harsh climate milder. In countries with a mild climate people spend less energy in the struggle with nature, and so man is gentler and more capable of tender feeling. In such countries people are beautiful, sensitive and flexible in spirit – their speech is elegant, their movements graceful. Science and the fine arts flourish among them; their philosophy is cheerful and there is great refinement and courtesy in their attitude towards women.

VOYNITSKY [*laughing*]. Bravo, bravo! . . . This is all very charming, but it isn't convincing . . . [*to* ASTROV] And so, my friend, you must allow me to go on burning logs in my stoves and building my barns of wood!

ASTROV. You can burn turf in your stoves and build your barns out of stone . . . Well, I would consent to cutting wood when people really need it, but why destroy the forests? The Russian forests are literally groaning under the axe, millions of trees are being destroyed, the homes of animals and birds are being laid waste, the rivers are getting shallow and drying up, wonderful scenery is disappearing for ever – and all this is happening just because people are too lazy and stupid to stoop down and pick up the fuel from the ground. [*to* YELENA] Isn't it so, Madam? Anyone who can burn up all that beauty in a stove, who can destroy something that we cannot create, must be a barbarian incapable of reason. Man is endowed with reason and creative power so that he can increase what has been given him, but up to the present he's been destroying and not creating. There are fewer and fewer forests, the rivers are drying up, the wild creatures are almost exterminated, the climate is being ruined, and the land is getting poorer and more hideous every day. [*to* VOYNITSKY] I can see your ironic expression, and I believe that what I say doesn't seem at all serious to you, and . . . and maybe it is just crankiness . . . All the same when I go walking by the woods that belong to the peasants, the woods I saved from being cut down, or when I hear the rustling of the young trees I planted with my own hands, I'm conscious of the fact that the climate is to some extent in my power too, and that if mankind is happy in a thousand years' time, I'll be responsible for it even though only to a very minute extent. When I plant a little birch tree and then see it growing green and swaying in the wind, my heart fills with pride, and I . . . [*sees the* WORKMAN *who has brought a glass of vodka on a tray*] However . . . [*drinks*] It's time for me to go. After all, that's probably just my crankiness. Permit me to take my leave! [*goes towards the house*]

SONYA [*takes his arm and walks with him*]. When are you coming to see us, then?

ASTROV. I don't know.

SONYA. Not for another month again?

ASTROV *and* SONYA *go into the house;* MARYA VASILYEVNA *and* TELEGIN *remain beside the table;* YELENA ANDREYEVNA *and* VOYNITSKY *walk towards the terrace.*

YELENA. And you have been behaving abominably again, Ivan Petrovich. Did you have to irritate Marya Vasilyevna with your talk about 'non-stop writers'? And at lunch today you argued with Alexandre again. How petty it all is!

VOYNITSKY. But if I detest him?

YELENA. There is nothing you can detest Alexandre for — he's just like anyone else. He's no worse than you are.

VOYNITSKY. If only you could see your face, your movements! . . . You give the impression that life is too much of an effort for you . . . Oh, such an effort!

YELENA. Oh, yes, such an effort and such a bore! Everyone blames my husband, everyone looks at me with compassion: an unfortunate woman – she's got an old husband! This sympathy for me – oh, how well I understand it! As Astrov said just now: you go on destroying the forests senselessly, and soon there won't be anything left on the earth. Just in the same way you senselessly ruin human beings, and soon, thanks to you, there will be no loyalty, no integrity, no capacity for self-sacrifice left. Why can't you look at a woman with indifference unless she's yours? Because – that doctor is right – there's a devil of destruction in every one of you. You spare neither woods, nor birds, nor women, nor one another.

VOYNITSKY. I don't like this sort of philosophy!

[a pause]

YELENA. The doctor has a tired, sensitive face. An interesting face. Sonya is obviously attracted by him; she's in love with him, and I understand her feelings. He's visited the house three times since I've been here, but I'm shy and I haven't once had a proper talk with him or been nice to him. He must have thought me bad-tempered. Perhaps, Ivan Petrovich, you and I are such good friends just because we both are such tiresome and boring people. Tiresome! Don't look at me like that, I don't like it!

VOYNITSKY. How else can I look at you if I love you? You are my happiness, my life, my youth! I know the chances of your returning my feelings are negligible, just zero – but I don't want anything – only let me look at you and hear your voice . . .

YELENA. Hush, they might hear you! [they go into the house]

VOYNITSKY [following her]. Let me talk of my love, don't drive me away – that in itself will be such great happiness to me . . .

YELENA. This is torture . . . [both enter the house]

[TELEGIN strikes the strings of his guitar and plays a polka. MARYA VASILYEVNA makes notes in the margin of her pamphlet]

CURTAIN

ACT TWO

Dining-room in SEREBRYAKOV's *house. Night-time; a watchman can be heard tapping in the garden.* SEREBRYAKOV *is sitting in an armchair in front of an open window, dozing.* YELENA ANDREYEVNA *is sitting beside him, also dozing.*

SEREBRYAKOV [*waking up*]. Who's that? Sonya, is it you?

YELENA. It's me . . .

SEREBRYAKOV. You, Lenochka . . . This pain's unbearable!

YELENA. Your rug's fallen on to the floor. [*wraps it round his legs*] I'll shut the window, Alexandre.

SEREBRYAKOV. No, I feel suffocated . . . I dozed off just now and I dreamt that my left leg didn't belong to me. I was woken up by an agonising pain. No, it's not gout; it's more like rheumatism. What time is it now?

YELENA. Twenty minutes past twelve.

[*a pause*]

SEREBRYAKOV. You might look out Batyushkov in the library in the morning. I believe we have his works.

YELENA. What?

SEREBRYAKOV. Look out Batyushkov in the morning. I seem to remember we had him. But why is it so difficult for me to breathe?

YELENA. You're tired. This is the second night you haven't slept.

SEREBRYAKOV. They say Turgenev got angina pectoris from gout. I'm afraid I might get it. This damnable, disgusting old age! The devil take it! Since I've aged so much I've become revolting even to myself. And you must find it revolting to look at me . . . all of you!

YELENA. You talk of your old age in a tone of voice which suggests we're all to blame for it.

SEREBRYAKOV. You are the first to find me repulsive.

[YELENA *gets up and sits down further away*]

SEREBRYAKOV. You are right, of course. I'm not a fool and I understand. You're young, healthy, good-looking, you want to live . . . whereas I am an old man, almost a corpse. Well . . . Do you suppose I don't understand? Of course, it's stupid of me to go on living. But wait a little while, I'll soon set you all free. I shan't have to linger on much longer.

YELENA. I'm worn out . . . for God's sake be quiet.

SEREBRYAKOV. It looks as if everyone's worn out, bored, wasting their youth thanks to me . . . and I am the only one who's content and enjoying life. Yes, yes, of course!

YELENA. Oh, do be quiet! You've worn me out!

SEREBRYAKOV. I've worn everyone out . . . Of course!

YELENA [*tearfully*]. It's intolerable! Tell me, what is it you want from me?

SEREBRYAKOV. Nothing at all.

YELENA. Well, be quiet then. I implore you.

SEREBRYAKOV. It's a strange business – when Ivan Petrovich starts talking – or that old idiot Marya Vasilyevna – it's all right, and everyone listens. But I only have to say a single word, and everyone begins to feel miserable. Even my voice disgusts them. Well, I suppose I am disgusting, an egoist, a despot – but haven't I a right to be selfish in my old age? Haven't I deserved it? I ask you, haven't I a right to a quiet old age, to a little personal attention?

YELENA. No-one is disputing your rights. [*the window bangs in the wind*] The wind's got up, I'll shut the window. [*shuts it*] It's going to rain presently. No-one disputes your rights.

[*a pause; in the garden the watchman taps and starts singing*]

SEREBRYAKOV. After devoting all my life to learning, after growing used to my study, to my lecture room, to esteemed colleagues – to find myself suddenly, for no reason at all, in this crypt, to have to meet stupid people every day, to have to listen to their trivial conversation! . . . I want to live, I love success, I like being a well-known figure, I like creating a stir – but here I feel an exile. To spend every minute regretting the past, watching others succeed, fearing death . . . I can't! It's more than I can bear! And they won't even forgive me for getting old!

YELENA. Wait a little, have patience! In five or six years I shall be old, too.

Enter SONYA.

SONYA. Papa, you told us to send for Doctor Astrov, and now he's come you refuse to see him. It's discourteous. We've troubled him for nothing. . . .

SEREBRYAKOV. What do I need your Astrov for? He knows as much about medicine as astronomy.

SONYA. We can't send for the whole medical faculty to attend to your gout.

SEREBRYAKOV. I won't even speak to that crank.

SONYA. Just as you please. [*sits down*] It's all the same to me.

SEREBRYAKOV. What time is it now?

YELENA. It's after midnight.

SEREBRYAKOV. I'm suffocating . . . Sonya, hand me my drops from the table.

SONYA. Just a moment. [*hands him the drops*]

SEREBRYAKOV [*irritably*]. Oh, not those! It's no use asking for anything!

SONYA. Please don't be peevish. Some people may like it, but do spare me, for goodness' sake! I don't like it. And I haven't the time, I must get up early tomorrow – I've got to see to the haymaking.

Enter VOYNITSKY *in a dressing-gown with a candle in his hand.*

VOYNITSKY. There's a storm getting up. [*a flash of lightning*] There, did you see? Hélène and Sonya, do go to bed, I've come to take your place.

SEREBRYAKOV [*alarmed*]. No, no! Don't leave me with him! Don't! He'll kill me with his talking!

VOYNITSKY. But they must have some rest! It's the second night they've had no sleep.

SEREBRYAKOV. Let them go to bed, but you go too. I'd be so grateful . . . I do implore you . . . For the sake of our past friendship, don't argue. We'll talk later on.

VOYNITSKY [*with a sneer*]. Our past friendship . . . Past . . .

SONYA. Be quiet, Uncle Vanya.

SEREBRYAKOV [*to his wife*]. My dear, don't leave me alone with him. He'll kill me with his talking!

VOYNITSKY. This is becoming ridiculous.

Enter MARINA *with a candle.*

SONYA. You ought to go to bed, Nanny. It's late.

MARINA. The samovar hasn't been cleared away. I can't very well go to bed.

SEREBRYAKOV. Everyone's awake, everyone's worn out – only I am thoroughly enjoying myself.

MARINA [*going up to* SEREBRYAKOV, *tenderly*]. What is it, my dear? Your pain again? I've got a grumbling pain in my legs, too, such a pain! [*tucks the rug in*] It's that old trouble of yours . . . Vera Petrovna, Sonyechka's mother, used to get so upset about it – she couldn't sleep of nights . . . Ever so fond of you she was . . . [*a pause*] The old are just the same as the little ones, they like someone to pity them – but nobody pities the old. [*kisses* SEREBRYAKOV *on the shoulder*] Come to bed, my dear . . . come, darling . . . I'll give you some lime-flower tea and warm your feet . . . and say a prayer for you . . .

SEREBRYAKOV [*moved*]. Let us go, Marina.

MARINA. I've got such a grumbling pain in my legs myself, such a grumbler! [*she and* SONYA *lead him off*] Vera Petrovna used to get so upset, she used to cry over you . . . You were little then, Sonyushka, you didn't understand . . . Come along, come along, sir.

[SEREBRYAKOV, SONYA *and* MARINA *go out*]

YELENA. I'm quite worn out with him. I can hardly keep on my feet.

VOYNITSKY. You with him, and I with myself. It's the third night I've had no sleep.

YELENA. Things have gone to pieces in this household. Your mother hates everything except her pamphlets and the professor; the professor is irritable – he doesn't trust me, and is afraid of you. Sonya is bad-tempered with her father, and angry with me: she hasn't spoken to me for a fortnight. You detest my husband and openly despise your mother; I am on edge – I have been on the point of crying twenty times today. Things have gone wrong in this house.

VOYNITSKY. Let's leave philosophy out of it!

YELENA. You are cultured and intelligent, Ivan Petrovich – surely you ought to realise that the world is being destroyed not by fire and pillage, but by hatred, enmity and all this petty quarrelling . . . Your job should be to reconcile people to one another, and not to grumble.

VOYNITSKY. Reconcile me to myself first! Dearest . . . [*bends down impulsively and kisses her hand*]

YELENA. Don't! [*draws away her hand*] Go away!

VOYNITSKY. In a minute or two the rain will be over, and everything in nature will be refreshed and sigh with relief. Only I shall not be refreshed by the storm. Day and night I feel suffocated by the thought that my life has been irretrievably lost. I have no past – it has all been stupidly wasted on trifles – while the present is awful because it's so meaningless. My life, my love – look at them – where do they belong? What am I to do with them? My feeling for you is just wasted like a ray of sunlight falling into a well – and I am wasted too.

YELENA. When you talk to me of your love I feel quite stupid and I don't know what to say. Forgive me, there's nothing I can say to you. [*starting to go out*] Good-night.

VOYNITSKY [*barring her way*]. And if you only knew how I suffer when I think that near to me, in the very same house, another life is being wasted – your life! What are you waiting for? What confounded philosophy is holding you back? Understand, do understand . . .

YELENA [*looks at him intently*]. Ivan Petrovich, you are drunk!

VOYNITSKY. Maybe, maybe . . .

YELENA. Where's the doctor?

VOYNITSKY. He's in there . . . He's staying the night with me. It may be, it may be . . . Anything may be!

YELENA. So you have been drinking again today! What ever for?

VOYNITSKY. At least it gives the illusion of life . . . Don't prevent me, Hélène . . .

YELENA. You never used to drink and you never used to talk so much . . . Do go to bed! You bore me.

VOYNITSKY [*impulsively kissing her hand*]. Dearest . . . You wonderful woman!

YELENA [*with annoyance*]. Leave me alone. This is really hateful! [*goes out*]

VOYNITSKY [*alone*]. She's gone. [*a pause*] Ten years ago I used to meet her at my sister's house. She was seventeen then and I was thirty-seven. Why didn't I fall in love with her then and ask her to marry me? It could have been done so easily! She would have been my wife now . . . Yes . . . and we two might have been awakened by this storm; she would have been frightened by the thunder and I would have held her in my arms and whispered: 'Don't be afraid, I'm here.' Oh, what a wonderful thought! How enchanting! It actually makes me laugh with happiness . . . but, oh, God! my thoughts are in a tangle . . . Why am I so old? Why won't she understand me? Her fine phrases, her easy moralising, her silly, facile ideas about the ruin of the world – how utterly hateful it all is to me! [*a pause*] And how I've been cheated! I adored the professor, the gouty old invalid, and I worked like an ox for him! Sonya and I squeezed all we could out of this estate . . . Like close-fisted peasants we traded in linseed oil, dried peas, and curds, we saved on our food so that we could scrape together halfpence and farthings and send him thousands of roubles. I was proud of him and his learning, he was the breath of my life! Everything he wrote or uttered seemed to me the work of a genius . . . And now what, good God? He's retired down here, and now you can see what his life really amounts to. Not a page of his writing will survive him . . . he's completely unknown, a nonentity! A soap bubble! And I've been cheated . . . I see it now . . . stupidly cheated . . .

Enter ASTROV; *he wears a coat but is without waistcoat or tie.*
He is slightly drunk. He is followed by TELEGIN *with a guitar.*

ASTROV. Play us something!
TELEGIN. Everyone's gone to bed!
ASTROV. Come on! Play!
[TELEGIN *plays softly*]
ASTROV [*to* VOYNITSKY]. Are you alone here? No ladies? [*putting his arms akimbo, sings quietly*] 'Dance my hut and dance my fire, the master's nowhere to retire.' . . . The thunderstorm woke me up. A nice spot of rain! What time is it now?
VOYNITSKY. The devil knows!
ASTROV. I thought I heard Yelena Andreyevna's voice.
VOYNITSKY. She was in here a moment ago.
ASTROV. An exceptionally attractive woman! [*examines the medicine bottles on the table*] What a variety of medicines! From Kharkov,

from Moscow, from Tula! . . . He must have plagued every town in Russia with his gout. Is he really ill, or shamming?

VOYNITSKY. He is ill.

[*a pause*]

ASTROV. Why are you so depressed today? Are you feeling sorry for the professor, or what?

VOYNITSKY. Leave me alone.

ASTROV. Or maybe you're in love with the professor's wife?

VOYNITSKY. She's my friend.

ASTROV. Already?

VOYNITSKY. What do you mean by 'already'?

ASTROV. A woman can only become a man's friend in three stages: first, she's an agreeable acquaintance, then a mistress, and only after that a friend.

VOYNITSKY. That's a crude sort of philosophy.

ASTROV. What? Well, yes . . . I must confess, I am becoming pretty crude . . . You see, I'm drunk, too. As a rule I get drunk like this once a month. When I'm in this state I get extremely provocative and audacious. Then there's nothing I don't feel equal to! I undertake the most difficult operations and do them beautifully, I draw up the most far-reaching plans for the future! At such times I no longer think of myself as a crank – I believe that I'm doing a tremendous job for the good of mankind . . . tremendous! On these occasions, too, I have my own special system of philosophy according to which all of you, my good friends, appear as insignificant as insects . . . or microbes. [*to* TELEGIN] Waffles, go on playing!

TELEGIN. My dear friend, I'd do anything for you, but do remember – everyone in the house has gone to bed!

ASTROV. Play, I tell you!

[TELEGIN *plays quietly*]

A drink would be nice. Come along, I believe there's still some brandy left. When it's daylight, shall we go to my place? All right for you? I've got an unqualified assistant who never says 'all right' but always 'aw-right'. He's an awful rogue. Aw-right, then?

[*sees* SONYA *entering*]

Excuse me, I haven't got my tie on.

[*goes out quickly;* TELEGIN *follows him*]

SONYA. Uncle Vanya, so you got drunk again with the doctor? You're a fine pair! It's not becoming at your age!

VOYNITSKY. Age has nothing to do with it. When people have no real life, they live on their illusions. Anyway, it's better than nothing.

SONYA. All the hay has been cut, it rains every day, everything is rotting, and you are living on illusions! You've been utterly neglecting the estate . . . I've had to work alone, I'm quite worn out . . . [*alarmed*] Uncle, there are tears in your eyes!

VOYNITSKY. Tears? It's nothing . . . nonsense! You looked at me then as your dear mother used to . . . My dearest girl! [*eagerly kisses her hands and face*] My sister . . . my dear sister . . . where is she now? If only she knew! Ah, if she only knew!

SONYA. What, uncle? Knew what?

VOYNITSKY. It's painful, wrong somehow . . . Never mind . . . Later on . . . it's nothing . . . I'll go . . . [*goes out*]

SONYA [*knocks at the door*]. Mikhail Lvovich! You're not asleep, are you? One minute!

ASTROV [*through the door*]. Coming! [*a moment later he comes out with his tie and waistcoat on*] What can I do for you?

SONYA. You can drink yourself if you don't find it disgusting, but don't let my uncle drink, I implore you! It's bad for him.

ASTROV. Very well. We won't drink any more. [*a pause*] I shall go home at once. That's settled and signed. It'll be daylight by the time they've got the horses ready.

SONYA. It's still raining. Wait till the morning.

ASTROV. The storm is passing us by, we'll only get a few drops. I'll go. And please don't ask me to see your father again. I tell him he has gout, and he tells me it's rheumatism; I ask him to stay in bed, and he sits up in a chair. And today he wouldn't even speak to me.

SONYA [*looks into the sideboard*]. Would you like something to eat?

ASTROV. Well, perhaps.

SONYA. I like having little snacks at night. I believe there's something in the sideboard. They say he's had great success with the women, and he's been spoilt by them. Here, have some cheese.
[*both stand at the sideboard and eat*]

ASTROV. I've had nothing to eat today, only drink. Your father is difficult. [*takes a bottle from the sideboard*] May I? [*drinks a glass*]

There's no-one here, and I can speak frankly. You know, I don't believe I could stick it in your house for a month, I should be suffocated in this atmosphere . . . Your father, completely absorbed in his gout and his books, Uncle Vanya with his depression, your grandmother, and your stepmother too . . .

SONYA. What about my stepmother?

ASTROV. Everything ought to be beautiful about a human being: face, clothes, soul, and thoughts . . . She's beautiful, there's no denying that, but . . . she does nothing but eat, sleep, go for walks, charm us all by her beauty . . . nothing else. She has no responsibilities, other people work for her . . . Isn't that so? And an idle life can't be virtuous. [*a pause*] However, perhaps I'm being too severe. I'm dissatisfied with life, like your uncle Vanya, and so we're both turning into old grumblers.

SONYA. You're dissatisfied with life then?

ASTROV. I love life as such – but our life, our everyday provincial life in Russia, I just can't endure. I despise it with all my soul. As for my own life, God knows I can find nothing good in it at all. You know, when you walk through a forest on a dark night and you see a small light gleaming in the distance, you don't notice your tiredness, nor the darkness, nor the prickly branches lashing you in the face . . . I work harder than anyone in the district – you know that – fate batters me continuously, at times I suffer unbearably – but there's no small light in the distance. I'm not expecting anything for myself any longer, I don't love human beings . . . I haven't cared for anyone for years.

SONYA. Not for anyone?

ASTROV. No-one. I feel a sort of fondness for your old nurse – for the sake of old times. The peasants are all too much alike, undeveloped, living in squalor. As for the educated people – it's hard to get on with them. They tire me so. All of them, all our good friends here are shallow in thought, shallow in feeling, unable to see further than their noses – or to put it quite bluntly, stupid. And the ones who are a bit more intelligent, of a higher mental calibre, are hysterical, positively rotten with introspection and futile cerebration. They whine, they are full of hatreds and morbidly malicious, they sidle up to a man, look at him out of the corner of their eyes, and pronounce their judgement: 'Oh, he's a psychopath!' or 'Just a phrase-monger'. And when they don't know how to label me, they say: 'He's a queer fellow, very queer!' I love forests – that's queer, I don't eat meat – that's queer too. There isn't any direct, objective, unprejudiced attitude to people or nature left . . . No, there isn't! [*about to drink*]

SONYA [*prevents him*]. No, I beg you, I implore you, don't drink any more.

ASTROV. Why not?

SONYA. It's so unlike you! You have such poise, your voice is so soft . . . More than that, you are beautiful as no-one else I know is beautiful. So why do you want to be like ordinary men, the kind who drink and play cards? Don't do it, I implore you! You always say that people don't create anything, but merely destroy what has been given them from above. Then why, why are you destroying yourself? You mustn't, you mustn't, I beseech you, I implore you!

ASTROV [*holds out his hand to her*]. I won't drink any more!

SONYA. Give me your word.

ASTROV. My word of honour.

SONYA [*presses his hand warmly*]. Thank you!

ASTROV. Enough! My head's clear now. You see I'm quite sober – and I'll stay sober to the end of my days. [*looks at his watch*] Well, to continue. As I said, my time's over, it's too late for me now . . . I've aged too much, I've worked myself to a standstill, I've grown coarse and insensitive . . . I believe I could never really become fond of another human being. I don't love anybody and . . . never shall now. What still does affect me is beauty. I can't remain indifferent to that. I believe that if Yelena Andreyevna wanted to, for instance, she could turn my head in a day . . . But that's not love, of course, that's not affection . . . [*covers his eyes with his hand and shudders*]

SONYA. What is it?

ASTROV. Nothing . . . In Lent one of my patients died under chloroform.

SONYA. It's time to forget about that. [*a pause*] Tell me, Mikhail Lvovich . . . If I had a girl friend, or a young sister and if you got to know that she . . . well, suppose that she loved you, what would you do?

ASTROV [*shrugging his shoulders*]. I don't know. Probably nothing. I should let her know that I couldn't love her . . . besides, I've got

too many other things on my mind. However, if I'm going, I'd
better start now. I'll say goodbye, my dear girl, or we'll not finish
till morning. [*shakes hands with her*] I'll go through the drawing-
room if I may, otherwise I'm afraid your uncle may keep me.
[*goes out*]

SONYA [*alone*]. He didn't say anything to me . . . His soul and his
heart are still hidden from me, so why do I feel so happy?
[*laughs with happiness*] I told him: you have poise and nobility of
mind and such a soft voice . . . Did it sound out of place? His
voice vibrates and caresses . . . I can almost feel it in the air
now. But when I said that to him about a younger sister, he
didn't understand . . . [*wringing her hands*] Oh, how dreadful it
is that I'm not good-looking! How dreadful! I know I'm plain,
I know, I know! . . . Last Sunday as people were coming out
of church I heard them talking about me and a woman said:
'She's kind and generous, but what a pity she is so plain.' . . .
So plain . . .

Enter YELENA ANDREYEVNA.

YELENA [*opens the windows*]. The storm's over. What lovely fresh
air! [*a pause*] Where's the doctor?
SONYA. He's gone.

[*a pause*]

YELENA. Sophie!
SONYA. What?
YELENA. How long are you going to go on being sulky with me?
We haven't done each other any harm . . . so why should we
behave like enemies? Come, do let us stop it . . .
SONYA. I wanted to myself . . . [*embraces her*] Yes, don't let us be
cross any more . . .
YELENA. That's fine!

[*both are moved*]

SONYA. Has papa gone to bed?
YELENA. No, he's sitting in the drawing-room . . . We don't speak
to each other for weeks on end, but Heaven alone knows
why . . . [*seeing that the sideboard is open*] What's this?
SONYA. Mikhail Lvovich has been having supper.
YELENA. There's wine too . . . Let's drink to our friendship.
SONYA. Yes, let's.

YELENA. Out of the same glass . . . [*fills it*] It's better like that. Now we are real friends?

SONYA. Friends. [*they drink and kiss each other*] I've been wanting to make it up for ever so long, but I felt so ashamed some-how . . . [*cries*]

YELENA. But why are you crying?

SONYA. Never mind . . . there's no reason.

YELENA. Come, there, there . . . [*cries*] I'm a queer creature – I've started crying too . . . [*a pause*] You're cross with me because you think I married your father for ulterior motives . . . If you are impressed by oaths, I'll vow to you that I married him for love. I was attracted by him as a learned man, a celebrity. It wasn't real love, it was all artificial, but you see at that time it seemed real to me. I'm not to blame. But from the day of our marriage you've been punishing me with those shrewd, suspicious eyes of yours.

SONYA. Come, peace, peace! Let's forget about it!

YELENA. You mustn't look at people like that – it doesn't suit you. You should believe everyone – or else you just can't live.

[*a pause*]

SONYA. Tell me honestly, as a friend . . . Are you happy?

YELENA. No.

SONYA. I knew that. One more question. Tell me frankly – wouldn't you have liked your husband to be young?

YELENA. What a little girl you are still! Of course I should. [*laughs*] Well, ask me something else, do . . .

SONYA. Do you like the doctor?

YELENA. Yes, very much.

SONYA [*laughs*]. Have I got a stupid face? . . . Yes? He's gone, but I can still hear his voice and his footsteps, and when I glance at that dark window I can see his face in it. Do let me tell you about it . . . But I mustn't speak so loudly, I feel ashamed. Come to my room, we'll talk there. Do I seem stupid to you? Own up . . . Tell me something about him.

YELENA. Well, what shall I tell you?

SONYA. He's so clever . . . He knows how to do things, he can do anything . . . He treats the sick, and he plants forests, too . . .

YELENA. It isn't a question of forests or medicine . . . My dear, don't you understand? . . . he's got talent! And do you know what that means? Courage, freedom of mind, breadth of outlook . . . He plants a tree and wonders what will come of it in a thousand years' time, and speculates on the future happiness of mankind. Such people are rare, and we must love them . . . He drinks, sometimes he seems a little coarse – but what does it matter? A talented man can't stay free from blemishes in Russia. Just think what sort of life this doctor leads! Impassable mud on the roads, frost, snow-storms, vast distances, crude, primitive people, poverty and disease all around him – it's hard for a man who works and struggles day after day in such surroundings to keep pure and sober till he's forty . . . [*kisses her*] I wish you happiness with all my heart, you deserve it . . . [*gets up*] As for me, I'm just a tiresome person of no importance. In my music studies, in my home life in my husband's house, in all my romantic affairs – in fact in everything I've just been a person of no importance. Really, Sonya, when you come to think of it, I'm a very, very unfortunate woman. [*walks about in agitation*]. There's no happiness for me on this earth. None! Why do you laugh?

SONYA [*laughs, hiding her face*]. I am so happy . . . so happy! . . .

YELENA. I should like to play something . . . I should like to play something now . . .

SONYA. Do play! [*embraces her*] I can't sleep . . . Do play!

YELENA. In a minute. Your father isn't asleep. When he's unwell, music irritates him. Go and ask him. If he doesn't mind, I'll play. Go.

SONYA. I'm going. [*goes out*]

[*watchman taps in the garden*]

YELENA. It's a long time since I played the piano. I shall play and cry . . . cry like a foolish girl. [*calling through the window*] Is it you tapping, Yefim?

WATCHMAN'S VOICE. Yes, me.

YELENA. Don't tap, the master's not well.

WATCHMAN'S VOICE. I'm just going. [*whistles*] Hey there! Good dog! Come, boy! Good dog!

[*a pause*]

SONYA [*returning*]. We mustn't!

CURTAIN

ACT THREE

A drawing-room in SEREBRYAKOV's *house. Three doors, right, left and centre. Daytime.*

   VOYNITSKY *and* SONYA *are seated, and* YELENA ANDREYEVNA *is walking about the stage, preoccupied.*

VOYNITSKY. The Herr Professor has graciously expressed a wish that we should assemble in this drawing-room at one o'clock. [*looks at his watch*] It is a quarter to. He wishes to make some communication to the world.

YELENA. Probably some business matter.

VOYNITSKY. He does no business of any kind. He just writes nonsense, grumbles and feels jealous – he does nothing else.

SONYA [*reproachfully*]. Uncle!

VOYNITSKY. Well, well, I apologise. [*pointing at* YELENA] Just look at her! She walks about staggering with sheer laziness. Wonderful! Wonderful!

YELENA. And you keep on droning away all the time, all day long! Aren't you tired of it? [*miserably*] I'm dying of boredom . . . I don't know what to do.

SONYA [*shrugging her shoulders*]. Isn't there plenty to do? If only you wanted to . . .

YELENA. For instance?

SONYA. You could help in running the estate, teach children, help to look after the sick. Isn't there plenty to do? For instance, before you and papa came to live here, Uncle Vanya and I used to go to the market ourselves and sell the flour.

YELENA. I don't know how to. And I'm not interested. It's only in idealistic novels that people teach and doctor the peasants . . . How am I suddenly to start teaching and doctoring them for no earthly reason?

SONYA. Well, I just don't understand how you can help wanting to go and teach them. Wait a little, you'll get accustomed to the idea. [*embraces her*] Don't get bored, dear! [*laughs*] You're bored and you don't know what to do with yourself, but boredom and idleness are infectious. Look: Uncle Vanya isn't doing anything either, just following you about like a shadow, and I've left my work and come running to you to have a chat. I've grown quite lazy, I can't help it! The doctor, Mikhail Lvovich, only used to come to see us very rarely, once a month — it was hard to persuade him to come. But now he comes here every day, he's neglecting his forestry and his practice. You must be a witch.

VOYNITSKY. Why be miserable? [*with enthusiasm*] Come, my dear, wonderful woman, be sensible! A mermaid's blood flows in your veins, so be a mermaid! Let yourself go for once in your life! Fall head over heels in love with some water-sprite — and plunge head first into deep water, so that the Herr Professor and all of us just throw up our hands in amazement!

YELENA [*angrily*]. Leave me alone! How cruel all this is! [*is about to go out*]

VOYNITSKY [*prevents her*]. Come, come, my treasure, forgive me! I apologise . . . [*kisses her hand*] Peace!

YELENA. Even an angel couldn't hold her patience with you, you know.

VOYNITSKY. As a token of peace and harmony I'll bring you a bunch of roses; I've had them ready for you since this morning. Autumn roses, exquisite, mournful roses . . . [*goes out*]

SONYA. Autumn roses, exquisite, mournful roses . . .

[*both look through the window*]

YELENA. It's September already. How are we going to live through the winter here! [*a pause*] Where's the doctor?

SONYA. In Uncle Vanya's room. Writing something. I'm glad Uncle Vanya's gone, I must have a talk with you.

YELENA. What about?

SONYA. What about! . . . [*lays her head on* YELENA'*s bosom*]

YELENA. Come, there, there . . . [*strokes her hair*] Don't . . .

SONYA. I'm not good-looking.

YELENA. You have beautiful hair.

SONYA. No! [*turns round to look at herself in a mirror*] No! When a woman is plain, they always say: 'You have beautiful eyes, you have beautiful hair . . .' I've loved him now for six years, I love him more than I did my mother; every moment I seem to hear him, to feel his hand in mine, and I look at the door waiting, expecting him to come in at any moment. And you can see how I keep coming to you just to talk about him. Now he comes here every day, but he doesn't look at me – doesn't see me . . . It's such a torment! I have no hope at all – none, none! [*in despair*] O Lord, give me strength . . . I've been praying all night . . . I often go up to him, start talking to him, look into his eyes . . . I have no more pride, no strength left to control myself . . . I couldn't help it, yesterday I confessed to Uncle Vanya that I'm in love . . . And all the servants know that I love him.

YELENA. And he?

SONYA. He doesn't notice me.

YELENA [*musing*]. He's a strange man . . . I've an idea . . . Let me have a talk with him . . . I'll be careful, I'll do it in a roundabout way . . . [*a pause*] Yes, really – after all, how much longer are you to remain in ignorance? . . . Let me!

[SONYA *nods her head in consent*]

YELENA. That's fine. It won't be difficult to find out whether he loves you or not. You must not feel ashamed, darling, you don't need to worry – I'll question him so carefully that he won't notice. All we want is to find out whether it's yes, or no. [*a pause*] If not, then he mustn't come here any more, must he?

[SONYA *nods in agreement*]

It's easier to bear when you don't see him. We won't put it off, I'll speak to him straight away. He was going to show me some charts. Go and tell him that I want to see him.

SONYA [*in great agitation*]. You will tell me the whole truth?

YELENA. Yes, of course. I think it's better to know the truth whatever it may be – it's not so dreadful as being kept in ignorance. Trust me, dear.

SONYA. Yes, yes . . . I'll tell him that you want to see his charts . . . [*is about to go, then stops near the door*] No, ignorance is better . . . At least there's some hope . . .

YELENA. What do you say?

SONYA. Nothing. [*goes out*]

YELENA [*alone*]. There's nothing worse than knowing someone's secret and not being able to help. [*musing*] He's not in love with her, that's obvious – but why shouldn't he marry her? She is not pretty, but she'd make an excellent wife for a country doctor at his time of life. She's intelligent, and so kind and pure . . . No, that's not the point . . . [*a pause*] I understand the poor girl so well. In the middle of all this desperate boredom, with just grey shadows wandering around instead of human beings, with nothing but commonplace tittle-tattle to listen to from people who do nothing but eat, drink, and sleep, he appears from time to time – so different from the rest of them, handsome, interesting, attractive, like a bright moon rising in the darkness . . . To fall under the fascination of a man like that, to forget oneself . . . I believe I'm a little attracted myself . . . Yes, I'm bored when he's not about, and here I am smiling when I think of him . . . Uncle Vanya here says I have mermaid's blood in my veins. 'Let yourself go for once in your life.' . . . Well, perhaps that's what I ought to do . . . To fly away, free as a bird, away from all of you, from your sleepy faces and talk, to forget that you exist at all – every one of you! . . . But I'm too timid and shy . . . My conscience would torment me to distraction . . . He comes here every day . . . I can guess why he comes and already I feel guilty . . . I want to fall on my knees before Sonya, to ask her forgiveness and cry . . .

ASTROV *comes in with a chart.*

ASTROV. Good-day to you! [*shakes hands*] You wanted to see my artistic handiwork?

YELENA. Yesterday you promised to show me some of your work. Are you free now?

ASTROV. But of course! [*spreads the chart on a card table and fixes it down with drawing-pins*] Tell me, where were you born?

YELENA [*helping him*]. In Petersburg.

ASTROV. And where did you study?

YELENA. At the School of Music.

ASTROV. I don't suppose this will interest you.

YELENA. Why not? It's true I don't know the country, but I've read a great deal.

ASTROV. I have a table of my own here . . . in Ivan Petrovich's room. When I'm completely tired out – to the point of utter stupefaction – I leave everything and escape here to amuse myself for an hour or two with this thing . . . Ivan Petrovich and Sofya Alexandrovna click away at their counting beads, and I sit beside them at my table and mess about with my paints – and I'm warm and quiet, and the cricket chirps. But I don't allow myself this pleasure very often, just once a month . . . [*pointing to the chart*] Now look at this. It's a map of our district as it was fifty years ago. The dark and light green stand for forest; half of the whole area was covered with forest. Where there's a sort of network of red over the green, elks and wild goats were common . . . I show both the flora and the fauna here. This lake was the home of swans, geese, and ducks. There was 'a power' of birds, as the old people say, of all kinds, no end of them: they used to fly about in clouds. Besides the villages and hamlets, you can see all sorts of small settlements scattered here and there – little farms, monasteries, water mills . . . Cattle and horses were numerous – that's shown by the blue colour. For instance, there's a lot of blue in this part of the region. There were any number of horses here, and every homestead had three on the average. [*a pause*] Now let us look lower down. This is how it was twenty-five years ago. Already only a third of the area is under forest. The goats have disappeared, but there are still some elks. The green and the blue colours are paler, and so on. Now look at the third section, the map showing the district as it is now. There's still some green here and there, but it's not continuous – it's in patches. The elks, swans, and woodgrouse have all disappeared. There's not a trace of the small farms and monasteries and mills that were there before . . . In general, it's an unmistakable picture of gradual decay which will obviously be completed in another ten or fifteen years. You may say that it is the influence of civilisation – that the old way of life naturally had to give place to the new. Yes, and I would agree – if on the site of these ruined forests there were now roads and railways, if there were workshops, and factories, and schools. Then the people would have been healthier, better off, and better educated – but there's nothing of the sort here! There are still the same swamps and mosquitoes, the same absence of roads, and the dire poverty, and typhus, and diphtheria, and fires. Here we have a picture of decay due to an insupportable struggle for existence, it is decay caused by inertia, by ignorance, by utter irresponsibility – as when a sick, hungry, shivering man, simply to save what is left of his life and to protect his children, instinctively, unconsciously clutches at anything which will satisfy his hunger and keep him warm, and in doing so destroys everything, without a thought for tomorrow . . . Already practically everything has been destroyed, but nothing has been created to take its place. [*coldly*] I see from your expression that it doesn't interest you.

YELENA. But I understand so little about all this . . .

ASTROV. There's nothing to understand: you're just not interested.

YELENA. To be quite frank, my mind was on something else. Forgive me. I want to put you through a little interrogation, and I feel rather embarrassed; I don't know how to begin.

ASTROV. An interrogation?

YELENA. Yes, an interrogation, but . . . a fairly innocent one. Let's sit down! [*they sit down*] It concerns a certain young person. We'll talk frankly, like friends, without beating about the bush. We'll talk it over and forget everything we said. Agreed?

ASTROV. Agreed.

YELENA. The matter concerns my stepdaughter, Sonya. Tell me, do you like her?

ASTROV. Yes, I respect her.

YELENA. Do you like her as a woman?

ASTROV [*after a brief pause*]. No.

YELENA. One thing more – and that'll be the end. Have you noticed anything?

ASTROV. Nothing.

YELENA [*taking him by the hand*]. You don't love her, I see it from your eyes . . . She is suffering . . . Understand that, and . . . stop coming here.

ASTROV [*rises*]. My time's past . . . Besides, I've got too much to do . . . [*shrugging his shoulders*] When could I find time? [*he is embarrassed*]

YELENA. Ough! What an unpleasant conversation! I feel as though I've been carrying a ton weight about. Anyway, we've finished now, thank Heaven! Let's forget it, as if we hadn't talked at all, and . . . and go away. You're an intelligent man, you will understand . . . [*a pause*] I feel I'm quite flushed.

ASTROV. If you'd told me a month or two ago, I might perhaps have considered it, but now . . . [*shrugs his shoulders*] But if she is suffering, then of course . . . There's only one thing I don't understand: why did you have to have this interrogation? [*looks into her eyes and shakes his finger at her*] You're a sly one!

YELENA. What does that mean?

ASTROV [*laughs*]. Sly! Suppose Sonya is suffering – I'm prepared to think it probable – but what was the purpose of this cross-examination? [*preventing her from speaking, with animation*] Please don't try to look astonished. You know perfectly well why I come here every day . . . Why, and on whose account – you know very well indeed. You charming bird of prey, don't look at me like that, I'm a wise old sparrow . . .

YELENA [*perplexed*]. Bird of prey! I don't understand at all!

ASTROV. A beautiful, fluffy weasel . . . You must have a victim! Here I've been doing nothing for a whole month. I've dropped everything, I seek you out hungrily – and you are awfully pleased about it, awfully . . . Well, what am I to say? I'm conquered, but you knew that without an interrogation! [*looks into her eyes and shakes his finger at her*] I submit. Here I am, devour me!

YELENA. Have you gone out of your mind?

ASTROV [*laughs sardonically*]. You are coy . . .

YELENA. Oh, I'm not so bad, or not so mean as you think! On my word of honour! [*tries to go out*]

ASTROV [*barring her way*]. I'll go away today, I won't come here again, but . . . [*takes her by the hand and glances round*] Where shall I see you? Tell me quickly, where? Someone may come in here, tell me quickly . . . [*passionately*] How wonderful, how glorious you are! One kiss . . . If I could only kiss your fragrant hair . . .

YELENA. I swear to you . . .

ASTROV [*prevents her from speaking*]. Why swear anything? There's no need to . . . No need for unnecessary words . . . Oh, how beautiful you are! What lovely hands! [*kisses her hands*]

YELENA. That's enough . . . go away . . . [*withdraws her hands*] You are forgetting yourself.

ASTROV. Speak, speak! Where shall we meet tomorrow? [*puts his arm round her waist*] You see, it's inevitable – we must see each other. [*kisses her*]

At that moment VOYNITSKY *comes in with a bunch of roses and stops just inside the door.*

YELENA [*not seeing* VOYNITSKY]. Spare me . . . leave me alone . . . [*lays her head on* ASTROV's *chest*] No! [*tries to go out*]

ASTROV [*holding her by the waist*]. Come to the plantation tomorrow . . . about two o'clock . . . Yes? yes? You will come?

YELENA [*seeing* VOYNITSKY]. Let me go! [*in extreme confusion goes to the window*] This is dreadful!

VOYNITSKY [*lays the roses on a chair; in agitation wipes his face and neck with a handkerchief*]. Never mind . . . no . . . never mind . . .

ASTROV [*with bravado*]. The weather is not too bad today, my dear Ivan Petrovich. It was overcast in the morning as though it were going to rain, but now it's sunny. It must be admitted that the autumn has turned out very fine . . . and the winter corn is quite promising. [*rolls up his chart*] The only thing is — the days are getting short . . . [*goes out*]

YELENA [*goes quickly up to* VOYNITSKY]. You will try, you will do your utmost to see that my husband and I leave here today for certain? Do you hear? Today for certain!

VOYNITSKY [*wiping his face*]. What? Oh, yes . . . very well . . .

YELENA [*nervously*]. Do you hear? I must get away from here this very day!

Enter SEREBRYAKOV, SONYA, TELEGIN *and* MARINA.

TELEGIN. I'm not feeling too well myself, your Excellency. I've been poorly for the last two days. Something the matter with my head . . .

SEREBRYAKOV. But where are the others? I don't like this house. It's like a sort of labyrinth. Twenty-six enormous rooms, people wander off in all directions, and there's no finding anyone. [*rings*] Ask Marya Vasilyevna and Yelena Andreyevna to come here!

YELENA. I'm here.

SEREBRYAKOV. Please sit down, my friends.

SONYA [*going up to* YELENA, *impatiently*]. What did he say?

YELENA. I'll tell you later.

SONYA. You're trembling? You're upset? [*looks searchingly into her face*] I understand . . . He said he wouldn't be coming here any more . . . yes? [*a pause*] Tell me: yes?

[YELENA *nods her head*]

SEREBRYAKOV [*to* TELEGIN]. One can put up with ill-health, after all. But what I can't stomach is the whole pattern of life in the country. I feel as if I had been cast off the earth on to some strange planet. Do sit down, friends, please! Sonya!

[SONYA *does not hear him; she stands and hangs her head sadly*]
Sonya! [*a pause*] She doesn't hear. [*to* MARINA] You sit down too, Nanny.

[*the nurse sits down and starts knitting a stocking*]
I beg you, my friends, lend me your ears, as the saying goes. [*laughs*]

VOYNITSKY [*agitated*]. Maybe I'm not needed here? Can I go?

SEREBRYAKOV. No, you're needed more than anyone.

VOYNITSKY. What do you require from me?

SEREBRYAKOV. Require from you . . . Why – are you annoyed at something? [*a pause*] If I've offended you in any way, please excuse me.

VOYNITSKY. You needn't adopt that tone. Let's come to business. What is it you want?

Enter MARYA VASILYEVNA.

SEREBRYAKOV. Here is *Maman*. Let me begin, my friends. [*a pause*] I have invited you here, ladies and gentlemen, to inform you that the Inspector General is coming to visit us. But, joking apart, this is a serious matter. I have called you together, my friends, to ask your help and advice and, knowing how obliging you always are, I hope to receive it. I'm an academic, bookish man, and I've never had anything to do with practical life. I must have guidance from people better informed than I am, and so I want to ask you, Ivan Petrovich, and also you, Ilya Ilyich, and you, *Maman* . . . The point is – *manet omnes una nox*: we are all mortal. I'm an old and ailing man, and I think it's high time to settle the matter of my property in so far as it concerns my family. My own life is over now, I'm not thinking of myself. But I have a young wife and an unmarried daughter. [*a pause*] It is impossible for me to go on living in the country. We are not made for country life. But to live in town on the income we are receiving from this estate is also impossible. Suppose we sold the forest – that would be an exceptional measure which could not be repeated every year. We must find ways which will guarantee us a permanent, more or less definite income. One such measure has occurred to me, and I would like to submit it for your consideration. Omitting the details, I will describe it in rough outline. Our estate yields on the average not more than two per cent on its capital value. I suggest we sell it. If we invest the money in suitable securities, we should get from four to five per cent, and I think we might even have a few thousand roubles to spare which would enable us to buy a small villa in Finland.

VOYNITSKY. Wait a moment . . . Surely, I haven't been hearing correctly. Say that again.

SEREBRYAKOV. I suggest putting the money in suitable securities and with whatever is left buying a villa in Finland.

VOYNITSKY. Not Finland . . . you said something else.

SEREBRYAKOV. I suggested we sell the estate.

VOYNITSKY. That's it. You sell the estate – that's a fine idea – magnificent . . . And where do you propose I should go – with my old mother and Sonya here?

SEREBRYAKOV. We shall discuss all that in due course. We can't do everything at once.

VOYNITSKY. Wait a moment. It looks as though I must have been incredibly stupid all this time. Until now I've been foolish enough to believe that this estate belonged to Sonya. My father bought it as a dowry for my sister. I've been too simple; not interpreting the law like a Turk, I thought that my sister's estate passed to Sonya.

SEREBRYAKOV. Yes, the estate belongs to Sonya. Who's disputing it? Without Sonya's consent I shall not venture to sell it. Besides, I am suggesting that this should be done for Sonya's benefit.

VOYNITSKY. It's inconceivable, inconceivable! Either I've gone out of my mind, or . . . or . . .

MARYA VASILYEVNA. Jean, don't contradict Alexandre. Believe me, he knows better than we do what's good for us and what isn't.

VOYNITSKY. No, give me some water. [drinks water] Say what you like, anything!

SEREBRYAKOV. I don't understand why you're so upset. I'm not saying that my plan is ideal. If everybody finds it unsuitable, I won't insist on it.

TELEGIN [*embarrassed*]. Towards learning, your Excellency, I have not merely a feeling of reverence, but a sort of family relationship as well. The brother of my brother's wife, Konstantin Erofimovich Lakedemonov – perhaps you know him? – was an M.A. . . .

VOYNITSKY. Stop, Waffles, we're talking business . . . Wait a little – later on . . . [*to* SEREBRYAKOV] Here, ask him. This estate was bought from his uncle.

SEREBRYAKOV. Indeed! But why should I ask him? Why ever . . . ?

VOYNITSKY. The estate was originally bought for ninety-five thousand roubles. My father only paid seventy thousand, and twenty-five thousand remained on mortgage. Now please do listen . . . This estate would never have been bought if I hadn't given up my share of the inheritance in favour of my sister, whom I loved dearly. What's more, I worked like an ox for ten years, and paid off the whole mortgage . . .

SEREBRYAKOV. I regret that I started this discussion.

VOYNITSKY. The estate is free from debt and in a good condition simply because of my own efforts. And now that I've grown old, I'm to be kicked out!

SEREBRYAKOV. I don't understand what you're driving at!

VOYNITSKY. For twenty-five years I've been managing this estate! I've been working and sending you money like the most conscientious bailiff you could have, but all this time you've never once thanked me for it. All this time – when I was young, and now just the same – I've been getting a salary of five hundred roubles a year from you – a pittance! – and never once have you thought of adding a single rouble to it!

SEREBRYAKOV. Ivan Petrovich, how was I to know? I'm not a practical man, I don't understand anything about these matters. You could have added as much as you liked.

VOYNITSKY. Yes indeed, why didn't I steal? Why don't you all laugh at me now because I didn't steal? It would have been fair enough, and I shouldn't have been a pauper now!

MARYA VASILYEVNA [sternly]. Jean!

TELEGIN [*in agitation*]. Vanya, my dear, don't, don't . . . I'm all of a tremble . . . Why spoil our good relations? [*embraces him*] You mustn't . . .

VOYNITSKY. For twenty-five years I sat with my mother here, buried like a mole in these four walls . . . All our thoughts and feelings belonged to you alone. By day we talked of you and your work; we were proud of you, we uttered your name with reverence. We wasted our nights reading books and magazines which now fill me with contempt.

TELEGIN. Don't, Vanya, don't . . . I can't bear it . . .

SEREBRYAKOV [*angrily*]. I don't understand what it is you want.

VOYNITSKY. To us you were a being of a higher order, and we knew your articles by heart . . . But now my eyes are opened! I can see it all! You write about art, but you don't understand anything about art! All your works, those works which I used to love, are not worth twopence! You've been deceiving us!

SEREBRYAKOV. Do make him stop this! I'll go!

YELENA. Ivan Petrovich, I insist that you stop. Do you hear?

VOYNITSKY. I will not be silent! [*barring* SEREBRYAKOV's *way*] Wait, I haven't finished yet! You've ruined my life! I haven't lived. I have not lived! Thanks to you I've destroyed, I've annihilated the best years of my life! You've been my worst enemy!

TELEGIN. I can't bear it . . . I can't . . . I'm going . . . [*goes out in great agitation*]

SEREBRYAKOV. What do you want from me? And what right have you to speak to me like this? You nonentity! If the estate is yours, take it! I don't need it!

YELENA. I'm going to get away from this hell this very minute! [*screams*] I can't stand it any longer!

VOYNITSKY. My life is ruined! I have talent, courage, intelligence . . . If I had had a normal life, I might have been a Schopenhauer, a Dostoyevsky . . . Oh, I'm talking rubbish! . . . I'm going out of my mind . . . Mother, I'm in despair! Mother!

MARYA VASILYEVNA [*sternly*]. Do as Alexandre tells you.

SONYA [*kneels before the nurse and huddles up against her*]. Nanny! Nanny!

VOYNITSKY. Mother! What am I to do? No, you needn't tell me! I know what I must do. [*to* SEREBRYAKOV] You'll remember me! [*goes out through middle door*]

[MARYA VASILYEVNA *follows him*]

SEREBRYAKOV. What does he mean by this behaviour? Take the madman away! I can't possibly live under the same roof with him. He lives there [*points at the middle door*] almost next door to me . . . Make him move into the village, or into the lodge – or I'll move – but I can't remain in the same house with him . . .

YELENA [*to her husband*]. We'll leave here today! We must make arrangements immediately.

SEREBRYAKOV. That nonentity!

SONYA [*on her knees, turns to her father and speaks tearfully and with agitation*]. You must have pity, Papa! Uncle Vanya and I are so unhappy! [*restraining her despair*] You must have pity! Remember – when you were younger Uncle Vanya and Grandmamma used to spend whole nights translating books for you, copying your papers . . . whole nights on end! . . . whole nights! Uncle Vanya and I worked incessantly, we were afraid to spend a penny on ourselves and sent it all to you . . . We really did earn our daily bread! I'm saying it all wrong – all wrong – but you must understand us, papa! You must be charitable!

YELENA [*in agitation, to her husband*]. Alexandre, for Heaven's sake, go and talk it over with him . . . I implore you!

SEREBRYAKOV. Very well, I will talk it over with him . . . I'm not accusing him of anything, I'm not angry. But you must agree with me that his behaviour is very strange, to say the least of it. Very well, I'll go and see him. [*goes out through the middle door*]

YELENA. Be as gentle as you can with him, try to reassure him . . . [*follows him*]

SONYA [*nestling up to the nurse*]. Nanny! Nanny!

MARINA. Never mind, child. The ganders will cackle a bit – and then they'll leave off . . . They'll cackle and leave off . . .

SONYA. Nanny!

MARINA [*stroking her head*]. You're shivering as if you were out in a frost! There, there, my little orphan, God is merciful. A drink of lime-flower tea, or hot raspberry, and it'll pass off . . . Don't get so upset, my little orphan . . . [*looking at the middle door, with annoyance*] What a row they're making, the ganders! Drat them!

[*a shot is heard off-stage, then a shriek from* YELENA; SONYA *starts*]

MARINA. Ough! Drat them!

SEREBRYAKOV [*runs in, staggering in terror*]. Stop him! Stop him! He's gone mad!

[YELENA *and* VOYNITSKY *struggle in the doorway*]

YELENA [*trying to take a revolver from him*]. Give it to me! Give it to me, I tell you!

VOYNITSKY. Let me go, Hélène! Let me go! [*freeing himself from her, runs in and looks round for* SEREBRYAKOV] Where is he? Ah, there he is! [*fires at him*] Bang! [*a pause*] Missed? Missed again! [*furiously*] Damnation! . . . devil . . . devil take it! [*flings the revolver on the floor and sinks on to a chair, exhausted.* SEREBRYAKOV *looks stunned;* YELENA *leans against the wall, almost fainting*]

YELENA. Take me away from here! Take me away, kill me . . . but I can't stay here, I can't!

VOYNITSKY [*in despair*]. Oh, what have I done? What am I doing?

SONYA [*softly*]. Nanny, dear! Nanny!

CURTAIN

ACT FOUR

VOYNITSKY's *room which serves both as his bedroom and his office. By the window, a large table with account books and various papers; also a bureau, bookcases and scales. A smaller table is set apart for* ASTROV *with paints, drawing materials, and a large portfolio. A cage with a starling in it. On the wall a map of Africa, obviously serving no useful purpose here. A large divan upholstered in American cloth. On the left a door leading to other rooms; on the right a door into the hall. In front of the right-hand door there is a mat to protect the floor from mud off the peasants' boots. It is an autumn evening, and very quiet.*

TELEGIN *and* MARINA, *sitting opposite one another, are winding wool.*

TELEGIN. Hurry up, Marina Timofeyevna. They'll soon be calling us to say goodbye. They've ordered the horses to be brought round.

MARINA [*tries to wind faster*]. There isn't much left.

TELEGIN. They're going to Kharkov. Going to live there . . .

MARINA. That will be much better.

TELEGIN. They've had a fright. Yelena Andreyevna keeps saying: 'I won't stay here another hour . . . Let's get away . . . Let's get away . . .' 'When we've lived in Kharkov for a bit and had a look round, we'll send for our things,' she says. They're travelling light. It seems they're not ordained to live here, Marina Timofeyevna. They're not ordained to . . . Such is the will of Providence.

MARINA. It's better so. The row they made this morning – and shooting, too – a regular disgrace!

TELEGIN. Yes . . . a subject worthy of the brush of Aivazovsky, one might say . . .

MARINA. What a sight for my old eyes! [*a pause*] We'll be living again as we used to – in the old way. Morning tea soon after seven, dinner at twelve, and in the evening we'll sit down to supper. Everything as it should be, just like other people . . . like Christians. [*with a sigh*] It's a long time since I tasted noodles, sinner that I am!

TELEGIN. Yes, it's a long time since they had noodles in this house. [*a pause*] A very long time . . . Marina Timofeyevna, as I was walking through the village this morning, the shopkeeper shouted after me: 'Hey, you scrounger . . . living on other people, you are!' I felt so hurt!

MARINA. You shouldn't take any notice, dearie. We all live on God. You, and Sonya, and Ivan Petrovich are just the same – none of us sits with folded hands, we are all working – all of us! . . . Where's Sonya?

TELEGIN. In the garden. She keeps walking round with the Doctor looking for Ivan Petrovich. They're afraid he may do himself harm.

MARINA. Where's his revolver?

TELEGIN [*in a whisper*]. I've hidden it in the cellar.

MARINA [*with a smile*]. What goings-on!

Enter VOYNITSKY *and* ASTROV *from outside.*

VOYNITSKY. Leave me alone. [*to* MARINA *and* TELEGIN] Please do go away from here, leave me alone – if it's only for an hour! I can't stand this supervision.

TELEGIN. Of course, Vanya. [*goes out on tiptoe*]

MARINA. You old gander! Ga-ga-ga! [*gathers up her wool and goes out*]

VOYNITSKY. Leave me alone!

ASTROV. With the greatest pleasure! I ought to have left here hours ago, but I must repeat I'm not going away until you give me back what you took from me.

VOYNITSKY. I haven't taken anything from you.

ASTROV. I'm speaking seriously – don't keep me waiting. I ought to have gone long ago.

VOYNITSKY. I didn't take anything from you.
[*both sit down*]

ASTROV. No? Well, I'll wait a little longer, and then, I'm sorry, but I'll have to use force. We'll tie your hands together and search you. I'm speaking absolutely in earnest.

VOYNITSKY. As you please. [*a pause*] To have made such a fool of myself – firing twice and missing both times! I shall never forgive myself for that!

ASTROV. If you really felt like shooting someone, you might as well have taken a pot-shot at yourself.

VOYNITSKY [*shrugging his shoulders*]. It's queer! Here I've tried to commit a murder, and yet no-one arrests me, no-one charges me with anything . . . It must mean they think I'm a madman. [*with an angry laugh*] I'm mad – but people who conceal their utter lack of talent, their dullness, their complete heartlessness under the guise of the professor, the purveyor of learned magic – they aren't mad. Women aren't mad who marry old men and then deceive them for everyone to see. I saw you with your arms round her, I saw it!

ASTROV. Yes, I did put my arms round her, and as for you – you can take this . . . [*thumbs his nose at him*]

VOYNITSKY [*looking at the door*]. The earth must be mad because it still supports you.

ASTROV. Now you're being just silly!

VOYNITSKY. Well, I'm mad, I'm irresponsible. I have the right to say silly things.

ASTROV. That's an old trick. You're not mad, you're simply a crank. A silly old fool. I used to think that every crank was sick or abnormal. But now I believe it's normal for a man to be a crank. You are perfectly normal.

VOYNITSKY [*covers his face with his hands*]. I feel so ashamed. If you only knew how ashamed I feel! This acute sense of shame – it's worse than any pain! [*wretchedly*] It's unbearable. [*leans over the table*] What am I to do? What am I to do?

ASTROV. Nothing.

VOYNITSKY. Give me something! Oh, my God! I'm forty-seven. If I live to be sixty, I've got another thirteen years. What a time! How am I to get through those thirteen years? What shall I do, how shall I fill in the time? Ah, don't you see . . . [*squeezing* ASTROV's *hand convulsively*], don't you see, if only you could live the rest of your life in some new way! To wake up on a clear, calm morning and feel that you're starting your life over again, that all your past is forgotten, blown away like smoke. [*weeps*] To begin a new life . . . Tell me how to begin . . . what with . . .

ASTROV [*with annoyance*]. Oh, get away with you! A new life indeed! Our situation's hopeless – yours and mine!

VOYNITSKY. Do you mean that?

ASTROV. I'm certain of it.

VOYNITSKY. Give me something . . . [*pointing at his heart*] I've a burning sensation here.

ASTROV [*shouts angrily*]. Shut up! [*softening*] The people who come a hundred years or a couple of hundred years after us and despise us for having lived in so stupid and tasteless a fashion – perhaps they'll find a way to be happy . . . As for us . . . There's only one hope for you and me . . . The hope that when we're at rest in our graves we may see visions – perhaps even pleasant ones. [*with a sigh*] Yes, my friend! In the whole of this province there have only been two decent, cultured people – you and I. But ten years of this contemptible routine, this trivial provincial life has swallowed us up, poisoned our blood with its putrid vapours, until now we've become just as petty as all the rest. [*with a sudden animation*] But don't you try to talk me out of it: give me back what you took from me.

VOYNITSKY. I didn't take anything from you.

ASTROV. You took a bottle of morphia out of my travelling medicine chest. [*a pause*] Look here now: if you really feel you must put an end to yourself, why don't you go to the woods and shoot yourself there? But do give me back the morphia, or else there will be talk and suspicion. People might think I'd given it you . . . It'll be quite enough to have to do your post-mortem. Do you think I shall find it interesting?

Enter SONYA.

VOYNITSKY. Leave me alone.

ASTROV [*to* SONYA]. Sofya Alexandrovna, your uncle has stolen a bottle of morphia from my medicine chest and won't give it back. Tell him that it's . . . well . . . it's not a bit clever of him. Besides, I haven't the time to waste. I ought to be going.

SONYA. Uncle Vanya, did you take the morphia?

[*a pause*]

ASTROV. He did. I'm certain of it.

SONYA. Give it back. Why do you frighten us like this? [*with tenderness*] Give it back, Uncle Vanya! I dare say I'm just as unhappy as you are, but I don't despair all the same. I bear it, and I shall continue to bear it till my life comes to its natural end . . . You must bear it, too. [*a pause*] Give it back! [*kisses his hand*] My dear, kind uncle – give it up, dear! [*weeps*] You're so good, I know you'll feel sorry for us and give it back. You'll have to bear it, uncle! You must bear it!

VOYNITSKY [*takes a bottle out of his desk and hands it to* ASTROV] Here, take it! [*to* SONYA.] But we must start work at once, we must start doing something, or else I can't . . . I can't . . .

SONYA. Yes, yes, work. As soon as we've seen the others off, we'll settle down to work . . . [*nervously turning over the papers on the table*] We've been neglecting everything.

ASTROV [*puts the bottle into his case and tightens the straps*]. Now I can be on my way.

Enter YELENA.

YELENA. Ivan Petrovich, are you here? We're just going. Go and see Alexandre, he wants to say something to you.

SONYA. Go along, Uncle Vanya. [*takes* VOYNITSKY's *arm*] Let's go. You and Papa must make it up. It's essential.

[SONYA *and* VOYNITSKY *go out*]

YELENA. I'm going away. [*gives* ASTROV *her hand*]

ASTROV. Already?

YELENA. The horses are waiting.

ASTROV. Goodbye.

YELENA. Today you promised me you'd go away from here.

ASTROV. I've not forgotten. I'm just going. [*a pause*] Did you get frightened? [*takes her hand*] Is it really so frightening?

YELENA. Yes.

ASTROV. Why not stay, all the same? . . . Well? Tomorrow, at the plantation. . . .

YELENA. No . . . It's settled . . . The reason I'm looking at you so fearlessly now is just that our departure has been settled . . . I only ask one thing of you: do think better of me. I should like you to respect me.

ASTROV. Oh! [*makes a gesture of impatience*] Do stay, I beg you. You must admit you have nothing whatever to do, you have absolutely no object in life, nothing to occupy your mind with, so that, sooner or later, you'll be bound to give way to your feelings – it's inevitable. And it will be better if that happens not in Kharkov, or somewhere in Kursk, but down here, in the lap of nature. At least it's poetical here, quite beautiful in fact . . . There are forestry plantations, half-ruined country houses in the Turgenev style. . . .

YELENA. How droll you are . . . I'm angry with you, and yet . . . I'll remember you with pleasure. You're an interesting, original man. We shall never see each other again, and so why should I conceal it? – you did turn my head a little. Come, let us shake hands and part friends. Think well of me.

ASTROV [*shakes hands with her*]. Yes, you'd better go . . . [*musing*] You seem to be so good and warm-hearted, and yet there's something strange about your personality . . . You just happened to come along with your husband and all of us here, who'd been working and running around and trying to create something, we all had to drop everything and occupy ourselves wholly with you and your husband's gout. You two infected all of us with your indolence. I was attracted by you and I've done nothing for a whole month, and in the meantime people have been ill and the peasants have been using my woods, my plantations of young trees, as pasture for their cattle . . . So you see, wherever you and your husband go, you bring along destruction with you . . . I'm joking, of course, but still . . . it is strange. I'm convinced that if you'd stayed on here the devastation would have been immense. I should have been ruined . . . and you wouldn't have fared too well, either. Go away, then. *Finita la commedia*!

YELENA [*takes a pencil from his table and quickly puts it in her pocket*]. I'm taking this pencil as a keepsake.

ASTROV. It is strange somehow . . . Here we've known one another, and all at once for some reason . . . we shall never see each other again. That's the way with everything in this world . . . While there's no-one here – before Uncle Vanya comes in with a bunch of flowers, allow me . . . to kiss you . . . goodbye . . . Yes? [*kisses her on the cheek*] There . . . that's fine.

YELENA. I wish you every happiness . . . [*looks round*] Well, here goes – for once in my life! [*embraces him impulsively, and both at once quickly step back from each other*] I must be off.

ASTROV. Go as soon as you can. If the horses are ready, you'd better be off!

YELENA. I think someone's coming. [*both listen*]

ASTROV. *Finita!*

Enter SEREBRYAKOV, VOYNITSKY, MARYA VASILYEVNA
carrying a book, TELEGIN *and* SONYA.

SEREBRYAKOV. Let us let bygones be bygones. What with everything that's happened, I've thought and lived through so much in the last few hours that I believe I could write a whole treatise on how one should conduct one's life – for the benefit of posterity. I gladly accept your apologies and I ask you to forgive me, too. Goodbye! [*he and* VOYNITSKY *embrace and kiss each other three times*]

VOYNITSKY. You'll be receiving the same amount as before, regularly. Everything shall be as it was before.

[YELENA *embraces* SONYA]

SEREBRYAKOV [*kisses* MARYA VASILYEVNA's *hand*]. Maman . . .

MARYA VASILYEVNA [*kissing him*]. Alexandre, do have your photograph taken again and send it to me. You know how much you mean to me.

TELEGIN. Goodbye, your Excellency! Don't forget us!

SEREBRYAKOV [*kisses his daughter*]. Goodbye . . . Goodbye everyone! [*shakes hands with* ASTROV] Thank you for the pleasure of your society. I respect your attitude of mind, your enthusiasms, your spontaneity, but permit an old man to add one thing to his farewell greetings: you must try to do real work, my friends, yes, real work! [*he bows to them all*] I wish you all happiness and good fortune! [*goes out, followed by* MARYA VASILYEVNA *and* SONYA]

VOYNITSKY [*warmly kisses* YELENA's *hand*]. Goodbye . . . Forgive me . . . We shall never see one another again.

YELENA [*moved*]. Goodbye, dear Ivan Petrovich. [*kisses him on the head and goes out*]

ASTROV [*to* TELEGIN]. Waffles, you might tell them to bring my horses round too.

TELEGIN. Certainly, my dear friend. [*goes out*]

[ASTROV *and* VOYNITSKY *remain alone*]

ASTROV [*clears the paints from the table and puts them away in his case*]. Well, why don't you go and see them off?

VOYNITSKY. Let them go. As for me – I . . . I can't. I'm depressed.
I must occupy myself with something as soon as I can . . . Work,
work! [*rummages among the papers*]
    [*a pause; the sound of harness bells is heard*]
ASTROV. They've gone. The professor's glad, that's certain. Wild
horses won't drag him back.

MARINA enters.

MARINA. They've gone. [*sits down in an easy chair and knits a stocking*]

SONYA enters.

SONYA. They've gone. [*wipes her eyes*] God grant them a safe
journey. [*to her uncle*] Well, Uncle Vanya, let's start doing
something.
VOYNITSKY. Work, work. . . .
SONYA. It's a long, long time since we sat at this table, just the two
of us. [*lights the lamp on the table*] There doesn't seem to be any
ink . . . [*takes the inkstand, goes to the cupboard and fills it with ink*]
But I feel sad now they've gone.

MARYA VASILYEVNA comes in slowly.

MARYA VASILYEVNA. Gone! [*sits down and becomes absorbed in reading*]
SONYA [*sits down at the table and turns over the pages of the account
book*]. First of all, Uncle Vanya, let's write out the bills . . . We've
neglected it all dreadfully. Someone sent for his account again
today. You make it out. While you do one, I'll do another . . .
VOYNITSKY [*writes*]. Delivered . . . to . . . Mr . . .
    [*both write in silence*]
MARINA [*yawns*]. I feel like going bye-bye . . .
ASTROV. How quiet it is! The pens scratch, the cricket sings. It's
warm and snug . . . I don't feel like leaving here.
    [*the sound of harness is heard*]
My horses are coming . . . There's nothing left for me but to
say goodbye to you, my friends, – to say goodbye to my table
and – be off! [*packs up his maps in the portfolio*]
MARINA. Why are you in such a hurry? I'd stay on if I were you.
ASTROV. I can't.
VOYNITSKY [*writes*]. Remaining to your debit: two roubles seventy-
five kopecks.

A WORKMAN *comes in.*

WORKMAN. Mikhail Lvovich, the horses are ready.

ASTROV. I heard them. [*hands him the medicine chest, the bag, and the portfolio*] Here, take these. Mind you don't bend the portfolio.

WORKMAN. Very good, sir. [*goes out*]

ASTROV. Well . . . [*approaches them to say goodbye*]

SONYA. When shall we see you again?

ASTROV. Not before next summer, I expect. Hardly in the winter . . . Naturally, if anything happens you'll let me know and I'll come. [*shakes hands with them*] Thank you for your hospitality, your kindness . . . for everything, in fact. [*goes to the nurse and kisses her on the head*] Goodbye, old woman!

MARINA. So you're going before you've had tea?

ASTROV. I don't want any, Nurse.

MARINA. Perhaps you'll have a drop of vodka?

ASTROV [*irresolutely*]. Perhaps . . .

[MARINA *goes out*]

ASTROV [*after a pause*]. One of my horses has gone lame for some reason. I noticed it yesterday when Petrushka took it to water.

VOYNITSKY. You must change its shoes.

ASTROV. I'll have to call in at the blacksmith's in Rozhdestvennoye. It can't be helped. [*walks up to the map of Africa and looks at it*] I suppose down there in Africa the heat must be terrific now!

VOYNITSKY. Yes, very likely.

MARINA [*returns carrying a tray with a glass of vodka and a piece of bread*]. Here you are.

[ASTROV *drinks vodka*]

MARINA. Good health, my dear. [*makes a low bow*] Why don't you eat some bread with it?

ASTROV. No, that'll do for me . . . Well, good luck to you all! [*to* MARINA] Don't see me off, Nurse. There's no need to. [*he goes out,* SONYA *following with a candle to see him off.* MARINA *sits down in her easy chair*]

VOYNITSKY [*writing*]. February the second, linseed oil, twenty pounds . . . February the sixteenth, linseed oil again . . . twenty pounds. Buckwheat . . .

[*a pause. The sound of harness bells*]

MARINA. He's gone.

[*a pause*]

SONYA [*comes back and puts the candle on the table*]. He's gone.

VOYNITSKY [*counts on the abacus and writes down*]. Total . . . fifteen . . . twenty-five . . .

MARINA [*yawns*]. Lord forgive us our sins . . .

> TELEGIN *enters on tiptoe, sits down by the door*
> *and quietly tunes his guitar.*

VOYNITSKY [*to* SONYA, *passing his hand over her hair*]. My child, there's such a weight on my heart! Oh, if only you knew how my heart aches!

SONYA. Well, what can we do? We must go on living! [*a pause*] We shall go on living, Uncle Vanya. We shall live through a long, long succession of days and tedious evenings. We shall patiently suffer the trials which Fate imposes on us; we shall work for others, now and in our old age, and we shall have no rest. When our time comes we shall die submissively, and over there, beyond the grave, we shall say that we've suffered, that we've wept, that we've had a bitter life, and God will take pity on us. And then, uncle dear, we shall both begin to know a life that is bright and beautiful, and lovely. We shall rejoice and look back at these troubles of ours with tender feelings, with a smile – and we shall have rest. I believe it, uncle, I believe it fervently, passionately . . . [*kneels before him and lays her head on his hands, in a tired voice*] We shall have rest!

> [TELEGIN *plays softly on the guitar*]

We shall rest! We shall hear the angels, we shall see all the heavens covered with stars like diamonds, we shall see all earthly evil, all our sufferings swept away by the grace which will fill the whole world, and our life will become peaceful, gentle, and sweet as a caress. I believe it, I believe it . . . [*wipes his eyes with her handkerchief*] Poor, poor Uncle Vanya, you're crying . . . [*tearfully*] You've had no joy in your life, but wait, Uncle Vanya, wait . . . We shall rest . . . [*embraces him*] We shall rest!

> [*the watchman taps*]
> [MARYA VASILYEVNA *makes notes on the margin of her pamphlet,*
> MARINA *knits her stocking*]

SONYA. We shall rest!

THE CURTAIN FALLS SLOWLY

THREE SISTERS

A Drama in Four Acts

Characters In The Play

PROZOROV, Andrey Sergeyevich
NATASHA (Natalya Ivanovna), his fiancée, afterwards his wife
OLGA (Olga Sergeyevna, Olya) ⎫
MASHA (Marya Sergeyevna)   ⎬ his sisters
IRINA (Irina Sergeyevna)   ⎭
KULYGIN, Fyodor Ilyich, master at the High School for boys,
   husband of Masha
VERSHININ, Alexandr Ignatyevich, Lieutenant-Colonel, battery
   commander
TUZENBAKH, Nikolay Lvovich, Baron, Lieutenant in the army
SOLYONY, Vasiliy Vasiliyich, Captain
CHEBUTYKIN, Ivan Romanich, army doctor
FEDOTIK, Alexey Petrovich, Second Lieutenant
RODÉ, Vladimir Karlovich, Second Lieutenant
FERAPONT (Ferapont Spiridonich), an old porter from the
   County Office
ANFISA, the Prozorovs' former nurse, an old woman of 80

The action takes place in a county town.

ACT ONE

A drawing-room in the Prozorovs' house; it is separated from a large ballroom at the back by a row of columns. It is midday; there is cheerful sunshine outside. In the ballroom the table is being laid for lunch. OLGA, *wearing the regulation dark-blue dress of a secondary school mistress, is correcting her pupils' work, standing or walking about as she does so.* MASHA, *in a black dress, is sitting reading a book, her hat on her lap.* IRINA, *in white, stands lost in thought.*

OLGA. It's exactly a year ago that Father died, isn't it? This very day, the fifth of May – your Saint's day, Irina. I remember it was very cold and it was snowing. I felt then as if I should never survive his death; and you had fainted and were lying quite still, as if you were dead. And now – a year's gone by, and we talk about it so easily. You're wearing white, and your face is positively radiant . . .
      [a clock strikes twelve]
The clock struck twelve then, too. *[a pause]* I remember when Father was being taken to the cemetery there was a military band, and a salute with rifle fire. That was because he was a general, in command of a brigade. And yet there weren't many people at the funeral. Of course, it was raining hard, raining and snowing.

IRINA. Need we bring up all these memories?

Baron TUZENBAKH, CHEBUTYKIN *and* SOLYONY *appear behind the columns by the table in the ballroom.*

OLGA. It's so warm today that we can keep the windows wide open, and yet there aren't any leaves showing on the birch trees. Father was made a brigadier eleven years ago, and then he left Moscow and took us with him. I remember so well how everything in Moscow was in blossom by now, everything was soaked in sunlight and warmth. Eleven years have gone by, yet I remember everything about it, as if we'd only left yesterday. Oh, Heavens! When I woke up this morning and saw this flood of sunshine, all this spring sunshine, I felt so moved and so happy! I felt such a longing to get back home to Moscow!

CHEBUTYKIN [*to* TUZENBAKH]. The devil you have!

TUZENBAKH. It's nonsense, I agree.

MASHA [*absorbed in her book, whistles a tune under her breath*].

OLGA. Masha, do stop whistling! How can you? [*a pause*] I suppose I must get this continual headache because I have to go to school every day and go on teaching right into the evening. I seem to have the thoughts of someone quite old. Honestly, I've been feeling as if my strength and youth were running out of me drop by drop, day after day. Day after day, all these four years that I've been working at the school . . . I just have one longing and it seems to grow stronger and stronger . . .

IRINA. If only we could go back to Moscow! Sell the house, finish with our life here, and go back to Moscow.

OLGA. Yes, Moscow! As soon as we possibly can.

[CHEBUTYKIN *and* TUZENBAKH *laugh*]

IRINA. I suppose Andrey will soon get a professorship. He isn't likely to go on living here. The only problem is our poor Masha.

OLGA. Masha can come and stay the whole summer with us every year in Moscow.

MASHA [*whistles a tune under her breath*].

IRINA. Everything will settle itself, with God's help. [*looks through the window*] What lovely weather it is today! Really, I don't know why there's such joy in my heart. I remembered this morning that it was my Saint's day, and suddenly I felt so happy, and I thought of the time when we were children, and Mother was still alive. And then such wonderful thoughts came to me, such wonderful stirring thoughts!

OLGA. You're so lovely today, you really do look most attractive. Masha looks pretty today, too. Andrey could be good-looking, but he's grown so stout. It doesn't suit him. As for me, I've just aged and grown a lot thinner. I suppose it's through getting so irritated with the girls at school. But today I'm at home, I'm free, and my headache's gone, and I feel much younger than I did yesterday. I'm only twenty-eight, after all . . . I suppose everything that God wills must be right and good, but I can't help thinking sometimes that if I'd got married and stayed at home, it would have been a better thing for me. [*a pause*] I would have been very fond of my husband.

TUZENBAKH [*to* SOLYONY]. Really, you talk such a lot of nonsense, I'm tired of listening to you. [*comes into the drawing-room*] I forgot to tell you: Vershinin, our new battery commander, is going to call on you today. [*sits down by the piano*]

OLGA. I'm very glad to hear it.

IRINA. Is he old?

TUZENBAKH. No, not particularly. Forty, forty-five at the most. [*plays quietly*] He seems a nice fellow. Certainly not a fool. His only weakness is that he talks too much.

IRINA. Is he interesting?

TUZENBAKH. He's all right, only he's got a wife, a mother-in-law and two little girls. What's more, she's his second wife. He calls on everybody and tells them that he's got a wife and two little girls. He'll tell you about it, too, I'm sure of that. His wife seems to be a bit soft in the head. She wears a long plait like a girl, she is always philosophising and talking in high-flown language, and then she often tries to commit suicide, apparently just to annoy her husband. I would have run away from a wife like that years ago, but he puts up with it, and just grumbles about it.

SOLYONY [*enters the drawing-room with* CHEBUTYKIN]. Now I can only lift sixty pounds with one hand, but with two I can lift two hundred pounds, or even two hundred and forty. So I conclude from that that two men are not just twice as strong as one, but three times as strong, if not more.

CHEBUTYKIN [*reads the paper as he comes in*]. Here's a recipe for hair that falls out . . . two ounces of naphthaline, half a bottle of methylated spirit . . . dissolve and apply once a day . . . [*writes it down in a notebook*] Must make a note of it. [to SOLYONY] Well, as I was trying to explain to you, you cork the bottle and pass a glass tube through the cork. Then you take a pinch of ordinary powdered alum, and . . .

IRINA. Ivan Romanich, dear Ivan Romanich!

CHEBUTYKIN. What is it, my child, what is it?

IRINA. Tell me, why is it I'm so happy today? Just as if I were sailing along in a boat with big white sails, and above me the wide, blue sky, and in the sky great white birds floating around.

CHEBUTYKIN [*kisses both her hands, tenderly*]. My little white bird!

IRINA. You know, when I woke up this morning, and after I'd got up and washed, I suddenly felt as if everything in the world had become clear to me, and I knew the way I ought to live. I know it all now, my dear Ivan Romanich. Man must work by the sweat of his brow whatever his class, and that should make up the whole meaning and purpose of his life and happiness and contentment. Oh, how good it must be to be a workman, getting up with the sun and breaking stones by the roadside – or a shepherd – or a schoolmaster teaching the children – or an engine-driver on the railway. Good heavens! It's better to be a mere ox or horse, and work, than the sort of young woman who wakes up at twelve, and drinks her coffee in bed, and then takes two hours dressing . . . How dreadful! You know how you long for a cool drink in hot weather? Well, that's the way I long for work. And if I don't get up early from now on and really work, you can refuse to be friends with me any more, Ivan Romanich.

CHEBUTYKIN [*tenderly*]. So I will, so I will . . .

OLGA. Father taught us to get up at seven o'clock and so Irina always wakes up at seven – but then she stays in bed till at least nine, thinking about something or other. And with such a serious expression on her face, too! [*laughs*]

IRINA. You think it's strange when I look serious because you always think of me as a little girl. I'm twenty, you know!

TUZENBAKH. All this longing for work . . . Heavens! how well I can understand it! I've never done a stroke of work in my life. I was born in Petersburg, an unfriendly, idle city – born into a family where work and worries were simply unknown. I remember a valet pulling off my boots for me when I came home from the cadet school . . . I grumbled at the way he did it, and my mother looked on in admiration. She was quite surprised when other people looked at me in any other way. I was so carefully protected from work! But I doubt whether they succeeded in protecting me for good and all – yes, I doubt it very much! The time's come: there's a terrific thunder-cloud advancing upon us, a mighty storm is coming to freshen us up! Yes, it's coming all right, it's quite near already, and it's going to blow away all this idleness and indifference, and prejudice against work, this rot of boredom that our society is suffering from. I'm going to work, and in twenty-five or thirty years' time every man and woman will be working. Every one of us!

CHEBUTYKIN. I'm not going to work.

TUZENBAKH. You don't count.

SOLYONY. In twenty-five years' time you won't be alive, thank goodness. In a couple of years you'll die from a stroke – or I'll lose my temper with you and put a bullet in your head, my good fellow. [*takes a scent bottle from his pocket and sprinkles the scent over his chest and hands*]

CHEBUTYKIN [*laughs*]. It's quite true that I never have done any work. Not a stroke since I left the university. I haven't even read a book, only newspapers. [*Takes another newspaper out of his pocket*] For instance, here . . . I know from the paper that there was a person called Dobrolyubov, but what he wrote about I've not the faintest idea . . . God alone knows . . .

[*someone knocks on the floor from downstairs*]

There! They're calling me to come down: there's someone come to see me. I'll be back in a moment . . . [*goes out hurriedly, stroking his beard*]

IRINA. He's up to one of his little games.

TUZENBAKH. Yes. He looked very solemn as he left. He's obviously going to give you a present.

IRINA. I do dislike that sort of thing . . .

OLGA. Yes, isn't it dreadful? He's always doing something silly.

MASHA. 'A green oak grows by a curving shore, And round that oak hangs a golden chain' . . . [*gets up as she sings under her breath*]

OLGA. You're sad today, Masha.

[MASHA *puts on her hat, singing*]

Where are you going?

MASHA. Home.

IRINA. What a strange thing to do.

TUZENBAKH. What! Going away from your sister's party?

MASHA. What does it matter? I'll be back this evening. Goodbye, my darling. [*kisses* IRINA] And once again – I wish you all the happiness in the world. In the old days when Father was alive we used to have thirty or forty officers at our parties. What gay parties we had! And today – what have we got today? A man and a half, and the place is as quiet as a tomb. I'm going home. I'm depressed today, I'm sad, so don't listen to me. [*laughs through her tears*] We'll have a talk later, but goodbye for now, my dear. I'll go somewhere or other . . .

IRINA [*displeased*]. Really, you are a . . .

OLGA [*tearfully*]. I understand you, Masha.

SOLYONY. If a man starts philosophising, you call that philosophy, or possibly just sophistry, but if a woman or a couple of women start philosophising you call that . . . what would you call it, now? Ask me another!

MASHA. What are you talking about? You are a disconcerting person!

SOLYONY. Nothing.

      'He had no time to say "Oh, oh!"
      Before that bear had struck him low' . . .

            [*a pause*]

MASHA [*to* OLGA, *crossly*]. Do stop snivelling!

Enter ANFISA *and* FERAPONT, *the latter carrying a large cake.*

ANFISA. Come along, my dear, this way. Come in, your boots are quite clean. [*to* IRINA] A cake from Protopopov, at the Council Office.

IRINA. Thank you. Tell him I'm very grateful to him. [*takes the cake*]

FERAPONT. What's that?

IRINA [*louder*]. Tell him I sent my thanks.

OLGA. Nanny, will you give him a piece of cake? Go along, Ferapont, they'll give you some cake.

FERAPONT. What's that?

ANFISA. Come along with me, Ferapont Spiridonich, my dear. Come along. [*goes out with* FERAPONT]

MASHA. I don't like that Protopopov fellow, Mikhail Potapich, or Ivanich, or whatever it is. It's best not to invite him here.

IRINA. I haven't invited him.

MASHA. Thank goodness.

Enter CHEBUTYKIN, *followed by a soldier carrying a silver samovar.*
Murmurs of astonishment and displeasure.

OLGA [*covering her face with her hands*]. A samovar! But this is dreadful! [*goes through to the ballroom and stands by the table*]

IRINA. My dear Ivan Romanich, what are you thinking about?

TUZENBAKH [*laughs*]. Didn't I tell you?

MASHA. Ivan Romanich, you really ought to be ashamed of yourself!

CHEBUTYKIN. My dear, sweet girls, I've no-one in the world but you. You're dearer to me than anything in the world! I'm nearly sixty, I'm an old man, a lonely, utterly unimportant old man. The only thing that's worth anything in me is my love for you, and if it weren't for you, really I would have been dead long ago. [*to* IRINA] My dear, my sweet little girl, haven't I known you since the very day you were born? Didn't I carry you about in my arms? . . . didn't I love your dear mother?

IRINA. But why do you get such expensive presents?

CHEBUTYKIN [*tearfully and crossly*]. Expensive presents! . . . Get along with you! [*to the orderly*] Put the samovar over there. [*mimics* IRINA] Expensive presents!

[*the orderly takes the samovar to the ballroom*]

ANFISA [*crosses the drawing-room*]. My dears, there's a strange colonel just arrived. He's taken off his coat and he's coming up now. Irinushka, do be nice and polite to him, won't you? [*in the doorway*] And it's high time we had lunch, too . . . Oh, dear! [*goes out*]

TUZENBAKH. It's Vershinin, I suppose.

Enter VERSHININ.

TUZENBAKH. Lieutenant-Colonel Vershinin!

VERSHININ [*to* MASHA *and* IRINA]. Allow me to introduce myself – Lieutenant-Colonel Vershinin. I'm so glad, so very glad to be here at last. How you've changed! Dear, dear, how you've changed!

IRINA. Please, do sit down. We're very pleased to see you, I'm sure.

VERSHININ [*gaily*]. I'm so glad to see you, so glad! But there were three of you, weren't there? – three sisters. I remember there were three little girls. I don't remember their faces, but I knew your father, Colonel Prozorov, and I remember he had three

little girls. Oh, yes, I saw them myself. I remember them quite
well. How time flies! Dear, dear, how it flies!

TUZENBAKH. Alexandr Ignatyevich comes from Moscow.

IRINA. From Moscow? You come from Moscow?

VERSHININ. Yes, from Moscow. Your father was a battery commander there, and I was an officer in the same brigade. [to
MASHA] I seem to remember your face a little.

MASHA. I don't remember you at all.

IRINA. Olya, Olya! [calls towards the ballroom] Olya, do come!

OLGA *enters from the ballroom.*

It seems that Lieutenant-Colonel Vershinin comes from Moscow.

VERSHININ. You must be Olga Sergeyevna, the eldest. And you are
Marya . . . And you are Irina, the youngest . . .

OLGA. You come from Moscow?

VERSHININ. Yes. I studied in Moscow and entered the service
there. I stayed there quite a long time, but then I was put in
charge of a battery here – so I moved out here, you see. I don't
really remember you, you know, I only remember that there
were three sisters. I remember your father, though, I remember
him very well. All I need to do is to close my eyes and I can see
him standing there as if he were alive. I used to visit you in
Moscow.

OLGA. I thought I remembered everybody, and yet . . .

VERSHININ. My Christian names are Alexandr Ignatyevich.

IRINA. Alexandr Ignatyevich, and you come from Moscow! Well,
what a surprise!

OLGA. We're going to live there, you know.

IRINA. We hope to be there by the autumn. It's our home town,
we were born there . . . In Staraya Basmannaya Street.

[*both laugh happily*]

MASHA. Fancy meeting a fellow townsman so unexpectedly! [*eagerly*]
I remember now. Do you remember, Olga, there was someone
they used to call 'the lovesick Major'? You were a Lieutenant
then, weren't you, and you were in love with someone or other,
and everyone used to tease you about it. They called you
'Major' for some reason or other.

VERSHININ [*laughs*]. That's it, that's it . . . 'The lovesick Major',
that's what they called me.

MASHA. In those days you only had a moustache . . . Oh, dear, how much older you look! [*tearfully*] How much older!

VERSHININ. Yes, I was still a young man in the days when they called me 'the lovesick Major'. I was in love then. It's different now.

OLGA. But you haven't got a single grey hair! You've aged, yes, but you're certainly not an old man.

VERSHININ. Nevertheless, I'm turned forty-two. Is it long since you left Moscow?

IRINA. Eleven years. Now what are you crying for, Masha, you funny girl? . . . [*tearfully*] You'll make me cry, too.

MASHA. I'm not crying. What was the street you lived in?

VERSHININ. In the Staraya Basmannaya.

OLGA. We did, too.

VERSHININ. At one time I lived in the Nemyetzkaya Street. I used to walk from there to the Krasniy Barracks, and I remember there was such a gloomy bridge I had to cross. I used to hear the noise of the water rushing under it. I remember how lonely and sad I felt there. [*a pause*] But what a magnificently wide river you have here! It's a marvellous river!

OLGA. Yes, but this is a cold place. It's cold here, and there are too many mosquitoes.

VERSHININ. Really? I should have said you had a really good healthy climate here, a real Russian climate. Forest, river . . . birch-trees, too. The dear, unpretentious birch-trees – I love them more than any of the other trees. It's nice living here. But there's one rather strange thing, the station is fifteen miles from the town. And no-one knows why.

SOLYONY. I know why it is.

[*everyone looks at him*]

Because if the station were nearer, it wouldn't be so far away, and as it is so far away, it can't be nearer.

[*an awkward silence*]

TUZENBAKH. You like your little joke, Vasiliy Vasiliyich.

OLGA. I'm sure I remember you now. I know I do.

VERSHININ. I knew your mother.

CHEBUTYKIN. She was a good woman, God bless her memory!

IRINA. Mamma was buried in Moscow.

OLGA. At the convent of Novo-Devichye.

MASHA. You know, I'm even beginning to forget what she looked like. I suppose people will lose all memory of us in just the same way. We'll be forgotten.

VERSHININ. Yes, we shall all be forgotten. Such is our fate, and we can't do anything about it. And all the things that seem serious, important and full of meaning to us now will be forgotten one day – or anyway they won't seem important any more.

[a pause]

It's strange to think that we're utterly unable to tell what will be regarded as great and important in the future and what will be thought of as just paltry and ridiculous. Didn't the great discoveries of Copernicus – or of Columbus, if you like – appear useless and unimportant to begin with? – whereas some rubbish, written up by an eccentric fool, was regarded as a revelation of great truth? It may well be that in time to come the life we live today will seem strange and uncomfortable and stupid and not too clean, either, and perhaps even wicked . . .

TUZENBAKH. Who can tell? It's just as possible that future generations will think that we lived our lives on a very high plane and remember us with respect. After all, we no longer have tortures and public executions and invasions, though there's still a great deal of suffering!

SOLYONY [*in a high-pitched voice as if calling to chickens*]. Cluck, cluck, cluck! There's nothing our good Baron loves as much as a nice bit of philosophising.

TUZENBAKH. Vasiliy Vasiliyich, will you kindly leave me alone? [*moves to another chair*] It's becoming tiresome.

SOLYONY [*as before*]. Cluck, cluck, cluck! . . .

TUZENBAKH [*to* VERSHININ]. The suffering that we see around us – and there's so much of it – itself proves that our society has at least achieved a level of morality which is higher . . .

VERSHININ. Yes, yes, of course.

CHEBUTYKIN. You said just now, Baron, that our age will be called great; but people are small all the same . . . [*gets up*] Look how small I am.

[a violin is played off-stage]

MASHA. That's Andrey playing the violin; he's our brother, you know.

IRINA. We've got quite a clever brother . . . We're expecting him to be a professor. Papa was a military man, but Andrey chose an academic career.

OLGA. We've been teasing him today. We think he's in love, just a little.

IRINA. With a girl who lives down here. She'll be calling in today, most likely.

MASHA. The way she dresses herself is awful! It's not that her clothes are just ugly and old-fashioned, they're simply pathetic. She'll put on some weird-looking, bright yellow skirt with a crude sort of fringe affair, and then a red blouse to go with it. And her cheeks look as though they've been scrubbed, they're so shiny! Andrey's not in love with her – I can't believe it; after all, he has got some taste. I think he's just playing the fool, just to annoy us. I heard yesterday that she's going to get married to Protopopov, the chairman of the local council. I thought it was an excellent idea. [calls through the side door] Andrey, come here, will you? Just for a moment, dear.

Enter ANDREY.

OLGA. This is my brother, Andrey Sergeyevich.

VERSHININ. Vershinin.

ANDREY. Prozorov. [wipes the perspiration from his face] I believe you've been appointed battery commander here?

OLGA. What do you think, dear? Alexandr Ignatyevich comes from Moscow.

ANDREY. Do you, really? Congratulations! You'll get no peace from my sisters now.

VERSHININ. I'm afraid your sisters must be getting tired of me already.

IRINA. Just look, Andrey gave me this little picture frame today. [shows him the frame] He made it himself.

VERSHININ [looks at the frame, not knowing what to say]. Yes, it's . . . it's very nice indeed . . .

IRINA. Do you see that little frame over the piano? He made that one, too.

[ANDREY *waves his hand impatiently and walks off*]

OLGA. He's awfully clever, and he plays the violin, and he makes all sorts of things, too. In fact, he's very gifted all round. Andrey, please, don't go. He's got such a bad habit – always going off like this. Come here!

[MASHA *and* IRINA *take him by the arms and lead him back, laughing*]

MASHA. Now just you come here!

ANDREY. Do leave me alone, please do!

MASHA. You are a silly! They used to call Alexandr Ignatyevich 'the lovesick Major', and he didn't get annoyed.

VERSHININ. Not in the least.

MASHA. I feel like calling you a 'lovesick fiddler'.

IRINA. Or a 'lovesick professor'.

OLGA. He's fallen in love! Our Andryusha's in love!

IRINA [*clapping her hands*]. Three cheers for Andryusha! Andryusha's in love!

CHEBUTYKIN [*comes up behind* ANDREY *and puts his arms round his waist*]. 'Nature created us for love alone.' . . . [*laughs loudly, still holding his paper in his hand*]

ANDREY. That's enough of it, that's enough . . . [*wipes his face*] I couldn't get to sleep all night, and I'm not feeling too grand just now. I read till four o'clock, and then I went to bed, but nothing happened. I kept thinking about one thing and another . . . and it gets light so early; the sun just pours into my room. I'd like to translate a book from the English while I'm here during the summer.

VERSHININ. You read English, then?

ANDREY. Yes. My father – God bless his memory – used to simply wear us out with learning. It sounds silly, I know, but I must confess that since he died I've begun to grow stout, as if I'd been physically relieved of the strain. I've grown quite stout in a year. Yes, thanks to Father, my sisters and I know French and German and English, and Irina here knows Italian, too. But what an effort it all cost us!

MASHA. Knowing three languages in a town like this is an unnecessary luxury. In fact, not even a luxury, but just a sort of useless encumbrance . . . it's rather like having a sixth finger on your hand. We know a lot of stuff that's just useless.

VERSHININ. Really! [*laughs*] You know a lot of stuff that's useless! It seems to me that there's no place on earth, however dull and depressing it may be, where intelligence and education can be useless. Let us suppose that among the hundred thousand people

in this town, all of them, no doubt, very backward and un-
cultured, there are just three people like yourselves. Obviously,
you can't hope to triumph over all the mass of ignorance around
you; as your life goes by, you'll have to keep giving in little by
little until you get lost in the crowd, in the hundred thousand.
Life will swallow you up, but you'll not quite disappear, you'll
make some impression on it. After you've gone, perhaps six
more people like you will turn up, then twelve, and so on, until
in the end most people will have become like you. So in two or
three hundred years life on this old earth of ours will have
become marvellously beautiful. Man longs for a life like that, and
if it isn't here yet, he must imagine it, wait for it, dream about it,
prepare for it, he must know and see more than his father and his
grandfather did. [*laughs*] And you're complaining because you
know a lot of stuff that's useless.

MASHA [*takes off her hat*]. I'll be staying to lunch.

IRINA [*with a sigh*]. Really, someone should have written all that
down.

[ANDREY *has left the room, unnoticed*]

TUZENBAKH. You say that in time to come life will be marvellously
beautiful. That's probably true. But in order to share in it now,
at a distance so to speak, we must prepare for it and work for it.

VERSHININ [*gets up*]. Yes . . . What a lot of flowers you've got here!
[*looks round*] And what a marvellous house! I do envy you! All
my life I seem to have been pigging it in small flats, with two
chairs and a sofa and a stove which always smokes. It's the
flowers that I've missed in my life, flowers like these! . . . [*rubs his
hands*] Oh, well, never mind!

TUZENBAKH. Yes, we must work. I suppose you're thinking I'm a
sentimental German. But I assure you I'm not – I'm Russian. I
don't speak a word of German. My father was brought up in the
Greek Orthodox faith. [*a pause*]

VERSHININ [*walks up and down the room*]. You know, I often wonder
what it would be like if you could start your life over again –
deliberately, I mean, consciously . . . Suppose you could put
aside the life you'd lived already, as though it was just a sort
of rough draft, and then start another one like a fair copy. If
that happened, I think the thing you'd want most of all would
be not to repeat yourself. You'd try at least to create a new

environment for yourself, a flat like this one, for instance, with some flowers and plenty of light . . . I have a wife, you know, and two little girls; and my wife's not very well, and all that . . . Well, if I had to start my life all over again, I wouldn't marry . . . No, no!

Enter KULYGIN, *in the uniform of a teacher.*

KULYGIN [*approaches* IRINA]. Congratulations, dear sister – from the bottom of my heart, congratulations on your Saint's day. I wish you good health and everything a girl of your age ought to have! And allow me to present you with this little book . . . [*hands her a book*] It's the history of our school covering the whole fifty years of its existence. I wrote it myself. Quite a trifle, of course – I wrote it in my spare time when I had nothing better to do – but I hope you'll read it nevertheless. Good morning to you all! [*to* VERSHININ] Allow me to introduce myself. Kulygin's the name; I'm a master at the secondary school here. And a town councillor. [*to* IRINA] You'll find a list in the book of all the pupils who have completed their studies at our school during the last fifty years. *Feci quod potui, faciant meliora potentes.* [*kisses* MASHA]

IRINA. But you gave me this book last Easter!

KULYGIN [*laughs*]. Did I really? In that case, give it me back – or no, better give it to the Colonel. Please do take it, Colonel. Maybe you'll read it some time when you've nothing better to do.

VERSHININ. Thank you very much. [*prepares to leave*] I'm so very glad to have made your acquaintance . . .

OLGA. You aren't going, are you? . . . Really, you mustn't.

IRINA. But you'll stay and have lunch with us! Please do.

OLGA. Please do.

VERSHININ [*bows*]. I see I've intruded on your Saint's day party. I didn't know. Forgive me for not offering you my congratulations. [*goes into the ballroom with* OLGA]

KULYGIN. Today is Sunday, my friends, a day of rest; let us rest and enjoy it, each according to his age and position in life! We shall have to roll up the carpets and put them away till the winter . . . We must remember to put some naphthaline on them, or Persian powder . . . The Romans enjoyed good health because they knew how to work and how to rest. They had *mens sana in corpore sano*. Their life had a definite shape, a form . . . The director of the school says that the most important thing about life is form . . . A thing that loses its form is finished – that's just as true of our ordinary, everyday lives. [*takes* MASHA *by the waist and laughs*] Masha loves me. My wife loves me. Yes, and the curtains will have to be put away with the carpets, too . . . I'm cheerful today, I'm in quite excellent spirits . . . Masha, we're invited to the director's at four o'clock today. A country walk has been arranged for the teachers and their families.

MASHA. I'm not going.

KULYGIN [*distressed*]. Masha, darling, why not?

MASHA. I'll tell you later . . . [*crossly*] All right, I'll come, only leave me alone now . . . [*walks off*]

KULYGIN. And after the walk we shall all spend the evening at the director's house. In spite of weak health, that man is certainly sparing no pains to be sociable. A first-rate, thoroughly enlightened man! A most excellent person! After the conference yesterday he said to me: 'I'm tired, Fyodor Ilyich. I'm tired!' [*looks at the clock, then at his watch*] Your clock is seven minutes fast. Yes, 'I'm tired,' he said.

[*the sound of the violin is heard off stage*]

OLGA. Will you all come and sit down, please! Lunch is ready. There's a pie.

KULYGIN. Ah, Olga, my dear girl! Last night I worked up to eleven o'clock, and I felt tired, but today I'm quite happy. [*goes to the table in the ballroom*] My dear Olga!

CHEBUTYKIN [*puts the newspaper in his pocket and combs his beard*]. A pie? Excellent!

MASHA [*sternly to* CHEBUTYKIN]. Remember, you mustn't take anything to drink today. Do you hear? It's bad for you.

CHEBUTYKIN. Never mind. I've got over that weakness long ago! I haven't done any heavy drinking for two years. [*impatiently*] Anyway, my dear, what does it matter?

MASHA. All the same, don't you dare to drink anything. Mind you don't now! [*crossly, but taking care that her husband does not hear*] So now I've got to spend another of these damnably boring evenings at the director's!

TUZENBAKH. I wouldn't go if I were you, and that's that.

CHEBUTYKIN. Don't you go, my dear.

MASHA. Don't go, indeed! Oh, what a damnable life! It's intolerable . . . [goes into the ballroom]

CHEBUTYKIN [follows her]. Well, well! . . .

SOLYONY [as he passes TUZENBAKH on the way to the ballroom]. Cluck, cluck, cluck!

TUZENBAKH. Do stop it, Vasiliy Vasiliyich. I've really had enough of it . . .

SOLYONY. Cluck, cluck, cluck! . . .

KULYGIN [gaily]. Your health, Colonel! I'm a schoolmaster . . . and I'm quite one of the family here, as it were. I'm Masha's husband. She's got a sweet nature, such a very sweet nature!

VERSHININ. I think I'll have a little of this dark vodka. [drinks] Your health! [to OLGA] I do feel so happy with you people!

[only IRINA and TUZENBAKH remain in the drawing-room]

IRINA. Masha's a bit out of humour today. You know, she got married when she was eighteen, and then her husband seemed the cleverest man in the world to her. It's different now. He's the kindest of men, but not the cleverest.

OLGA [impatiently]. Andrey, will you please come?

ANDREY [off stage]. Just coming.

ANDREY enters and goes to the table.

TUZENBAKH. What are you thinking about?

IRINA. Oh, nothing special. You know, I don't like this man Solyony, I'm quite afraid of him. Whenever he opens his mouth he says something silly.

TUZENBAKH. He's a strange fellow. I'm sorry for him, even though he irritates me. In fact, I feel more sorry for him than irritated. I think he's shy. When he's alone with me, he can be quite sensible and friendly, but in company he's offensive and bullying. Don't go over there just yet, let them get settled down at the table. Let me stay beside you for a bit. Tell me what you're thinking about. [a pause] You're twenty . . . and I'm not thirty yet myself. What years and years we still have ahead of us, a whole long succession of years, all full of my love for you! . . .

IRINA. Don't talk to me about love, Nikolay Lvovich.

TUZENBAKH [not listening]. Oh, I long so passionately for life, I long to work and strive so much, and all this longing is somehow mingled with my love for you, Irina. And just because you happen to be beautiful, life appears beautiful to me! What are you thinking about?

IRINA. You say that life is beautiful. Maybe it is — but what if it only seems to be beautiful? Our lives, I mean the lives of us three sisters, haven't been beautiful up to now. The truth is that life has been stifling us, like weeds in a garden. I'm afraid I'm crying . . . So unnecessary . . . [*quickly dries her eyes and smiles*] We must work, work! The reason we feel depressed and take such a gloomy view of life is that we've never known what it is to make a real effort. We're the children of parents who despised work . . .

Enter NATALYA IVANOVNA. *She is wearing a pink dress
with a green belt.*

NATASHA. They've gone in to lunch already . . . I'm late . . . [*glances at herself in a mirror, adjusts her dress*] My hair seems to be all right . . . [*catches sight of* IRINA] My dear Irina Sergeyevna, congratulations! [*gives her a vigorous and prolonged kiss*] You've got such a lot of visitors . . . I feel quite shy . . . How do you do, Baron?

OLGA [*enters the drawing-room*]. Oh, there you are, Natalya Ivanovna! How are you, my dear?

[*they kiss each other*]

NATASHA. Congratulations! You've such a lot of people here, I feel dreadfully shy . . .

OLGA. It's all right, they're all old friends. [*alarmed, dropping her voice*] You've got a green belt on! My dear, that's surely a mistake!

NATASHA. Why, is it a bad omen, or what?

OLGA. No, but it just doesn't go with your dress . . . it looks so strange . . .

NATASHA [*tearfully*]. Really? But it isn't really green, you know, it's a sort of dull colour . . . [*follows* OLGA *to the ballroom*]

[*all are now seated at the table; the drawing-room is empty*]

KULYGIN. Irina, you know, I do wish you'd find yourself a good husband. In my view it's high time you got married.

CHEBUTYKIN. You ought to get yourself a nice little husband, too, Natalya Ivanovna.

KULYGIN. Natalya Ivanovna already has a husband in view.

MASHA [*strikes her plate with her fork*]. A glass of wine for me, please! Three cheers for our jolly old life! We keep our end up, we do!

KULYGIN. Masha, you won't get more than five out of ten for good conduct!

VERSHININ. I say, this liqueur's very nice. What is it made of?

SOLYONY. Black beetles!

IRINA. Ugh! ugh! How disgusting!

OLGA. We're having roast turkey for dinner tonight, and then apple tart. Thank goodness, I'll be here all day today . . . this evening, too. You must all come this evening.

VERSHININ. May I come in the evening, too?

IRINA. Yes, please do.

NATASHA. They don't stand on ceremony here.

CHEBUTYKIN. 'Nature created us for love alone.' . . . [*laughs*]

ANDREY [*crossly*]. Will you stop it, please? Aren't you tired of it yet?

FEDOTIK *and* RODÉ *come in with a large basket of flowers.*

FEDOTIK. Just look here, they're having lunch already!

RODÉ [*in a loud voice*]. Having their lunch? So they are, they're having lunch already.

FEDOTIK. Wait half a minute. [*takes a snapshot*] One! Just a minute more! . . . [*takes another snapshot*] Two! all over now.

[*they pick up the basket and go into the ballroom where
they are greeted uproariously*]

RODÉ [*loudly*]. Congratulations, Irina Sergeyevna! I wish you all the best, everything you'd wish for yourself! Gorgeous weather today, absolutely marvellous. I've been out walking the whole morning with the boys. You do know that I teach gym at the high school, don't you? . . .

FEDOTIK. You may move now, Irina Sergeyevna, that is, if you want to. [*takes a snapshot*] You do look attractive today [*takes a top out of his pocket*] By the way, look at this top. It's got a wonderful hum.

IRINA. What a sweet little thing!

MASHA. 'A green oak grows by a curving shore, And round that oak hangs a golden chain.' . . . A green chain around that oak . . . [*peevishly*] Why do I keep on saying that? Those lines have been worrying me all day long!

KULYGIN. Do you know, we're thirteen at table?

RODÉ [*loudly*]. You don't really believe in these old superstitions, do you? [*laughter*]

KULYGIN. When thirteen people sit down to table, it means that some of them are in love. Is it you, by any chance, Ivan Romanich?

CHEBUTYKIN. Oh, I'm just an old sinner . . . But what I can't make out is why Natalya Ivanovna looks so embarrassed.

[*loud laughter;* NATASHA *runs out into the drawing-room,* ANDREY *following her*]

ANDREY. Please, Natasha, don't take any notice of them! Stop . . . wait a moment . . . Please!

NATASHA. I feel so ashamed . . . I don't know what's the matter with me, and they're all laughing at me. It's awful of me to leave the table like that, but I couldn't help it . . . I just couldn't . . . [*covers her face with her hands*]

ANDREY. My dear girl, please, please don't get upset. Honestly, they don't mean any harm, they're just teasing. My dear, sweet girl, they're really good-natured folks, they all are, and they're fond of us both. Come over to the window, they can't see us there . . . [*looks round*]

NATASHA. You see, I'm not used to being with a lot of people.

ANDREY. Oh, how young you are, Natasha, how wonderfully, beautifully young! My dear, sweet girl, don't get so upset! Do believe me, believe me . . . I'm so happy, so full of love, of joy . . . No, they can't see us here! They can't see us! How did I come to love you, when was it? . . . I don't understand anything. My precious, my sweet, my innocent girl, please – I want you to marry me! I love you, I love you as I've never loved anybody . . . [*kisses her*]

Enter two officers who, seeing NATASHA *and* ANDREY *kissing, stand and stare in amazement.*

CURTAIN

ACT TWO

The scene is the same as in Act One. It is eight o'clock in the evening. The faint sound of an accordion is heard coming from the street.

The stage is unlit. Enter NATALYA IVANOVNA *in a dressing-gown, carrying a candle. She crosses the stage and stops by the door leading to* ANDREY'S *room.*

NATASHA. What are you doing, Andryusha? Reading? It's all right, I only wanted to know . . . [*goes to another door, opens it, looks inside and shuts it again*] No-one's left a light anywhere . . .

ANDREY [*enters with a book in his hand*]. What is it, Natasha?

NATASHA. I was just going round to see if anyone had left a light anywhere. It's carnival week, and the servants are so excited about it . . . anything might happen! You've got to watch them. Last night about twelve o'clock I happened to go into the dining-room, and — would you believe it? — there was a candle alight on the table. I've not found out who lit it. [*puts the candle down*] What time is it?

ANDREY [*glances at his watch*]. Quarter past eight.

NATASHA. And Olga and Irina still out. They aren't back from work yet, poor things! Olga's still at some teachers' conference, and Irina's at the post office. [*sighs*] This morning I said to Irina: 'Do take care of yourself, my dear.' But she won't listen. Did you say it was a quarter past eight? I'm afraid Bobik is not at all well. Why does he get so cold? Yesterday he had a temperature, but today he feels quite cold when you touch him . . . I'm so afraid!

ANDREY. It's all right, Natasha. The boy's well enough.

NATASHA. Still, I think he ought to have a special diet. I'm so anxious about him. By the way, they tell me that some carnival party's supposed to be coming here soon after nine. I'd rather they didn't come, Andryusha.

ANDREY. Well, I really don't know what I can do. They've been asked to come.

NATASHA. This morning the dear little fellow woke up and looked at me, and then suddenly he smiled. He recognised me, you see. 'Good morning, Bobik,' I said, 'good morning, darling precious!' And then he laughed. Babies understand everything, you know, they understand us perfectly well. Anyway, Andryusha, I'll tell the servants not to let that carnival party in.

ANDREY [*irresolutely*]. Well . . . it's really for my sisters to decide, isn't it? It's their house, after all.

NATASHA. Yes, it's their house as well. I'll tell them, too . . . They're so kind . . . [*walks off*] I've ordered sour milk for supper. The doctor says you ought to eat nothing but sour milk, or you'll never get any thinner. [*stops*] Bobik feels so cold. I'm afraid his room is too cold for him. He ought to move into a warmer room, at least until the warm weather comes. Irina's room, for instance – that's just a perfect room for a baby: it's dry, and it gets the sun all day long. We must tell her: perhaps she'd share Olga's room for a bit . . . In any case, she's never at home during the day, she only sleeps there . . . [*a pause*] Andryusha, why don't you say anything?

ANDREY. I was just day-dreaming . . . There's nothing to say, anyway . . .

NATASHA. Well . . . What was it I was going to tell you? Oh, yes! Ferapont from the Council Office wants to see you about something.

ANDREY [*yawns*]. Tell him to come up.

NATASHA *goes out.* ANDREY, *bending over the candle which she has left behind, begins to read his book. Enter* FERAPONT *in an old shabby overcoat, his collar turned up, his ears muffled in a scarf.*

ANDREY. Hullo, old chap! What did you want to see me about?

FERAPONT. The chairman's sent you the register and a letter or something. Here they are. [*hands him the book and the letter*]

ANDREY. Thanks. That's all right. Incidentally, why have you come so late? It's gone eight already.

FERAPONT. What's that?

ANDREY [*raising his voice*]. I said, why have you come so late? It's gone eight already.

FERAPONT. That's right. It was still daylight when I came first, but they wouldn't let me see you. The master's engaged, they said. Well, if you're engaged, you're engaged, I'm not in a hurry. [*thinking that* ANDREY *has said something*] What's that?

ANDREY. Nothing. [*turns over the pages of the register*] Tomorrow's Friday, there's no meeting, but I'll go to the office just the same . . . do some work. I'm so bored at home! . . . [*a pause*] Yes, my dear old fellow, how things do change, what a fraud life is! So strange! Today I picked up this book, just out of boredom, because I hadn't anything to do. It's a copy of some lectures I attended at the University . . . Good Heavens! Just think – I'm secretary of the local council now, and Protopopov's chairman, and the most I can ever hope for is to become a member of the council myself! I – a member of the local council! I, who dream every night that I'm a professor in Moscow University, a famous academician, the pride of all Russia!

FERAPONT. I'm sorry, I can't tell you. I don't hear very well.

ANDREY. If you could hear properly I don't think I'd be talking to you like this. I must talk to someone, but my wife doesn't seem to understand me, and as for my sisters . . . I'm afraid of them for some reason or other, I'm afraid of them laughing at me and pulling my leg . . . I don't drink and I don't like going to pubs, but my word! how I'd enjoy an hour or so at Tyestov's, or the Great Moscow restaurant! Yes, my dear fellow, I would indeed!

FERAPONT. The other day at the office a contractor was telling me about some business men who were eating pancakes in Moscow. One of them ate forty pancakes and died. It was either forty or fifty, I can't remember exactly.

ANDREY. You can sit in some huge restaurant in Moscow without knowing anyone, and no-one knowing you; yet somehow you don't feel that you don't belong there . . . Whereas here you know everybody, and everybody knows you, and yet you don't feel you belong here, you feel you don't belong at all . . . You're lonely and you feel a stranger.

FERAPONT. What's that? [*a pause*] It was the same man that told me – of course, he may have been lying – he said that there's an enormous rope stretched right across Moscow.

ANDREY. Whatever for?

FERAPONT. I'm sorry, I can't tell you. That's what he said.

ANDREY. What nonsense! [*reads the book*] Have you ever been to Moscow?

FERAPONT [*after a pause*]. No. It wasn't God's wish. [*a pause*] Shall I go now?

ANDREY. Yes, you may go. Goodbye.

      [FERAPONT *goes out*]

Goodbye. [*reading*] Come in the morning to take some letters . . . You can go now. [*a pause*] He's gone.

      [*a bell rings*]

Yes, that's how it is . . . [*stretches and slowly goes to his room*]

 Singing is heard off stage; a nurse is putting a baby to sleep.
 Enter MASHA *and* VERSHININ. *While they talk together, a maid*
  lights a lamp and candles in the ballroom.

MASHA. I don't know. [*a pause*] I don't know. Habit's very important, of course. For instance, after Father died, for a long time we couldn't get accustomed to the idea that we hadn't any orderlies to wait on us. But, habit apart, I think it's quite right what I was saying. Perhaps it's different in other places, but in this town the military certainly do seem to be the nicest and most generous and best-mannered people.

VERSHININ. I'm thirsty. I could do with a nice glass of tea.

MASHA [*glances at her watch*]. They'll bring it in presently. You see, they married me off when I was eighteen. I was afraid of my husband because he was a schoolmaster, and I had only just left school myself. He seemed terribly learned then, very clever and important. Now it's quite different, unfortunately.

VERSHININ. Yes . . . I see . . .

MASHA. I don't say anything against my husband – I'm used to him now – but there are such a lot of vulgar and unpleasant and offensive people among the other civilians. Vulgarity upsets me, it makes me feel insulted, I actually suffer when I meet someone who lacks refinement and gentle manners, and courtesy. When I'm with the other teachers, my husband's friends, I just suffer.

VERSHININ. Yes, of course. But I should have thought that in a town like this the civilians and the army people were equally uninteresting. There's nothing to choose between them. If you talk to any educated person here, civilian or military, he'll generally tell you that he's just worn out. It's either his wife, or his house, or his estate, or his horse, or something . . . We Russians are capable of such elevated thoughts – then why do we have such low ideals in practical life? Why is it, why?

MASHA. Why?

VERSHININ. Yes, why does his wife wear him out, why do his children wear him out? And what about him wearing out his wife and children?

MASHA. You're a bit low-spirited today, aren't you?

VERSHININ. Perhaps. I haven't had any dinner today. I've had nothing to eat since morning. One of my daughters is a bit off colour, and when the children are ill, I get so worried. I feel utterly conscience-stricken at having given them a mother like theirs. Oh, if only you could have seen her this morning! What a despicable woman! We started quarrelling at seven o'clock, and at nine I just walked out and slammed the door. [*a pause*] I never talk about these things in the ordinary way. It's a strange thing, but you're the only person I feel I dare complain to. [*kisses her hand*] Don't be angry with me. I've nobody, nobody but you . . . [*a pause*]

MASHA. What a noise the wind's making in the stove! Just before Father died the wind howled in the chimney just like that.

VERSHININ. Are you superstitious?

MASHA. Yes.

VERSHININ. How strange. [*kisses her hand*] You really are a wonderful creature, a marvellous creature! Wonderful, marvellous! It's quite dark here, but I can see your eyes shining.

MASHA [*moves to another chair*]. There's more light over here.

VERSHININ. I love you, I love you, I love you . . . I love your eyes, I love your movements . . . I dream about them. A wonderful, marvellous being!

MASHA [*laughing softly*]. When you talk to me like that, somehow I can't help laughing, although I'm afraid at the same time. Don't say it again, please. [*half-audibly*] Well, no . . . go on. I don't mind . . . [*covers her face with her hands*] I don't mind . . . Someone's coming . . . Let's talk about something else . . .

Enter IRINA *and* TUZENBAKH *through the ballroom.*

TUZENBAKH. I have a triple-barrelled name – Baron Tuzenbakh-Krone-Alschauer – but actually I'm a Russian. I was baptised in the Greek Orthodox faith, just like yourself. I haven't really got any German characteristics, except maybe the obstinate patient way I keep on pestering you. Look how I bring you home every evening.

IRINA. How tired I am!

TUZENBAKH. And I'll go on fetching you from the post office and bringing you home every evening for the next twenty years — unless you send me away . . . [*noticing* MASHA *and* VERSHININ, *with pleasure*] Oh, it's you! How are you?

IRINA. Well, here I am, home at last! [*to* MASHA] A woman came into the post office just before I left. She wanted to send a wire to her brother in Saratov to tell him her son had just died, but she couldn't remember the address. So we had to send the wire without an address, just to Saratov. She was crying and I was rude to her, for no reason at all. 'I've no time to waste,' I told her. So stupid of me. We're having the carnival crowd today, aren't we?

MASHA. Yes.

IRINA [*sits down*]. How nice it is to rest! I am tired!

TUZENBAKH [*smiling*]. When you come back from work, you look so young, so pathetic, somehow . . . [*a pause*]

IRINA. I'm tired. No, I don't like working at the post office, I don't like it at all.

MASHA. You've got thinner . . . [*whistles*] You look younger, too, and your face looks quite boyish.

TUZENBAKH. It's the way she does her hair.

IRINA. I must look for another job. This one doesn't suit me. It hasn't got what I always longed for and dreamed about. It's the sort of work you do without inspiration, without even thinking.

[*someone knocks at the floor from below*]

That's the Doctor knocking. [*to* TUZENBAKH] Will you answer him, dear? . . . I can't . . . I'm so tired.

TUZENBAKH [*knocks on the floor*].

IRINA. He'll be up in a moment. We must do something about all this. Andrey and the Doctor went to the club last night and lost at cards again. They say Andrey lost two hundred roubles.

MASHA [*with indifference*]. Well, what are we to do about it?

IRINA. He lost a fortnight ago, and he lost in December, too. I wish to goodness he'd lose everything we've got, and soon, too, and then perhaps we'd move out of this place. Good Heavens, I dream of Moscow every night. Sometimes I feel as if I were going mad. [*laughs*] We're going to Moscow in June. How many months are there till June? . . . February, March, April, May . . . nèarly half-a-year!

MASHA. We must take care that Natasha doesn't get to know about him losing at cards.

IRINA. I don't think she cares.

Enter CHEBUTYKIN. *He has been resting on his bed since dinner and has only just got up. He combs his beard, then sits down at the table and takes out a newspaper.*

MASHA. There he is. Has he paid his rent yet?

IRINA [*laughs*]. No. Not a penny for the last eight months. I suppose he's forgotten.

MASHA [*laughs*]. How solemn he looks sitting there!
[*they all laugh; a pause*]

IRINA. Why don't you say something, Alexandr Ignatyevich?

VERSHININ. I don't know. I'm just longing for some tea. I'd give my life for a glass of tea! I've had nothing to eat since morning . . .

CHEBUTYKIN. Irina Sergeyevna!

IRINA. What is it?

CHEBUTYKIN. Please come here. *Venez ici*!
[IRINA *goes over to him and sits down at the table*]
I can't do without you.
[IRINA *lays out the cards for a game of patience*]

VERSHININ. Well, if we can't have any tea, let's do a bit of philosophising, anyway.

TUZENBAKH. Yes, let's. What about?

VERSHININ. What about? Well . . . let's try to imagine what life will be like after we're dead, say in two or three hundred years.

TUZENBAKH. All right, then . . . After we're dead, people will fly about in balloons, the cut of their coats will be different, the sixth sense will be discovered, and possibly even developed and used, for all I know . . . But I believe life itself will remain the same; it will still be difficult and full of mystery and full of happiness. And in a thousand years' time people will still be sighing and complaining: 'How hard this business of living is!' –

and yet they'll still be scared of death and unwilling to die, just as
they are now.

VERSHININ [*after a moment's thought*]. Well, you know . . . how shall
I put it? I think everything in the world is bound to change
gradually – in fact, it's changing before our very eyes. In two or
three hundred years, or maybe in a thousand years – it doesn't
matter how long exactly – life will be different. It will be happy.
Of course, we shan't be able to enjoy that future life, but all the
same, what we're living for now is to create it, we work and . . .
yes, we suffer in order to create it. That's the goal of our life, and
you might say that's the only happiness we shall ever achieve.

MASHA [*laughs quietly*].

TUZENBAKH. Why are you laughing?

MASHA. I don't know. I've been laughing all day today.

VERSHININ [*to* TUZENBAKH]. I went to the same cadet school as you
did but I never went on to the Military Academy. I read a great
deal, of course, but I never know what books I ought to choose,
and probably I read a lot of stuff that's not worth anything. But
the longer I live the more I seem to long for knowledge. My
hair's going grey and I'm getting on in years, and yet how little I
know, how little! All the same, I think I do know one thing
which is not only true but also most important. I'm sure of it.
Oh, if only I could convince you that there's not going to be any
happiness for our own generation, that there mustn't be and
won't be . . . We've just got to work and work. All the happiness
is reserved for our descendants, our remote descendants. [*a pause*]
Anyway, if I'm not to be happy, then at least my children's
children will be.

FEDOTIK *and* RODÉ *enter the ballroom; they sit down and sing
quietly, one of them playing on a guitar.*

TUZENBAKH. So you won't even allow us to dream of happiness!
But what if I am happy?

VERSHININ. You're not.

TUZENBAKH [*flinging up his hands and laughing*]. We don't understand one another, that's obvious. How can I convince you?

MASHA [*laughs quietly*].

TUZENBAKH [*holds up a finger to her*]. Show a finger to her and she'll
laugh! [*to* VERSHININ] And life will be just the same as ever not

merely in a couple of hundred years' time, but in a million years. Life doesn't change, it always goes on the same; it follows its own laws, which don't concern us, which we can't discover anyway. Think of the birds that migrate in the autumn, the cranes, for instance: they just fly on and on. It doesn't matter what sort of thoughts they've got in their heads, great thoughts or little thoughts, they just fly on and on, not knowing where or why. And they'll go on flying no matter how many philosophers they happen to have flying with them. Let them philosophise as much as they like, as long as they go on flying.

MASHA. Isn't there some meaning?

TUZENBAKH. Meaning? . . . Look out there, it's snowing. What's the meaning of that? [*a pause*]

MASHA. I think a human being has got to have some faith, or at least he's got to seek faith. Otherwise his life will be empty, empty . . . How can you live and not know why the cranes fly, why children are born, why the stars shine in the sky! . . . You must either know why you live, or else . . . nothing matters . . . everything's just wild grass . . . [*a pause*]

VERSHININ. All the same, I'm sorry my youth's over.

MASHA. 'It's a bore to be alive in this world, friends,' that's what Gogol says.

TUZENBAKH. And I feel like saying: it's hopeless arguing with you, friends! I give you up.

CHEBUTYKIN [*reads out of the paper*]. Balzac's marriage took place at Berdichev.*

IRINA [*sings softly to herself*].

CHEBUTYKIN. Must write this down in my notebook. [*writes*] Balzac's marriage took place at Berdichev. [*reads on*]

IRINA [*playing patience, pensively*]. Balzac's marriage took place at Berdichev.

TUZENBAKH. Well, I've thrown in my hand. Did you know that I'd sent in my resignation, Marya Sergeyevna?

MASHA. Yes, I heard about it. I don't see anything good in it, either. I don't like civilians.

TUZENBAKH. Never mind. [*gets up*] What sort of a soldier do I make, anyway? I'm not even good-looking. Well, what does it

---

* A town in western Russia well known for its almost exclusively Jewish population.

matter? I'll work. I'd like to do such a hard day's work that when I came home in the evening I'd fall on my bed exhausted and go to sleep at once. [*goes to the ballroom*] I should think working men sleep well at nights!

FEDOTIK [*to* IRINA]. I've got you some coloured crayons at Pyzhikov's, in Moscow Street. And this little penknife, too . . .

IRINA. You still treat me as if I were a little girl. I wish you'd remember I'm grown up now. [*takes the crayons and the penknife, joyfully*] They're awfully nice!

FEDOTIK. Look, I bought a knife for myself, too. You see, it's got another blade here, and then another . . . this thing's for cleaning your ears, and these are nail-scissors, and this is for cleaning your nails. . . .

RODÉ [*in a loud voice*]. Doctor, how old are you?

CHEBUTYKIN. I? Thirty-two.

[*laughter*]

FEDOTIK. I'll show you another kind of patience. [*sets out the cards*]

The samovar is brought in, and ANFISA *attends to it. Shortly afterwards* NATASHA *comes in and begins to fuss around the table.* SOLYONY *enters, bows to the company and sits down at the table.*

VERSHININ. What a wind, though!

MASHA. Yes. I'm tired of winter. I've almost forgotten what summer is like.

IRINA [*playing patience*]. It's coming out. We'll get to Moscow!

FEDOTIK. No, it's not coming out. You see, the eight has to go on the two of spades. [*laughs*] That means you won't go to Moscow.

CHEBUTYKIN [*reads the paper*]. Tzitzikar. Smallpox is raging . . .

ANFISA [*goes up to* MASHA]. Masha, the tea's ready, dear. [*to* VERSHININ] Will you please come to the table, your Excellency? Forgive me, your name's slipped my memory . . .

MASHA. Bring it here, Nanny. I'm not coming over there.

IRINA. Nanny!

ANFISA. Comi-ing!

NATASHA [*to* SOLYONY]. You know, even tiny babies understand what we say perfectly well! 'Good morning, Bobik,' I said to him only today, 'Good morning, my precious!' – and then he looked at me in such a special sort of way. You may say it's only a mother's imagination, but it isn't, I do assure you. No, no! He really is an extraordinary child!

SOLYONY. If that child were mine, I'd cook him up in a frying pan and eat him. [*picks up his glass, goes into the drawing-room and sits down in a corner*]

NATASHA [*covers her face with her hands*]. What a rude, ill-mannered person!

MASHA. People who don't even notice whether it's summer or winter are lucky! I think I'd be indifferent to the weather if I were living in Moscow.

VERSHININ. I've just been reading the diary of some French cabinet minister — he wrote it in prison. He got sent to prison in connection with the Panama affair. He writes with such a passionate delight about the birds he can see through the prison window — the birds he never even noticed when he was a cabinet minister. Of course, now he's released he won't notice them any more . . . And in the same way, you won't notice Moscow once you live there again. We're not happy and we can't be happy: we only want happiness.

TUZENBAKH [*picks up a box from the table*]. I say, where are all the chocolates?

IRINA. Solyony's eaten them.

TUZENBAKH. All of them?

ANFISA [*serving* VERSHININ *with tea*]. Here's a letter for you, sir.

VERSHININ. For me? [*takes the letter*] From my daughter. [*reads it*] Yes, of course . . . Forgive me, Marya Sergeyevna, I'll just leave quietly. I won't have any tea. [*gets up, agitated*] Always the same thing. . . .

MASHA. What is it? Secret?

VERSHININ [*in a low voice*]. My wife's taken poison again. I must go. I'll get away without them seeing me. All this is so dreadfully unpleasant. [*kisses* MASHA's *hand*] My dear, good, sweet girl . . . I'll go out this way, quietly . . . [*goes out*]

ANFISA. Where's he off to? And I've just brought him some tea! What a queer fellow!

MASHA [*flaring up*]. Leave me alone! Why do you keep worrying me? Why don't you leave me in peace? [*goes to the table, cup in hand*] I'm sick and tired of you, silly old woman!

ANFISA. Why . . . I didn't mean to offend you, dear.

ANDREY [*off stage*]. Anfisa!

ANFISA [*mimics him*]. Anfisa! Sitting there in his den! . . . [*goes out*]

MASHA [*by the table in the ballroom, crossly*]. Do let me sit down somewhere! [*jumbles up the cards laid out on the table*] You take up the whole table with your cards! Why don't you get on with your tea?

IRINA. How bad-tempered you are, Mashka!

MASHA. Well, if I'm bad-tempered, don't talk to me, then. Don't touch me!

CHEBUTYKIN [*laughs*]. Don't touch her! . . . Take care you don't touch her!

MASHA. You may be sixty, but you're always gabbling some damn nonsense or other, just like a child. . . .

NATASHA [*sighs*]. My dear Masha, need you use such expressions? You know, with your good looks you'd be thought so charming, even by the best people — yes, I honestly mean it — if only you wouldn't use these expressions of yours! *Je vous prie, pardonnez moi, Marie, mais vous avez des manières un peu grossières.*

TUZENBAKH [*with suppressed laughter*]. Pass me . . . I say, will you please pass me . . . Is that cognac over there, or what? . . .

NATASHA. *Il paraît que mon Bobik déjà ne dort pas* . . . I think he's awake. He's not been too well today. I must go and see him . . . excuse me. [*goes out*]

IRINA. I say, where has Alexandr Ignatyevich gone to?

MASHA. He's gone home. His wife's done something queer again.

TUZENBAKH [*goes over to* SOLYONY *with a decanter of cognac*]. You always sit alone brooding over something or other — though what it's all about nobody knows. Well, let's make it up. Let's have a cognac together. [*they drink*] I suppose I'll have to play the piano all night tonight — a lot of rubbishy tunes, of course . . . Never mind!

SOLYONY. Why did you say 'let's make it up'? We haven't quarrelled.

TUZENBAKH. You always give me the feeling that there's something wrong between us. You're a strange character, no doubt about it.

SOLYONY [*recites*]. 'I am strange, but who's not so? Don't be angry, Aleko!'

TUZENBAKH. What's Aleko got to do with it? . . . [*a pause*]

SOLYONY. When I'm alone with somebody I'm all right, I'm just like other people. But in company, I get depressed and shy, and . . . I talk all sorts of nonsense. All the same, I'm a good deal more honest and well-intentioned than plenty of others. I can prove I am.

TUZENBAKH. You often make me angry because you keep on pestering me when we're in company – but all the same, I do like you for some reason . . . I'm going to get drunk tonight, whatever happens! Let's have another drink!

SOLYONY. Yes, let's. [*a pause*] I've never had anything against you personally, Baron. But my temperament's rather like Lermontov's. [*in a low voice*] I even look a little like Lermontov, I've been told . . . [*takes a scent bottle from his pocket and sprinkles some scent on his hands*]

TUZENBAKH. I have sent in my resignation! Finished! I've been considering it for five years, and now I've made up my mind at last. I'm going to work.

SOLYONY [*recites*]. 'Don't be angry, Aleko . . . Away, away with all your dreams!'

During the conversation ANDREY *enters quietly with a book in his hand and sits down by the candle.*

TUZENBAKH. I'm going to work!

CHEBUTYKIN [*comes into the drawing-room with* IRINA]. And the food they treated me to was the genuine Caucasian stuff; onion soup, followed by *chekhartma* – that's a meat dish, you know.

SOLYONY. *Cheremsha* isn't meat at all; it's a plant, something like an onion.

CHEBUTYKIN. No-o, my dear friend. *Chekhartma* isn't an onion, it's roast mutton.

SOLYONY. I tell you *cheremsha* is a kind of onion.

CHEBUTYKIN. Well, why should I argue about it with you? You've never been to the Caucasus and you've never tasted *chekhartma*.

SOLYONY. I haven't tasted it because I can't stand the smell of it. *Cheremsha* stinks just like garlic.

ANDREY [*imploringly*]. Do stop it, friends! Please stop it!

TUZENBAKH. When's the carnival crowd coming along?

IRINA. They promised to be here by nine – that means any moment now.

TUZENBAKH [*embraces* ANDREY *and sings*]. 'Ah, my beautiful porch, my lovely new porch, my . . . '*

ANDREY [*dances and sings*]. 'My new porch all made of maple-wood . . . '

CHEBUTYKIN [*dances*]. 'With fancy carving over the door . . .'
                              [*laughter*]

TUZENBAKH [*kisses* ANDREY]. Let's have a drink, the devil take it! Andryusha, let's drink to eternal friendship. I'll come with you when you go back to Moscow University.

SOLYONY. Which university? There are two universities in Moscow.

ANDREY. There's only one.

SOLYONY. I tell you there are two.

ANDREY. Never mind, make it three. The more the merrier.

SOLYONY. There are two universities in Moscow.
            [*murmurs of protest and cries of 'Hush!'*]
There are two universities in Moscow, an old one and a new one. But if you don't want to listen to what I'm saying, if my conversation irritates you, I can keep silent. In fact I can go to another room . . . [*goes out through one of the doors*]

TUZENBAKH. Bravo, bravo! [*laughs*] Let's get started, my friends, I'll play for you. What a funny creature that Solyony is! . . . [*sits down at the piano and plays a waltz*]

MASHA [*dances alone*]. The Baron is drunk, the Baron is drunk, the Baron is drunk . . .

Enter NATASHA.

NATASHA [*to* CHEBUTYKIN]. Ivan Romanich! [*speaks to him, then goes out quietly.* CHEBUTYKIN *touches* TUZENBAKH *on the shoulder and whispers to him*]

IRINA. What is it?

CHEBUTYKIN. It's time we were going. Good-night.

IRINA. But really . . . What about the carnival party?

ANDREY [*embarrassed*]. The carnival party's not coming. You see, my dear, Natasha says that Bobik isn't very well, and so . . . Anyway, I don't know . . . and I certainly don't care . . .

IRINA [*shrugs her shoulders*]. Bobik's not very well! . . .

MASHA. Never mind, we'll keep our end up! If they turn us out, out we must go! [*to* IRINA] It isn't Bobik who's not well, it's

* A traditional Russian dance-song.

her . . . There! . . . [*taps her forehead with her finger*] Petty little bourgeois housewife!

[ANDREY *goes to his room on the right.* CHEBUTYKIN *follows him.*
The guests say goodbye in the ballroom]

FEDOTIK. What a pity! I'd been hoping to spend the evening here, but of course, if the baby's ill . . . I'll bring him some toys tomorrow.

RODÉ [*in a loud voice*]. I had a good long sleep after lunch today on purpose, I thought I'd be dancing all night. I mean to say, it's only just nine o'clock.

MASHA. Let's go outside and talk it over. We can decide what to do then.

Voices are heard saying 'Goodbye! God bless you!' and TUZENBAKH
is heard laughing gaily. Everyone goes out. ANFISA *and a maid clear the table and put out the lights. The nurse sings to the baby off-stage.*
Enter ANDREY, *wearing an overcoat and hat, followed by*
CHEBUTYKIN. *They move quietly.*

CHEBUTYKIN. I've never found time to get married, somehow . . . partly because my life's just flashed past me like lightning, and partly because I was always madly in love with your mother and she was married . . .

ANDREY. One shouldn't marry. One shouldn't marry because it's so boring.

CHEBUTYKIN. That may be so, but what about loneliness? You can philosophise as much as you like, dear boy, but loneliness is a dreadful thing. Although, really . . . well, it doesn't matter a damn, of course! . . .

ANDREY. Let's get along quickly.

CHEBUTYKIN. What's the hurry? There's plenty of time.

ANDREY. I'm afraid my wife may try to stop me.

CHEBUTYKIN. Ah!

ANDREY. I won't play cards tonight, I'll just sit and watch. I'm not feeling too well . . . What ought I to do for this breathlessness, Ivan Romanich?

CHEBUTYKIN. Why ask me, dear boy? I can't remember – I simply don't know.

ANDREY. Let's go through the kitchen. [*they go out. A bell rings. The ring is repeated, then voices and laughter are heard*]

IRINA [*coming in*]. What's that?

ANFISA [*in a whisper*]. The carnival party.

[*the bell rings again*]

IRINA. Tell them there's no-one at home, Nanny. Apologise to them.

ANFISA *goes out.* IRINA *walks up and down the room, lost in thought, she seems agitated. Enter* SOLYONY.

SOLYONY [*puzzled*]. There's no-one here . . . Where is everybody?

IRINA. They've gone home.

SOLYONY. How strange! Then you're alone here?

IRINA. Yes, alone. [*a pause*] Well . . . good-night.

SOLYONY. I know I behaved tactlessly just now, I lost control of myself. But you're different from the others, you stand out high above them — you're pure, you can see where the truth lies . . . You're the only person in the world who can possibly understand me. I love you . . . I love you with a deep, infinite . . .

IRINA. Do please go away. Good-night!

SOLYONY. I can't live without you. [*follows her*] Oh, it's such a delight just to look at you! [*with tears*] Oh, my happiness! Your glorious, marvellous, entrancing eyes — eyes like no other woman's I've ever seen . . .

IRINA [*coldly*]. Please stop it, Vasiliy Vasiliyich!

SOLYONY. I've never spoken to you of my love before . . . it makes me feel as if I were living on a different planet . . . [*rubs his forehead*] Never mind! I can't force you to love me, obviously. But I don't intend to have any rivals — successful rivals, I mean . . . No, no! I swear to you by everything I hold sacred that if there's anyone else, I'll kill him. Oh, how wonderful you are!

Enter NATASHA *carrying a candle.*

NATASHA [*pokes her head into one room, then into another, but passes the door leading to her husband's room*]. Andrey's reading in there. Better let him read. Forgive me, Vasiliy Vasiliyich, I didn't know you were here. I'm afraid I'm not properly dressed.

SOLYONY. I don't care. Goodbye. [*goes out*]

NATASHA. You must be tired, my poor dear girl. [*kisses* IRINA] You ought to go to bed earlier.

IRINA. Is Bobik asleep?

NATASHA. Yes, he's asleep. But he's not sleeping peacefully. By the way, my dear, I've been meaning to speak to you for some time but there's always been something . . . either you're not here, or I'm too busy . . . You see, I think that Bobik's nursery is so cold and damp . . . And your room is just ideal for a baby. Darling, do you think you could move into Olga's room?

IRINA [*not understanding her*]. Where to? [*the sound of bells is heard outside, as a troika is driven up to the house*]

NATASHA. You can share a room with Olya for the time being, and Bobik can have your room. He is such a darling! This morning I said to him: 'Bobik, you're my very own! My very own!' And he just gazed at me with his dear little eyes.

[*the door bell rings*]

That must be Olga. How late she is!

[*a maid comes up to* NATASHA *and whispers in her ear*]

Protopopov! What a funny fellow! Protopopov's come to ask me to go for a drive with him. In a troika! [*laughs*] Aren't these men strange creatures! . . .

[*the door bell rings again*]

Someone's ringing. Shall I go for a short drive? Just for a quarter of an hour? [*to the maid*] Tell him I'll be down in a minute.

[*the door bell rings again*]

That's the bell again. I suppose it's Olga. [*goes out*]

The maid runs out; IRINA *sits lost in thought. Enter* KULYGIN *and* OLGA, *followed by* VERSHININ.

KULYGIN. Well! What's the meaning of this? You said you were going to have a party.

VERSHININ. It's a strange thing. I left here about half an hour ago, and they were expecting a carnival party then.

IRINA. They've all gone.

KULYGIN. Masha's gone, too? Where has she gone to? And why is Protopopov waiting outside in a troika? Who's he waiting for?

IRINA. Please don't ask me questions. I'm tired.

KULYGIN. You . . . spoilt child!

OLGA. The conference has only just ended. I'm quite worn out. The headmistress is ill and I'm deputising for her. My head's aching, oh, my head, my head . . . [*sits down*] Andrey lost two hundred roubles at cards last night. The whole town's talking about it . . .

KULYGIN. Yes, the conference exhausted me, too. [*sits down*]

VERSHININ. So now my wife's taken it into her head to try to frighten me. She tried to poison herself. However, everything's all right now, so I can relax, thank goodness . . . So we've got to go away? Well, good-night to you, all the best. Fyodor Ilyich, would you care to come along with me somewhere or other? I can't stay at home tonight, I really can't . . . Do come!

KULYGIN. I'm tired. I don't think I'll come. [*gets up*] I'm tired. Has my wife gone home?

IRINA. I think so.

KULYGIN [*kisses* IRINA's *hand*]. Good-night. We can rest tomorrow and the day after tomorrow, two whole days! Well, I wish you all the best. [*going out*] How I long for some tea! I reckoned on spending the evening in congenial company, but – *O, fallacem hominum spem!* Always use the accusative case in exclamations.

VERSHININ. Well, it looks as if I'll have to go somewhere by myself. [*goes out with* KULYGIN, *whistling*]

OLGA. My head aches, oh, my head . . . Andrey lost at cards . . . the whole town's talking . . . I'll go and lie down. [*going out*] Tomorrow I'm free. Heavens, what a joy! Tomorrow I'm free, and the day after tomorrow I'm free . . . My head's aching, oh, my poor head . . .

IRINA [*alone*]. They've all gone. No-one's left. [*Someone is playing an accordion in the street. The nurse sings in the next room.*]

NATASHA [*crosses the ballroom, wearing a fur coat and cap. She is followed by the maid*]. I'll be back in half an hour. I'm just going for a little drive. [*goes out*]

IRINA [*alone, with intense longing*]. Moscow! Moscow! Moscow!

CURTAIN

ACT THREE

A bedroom now shared by OLGA *and* IRINA. *There are two beds, one on the right, the other on the left, each screened off from the centre of the room. It is past two o'clock in the morning. Off-stage the alarm is being sounded on account of a fire which has been raging for some time. The inmates of the house have not yet been to bed.* MASHA *is lying on a couch, dressed, as usual, in black.* OLGA *and* ANFISA *come in.*

ANFISA. Now they're sitting down there, under the stairs . . . I keep telling them to come upstairs, that they shouldn't sit down there, but they just cry. 'We don't know where our papa is,' they say, 'perhaps he's got burned in the fire.' What an idea! And there are people in the yard, too . . . half-dressed . . .

OLGA [*takes a dress out of a wardrobe*]. Take this grey frock, Nanny . . . And this one . . . This blouse, too . . . And this skirt. Oh, Heavens! what is happening! Apparently the whole of the Kirsanovsky Street's been burnt down . . . Take this . . . and this, too . . . [*throws the clothes into* ANFISA's *arms*] The poor Vershinins had a fright. Their house only just escaped being burnt down. They'll have to spend the night here . . . we mustn't let them go home. Poor Fedotik's lost everything, he's got nothing left . . .

ANFISA. I'd better call Ferapont, Olyushka, I can't carry all this.

OLGA [*rings*]. No-one takes any notice when I ring. [*calls through the door*] Is anyone there? Will someone come up, please!

[*a window, red with the glow of the fire, can be seen through the open door. The sound of a passing fire engine is heard*]

How dreadful it all is! And how tired of it I am!

Enter FERAPONT.

Take this downstairs please . . . The Kolotilin girls are sitting under the stairs . . . give it to them. And this, too . . .

FERAPONT. Very good, madam. Moscow was burned down in 1812 just the same. Mercy on us! . . . Yes, the French were surprised all right.

OLGA. Go along now, take this down.

FERAPONT. Very good. [*goes out*]

OLGA. Give it all away, Nanny dear. We won't keep anything, give it all away . . . I'm so tired, I can hardly keep on my feet. We mustn't let the Vershinins go home. The little girls can sleep in the drawing-room, and Alexandr Ignatyevich can share the down-stairs room with the Baron. Fedotik can go in with the Baron, too, or maybe he'd better sleep in the ballroom. The doctor's gone and got drunk – you'd think he'd done it on purpose; he's so hopelessly drunk that we can't let anyone go into his room. Vershinin's wife will have to go into the drawing-room, too.

ANFISA [*wearily*]. Don't send me away, Olyushka, darling! Don't send me away!

OLGA. What nonsense you're talking, Nanny! No-one's sending you away.

ANFISA [*leans her head against* OLGA's *breast*]. My dearest girl! I do work, you know, I work as hard as I can . . . I suppose now I'm getting weaker, I'll be told to go. But where can I go? Where? I'm eighty years old. I'm over eighty-one!

OLGA. You sit down for a while, Nanny . . . You're tired, you poor dear . . . [*makes her sit down*] Just rest a bit. You've turned quite pale.

Enter NATASHA.

NATASHA. They're saying we ought to start a subscription in aid of the victims of the fire. You know – form a society or something for the purpose. Well, why not? It's an excellent idea! In any case it's up to us to help the poor as best we can. Bobik and Sofochka are fast asleep as if nothing had happened. We've got such a crowd of people in the house; the place seems full of people whichever way you turn. There's 'flu about in the town . . . I'm so afraid the children might catch it.

OLGA [*without listening to her*]. You can't see the fire from this room; it's quiet in here.

NATASHA. Yes . . . I suppose my hair is all over the place. [*stands in front of the mirror*] They say I've got stouter, but it's not true! I'm

not a bit stouter. Masha's asleep . . . she's tired, poor girl . . .
[*to* ANFISA, *coldly*] How dare you sit down in my presence? Get
up! Get out of here!

                    [ANFISA *goes out. A pause*]

I can't understand why you keep that old woman in the house.

OLGA [*taken aback*]. Forgive me for saying it, but I can't understand
how you . . .

NATASHA. She's quite useless here. She's just a peasant woman, her
right place is in the country. You're spoiling her. I do like order
in the home, I don't like having useless people about. [*strokes*
OLGA's *cheek*] You're tired, my poor dear! Our headmistress is
tired! You know, when my Sofochka grows up and goes to
school, I'll be frightened of you.

OLGA. I'm not going to be a headmistress.

NATASHA. You'll be asked to, Olechka. It's settled.

OLGA. I'll refuse. I couldn't do it . . . I wouldn't be strong enough.
[*drinks water*] You spoke so harshly to Nanny just now . . . You
must forgive me for saying so, but I just can't stand that sort of
thing . . . it made me feel quite faint . . .

NATASHA [*agitated*]. Forgive me, Olya, forgive me. I didn't mean to
upset you.

        [MASHA *gets up, picks up a pillow and goes out in a huff*]

OLGA. Please try to understand me, dear . . . It may be that we've
been brought up in a peculiar way, but anyway I just can't bear
it. When people are treated like that, it gets me down, I feel
quite ill . . . I simply get unnerved . . .

NATASHA. Forgive me, dear, forgive me! . . . [*kisses her*]

OLGA. Any cruel or tactless remark, even the slightest discourtesy,
upsets me . . .

NATASHA. It's quite true, I know I often say things which would be
better left unsaid – but you must agree with me, dear, that she'd
be better in the country somewhere.

OLGA. She's been with us for thirty years.

NATASHA. But she can't do any work now, can she? Either I don't
understand you, or you don't want to understand me. She can't
work, she just sleeps or sits about.

OLGA. Well, let her sit about.

NATASHA [*in surprise*]. What do you mean, let her sit about? Surely
she is a servant! [*tearfully*] No, I don't understand you, Olya! I

have a nurse for the children and a wet nurse and we share a
maid and a cook. Whatever do we want this old woman for?
What for?

[*the alarm is sounded again*]

OLGA. I've aged ten years tonight.

NATASHA. We must sort things out, Olya. You're working at your
school, and I'm working at home. You're teaching and I'm
running the house. And when I say anything about the servants,
I know what I'm talking about . . . That old thief, that old witch
must get out of this house tomorrow! . . . [*stamps her feet*] How
dare you vex me so? How dare you? [*recovering her self-control*]
Really, if you don't move downstairs, we'll always be quarrelling. This is quite dreadful!

Enter KULYGIN.

KULYGIN. Where's Masha? It's time we went home. They say the
fire's getting less fierce. [*stretches*] Only one block got burnt
down, but to begin with it looked as if the whole town was
going to be set on fire by that wind. [*sits down*] I'm so tired,
Olechka, my dear. You know, I've often thought that if I hadn't
married Masha, I'd have married you, Olechka. You're so kind.
I'm worn out. [*listens*]

OLGA. What is it?

KULYGIN. The doctor's got drunk just as if he'd done it on purpose.
Hopelessly drunk . . . As if he'd done it on purpose. [*gets up*] I
think he's coming up here . . . Can you hear him? Yes, he's
coming up. [*laughs*] What a fellow, really! . . . I'm going to hide
myself. [*goes to the wardrobe and stands between it and the wall*] What
a scoundrel!

OLGA. He's been off drinking for two years, and now suddenly
he goes and gets drunk . . . [*walks with* NATASHA *towards the back
of the room*]

CHEBUTYKIN *enters; walking firmly and soberly he crosses the room, stops,
looks round, then goes to the wash-stand and begins to wash his hands.*

CHEBUTYKIN [*glumly*]. The devil take them all . . . all the lot of
them! They think I can treat anything just because I'm a doctor,
but I know positively nothing at all. I've forgotten everything I
used to know. I remember nothing, positively nothing . . .

[OLGA *and* NATASHA *leave the room without his noticing*]
The devil take them! Last Wednesday I attended a woman at
Zasyp. She died, and it's all my fault that she did die. Yes . . .
I used to know a thing or two twenty-five years ago, but
now I don't remember anything. Not a thing! Perhaps I'm
not a man at all, but I just imagine that I've got hands and
feet and a head. Perhaps I don't exist at all, and I only imagine that I'm walking about and eating and sleeping. [*weeps*]
Oh, if only I could simply stop existing! [*stops crying, glumly*]
God knows . . . The other day they were talking about
Shakespeare and Voltaire at the club . . . I haven't read either,
never read a single line of either, but I tried to make out
by my expression that I had. The others did the same. How
petty it all is! How despicable! And then suddenly I thought
of the woman I killed on Wednesday. It all came back to me,
and I felt such a swine, so sick of myself that I went and got
drunk . . .

Enter IRINA, VERSHININ *and* TUZENBAKH. TUZENBAKH *is wearing
a fashionable new civilian suit.*

IRINA. Let's sit down here for a while. No-one will come in here.
VERSHININ. The whole town would have been burnt down but for
the soldiers. They're a fine lot of fellows! [*rubs his hands with
pleasure*] Excellent fellows! Yes, they're a fine lot!
KULYGIN [*approaches them*]. What's the time?
TUZENBAKH. It's gone three. It's beginning to get light.
IRINA. Everyone's sitting in the ballroom and nobody thinks of
leaving. That man Solyony there, too . . . [*to* CHEBUTYKIN] You
ought to go to bed, Doctor.
CHEBUTYKIN. I'm all right . . . Thanks . . . [*combs his beard*]
KULYGIN [*laughs*]. Half seas over, Ivan Romanich! [*slaps him on
the shoulder*] You're a fine one! *In vino veritas*, as they used to say
in Rome.
TUZENBAKH. Everyone keeps asking me to arrange a concert in aid
of the victims of the fire.
IRINA. Well, who'd you get to perform in it?
TUZENBAKH. It could be done if we wanted to. Marya Sergeyevna
plays the piano wonderfully well, in my opinion.
KULYGIN. Yes, wonderfully well!

IRINA. She's forgotten how to. She hasn't played for three years . . . or maybe it's four.

TUZENBAKH. Nobody understands music in this town, not a single person. But I do – I really do – and I assure you quite definitely that Marya Sergeyevna plays magnificently. She's almost a genius for it.

KULYGIN. You're right, Baron. I'm very fond of Masha. She's such a nice girl.

TUZENBAKH. Fancy being able to play so exquisitely, and yet having nobody, nobody at all, to appreciate it!

KULYGIN [sighs]. Yes . . . But would it be quite proper for her to play in a concert? [a pause] I don't know anything about these matters, my friends. Perhaps it'll be perfectly all right. But you know, although our director is a good man, a very good man indeed, and most intelligent, I know that he does hold certain views . . . Of course, this doesn't really concern him, but I'll have a word with him about it, all the same, if you like.

CHEBUTYKIN [picks up a china clock and examines it].

VERSHININ. I've got my clothes in such a mess helping to put out the fire, I must look like nothing on earth. [a pause] I believe they were saying yesterday that our brigade might be transferred to somewhere a long way away. Some said it was to be Poland, and some said it was Chita, in Siberia.

TUZENBAKH. I heard that, too. Well, the town will seem quite deserted.

IRINA. We'll go away, too!

CHEBUTYKIN [drops the clock and breaks it]. Smashed to smithereens!
       [a pause; everyone looks upset and embarrassed]

KULYGIN [picks up the pieces]. Fancy breaking such a valuable thing! Ah, Ivan Romanich, Ivan Romanich! You'll get a bad mark for that!

IRINA. It was my mother's clock.

CHEBUTYKIN. Well, supposing it was. If it was your mother's, then it was your mother's. Perhaps I didn't smash it. Perhaps it only appears that I did. Perhaps it only appears to us that we exist, whereas in reality we don't exist at all. I don't know anything, no-one knows anything. [stops at the door] Why are you staring at me? Natasha's having a nice little affair with Protopopov, and you don't see it. You sit here seeing nothing, and meanwhile

Natasha's having a nice little affair with Protopopov . . . [*sings*] Would you like a date? . . . [*goes out*]

VERSHININ. So . . . [*laughs*] How odd it all is, really! [*a pause*] When the fire started, I ran home as fast as I could. When I got near, I could see that our house was all right and out of danger, but the two little girls were standing there, in the doorway in their night clothes. Their mother wasn't there. People were rushing about, horses, dogs . . . and in the kiddies' faces I saw a frightened, anxious, appealing look, I don't know what! . . . My heart sank when I saw their faces. My God, I thought, what will these children have to go through in the course of their poor lives? And they may live a long time, too! I picked them up and ran back here with them, and all the time I was running, I was thinking the same thing: what will they have to go through?

[*the alarm is sounded; a pause*]

When I got here, my wife was here already . . . angry, shouting!

Enter MASHA *carrying a pillow; she sits down on the couch.*

And when my little girls were standing in the doorway with nothing on but their night clothes, and the street was red with the glow of the fire and full of terrifying noises, it struck me that the same sort of thing used to happen years ago, when armies used to make sudden raids on towns, and plunder them and set them on fire . . . Anyway, is there any essential difference between things as they were and as they are now? And before very long, say, in another two or three hundred years, people may be looking at our present life just as we look at the past now, with horror and scorn. Our own times may seem uncouth to them, boring and frightfully uncomfortable and strange . . . Oh, what a great life it'll be then, what a life! [*laughs*] Forgive me, I'm philosophising my head off again . . . but may I go on, please? I'm bursting to philosophise just at the moment. I'm in the mood for it. [*a pause*] You seem as if you've all gone to sleep. As I was saying: what a great life it will be in the future! Just try to imagine it . . . At the present time there are only three people of your intellectual calibre in the whole of this town, but future generations will be more productive of people like you. They'll go on producing more and more of the same sort until at last the time will come when everything will be just as you'd wish it yourselves. People will live their lives in your way, and then even you may be outmoded, and a new lot will come along who will be even better than you are . . . [*laughs*] I'm in quite a special mood today. I feel full of a tremendous urge to live . . . [*sings*]

> To Love all ages are in fee,
> The passion's good for you and me . . . [*laughs*]

MASHA [*sings*]. Tara-tara-tara . . .

VERSHININ. Tum-tum . . .

MASHA. Tara-tara . . .

VERSHININ. Tum-tum, tum-tum . . . [*laughs*]

Enter FEDOTIK.

FEDOTIK [*dancing about*]. Burnt, burnt! Everything I've got burnt!
[*all laugh*]

IRINA. It's hardly a joking matter. Has everything really been burnt?

FEDOTIK [*laughs*]. Everything, completely. I've got nothing left. My guitar's burnt, my photographs are burnt, all my letters are burnt. Even the little note-book I was going to give you has been burnt.

Enter SOLYONY.

IRINA. No, please go away, Vasiliy Vasiliyich. You can't come in here.

SOLYONY. Can't I? Why can the Baron come in here if I can't?

VERSHININ. We really must go, all of us. What's the fire doing?

SOLYONY. It's dying down, they say. Well, I must say it's a peculiar thing that the Baron can come in here, and I can't. [*takes a scent bottle from his pocket and sprinkles himself with scent*]

VERSHININ. Tara-tara.

MASHA. Tum-tum, tum-tum.

VERSHININ [*laughs, to* SOLYONY]. Let's go to the ballroom.

SOLYONY. Very well, we'll make a note of this. 'I hardly need to make my moral yet more clear: That might be teasing geese, I fear!' * [*looks at* TUZENBAKH] Cluck, cluck, cluck! [*goes out with* VERSHININ *and* FEDOTIK]

IRINA. That Solyony has smoked the room out . . . [*puzzled*] The Baron's asleep. Baron! Baron!

* From Krylov's fable *Geese*.

TUZENBAKH [*waking out of his doze*]. I must be tired. The brick-
works . . . No, I'm not talking in my sleep. I really do intend to
go to the brick-works and start working there quite soon. I've
had a talk with the manager. [*to* IRINA, *tenderly*] You are so pale,
so beautiful, so fascinating . . . Your pallor seems to light up the
darkness around you, as if it were luminous, somehow . . .
You're sad, you're dissatisfied with the life you have to live . . .
Oh, come away with me, let's go away and work together!

MASHA. Nikolay Lvovich, I wish you'd go away.

TUZENBAKH [*laughs*]. Oh, you're here, are you? I didn't see you.
[*kisses* IRINA's *hand*] Goodbye, I'm going. You know, as I look at
you now, I keep thinking of the day – it was a long time
ago, your Saint's day – when you talked to us about the joy of
work . . . You were so gay and high-spirited then . . . And what
a happy life I saw ahead of me! Where is it all now? [*kisses her
hand*] There are tears in your eyes. You should go to bed, it's
beginning to get light . . . it's almost morning . . . Oh, if only I
could give my life for you!

MASHA. Nikolay Lvovich, please go away! Really now . . .

TUZENBAKH. I'm going. [*goes out*]

MASHA [*lies down*]. Are you asleep, Fyodor?

KULYGIN. Eh?

MASHA. Why don't you go home?

KULYGIN. My darling Masha, my sweet, my precious Masha . . .

IRINA. She's tired. Let her rest a while, Fedya.

KULYGIN. I'll go in a moment. My wife, my dear, good wife! . . .
How I love you! . . . only you!

MASHA [*crossly*]. *Amo, amas, amat, amamus, amatis, amant*!

KULYGIN [*laughs*]. Really, she's an amazing woman! – I've been
married to you for seven years, but I feel as if we were only
married yesterday. Yes, on my word of honour, I do! You really
are amazing! Oh, I'm so happy, happy, happy!

MASHA. And I'm so bored, bored, bored! [*sits up*] I can't get it out
of my head . . . It's simply disgusting. It's like having a nail
driven into my head. No, I can't keep silent about it any more.
It's about Andrey . . . He's actually mortgaged this house to a
bank, and his wife's got hold of all the money – and yet the
house doesn't belong to him, it belongs to all four of us! Surely,
he must realise that, if he's got any honesty.

KULYGIN. Why bring all this up, Masha? Why bother about it now? Andryusha owes money all round . . . Leave him alone.

MASHA. Anyway, it's disgusting. [*lies down*]

KULYGIN. Well, we aren't poor, Masha. I've got work, I teach at the county school, I give private lessons in my spare time . . . I'm just a plain, honest man . . . *Omnia mea mecum porto*, as they say.

MASHA. I don't ask for anything, but I'm just disgusted by injustice. [*a pause*] Why don't you go home, Fyodor?

KULYGIN [*kisses her*]. You're tired. Just rest here for a while . . . I'll go home and wait for you . . . Go to sleep. [*goes to the door*] I'm happy, happy, happy! [*goes out*]

IRINA. The truth is that Andrey is getting to be shallow-minded. He's ageing and since he's been living with that woman he's lost all the inspiration he used to have! Not long ago he was working for a professorship, and yet yesterday he boasted of having at last been elected a member of the County Council. Fancy him a member, with Protopopov as chairman! They say the whole town's laughing at him, he's the only one who doesn't know anything or see anything. And now, you see, everyone's at the fire, while he's just sitting in his room, not taking the slightest notice of it. Just playing his violin. [*agitated*] Oh, how dreadful it is, how dreadful, how dreadful! I can't bear it any longer, I can't, I really can't! . . .

Enter OLGA. *She starts arranging things on her bedside table.*

IRINA [*sobs loudly*]. You must turn me out of here! Turn me out; I can't stand it any more!

OLGA [*alarmed*]. What is it? What is it, darling?

IRINA [*sobbing*]. Where . . . Where has it all gone to? Where is it? Oh, God! I've forgotten . . . I've forgotten everything . . . there's nothing but a muddle in my head . . . I don't remember what the Italian for 'window' is, or for 'ceiling' . . . Every day I'm forgetting more and more, and life's slipping by, and it will never, never come back . . . We shall never go to Moscow . . . I can see that we shall never go . . .

OLGA. Don't, my dear, don't . . .

IRINA [*trying to control herself*]. Oh, I'm so miserable! . . . I can't work, I won't work! I've had enough of it, enough! . . . First I worked on the telegraph, now I'm in the County Council office, and I hate and despise everything they give me to do there . . . I'm twenty-three years old, I've been working all this time, and I feel as if my brain's dried up. I know I've got thinner and uglier and older, and I find no kind of satisfaction in anything, none at all. And the time's passing . . . and I feel as if I'm moving away from any hope of a genuine, fine life, I'm moving further and further away and sinking into a kind of abyss. I feel in despair, and I don't know why I'm still alive, why I haven't killed myself . . .

OLGA. Don't cry, my dear child, don't cry . . . It hurts me.

IRINA. I'm not crying any more. That's enough of it. Look, I'm not crying now. Enough of it, enough! . . .

OLGA. Darling, let me tell you something . . . I just want to speak as your sister, as your friend . . . That is, if you want my advice . . . Why don't you marry the Baron?

IRINA [weeps quietly].

OLGA. After all, you do respect him, you think a lot of him . . . It's true, he's not good-looking, but he's such a decent, clean-minded sort of man . . . After all, one doesn't marry for love, but to fulfil a duty. At least, I think so, and I'd marry even if I weren't in love. I'd marry anyone that proposed to me, as long as he was a decent man. I'd even marry an old man.

IRINA. I've been waiting all this time, imagining that we'd be moving to Moscow, and I'd meet the man I'm meant for there. I've dreamt about him and I've loved him in my dreams . . . But it's all turned out to be nonsense . . . nonsense . . .

OLGA [embracing her]. My darling sweetheart, I understand everything perfectly. When the Baron resigned his commission and came to see us in his civilian clothes, I thought he looked so plain that I actually started to cry . . . He asked me why I was crying . . . How could I tell him? But, of course, if it were God's will that he should marry you, I'd feel perfectly happy about it. That's quite a different matter, quite different!

[NATASHA, carrying a candle, comes out of the door on the right, crosses the stage and goes out through the door on the left without saying anything]

MASHA [sits up]. She goes about looking as if she'd started the fire.

OLGA. You're silly, Masha. You're the stupidest person in our family. Forgive me for saying so.

[*a pause*]

MASHA. My dear sisters, I've got something to confess to you. I must get some relief, I feel the need of it in my heart. I'll confess it to you two alone, and then never again, never to anybody! I'll tell you in a minute. [*in a low voice*] It's a secret, but you'll have to know everything. I can't keep silent any more. [*a pause*] I'm in love, in love . . . I love that man . . . You saw him there just now . . . Well, what's the good? . . . I love Vershinin . . .

OLGA [*goes behind her screen*]. Don't say it. I don't want to hear it.

MASHA. Well, what's to be done? [*holding her head*] I thought he was queer at first, then I started to pity him . . . then I began to love him . . . love everything about him – his voice, his talk, his misfortunes, his two little girls . . .

OLGA. Nevertheless, I don't want to hear it. You can say any nonsense you like, I'm not listening.

MASHA. Oh, you're stupid, Olya! If I love him, well – that's my fate! That's my destiny . . . He loves me, too. It's all rather frightening, isn't it? Not a good thing, is it? [*takes* IRINA *by the hand and draws her to her*] Oh, my dear! . . . How are we going to live through the rest of our lives? What's going to become of us? When you read a novel, everything in it seems so old and obvious, but when you fall in love yourself, you suddenly discover that you don't really know anything, and you've got to make your own decisions . . . My dear sisters, my dear sisters! . . . I've confessed it all to you, and now I'll keep quiet . . . I'll be like that madman in the story by Gogol – silence . . . silence! . . .

Enter ANDREY *followed by* FERAPONT.

ANDREY [*crossly*]. What do you want? I don't understand you.

FERAPONT [*stopping in the doorway, impatiently*]. I've asked you about ten times already, Andrey Sergeyevich.

ANDREY. In the first place, you're not to call me Andrey Sergeyevich – call me 'Your Honour'.

FERAPONT. The firemen are asking Your Honour if they may drive through your garden to get to the river. They've been going a long way round all this time – it's a terrible business!

ANDREY. All right. Tell them it's all right.

[FERAPONT *goes out*]

They keep on plaguing me. Where's Olga?

[OLGA *comes from behind the screen*]

I wanted to see you. Will you give me the key to the cupboard? I've lost mine. You know the key I mean, the small one you've got . . .

[OLGA *silently hands him the key.* IRINA *goes behind the screen on her side of the room*]

ANDREY. What a terrific fire! It's going down though. That Ferapont annoyed me, the devil take him! Silly thing he made me say . . . Telling him to call me 'Your Honour'! . . . [*a pause*] Why don't you say anything, Olya? [*a pause*] It's about time you stopped this nonsense . . . sulking like this for no reason whatever . . . You here, Masha? And Irina's here, too. That's excellent! We can talk it over then, frankly and once for all. What have you got against me? What is it?

OLGA. Drop it now, Andryusha. Let's talk it over tomorrow. [*agitated*] What a dreadful night!

ANDREY [*in great embarrassment*]. Don't get upset. I'm asking you quite calmly, what have you got against me? Tell me frankly.

VERSHININ'S VOICE [*off stage*]. Tum-tum-tum!

MASHA [*in a loud voice, getting up*]. Tara-tara-tara! [*to* OLGA] Goodbye, Olya, God bless you! [*goes behind the screen and kisses* IRINA] Sleep well . . . Goodbye, Andrey. I should leave them now, they're tired . . . talk it over tomorrow . . . [*goes out*]

OLGA. Really, Andryusha, let's leave it till tomorrow . . . [*goes behind the screen on her side of the room*] It's time to go to bed.

ANDREY. I only want to say one thing, then I'll go. In a moment . . . First of all, you've got something against my wife, against Natasha. I've always been conscious of it from the day we got married. Natasha is a fine woman, she's honest and straightforward and high-principled . . . That's my opinion. I love and respect my wife. You understand that I respect her, and I expect others to respect her, too. I repeat: she's an honest, high-principled woman, and all your grievances against her – if you don't mind my saying so – are just imagination, and nothing more . . . [*a pause*] Secondly, you seem to be annoyed with me for not making myself a professor, and not doing any academic work. But I'm working in the Council Office, I'm a member of the County Council, and I feel my service there is just as fine and valuable as any academic work I might do. I'm a member of the County Council, and if you want to know, I'm proud of it! [*a pause*] Thirdly . . . there's something else I must tell you . . . I know I mortgaged the house without asking your permission . . . That was wrong, I admit it, and I ask you to forgive me . . . I was driven to it by my debts . . . I'm in debt for about thirty-five thousand roubles. I don't play cards any more, I've given it up long ago . . . The only thing I can say to justify myself is that you girls get an annuity, while I don't get anything . . . no income, I mean . . . [*a pause*]

KULYGIN [*calling through the door*]. Is Masha there? She's not there? [*alarmed*] Where can she be then? It's very strange . . . [*goes away*]

ANDREY. So you won't listen? Natasha is a good, honest woman, I tell you. [*walks up and down the stage, then stops*] When I married her, I thought we were going to be happy, I thought we should all be happy . . . But . . . oh, my God! . . . [*weeps*] My dear sisters, my dear, good sisters, don't believe what I've been saying, don't believe it . . . [*goes out*]

KULYGIN [*through the door, agitated*]. Where's Masha? Isn't Masha here? Extraordinary! [*goes away*]

[*the alarm is heard again; the stage is empty*]

IRINA [*speaking from behind the screen*]. Olya! Who's that knocking on the floor?

OLGA. It's the doctor, Ivan Romanich. He's drunk.

IRINA. It's been one thing after another all night. [*a pause*] Olya! [*peeps out from behind the screen*] Have you heard? The troops are being moved from the district . . . they're being sent somewhere a long way off.

OLGA. That's only a rumour.

IRINA. We'll be left quite alone then . . . Olya!

OLGA. Well?

IRINA. Olya, darling, I do respect the Baron . . . I think a lot of him, he's a very good man . . . I'll marry him, Olya, I'll agree to marry him, if only we can go to Moscow! Let's go, please do let's go! There's nowhere in all the world like Moscow. Let's go, Olya! Let's go!

CURTAIN

ACT FOUR

The old garden belonging to the Prozorovs' house. A river is seen at the end of a long avenue of fir trees, and on the far bank of the river a forest. On the right of the stage there is a verandah with a table on which champagne bottles and glasses have been left. It is midday. From time to time people from the street pass through the garden to get to the river. Five or six soldiers march through quickly.

CHEBUTYKIN, radiating a mood of benevolence which does not leave him throughout the Act, is sitting in a chair in the garden. He is wearing his army cap and is holding a walking stick, as if ready to be called away at any moment. KULYGIN, with a decoration round his neck and with his moustache shaved off, TUZENBAKH and IRINA are standing on the verandah saying goodbye to FEDOTIK and RODÉ, who are coming down the steps. Both officers are in marching uniform.

TUZENBAKH [*embracing* FEDOTIK]. You're a good fellow, Fedotik; we've been good friends! [*embraces* RODÉ] Once more, then . . . Goodbye, my dear friends!

IRINA. *Au revoir!*

FEDOTIK. It's not '*au revoir*'. It's goodbye. We shall never meet again!

KULYGIN. Who knows? [*wipes his eyes, smiling*] There! you've made me cry.

IRINA. We'll meet some time.

FEDOTIK. Perhaps in ten or fifteen years' time. But then we'll hardly know one another . . . We shall just meet and say: 'How are you?' coldly . . . [*takes a snapshot*] Wait a moment . . . Just one more, for the last time.

RODÉ [*embraces* TUZENBAKH]. We're not likely to meet again . . . [*kisses* IRINA'*s hand*] Thank you for everything . . . everything!

FEDOTIK [*annoyed*]. Do just wait a second!

TUZENBAKH. We'll meet again if we're fated to meet. Do write to us. Be sure to write.

RODÉ [*glancing round the garden*]. Goodbye, trees! [*shouts*] Heigh-ho! [*a pause*] Goodbye, echo!

KULYGIN. I wouldn't be surprised if you got married out there, in Poland . . . You'll get a Polish wife, and she'll put her arms round you and say: *Kohane!** [*laughs*]

FEDOTIK [*glances at his watch*]. There's less than an hour to go. Solyony is the only one from our battery who's going down the river on the barge. All the others are marching with the division. Three batteries are leaving today by road and three more tomorrow – then the town will be quite peaceful.

TUZENBAKH. Yes, and dreadfully dull, too.

RODÉ. By the way, where's Marya Sergeyevna?

KULYGIN. She's somewhere in the garden.

FEDOTIK. We must say goodbye to her.

RODÉ. Goodbye. I really must go, or I'll burst into tears. [*quickly embraces* TUZENBAKH *and* KULYGIN, *kisses* IRINA's *hand*] Life's been very pleasant here . . .

FEDOTIK [*to* KULYGIN]. Here's something for a souvenir for you – a note-book with a pencil . . . We'll go down to the river through here. [*they go off, glancing back*]

RODÉ [*shouts*]. Heigh-ho!

KULYGIN [*shouts*]. Goodbye!

[*at the back of the stage* FEDOTIK *and* RODÉ *meet* MASHA, *and say goodbye to her; she goes off with them*]

IRINA. They've gone . . . [*sits down on the bottom step of the verandah*]

CHEBUTYKIN. They forgot to say goodbye to me.

IRINA. Well, what about you?

CHEBUTYKIN. That's true, I forgot, too. Never mind, I'll be seeing them again quite soon. I'll be leaving tomorrow. Yes . . . only one more day. And then, in a year's time I'll be retiring. I'll come back here and finish the rest of my life near you. There's just one more year to go and then I get my pension . . . [*puts a newspaper in his pocket and takes out another*] I'll come back here and lead a reformed life. I'll be a nice, quiet, well-behaved little man.

IRINA. Yes, it's really time you reformed, my dear friend. You ought to live a different sort of life, somehow.

CHEBUTYKIN. Yes . . . I think so, too. [*sings quietly*] Tarara-boom-di-ay . . . I'm sitting on a tomb-di-ay . . .

* A Polish word meaning 'beloved'.

KULYGIN. Ivan Romanich is incorrigible! Incorrigible!

CHEBUTYKIN. Yes, you ought to have taken me in hand. You'd have reformed me!

IRINA. Fyodor's shaved his moustache off. I can't bear to look at him.

KULYGIN. Why not?

CHEBUTYKIN. If I could just tell you what your face looks like now — but I daren't.

KULYGIN. Well! Such are the conventions of life! Modus vivendi, you know. The director shaved his moustache off, so I shaved mine off when they gave me an inspectorship. No-one likes it, but personally I'm quite indifferent. I'm content. Whether I've got a moustache or not, it's all the same to me. [*sits down*]

[ANDREY *passes across the back of the stage pushing a pram with a child asleep in it*]

IRINA. Ivan Romanich, my dear friend, I'm awfully worried about something. You were out in the town garden last night — tell me what happened there?

CHEBUTYKIN. What happened? Nothing. Just a trifling thing. [*reads his paper*] It doesn't matter anyway.

KULYGIN. They say that Solyony and the Baron met in the town garden outside the theatre last night and . . .

TUZENBAKH. Don't, please! What's the good? . . . [*waves his hand at him deprecatingly and goes into the house*]

KULYGIN. It was outside the theatre . . . Solyony started badgering the Baron, and he lost patience and said something that offended him.

CHEBUTYKIN. I don't know anything about it. It's all nonsense.

KULYGIN. A schoolmaster once wrote 'nonsense' in Russian over a pupil's essay, and the pupil puzzled over it, thinking it was a Latin word. [*laughs*] Frightfully funny, you know! They say that Solyony's in love with Irina and that he got to hate the Baron more and more . . . Well, that's understandable. Irina's a very nice girl. She's a bit like Masha, she tends to get wrapped up in her own thoughts. [*to* IRINA] But your disposition is more easy-going than Masha's. And yet Masha has a very nice disposition, too. I love her, I love my Masha.

[*from the back of the stage comes a shout: 'Heigh-ho!'*]

IRINA [*starts*]. Anything seems to startle me today. [*a pause*] I've got everything ready, too. I'm sending my luggage off after lunch. The Baron and I are going to get married tomorrow, and directly afterwards we're moving to the brick-works, and the day after tomorrow I'm starting work at the school. So our new life will begin, God willing! When I was sitting for my teacher's diploma, I suddenly started crying for sheer joy, with a sort of feeling of blessedness . . . [*a pause*] The carrier will be coming for my luggage in a minute . . .

KULYGIN. That's all very well, but somehow I can't feel that it's meant to be serious. All ideas and theories, but nothing really serious. Anyway, I wish you luck from the bottom of my heart.

CHEBUTYKIN [*moved*]. My dearest girl, my precious child! You've gone on so far ahead of me, I'll never catch you up now. I've got left behind like a bird which has grown too old and can't keep up with the rest of the flock. Fly away, my dears, fly away, and God be with you! [*a pause*] It's a pity you've shaved your moustache off, Fyodor Ilyich.

KULYGIN. Don't keep on about it, please! [*sighs*] Well, the soldiers will be leaving today, and everything will go back to what it was before. Anyway, whatever they say, Masha is a good, loyal wife. Yes, I love her dearly and I'm thankful for what God has given me. Fate treats people so differently. For instance, there's an excise clerk here called Kozyrev. He was at school with me and he was expelled in his fifth year because he just couldn't grasp the *ut consecutivum*. He's dreadfully hard up now, and in bad health, too, and whenever I meet him, I just say to him: 'Hullo, *ut consecutivum*!' 'Yes', he replies, 'that's just the trouble – *consecutivum*' . . . and he starts coughing. Whereas I – I've been lucky all my life. I'm happy, I've actually been awarded the order of Saint Stanislav, second class – and now I'm teaching the children the same old *ut consecutivum*. Of course, I'm clever, cleverer than plenty of other people, but happiness does not consist of merely being clever . . .

[*in the house someone plays 'The Maiden's Prayer'*]

IRINA. Tomorrow night I shan't have to listen to the 'Maiden's Prayer'. I shan't have to meet Protopopov . . . [*a pause*] By the way, he's in the sitting-room. He's come again.

KULYGIN. Hasn't our headmistress arrived yet?

IRINA. No, we've sent for her. If you only knew how difficult it is

OLGA

for me to live here by myself, without Olya! She lives at the
school now; she's the headmistress and she's busy the whole day.
And I'm here alone, bored, with nothing to do, and I hate the
very room I live in. So I've just made up my mind – if I'm really
not going to be able to live in Moscow, that's that. It's my
fate, that's all. Nothing can be done about it. It's God's will,
everything that happens, and that's the truth. Nikolay Lvovich
proposed to me . . . Well, I thought it over, and I made up
my mind. He's such a nice man, it's really extraordinary how
nice he is . . . And then suddenly I felt as though my soul had
grown wings, I felt more cheerful and so relieved somehow
that I wanted to work again. Just to start work! . . . Only
something happened yesterday, and now I feel as though something mysterious is hanging over me . . .

CHEBUTYKIN. Nonsense!

NATASHA [*speaking through the window*]. Our headmistress!

KULYGIN. Our headmistress has arrived! Let's go indoors.

[*goes indoors with* IRINA]

CHEBUTYKIN [*reads his paper and sings quietly to himself*]. Tarara-
boom-di-ay . . . I'm sitting on a tomb-di-ay . . .

[MASHA *walks up to him;* ANDREY *passes across the back
of the stage pushing the pram*]

MASHA. You look very comfortable sitting here . . .

CHEBUTYKIN. Well, why not? Anything happening?

MASHA [*sits down*]. No, nothing. [*a pause*] Tell me something.
Were you in love with my mother?

CHEBUTYKIN. Yes, very much in love.

MASHA. Did she love you?

CHEBUTYKIN [*after a pause*]. I can't remember now.

MASHA. Is my man here? Our cook Marfa always used to call her
policeman 'my man'. Is he here?

CHEBUTYKIN. Not yet.

MASHA. When you have to take your happiness in snatches, in little
bits, as I do, and then lose it, as I've lost it, you gradually get
hardened and bad-tempered. [*points at her breast*] Something's
boiling over inside me, here. [*looking at* ANDREY, *who again crosses
the stage with the pram*] There's Andrey, our dear brother . . .
All our hopes are gone. It's the same as when thousands of people
haul a huge bell up into a tower. Untold labour and money is

spent on it, and then suddenly it falls and gets smashed. Suddenly, without rhyme or reason. It was the same with Andrey . . .

ANDREY. When are they going to settle down in the house? They're making such a row.

CHEBUTYKIN. They will soon. [looks at his watch] This is an old-fashioned watch: it strikes . . . [winds his watch which then strikes] The first, second and fifth batteries will be leaving punctually at one o'clock. [a pause] And I shall leave tomorrow.

ANDREY. For good?

CHEBUTYKIN. I don't know. I may return in about a year. Although, God knows . . . It's all the same . . .

[the sounds of a harp and a violin are heard]

ANDREY. The town will seem quite empty. Life will be snuffed out like a candle. [a pause] Something happened yesterday outside the theatre; everybody's talking about it. I'm the only one that doesn't seem to know about it.

CHEBUTYKIN. It was nothing. A lot of nonsense. Solyony started badgering the Baron, or something. The Baron lost his temper and insulted him, and in the end Solyony had to challenge him to a duel. [looks at his watch] I think it's time to go . . . At half-past twelve, in the forest over there, on the other side of the river . . . Bang–bang! [laughs] Solyony imagines he's like Lermontov. He actually writes poems. But, joking apart, this is his third duel.

MASHA. Whose third duel?

CHEBUTYKIN. Solyony's.

MASHA. What about the Baron?

CHEBUTYKIN. Well, what about him? [a pause]

MASHA. My thoughts are all in a muddle . . . But what I mean to say is that they shouldn't be allowed to fight. He might wound the Baron or even kill him.

CHEBUTYKIN. The Baron's a good enough fellow, but what does it really matter if there's one Baron more or less in the world? Well, let it be! It's all the same.

[the shouts of 'Ah-oo!' and 'Heigh-ho!' are heard from beyond the garden]

That's Skvortsov, the second, shouting from the boat. He can wait.

ANDREY. I think it's simply immoral to fight a duel, or even to be present at one as a doctor.

CHEBUTYKIN. That's only how it seems . . . We don't exist, nothing exists, it only seems to us that we do . . . And what difference does it make?

MASHA. Talk, talk, nothing but talk all day long! . . . [*starts to go*] Having to live in this awful climate with the snow threatening to fall at any moment, and then on the top of it having to listen to all this sort of talk . . . [*stops*] I won't go into the house, I can't bear going in there . . . Will you let me know when Vershinin comes? . . . [*walks off along the avenue*] Look, the birds are beginning to fly away already! [*looks up*] Swans or geese . . . Dear birds, happy birds . . . [*goes off*]

ANDREY. Our house will seem quite deserted. The officers will go, you'll go, my sister will get married, and I'll be left alone in the house.

CHEBUTYKIN. What about your wife?

Enter FERAPONT *with some papers.*

ANDREY. My wife is my wife. She's a good, decent sort of woman . . . she's really very kind, too, but there's something about her which pulls her down to the level of an animal . . . a sort of mean, blind, thick-skinned animal — anyway, not a human being. I'm telling you this as a friend, the only person I can talk openly to. I love Natasha, it's true. But at times she appears to me so utterly vulgar, that I feel quite bewildered by it, and then I can't understand why, for what reasons I love her — or, anyway, did love her . . .

CHEBUTYKIN [*gets up*]. Well, dear boy, I'm going away tomorrow and it may be we shall never see each other again. So I'll give you a bit of advice. Put on your hat, take a walking stick, and go away . . . Go away, and don't ever look back. And the further you go, the better.

[SOLYONY *passes across the back of the stage accompanied by two officers. Seeing* CHEBUTYKIN, *he turns towards him, while the officers walk on*]

SOLYONY. It's time, Doctor. Half past twelve already. [*shakes hands with* ANDREY]

CHEBUTYKIN. In a moment. Oh, I'm tired of you all. [*to* ANDREY] Andryusha, if anyone asks for me, tell them I'll be back presently. [*sighs*] Oh-ho-ho!

SOLYONY.   'He had not time to say "Oh, oh!"
            Before that bear had struck him low.' . . .
[walks off with him] What are you groaning about, old man?

CHEBUTYKIN. Oh, well!

SOLYONY. How do you feel?

CHEBUTYKIN [crossly]. Like a last year's bird's-nest.

SOLYONY. You needn't be so agitated about it, old boy. I shan't
    indulge in anything much, I'll just scorch his wings a little, like
    a woodcock's. [takes out a scent bottle and sprinkles scent over his
    hands] I've used up a whole bottle today, but my hands still
    smell. They smell like a corpse. [a pause] Yes . . . Do you
    remember that poem of Lermontov's?
            'And he, rebellious, seeks a storm,
            As if in storms there were tranquillity.' . . .

CHEBUTYKIN. Yes.
            'He had not time to say "Oh, oh!"
            Before that bear had struck him low.'
                    [goes out with SOLYONY]

    Shouts of 'Heigh-ho!' 'Ah-hoo!' are heard. Enter ANDREY
                    and FERAPONT.

FERAPONT. Will you sign these papers, please?

ANDREY [with irritation]. Leave me alone! Leave me alone, for
    Heaven's sake. [goes off with the pram]

FERAPONT. Well, what am I supposed to do with the papers then?
    They are meant to be signed, aren't they? [goes to back of stage]

    Enter IRINA and TUZENBAKH, the latter wearing a straw hat.
    KULYGIN crosses the stage, calling: 'Ah-oo! Masha! Ah-oo!'

TUZENBAKH. I think he's the only person in the whole town who's
    glad that the army is leaving.

IRINA. That's quite understandable, really. [a pause] The town will
    look quite empty.

TUZENBAKH. My dear, I'll be back in a moment.

IRINA. Where are you going?

TUZENBAKH. I must slip back to the town, and then . . . I want to
    see some of my colleagues off.

IRINA. It's not true . . . Nikolay, why are you so absent-minded
    today? [a pause] What happened outside the theatre last night?

TUZENBAKH [*with a movement of impatience*]. I'll be back in an hour . . . I'll be back with you again. [*kisses her hands*] My treasure! . . . [*gazes into her eyes*] It's five years since I first began to love you, and still I can't get used to it, and you seem more beautiful every day. What wonderful, lovely hair! What marvellous eyes! I'll take you away tomorrow. We'll work, we'll be rich, my dreams will come to life again. And you'll be happy! But – there's only one 'but', only one – you don't love me!

IRINA. I can't help that! I'll be your wife, I'll be loyal and obedient to you, but I can't love you . . . What's to be done? [*weeps*] I've never loved anyone in my life. Oh, I've had such dreams about being in love! I've been dreaming about it for ever so long, day and night . . . but somehow my soul seems like an expensive piano which someone has locked up and the key's got lost. [*a pause*] Your eyes are so restless.

TUZENBAKH. I was awake all night. Not that there's anything to be afraid of in my life, nothing threatening . . . Only the thought of that lost key torments me and keeps me awake. Say something to me . . . [*a pause*] Say something!

IRINA. What? What am I to say? What?

TUZENBAKH. Anything.

IRINA. Don't, my dear, don't . . . [*a pause*]

TUZENBAKH. Such trifles, such silly little things sometimes become so important suddenly, for no apparent reason! You laugh at them, just as you always have done, you still regard them as trifles, and yet you suddenly find they're in control, and you haven't the power to stop them. But don't let us talk about all that! Really, I feel quite elated. I feel as if I was seeing those fir trees and maples and birches for the first time in my life. They all seem to be looking at me with a sort of inquisitive look and waiting for something. What beautiful trees – and how beautiful, when you think of it, life ought to be with trees like these!

[*shouts of 'Ah-oo! Heigh-ho!' are heard*]

I must go, it's time . . . Look at that dead tree, it's all dried-up, but it's still swaying in the wind along with the others. And in the same way, it seems to me that, if I die, I shall still have a share in life somehow or other. Goodbye, my dear . . . [*kisses her hands*] Your papers, the ones you gave me, are on my desk, under the calendar.

IRINA. I'm coming with you.

TUZENBAKH [*alarmed*]. No, no! [*goes off quickly, then stops in the avenue*] Irina!

IRINA. What?

TUZENBAKH [*not knowing what to say*]. I didn't have any coffee this morning. Will you tell them to get some ready for me? [*goes off quickly*]

IRINA *stands, lost in thought, then goes to the back of the stage and sits down on a swing. Enter* ANDREY *with the pram;* FERAPONT *appears.*

FERAPONT. Andrey Sergeyevich, the papers aren't mine, you know, they're the office papers. I didn't make them up.

ANDREY. Oh, where has all my past life gone to? – the time when I was young and gay and clever, when I used to have fine dreams and great thoughts, and the present and the future were bright with hope? Why do we become so dull and common-place and uninteresting almost before we've begun to live? Why do we get lazy, indifferent, useless, unhappy? . . . This town's been in existence for two hundred years; a hundred thousand people live in it, but there's not one who's any different from all the others! There's never been a scholar or an artist or a saint in this place, never a single man sufficiently outstanding to make you feel passionately that you wanted to emulate him. People here do nothing but eat, drink and sleep . . . Then they die and some more take their places, and they eat, drink and sleep, too – and just to introduce a bit of variety into their lives, so as to avoid getting completely stupid with boredom, they indulge in their disgusting gossip and vodka and gambling and law-suits. The wives deceive their husbands, and the husbands lie to their wives, and pretend they don't see anything and don't hear anything . . . And all this overwhelming vulgarity and pettiness crushes the children and puts out any spark they might have in them, so that they, too, become miserable, half-dead creatures, just like one another and just like their parents! . . . [*to* FERAPONT, *crossly*] What do you want?

FERAPONT. What? Here are the papers to sign.

ANDREY. What a nuisance you are!

FERAPONT [*hands him the papers*]. The porter at the finance depart-

ment told me just now . . . he said last winter they had two
hundred degrees of frost in Petersburg.

ANDREY. I hate the life I live at present, but oh! the sense of elation
when I think of the future! Then I feel so light-hearted, such a
sense of release! I seem to see light ahead, light and freedom. I see
myself free, and my children, too — free from idleness, free from
kvass, free from eternal meals of goose and cabbage, free from
after-dinner naps, free from all this degrading parasitism! . . .

FERAPONT. They say two thousand people were frozen to death.
They say everyone was scared stiff. It was either in Petersburg or
in Moscow, I can't remember exactly.

ANDREY [*with sudden emotion, tenderly*]. My dear sisters, my dear
good sisters! [*tearfully*] Masha, my dear sister! . . .

NATASHA [*through the window*]. Who's that talking so loudly there?
Is that you, Andryusha? You'll wake Sofochka. *Il ne faut pas faire
du bruit, la Sophie est dormie déjà. Vous êtes un ours.* [*getting angry*]
If you want to talk, give the pram to someone else. Ferapont,
take the pram from the master.

FERAPONT. Yes, Madam. [*takes the pram*]

ANDREY [*shamefacedly*]. I was talking quietly.

NATASHA [*in the window, caressing her small son*]. Bobik! Naughty
Bobik! Aren't you a naughty boy!

ANDREY [*glancing through the papers*]. All right, I'll go through them
and sign them if they need it. You can take them back to the
office later. [*goes into the house, reading the papers*]

    [FERAPONT *wheels the pram into the garden*]

NATASHA [*in the window*]. What's Mummy's name, Bobik? You
darling! And who's that lady? Auntie Olya. Say: 'Hullo, Auntie
Olya.'

Two street musicians, a man and a girl, enter and begin to play on a
violin and a harp; VERSHININ, OLGA *and* ANFISA *come out of the house*
and listen in silence for a few moments; then IRINA *approaches them.*

OLGA. Our garden's like a public road; everybody goes through it.
Nanny, give something to the musicians.

ANFISA [*giving them money*]. Go along now, God bless you, good
people!

    [*the musicians bow and go away*]

Poor, homeless folk! Whoever would go dragging round the

streets playing tunes if he had enough to eat? [*to* IRINA] How are you, Irenushka? [*kisses her*] Ah, my child, what a life I'm having! Such comfort! In a large flat at the school with Olyushka – and no rent to pay, either! The Lord's been kind to me in my old age. I've never had such a comfortable time in my life, old sinner that I am! A big flat, and no rent to pay, and a whole room to myself, with my own bed. All free. Sometimes when I wake up in the night I begin to think, and then – Oh, Lord! Oh, Holy Mother of God! – there's no-one happier in the world than me!

VERSHININ [*glances at his watch*]. We shall be starting in a moment, Olga Sergeyevna. It's time I went. [*a pause*] I wish you all the happiness in the world . . . everything . . . Where's Marya Sergeyevna?

IRINA. She's somewhere in the garden. I'll go and look for her.

VERSHININ. That's kind of you. I really must hurry.

ANFISA. I'll come and help to look for her. [*calls out*] Mashenka, ah-oo!

   [*goes with* IRINA *towards the far end of the garden*]
Ah-oo! Ah-oo!

VERSHININ. Everything comes to an end. Well, here we are – and now it's going to be goodbye. [*looks at his watch*] The city gave us a sort of farewell lunch. There was champagne, and the mayor made a speech, and I ate and listened, but in spirit I was with you here . . . [*glances round the garden*] I've grown so . . . so accustomed to you.

OLGA. Shall we meet again some day, I wonder?

VERSHININ. Most likely not! [*a pause*] My wife and the two little girls will be staying on here for a month or two. Please, if anything happens, if they need anything . . .

OLGA. Yes, yes, of course. You needn't worry about that. [*a pause*] Tomorrow there won't be a single officer or soldier in the town . . . All that will be just a memory, and, of course, a new life will begin for us here . . . [*a pause*] Nothing ever happens as we'd like it to. I didn't want to be a headmistress, and yet now I am one. It means we shan't be going to live in Moscow . . .

VERSHININ. Well . . . Thank you for everything. Forgive me if ever I've done anything . . . I've talked a lot too much, far too much . . . Forgive me for that, don't think too unkindly of me.

OLGA [*wipes her eyes*]. Now . . . why is Masha so long coming?

VERSHININ. What else can I tell you now it's time to say goodbye? What shall I philosophise about now? . . . [*laughs*] Yes,
life is difficult. It seems quite hopeless for a lot of us, just a kind
of impasse . . . And yet you must admit that it is gradually
getting easier and brighter, and it's clear that the time isn't
far off when the light will spread everywhere. [*looks at his
watch*] Time, it's time for me to go . . . In the old days the
human race was always making war, its entire existence
was taken up with campaigns, advances, retreats, victories . . .
But now all that's out of date, and in its place there's a huge
vacuum, clamouring to be filled. Humanity is passionately seeking something to fill it with and, of course, it will find something some day. Oh! If only it would happen soon! [*a pause*]
If only we could educate the industrious people and make
the educated people industrious . . . [*looks at his watch*] I really
must go . . .

OLGA. Here she comes!

Enter MASHA.

VERSHININ. I've come to say goodbye . . .
   [OLGA *walks off and stands a little to one side so as not to interfere
                    with their leave-taking*]

MASHA [*looking into his face*]. Goodbye! . . . [*a long kiss*]

OLGA. That'll do, that'll do.

MASHA [*sobs loudly*].

VERSHININ. Write to me . . . Don't forget me! Let me go . . . it's
time. Olga Sergeyevna, please take her away . . . I must go . . .
I'm late already . . . [*deeply moved, kisses* OLGA's *hands, then
embraces* MASHA *once again and goes out quickly*]

OLGA. That'll do, Masha! Don't, my dear, don't . . .

Enter KULYGIN.

KULYGIN [*embarrassed*]. Never mind, let her cry, let her . . . My
dear Masha, my dear, sweet Masha . . . You're my wife, and
I'm happy in spite of everything . . . I'm not complaining, I've
no reproach to make – not a single one . . . Olga here is my
witness . . . We'll start our life over again in the same old way,
and you won't hear a word from me . . . not a hint . . .

MASHA [*suppressing her sobs*]. 'A green oak grows by a curving shore, And round that oak hangs a golden chain.' . . . 'A golden chain round that oak.' . . . Oh, I'm going mad. . . . By a curving shore . . . a green oak . . .

OLGA. Calm yourself, Masha, calm yourself. . . . Give her some water.

MASHA. I'm not crying any more. . . .

KULYGIN. She's not crying any more . . . she's a good girl.

[*the hollow sound of a gun-shot is heard in the distance*]

MASHA. 'A green oak grows by a curving shore, And round that oak hangs a golden chain.' . . . A green cat . . . a green oak . . . I've got it all mixed up . . . [*drinks water*] My life's messed up . . . I don't want anything now . . . I'll calm down in a moment . . . It doesn't matter. . . . What is 'the curving shore'? Why does it keep coming into my head all the time? My thoughts are all mixed up.

Enter IRINA.

OLGA. Calm down, Masha. That's right . . . good girl! . . . Let's go indoors.

MASHA [*irritably*]. I'm not going in there! [*sobs, but immediately checks herself*] I don't go into that house now, and I'm not going to . . .

IRINA. Let's sit down together for a moment, and not talk about anything. I'm going away tomorrow, you know . . .

[*a pause*]

KULYGIN. Yesterday I took away a false beard and a moustache from a boy in the third form. I've got them here. [*puts them on*] Do I look like our German teacher? . . . [*laughs*] I do, don't I? The boys are funny.

MASHA. It's true, you do look like that German of yours.

OLGA [*laughs*] Yes, he does.

[MASHA *cries*]

IRINA. That's enough, Masha!

KULYGIN. Very much like him, I think!

Enter NATASHA.

NATASHA [*to the maid*]. What? Oh, yes. Mr Protopopov is going to keep an eye on Sofochka, and Andrey Sergeyevich is going to take Bobik out in the pram. What a lot of work these children make! . . . [*to* IRINA] Irina, you're really leaving tomorrow? What a pity! Do stay just another week, won't you? [*catching sight of* KULYGIN, *shrieks; he laughs and takes off the false beard and moustache*] Get away with you! How you scared me! [*to* IRINA] I've grown so accustomed to you being here . . . You mustn't think it's going to be easy for me to be without you. I'll get Andrey and his old violin to move into your room: he can saw away at it as much as he likes there. And then we'll move Sofochka into his room. She's such a wonderful child, really! Such a lovely little girl! This morning she looked at me with such a sweet expression, and then she said: 'Ma–mma!'

KULYGIN. It's quite true, she is a beautiful child.

NATASHA. So tomorrow I'll be alone here. [*sighs*] I'll have this fir-tree avenue cut down first, then that maple tree over there. It looks so awful in the evenings . . . [*to* IRINA] My dear, that belt you're wearing doesn't suit you at all. Not at all good taste. You want something brighter to go with that dress . . . I'll tell them to put flowers all round here, lots of flowers, so that we get plenty of scent from them . . . [*sternly*] Why is there a fork lying on this seat? [*going into the house, to the maid*] Why is that fork left on the seat there? [*shouts*] Don't answer me back!

KULYGIN. There she goes again!

    [*a band plays a military march off-stage; all listen*]

OLGA. They're going.

Enter CHEBUTYKIN.

MASHA. The soldiers are going. Well . . . Happy journey to them! [*to her husband*] We must go home . . . Where's my hat and cape? . . .

KULYGIN. I took them indoors. I'll bring them at once.

OLGA. Yes, we can go home now. It's time.

CHEBUTYKIN. Olga Sergeyevna!

OLGA. What is it? [*a pause*] What?

CHEBUTYKIN. Nothing . . . I don't know quite how to tell you . . . [*whispers into her ear*]

OLGA [*frightened*]. It can't be true!

CHEBUTYKIN. Yes . . . a bad business . . . I'm so tired . . . quite worn out . . . I don't want to say another word . . . [*with annoyance*] Anyway, nothing matters! . . .

MASHA. What's happened?

OLGA [*puts her arms round* IRINA]. What a dreadful day! . . . I don't know how to tell you, dear . . .

IRINA. What is it? Tell me quickly, what is it? For Heaven's sake! . . . [*cries*]

CHEBUTYKIN. The Baron's just been killed in a duel.

IRINA [*cries quietly*]. I knew it, I knew it . . .

CHEBUTYKIN [*goes to the back of the stage and sits down*]. I'm tired . . . [*takes a newspaper out of his pocket*] Let them cry for a bit . . . [*sings quietly to himself*] Tarara-boom-di-ay, I'm sitting on a tomb-di-ay . . . What difference does it make? . . .

[*the three sisters stand huddled together*]

MASHA. Oh, listen to that band! They're leaving us . . . one of them's gone for good . . . for ever! We're left alone . . . to start our lives all over again. We must go on living . . . we must go on living . . .

IRINA [*puts her head on* OLGA'*s breast*]. Some day people will know why such things happen, and what the purpose of all this suffering is . . . Then there won't be any more riddles . . . Meanwhile we must go on living . . . and working. Yes, we must just go on working! Tomorrow I'll go away alone and teach in a school somewhere; I'll give my life to people who need it . . . It's autumn now, winter will soon be here, and the snow will cover everything . . . but I'll go on working and working! . . .

OLGA [*puts her arms round both her sisters*]. How cheerfully and jauntily that band's playing – really I feel as if I wanted to live! Merciful God! The years will pass, and we shall all be gone for good and quite forgotten . . . Our faces and our voices will be forgotten and people won't even know that there were once three of us here . . . But our sufferings may mean happiness for the people who come after us . . . There'll be a time when peace and happiness reign in the world, and then we shall be remembered kindly and blessed. No, my dear sisters, life isn't finished for us yet! We're going to live! The band is playing so cheerfully and joyfully – maybe, if we wait a little longer, we shall find out why we live, why we suffer . . . Oh, if we only knew, if only we knew!

The music grows fainter and fainter. KULYGIN, *smiling happily,*
brings out the hat and the cape. ANDREY *enters; he is pushing*
the pram with BOBIK *sitting in it.*

CHEBUTYKIN [*sings quietly to himself*]. Tarara-boom-di-ay . . . I'm
sitting on a tomb-di-ay . . . [*reads the paper*] What does it matter?
Nothing matters!

OLGA. If only we knew, if only we knew! . . .

CURTAIN

THE CHERRY ORCHARD

A Comedy in Four Acts

Characters in the Play

RANEVSKAYA, Lyubov Andreyevna (Lyuba), a landowner
ANYA (Anichka), her daughter, aged 17
VARYA (Varvara Mikhailovna), her adopted daughter, aged 24
GAYEV, Leonid Andreyevich (Lyonya), brother of Mme Ranevskaya
LOPAKHIN, Yermolay Alexeyevich, a businessman
TROFIMOV, Pyotr Sergeyevich (Petya), a student
SIMEONOV-PISHCHIK, Boris Borisovich, a landowner
CHARLOTTA IVANOVNA, a German governess
YEPIKHODOV, Semyon Panteleyevich, a clerk on Ranevskaya's
  estate
DUNYASHA (Avdotya Fyodorovna), a parlourmaid
FIRS (Firs Nikolayevich), a man-servant, aged 87
YASHA, a young man-servant
A TRAMP
STATION-MASTER
POST-OFFICE CLERK
GUESTS, SERVANTS

The action takes place on the estate of Mme Ranevskaya.

ACT ONE

A room which used to be the children's bedroom and is still referred to as the 'nursery'. There are several doors: one of them leads into ANYA's *room. It is early morning: the sun is just coming up. The windows of the room are shut, but through them the cherry trees can be seen in blossom. It is May, but in the orchard there is morning frost.*

Enter DUNYASHA, *carrying a candle, and* LOPAKHIN *with a book in his hand.*

LOPAKHIN. The train's arrived, thank God. What time is it?

DUNYASHA. It's nearly two. [*blows out the candle*] It's light already.

LOPAKHIN. How late was the train then? Two hours at least. [*yawns and stretches*] How stupid I am! What a fool I've made of myself! Came here on purpose to go to the station and meet them – and then overslept! . . . Dropped off to sleep in the chair. Annoying . . . I wish you'd woken me up.

DUNYASHA. I thought you'd gone. [*listens*] Sounds as if they're coming.

LOPAKHIN [*also listens*]. No . . . They'll have to get their luggage out, and all that . . . [*pause*] Lyubov Andreyevna has been abroad for five years, I don't know what she's like now . . . She used to be a good soul. An easy-going, simple kind of person. I remember when I was a boy of about fifteen, my father – he had a small shop in the village then – hit me in the face and made my nose bleed . . . We had come to the manor for something or other, and he'd been drinking, I remember it as if it happened yesterday: Lyubov Andreyevna – she was still young and slender then – brought me in and took me to the washstand in this very room, the nursery it was then. 'Don't cry, little peasant,' she said, 'it'll be better before you're old enough to get married' . . . [*pause*] 'Little peasant'. . . . She was right enough, my father was a peasant. Yet here I am – all dressed up in a white waistcoat and brown shoes . . . But you can't make a silk purse out of a sow's ear. I am rich, I've got a lot of money, but anyone can see I'm just a peasant, anyone who takes the trouble to think about me and look under my skin. [*turning over pages in the book*] I've been reading this book, and I haven't understood a word of it. I fell asleep reading it. [*pause*]

DUNYASHA. The dogs didn't sleep all night: they know their masters are coming.

LOPAKHIN. What's the matter, Dunyasha?

DUNYASHA. My hands are trembling. I feel as if I'm going to faint.

LOPAKHIN. You're too refined and sensitive, Dunyasha. You dress yourself up like a lady, and you do your hair like one, too. That won't do, you know. You must remember your place.

Enter YEPIKHODOV *with a bunch of flowers; he wears a jacket and brightly polished high boots which squeak loudly; as he comes in, he drops the flowers.*

YEPIKHODOV [*picks up the flowers*]. The gardener sent these. He says they're to go in the dining-room. [*hands the flowers to* DUNYASHA]

LOPAKHIN. And bring me some *kvass*.

DUNYASHA. Very well. [*goes out*]

YEPIKHODOV. There's a frost outside, three degrees of it, and the cherry trees are covered with bloom. I can't approve of this climate of ours, you know. [*sighs*] No, I can't. It doesn't contribute to – to things, I mean. And do you know, Yermolay Alexeyevich, I bought myself a pair of boots the day before yesterday, and they squeak so terribly . . . well, I mean to say, it's utterly impossible, you know . . . What can I put on them?

LOPAKHIN. Oh, leave me alone. You make me tired.

YEPIKHODOV. Every day something or other unpleasant happens to me. But I don't complain; I'm accustomed to it, I even laugh at it.

Enter DUNYASHA; *she serves* LOPAKHIN *with kvass.*

I'll leave you now. [*bumps into a chair which falls over*] You see! [*triumphantly*] You can see for yourself what it is, I mean to say . . . so to speak . . . It's simply extraordinary! [*goes out*]

DUNYASHA. I want to tell you a secret, Yermolay Alexeyevich. Yepikhodov proposed to me.

LOPAKHIN. Ah!

DUNYASHA. I don't know what to do . . . He's a quiet man, but sometimes he gets talking, and then you can't understand anything he says. It sounds nice, it sounds very moving, but you just can't understand it. I think I like him a little, and he's madly in love with me. He's an unlucky sort of person, something unpleasant seems to happen to him every day. That's why they tease him and call him 'two-and-twenty misfortunes'.

LOPAKHIN [*listens*]. I think I can hear them coming . . .

DUNYASHA. Coming! . . . Oh, dear! I don't know what's the matter with me. . . . I feel cold all over.

LOPAKHIN. Yes, they really are coming! Let's go and meet them at the door. I wonder if she'll recognise me? We haven't met for five years.

DUNYASHA [*agitated*]. I'm going to faint . . . Oh, I'm fainting! . . .

The sound of two coaches driving up to the house is heard. LOPAKHIN *and* DUNYASHA *go out quickly. The stage is empty. Then there are sounds of people arriving in the adjoining room.* FIRS, *leaning on a stick, crosses the stage hurriedly: he has been to the station to meet* LYUBOV ANDREYEVNA. *He is dressed in an old-fashioned livery coat and a top hat and is muttering to himself, though it is impossible to make out what he is saying. The noises off-stage become louder. A voice says: 'Let's go through here'.*

Enter LYUBOV ANDREYEVNA, ANYA *and* CHARLOTTA IVANOVNA, *leading a small dog, all in travelling clothes,* VARYA, *wearing an overcoat and a kerchief over her head,* GAYEV, SIMEONOV–PISHCHIK, LOPAKHIN, DUNYASHA, *carrying a bundle and an umbrella, and other servants with luggage.*

ANYA. Let's go through here. You remember what room this is, mamma?

LYUBOV ANDREYEVNA [*joyfully, through her tears*]. The nursery!

VARYA. How cold it is! My hands are quite numb. [*to* LYUBOV ANDREYEVNA] Your rooms are just as you left them, mamma dear, the white one, and the mauve one.

LYUBOV ANDREYEVNA. The nursery, my dear, my beautiful room! . . . I used to sleep here when I was little . . . [*cries*] And now I feel as if I were little again . . . [*she kisses her brother, then* VARYA, *then her brother again*] And Varya is just the same as ever, looking like a nun. I recognised Dunyasha, too. [*kisses* DUNYASHA]

GAYEV. The train was two hours late. Just think of it! What efficiency!

CHARLOTTA [*to* PISHCHIK]. My dog actually eats nuts.

PISHCHIK [*astonished*]. Fancy that!

[*they all go out except* ANYA *and* DUNYASHA]

DUNYASHA. We've waited and waited for you . . . [*helps* ANYA *to take off her hat and coat*]

ANYA. I haven't slept for four nights . . . I'm frozen.

DUNYASHA. You went away during Lent and it was snowing and freezing then, but now it's spring-time. Darling! [*she laughs and kisses her*] I could hardly bear waiting for you, my pet, my precious . . . But I must tell you at once, I can't wait a minute longer . . .

ANYA [*without enthusiasm*]. What is it this time? . . .

DUNYASHA. Yepikhodov, the clerk, proposed to me just after Easter.

ANYA. You never talk about anything else . . . [*tidies her hair*] I've lost all my hairpins . . . [*she is very tired and can hardly keep on her feet*]

DUNYASHA. I really don't know what to think. He loves me . . . he does love me so!

ANYA [*looking through the door into her room, tenderly*]. My own room, my own windows, just as if I had never been away! I'm home again! Tomorrow I'm going to get up and run straight into the garden! Oh, if only I could go to bed and sleep now! I couldn't sleep all the way back, I was so worried.

DUNYASHA. Pyotr Sergeyevich arrived the day before yesterday.

ANYA [*joyfully*]. Petya!

DUNYASHA. He's sleeping in the bath-house, and living there, too. 'I wouldn't like to inconvenience them,' he said. [*looks at her watch*] I ought to wake him up, but Varvara Mikhailovna told me not to. 'Don't you wake him,' she said.

Enter VARYA *with a bunch of keys at her waist.*

VARYA. Dunyasha, make some coffee, quick! Mamma is asking for coffee.

DUNYASHA. It'll be ready in a moment. [*goes out*]

VARYA. Thank God, you've arrived. You're home again. [*embracing her*] My darling's come back! My precious!

ANYA. If you only knew the things I had to put up with!

VARYA. I can just imagine it.

ANYA. I left just before Easter: it was cold then. Charlotta never stopped talking, never left off doing her silly conjuring tricks all the way. Why did you make me take Charlotta?

VARYA. But how could you go alone, darling? At seventeen!

ANYA. When we arrived in Paris it was cold and snowing. My French was awful. Mamma was living on the fifth floor, and when I got there she had visitors. There were some French ladies there and an old priest with a little book, and the room was full of cigarette smoke, so untidy and uncomfortable. Suddenly I felt so sorry for mamma, so sorry, that I took her head between my hands, and just couldn't let it go . . . Afterwards mamma cried and was very sweet to me.

VARYA [*tearfully*]. I can hardly bear listening to you . . .

ANYA. She had already sold her villa near Mentone, and she had nothing left, positively nothing. And I hadn't any money left either, not a penny: I had hardly enough to get to Paris. And mamma couldn't grasp that! In station restaurants she would order the most expensive dishes and tip the waiters a rouble each. Charlotta was just the same. And Yasha expected a full-course dinner for himself: it was simply dreadful. You know, Yasha is mamma's valet, we brought him with us.

VARYA. Yes, I've seen the wretch.

ANYA. Well, how are things going? Have we paid the interest?

VARYA. Far from it.

ANYA. Oh dear! Oh dear!

VARYA. The estate will be up for sale in August.

ANYA. Oh dear!

LOPAKHIN [*puts his head through the door and bleats*]. Me-e-e . . . [*disappears*]

VARYA [*tearfully*]. I'd like to give him this . . . [*clenches her fist*]

ANYA [*her arms round* VARYA, *dropping her voice*]. Varya, has he proposed to you?

[VARYA *shakes her head*]

But he loves you . . . Why don't you talk it over with him, what are you waiting for?

VARYA. I don't believe anything will come of it. He's too busy, he's no time to think of me . . . He takes no notice of me at all. I'd rather he didn't come, it makes me miserable to see him. Everyone's talking of our wedding, everyone's congratulating me, but in fact there's nothing in it, it's all a kind of dream. [*in a changed tone of voice*] You've got a new brooch, a bee, isn't it?

ANYA [*sadly*]. Mamma bought it for me. [*she goes into her room and now speaks gaily, like a child*] You know, I went up in a balloon in Paris!

VARYA. My darling's home again! My precious girl!

DUNYASHA *returns with a coffee-pot and prepares coffee.*

VARYA [*standing by* ANYA's *door*]. You know, dearest, as I go about the house doing my odd jobs, I'm always dreaming and dreaming. If only we could marry you to some rich man, I feel my mind would be at ease. I'd go away then, first to a hermitage, then on to Kiev, to Moscow . . . walking from one holy place to another. I'd go on and on. Oh, what a beautiful life!

ANYA. The birds are singing in the garden. What time is it?

VARYA. It must be gone two. Time you went to bed, darling. [*goes into* ANYA's *room*] A beautiful life!

Enter YASHA, *carrying a travelling rug and a small bag.*

YASHA [*crossing the stage, in an affectedly genteel voice*]. May I go through here?

DUNYASHA. I can hardly recognise you, Yasha. You've changed so abroad.

YASHA. Hm! And who are you?

DUNYASHA. When you left here, I was no bigger than this . . . [*shows her height from the floor with her hand*] I'm Dunyasha, Fyodor Kosoyedov's daughter. You can't remember!

YASHA. Hm! Quite a little peach! [*looks round, puts his arms round her; she cries out and drops a saucer.* YASHA *goes out quickly*]

VARYA [*in the doorway, crossly*] What's going on here?

DUNYASHA [*tearfully*]. I've broken a saucer.

VARYA. That's a good omen.

ANYA [*coming out of her room*]. We ought to warn mamma that Petya is here.

VARYA. I gave orders not to wake him.

ANYA [*pensively*]. It was six years ago that father died, and then, only a month after that, little brother Grisha was drowned in the river. He was only seven, such a pretty little boy! Mamma couldn't bear it and went away . . . she never looked back. [*shivers*] How well I understand her! If she only knew how I understand her! [*pause*] And, of course, Petya Trofimov was Grisha's tutor, he might remind her . . .

Enter FIRS, *wearing a jacket and a white waistcoat.*

FIRS [*goes to the coffee-pot, preoccupied*]. Madam will have her coffee here. [*puts on white gloves*] Is the coffee ready? [*to* DUNYASHA, *severely*] What about the cream?

DUNYASHA. Oh, my goodness! [*goes out quickly*]

FIRS [*fussing around the coffee-pot*]. The girl's daft . . . [*mutters*] From Paris . . . The master used to go to Paris years ago . . . Used to go by coach . . . [*laughs*]

VARYA. Firs, what are you laughing at?

FIRS. What can I get you, Madam? [*happily*] The mistress is home again! Home at last! I don't mind if I die now . . . [*weeps with joy*]

Enter LYUBOV ANDREYEVNA, LOPAKHIN, GAYEV *and* SIMEONOV-PISHCHIK, *the last wearing a long peasant coat of finely-woven cloth and wide trousers tucked inside high boots.* GAYEV, *as he comes in, moves his arms and body as if he were playing billards.*

LYUBOV ANDREYEVNA. How does it go now? Let me think . . . I pot the red . . . I go in off into the middle pocket!

GAYEV. I pot into the corner pocket! . . . Years ago you and I slept in this room, little brother and sister together; and now I'm fifty-one, strange as it may seem.

LOPAKHIN. Yes, time flies.

GAYEV. What?

LOPAKHIN. Time flies, I say.

GAYEV. This place smells of patchouli . . .

ANYA. I think I'll go to bed. Good-night, mamma. [*kisses her*]

LYUBOV ANDREYEVNA. My precious child! [*kisses her hands*] You're glad to be home, aren't you? I still feel dazed.

ANYA. Good-night, uncle.

GAYEV [*kisses her face and hands*]. God bless you. How like your mother you are! [*to his sister*] You looked exactly like her at her age, Lyuba.

> [ANYA *shakes hands with* LOPAKHIN *and* PISHCHIK, *goes out and shuts the door after her*]

LYUBOV ANDREYEVNA. She's very tired.

PISHCHIK. It's a long journey.

VARYA [*to* LOPAKHIN *and* PISHCHIK]. Well, gentlemen? It's past two, time to break up the party.

LYUBOV ANDREYEVNA [*laughs*]. You're just the same, Varya. [*draws* VARYA *to her and kisses her*] Let me have some coffee, then we'll all go. [FIRS *places a cushion under her feet*] Thank you, my dear. I've got into the habit of drinking coffee. I drink it day and night. Thank you, my dear old friend. [*kisses* FIRS]

VARYA. I'd better see if all the luggage is there. [*goes out*]

LYUBOV ANDREYEVNA. Is it really me sitting here? [*laughs*] I feel like dancing and flinging my arms about. [*hides her face in her hands*] What if I'm just dreaming? God, how I love my own country! I love it so much, I could hardly see it from the train, I was crying all the time. [*through tears*] However, I must drink my coffee. Thank you, Firs, thank you, my dear old friend. I am so glad I found you still alive.

FIRS. The day before yesterday.

GAYEV. He doesn't hear very well.

LOPAKHIN. I've got to leave for Kharkov soon after four. What a nuisance! I'd like to have a good look at you, to have a talk . . . You look as lovely as ever.

PISHCHIK [*breathing heavily*]. She looks prettier. In her Parisian clothes . . . enough to turn anybody's head!

LOPAKHIN. Your brother here – Leonid Andreyevich – says that I'm a country bumpkin, a tight-fisted peasant, but I don't take any notice of that. Let him say what he likes. The only thing I want is for you to have faith in me as you did before. Merciful God! My father was your father's serf, and your grandfather's, too, but you did so much for me in the past that I forget everything and love you as if you were my own sister . . . more than my own sister.

LYUBOV ANDREYEVNA. I just can't sit still, I simply can't! [*she jumps up and walks about the room in great agitation*] This happiness is too much for me. You can laugh at me, I'm foolish . . . My dear bookcase! [*kisses bookcase*] My own little table!

GAYEV. You know, old Nanny died while you were away.

LYUBOV ANDREYEVNA [*sits down and drinks coffee*]. Yes, I know. May the kingdom of heaven be hers. They wrote to tell me.

GAYEV. Anastasiy died, too. Petrushka Kosoy has left me and is working for the police in town. [*takes a box of boiled sweets from his pocket and puts one in his mouth*]

PISHCHIK. My daughter, Dashenka, sends her greetings to you.

LOPAKHIN. I feel I'd like to tell you something nice, something jolly. [*glances at his watch*] I'll have to go in a moment, there's no time to talk. However, I could tell you in a few words. You know, of course, that your cherry orchard is going to be sold to pay your debts. The auction is to take place on the twenty-second of August, but there's no need for you to worry. You can sleep in peace, my dear; there's a way out. This is my plan, please listen carefully. Your estate is only twenty miles from town, and the railway line is not far away. Now, if your cherry orchard and the land along the river are divided into plots and leased out for summer residences you'll have a yearly income of at least twenty-five thousand roubles.

GAYEV. But what nonsense!

LYUBOV ANDREYEVNA. I don't quite understand you, Yermolay Alexeyevich.

LOPAKHIN. You'll charge the tenants at least ten roubles a year for a plot of one acre, and if you advertise now, I'm prepared to stake any amount you like that you won't have a spot of land unoccupied by the autumn: it will be snatched up. In fact, I really feel I must congratulate you, you're saved after all! It's a marvellous situation and the river's deep enough for bathing. But, of course, the place will have to be cleaned up, put in order. For instance, all the old outbuildings will have to be pulled down, as well as this house which is no good to anybody. The old cherry orchard should be cut down, too.

LYUBOV ANDREYEVNA. Cut down? My dear man, forgive me, you don't seem to understand. If there's one thing interesting, one thing really outstanding in the whole county, it's our cherry orchard.

LOPAKHIN. The only outstanding thing about this orchard is that it's very large. It only produces a crop every other year, and then there's nobody to buy it.

GAYEV. This orchard is actually mentioned in the *Encyclopaedia*.

LOPAKHIN [*glancing at his watch*]. If you can't think clearly about it, or come to a decision, the cherry orchard and the whole estate as well will be sold by auction. You must decide! There's no other way out, I assure you. There's no other way.

FIRS. In the old days, forty or fifty years ago, the cherries were dried, preserved, marinaded, made into jam, and sometimes . . .

GAYEV. Be quiet, Firs.

FIRS. And sometimes, whole cartloads of dried cherries were sent to Moscow and Kharkov. The money they fetched! And the dried cherries in those days were soft, juicy, sweet, tasty . . . They knew how to do it then . . . they had a recipe . . .

LYUBOV ANDREYEVNA. And where is that recipe now?

FIRS. Forgotten. No-one can remember it.

PISHCHIK [*to* LYUBOV ANDREYEVNA]. What was it like in Paris? Did you eat frogs?

LYUBOV ANDREYEVNA. I ate crocodiles.

PISHCHIK. Fancy that!

LOPAKHIN. Up to just recently there were only gentry and peasants living in the country, but now there are all these summer residents. All the towns, even quite small ones, are surrounded with villas. And probably in the course of the next twenty years or so, these people will multiply tremendously. At present they merely drink tea on the verandah, but they might start cultivating their plots of land, and then your cherry orchard would be gay with life and wealth and luxury . . .

GAYEV [*indignantly*]. What nonsense!

Enter VARYA *and* YASHA.

VARYA. Here are two telegrams for you, mamma dear. [*picks out a key and unlocks an old bookcase with a jingling noise*] Here they are.

LYUBOV ANDREYEVNA. They are from Paris. [*tears them up without reading them*] I've finished with Paris.

GAYEV. Do you know, Lyuba, how old this bookcase is? A week ago I pulled out the bottom drawer, and I found some figures burnt in the wood. It was made exactly a hundred years ago. What do you think of that, eh? We ought to celebrate its anniversary. An inanimate object, true, but still — a bookcase!

PISHCHIK [*astonished*]. A hundred years! Fancy that!

GAYEV. Yes . . . This is a valuable piece of furniture. [*feeling round the bookcase with his hands*] My dear, venerable bookcase! I salute you! For more than a hundred years you have devoted yourself to the highest ideals of goodness and justice. For a hundred years you have never failed to fill us with an urge to useful work; several generations of our family have had their courage sustained and their faith in a better future fortified by your silent call; you have fostered in us the ideal of public good and social consciousness.

[*pause*]

LOPAKHIN. Yes . . .

LYUBOV ANDREYEVNA. You're just the same, Lyonya.

GAYEV [*slightly embarrassed*]. I pot into the corner pocket! I pot into the middle pocket! . . .

LOPAKHIN [*glances at his watch*]. Well, it's time for me to be going.

YASHA [*brings medicine to* LYUBOV ANDREYEVNA]. Would you care to take your pills now?

PISHCHIK. Don't take medicines, my dear . . . they don't do you any good . . . or harm either. Let me have them. [*takes the box from her, pours the pills into the palm of his hand, blows on them, puts them all into his mouth and takes a drink of kvass*] There!

LYUBOV ANDREYEVNA [*alarmed*]. But you're mad!

PISHCHIK. I've taken all the pills.

LOPAKHIN. What a digestion!

[*all laugh*]

FIRS. His Honour came to see us in Holy Week, and ate half-a-bucketful of salt cucumbers. [*mutters*]

LYUBOV ANDREYEVNA. What is it he's saying?

VARYA. He's been muttering for the last three years. We're accustomed to it.

YASHA. It's his age. . . .

[CHARLOTTA IVANOVNA, *very thin and tightly laced in a white dress, with a lorgnette at her waist, passes across the stage*]

LOPAKHIN. Forgive me, Charlotta Ivanovna, I haven't yet had time to say how d'you do to you. [*tries to kiss her hand*].

CHARLOTTA [*withdrawing her hand*]. If you were permitted to kiss a lady's hand, you'd want to kiss her elbow next, and then her shoulder.

LOPAKHIN. I'm unlucky today.

[*all laugh*]

Charlotta Ivanovna, do a trick for us.

CHARLOTTA. There's no need to, now. I want to go to bed. [*goes out*]

LOPAKHIN. I'll see you in three weeks' time. [*kisses* LYUBOV ANDRE-YEVNA's *hand*] Meanwhile, goodbye. Time to go. [*to* GAYEV] *Au revoir.* [*embraces* PISHCHIK] *Au revoir.* [*shakes hands with* VARYA, *then with* FIRS *and* YASHA] I don't want to go, really. [*to* LYUBOV ANDREYEVNA] If you think over this question of country villas and come to a decision, let me know, and I'll get you a loan of fifty thousand or more. Think it over seriously.

VARYA [*crossly*]. Will you ever go away?

LOPAKHIN. I'm going, I'm going. [*goes out*]

GAYEV. What a boor! I beg your pardon . . . Varya's going to marry him, he's Varya's precious fiancé.

VARYA. Please don't say anything uncalled for, uncle dear.

LYUBOV ANDREYEVNA. Well, Varya, I shall be very glad. He's a good man.

PISHCHIK. He's a man . . . let's admit it . . . a most admirable fellow . . . My Dashenka says so, too . . . she says all sorts of things . . . [*he drops asleep and snores, but wakes up again at once*] Incidentally, my dear, will you lend me two hundred and forty roubles? I've got to pay the interest on the mortgage tomorrow . . .

VARYA [*in alarm*]. We haven't got it, we really haven't!

LYUBOV ANDREYEVNA. It's quite true, I have nothing.

PISHCHIK. It'll turn up. [*laughs*] I never lose hope. Sometimes I think everything's lost, I'm ruined, and then – lo and behold! – a railway line is built through my land, and they pay me for it! Something or other is sure to happen, tomorrow, if not today. Perhaps Dashenka will win two hundred thousand roubles. She's got a lottery ticket.

LYUBOV ANDREYEVNA. I've finished my coffee; now I can go and rest.

FIRS [*brushing* GAYEV, *admonishing him*]. You've put on the wrong pair of trousers again! What am I to do with you?

VARYA [*in a low voice*]. Anya's asleep. [*quietly opens a window*] The sun has risen, it's warmer already. Look, mamma dear, how wonderful the trees are! Heavens, what lovely air! The starlings are singing!

GAYEV [*opens another window*]. The orchard is all white. You haven't forgotten, Lyuba? How straight this long avenue is — quite straight, just like a ribbon that's been stretched taut. It glitters on moonlit nights. Do you remember? You haven't forgotten?

LYUBOV ANDREYEVNA [*looks through the window at the orchard*]. Oh, my childhood, my innocent childhood! I used to sleep in this nursery; I used to look on to the orchard from here, and I woke up happy every morning. In those days the orchard was just as it is now, nothing has changed. [*laughs happily*] All, all white! Oh, my orchard! After the dark, stormy autumn and the cold winter, you are young and joyous again; the angels have not forsaken you! If only this burden could be taken from me, if only I could forget my past!

GAYEV. Yes, and now the orchard is going to be sold to pay our debts, strange as it seems. . . .

LYUBOV ANDREYEVNA. Look, there's Mother walking through the orchard . . . in a white dress! [*laughs happily*] It is her!

GAYEV. Where?

VARYA. Bless you, mamma dear!

LYUBOV ANDREYEVNA. It's no-one, I only imagined it. Over there, you see, on the right, by the turning to the summer house there's a small white tree and it's bending over . . . it looks like a woman.

Enter TROFIMOV. *He is dressed in a shabby student's uniform, and wears glasses.*

LYUBOV ANDREYEVNA. What a wonderful orchard! Masses of white blossom, the blue sky. . . .

TROFIMOV. Lyubov Andreyevna! [*she turns to him*] I'll just make my bow and go at once. [*kisses her hand warmly*] I was told to wait until the morning, but it was too much for my patience.

[LYUBOV ANDREYEVNA *looks at him, puzzled*]

VARYA [*through tears*]. This is Petya Trofimov.

TROFIMOV. Petya Trofimov, I used to be tutor to your Grisha. Have I really changed so much?

[LYUBOV ANDREYEVNA *puts her arms round him and weeps quietly*]

GAYEV [*embarrassed*]. Now, now, Lyuba. . . .

VARYA [*weeps*]. Didn't I tell you to wait until tomorrow, Petya?

LYUBOV ANDREYEVNA. My Grisha . . . my little boy . . . Grisha . . . my son . . .

VARYA. There's nothing for it, mamma darling. It was God's will.

TROFIMOV [*gently, with emotion*]. Don't, don't . . .

LYUBOV ANDREYEVNA [*quietly weeping*]. My little boy was lost . . . drowned . . . What for? What for, my friend? [*more quietly*] Anya's asleep there, and here I am, shouting and making a scene. Well, Petya? How is it you've lost your good looks? Why have you aged so?

TROFIMOV. A peasant woman in the train called me 'that moth-eaten gent'.

LYUBOV ANDREYEVNA. In those days you were quite a boy, a nice young student, and now your hair is thin, you wear glasses . . . Are you still a student? [*walks to the door*]

TROFIMOV. I expect I shall be a student to the end of my days.

LYUBOV ANDREYEVNA [*kisses her brother, then* VARYA]. Well, go to bed now. You have aged, too, Leonid.

PISHCHIK [*following her*]. So you're going to bed now? Och, my gout! I'd better stay the night here. And tomorrow morning, Lyubov Andreyevna, my dear, I'd like to borrow those two hundred and forty roubles.

GAYEV. How the fellow keeps at it!

PISHCHIK. Two hundred and forty roubles . . . You see, I've got to pay the interest on the mortgage.

LYUBOV ANDREYEVNA. I have no money, my dear.

PISHCHIK. I'll pay you back, my dear lady. It's a trifling amount, after all.

LYUBOV ANDREYEVNA. Very well, then. Leonid will give you the money. You give him the money, Leonid.

GAYEV. I'll be delighted; anything he wants, of course!

LYUBOV ANDREYEVNA. What else can we do? He needs it. He'll pay it back.

[LYUBOV ANDREYEVNA, TROFIMOV, PISHCHIK *and* FIRS *go out*, GAYEV, VARYA *and* YASHA *remain*]

GAYEV. My sister hasn't lost her habit of throwing money away. [*to* YASHA] Out of the way, my man, you smell of the kitchen.

YASHA [*with a sneer*]. I see you're just the same as you used to be, Leonid Andreyevich.

GAYEV. What's that? [*to* VARYA] What did he say?

VARYA [*to* YASHA]. Your mother's come from the village, she's been sitting in the servants' hall since yesterday, wanting to see you.

YASHA. I wish she'd leave me alone!

VARYA. You . . . aren't you ashamed of yourself?

YASHA. It's quite unnecessary. She could have come tomorrow.
[YASHA *goes out*]

VARYA. Dear mamma is just the same as she used to be, she hasn't
changed a bit. If she had her own way, she'd give away
everything.

GAYEV. Yes . . . You know, if a lot of cures are suggested for a
disease, it means that the disease is incurable. I've been thinking
and puzzling my brains, and I've thought of plenty of ways out,
plenty – which means there aren't any. It would be a good thing
if somebody left us some money, or if we married off our Anya
to some very rich man, or if one of us went to Yaroslavl and
tried our luck with the old aunt, the Countess. You know she's
very rich.

VARYA [*weeping*]. If only God would help us.

GAYEV. Do stop blubbering! The Countess is very rich, but she
doesn't like us . . . First, because my sister married a solicitor, and
not a nobleman . . .
[ANYA *appears in the doorway*]
She married a man who wasn't of noble birth . . . and then you
can't say her behaviour's been exactly virtuous. She's a good,
kind, lovable person, and I'm very fond of her, but whatever
extenuating circumstances you may think of, you must admit
that she's a bit easy-going morally. You can sense it in every
movement . . .

VARYA [*in a whisper*]. Anya's standing in the doorway.

GAYEV. What? [*a pause*] Funny thing, something's got into my
right eye . . . I can't see properly. And on Thursday, when I was
at the District Court . . .

ANYA *comes in.*

VARYA. Well, why aren't you asleep, Anya?

ANYA. I can't get to sleep. I just can't.

GAYEV. My dear little girl! [*kisses* ANYA's *face and hands*] My dear
child! [*through tears*] You're not just a niece to me, you're an
angel, you're everything to me. Please believe me, believe . . .

ANYA. I believe you, uncle. Everyone loves you, respects you . . .
but, dear uncle, you oughtn't to talk, you ought to try to keep

quiet. What was that you were saying just now about my mother, about your own sister? Why were you saying it?

GAYEV. Yes, yes! [*He takes her hand and puts it over his face*] You're quite right, it's dreadful! My God! My God! And the speech I made today in front of the bookcase . . . so foolish! And it was only after I'd finished that I realised it was foolish.

VARYA. It's true, uncle dear, you ought to try to keep quiet. Just keep quiet, that's all.

ANYA. If you keep quiet, you'll be happier in yourself.

GAYEV. I'll be quiet. [*kisses* ANYA's *and* VARYA's *hands*] I'll be quiet. But I must tell you something important. Last Thursday I went to the District Court, and I got talking with some friends, and from what they said it looks as if it might be possible to get a loan on promissory notes, in order to pay the interest to the bank.

VARYA. If only God would help us!

GAYEV. I'll go there again on Tuesday and have another talk. [*to* VARYA] Don't keep crying. [*to* ANYA] Your mother's going to have a talk with Lopakhin: he won't refuse her, of course. And after you've had a rest, you will go to Yaroslavl, to see the Countess, your grandmother. And so we'll approach the matter from three angles, and – the thing's done! We shall pay the interest, I'm sure of it. [*he puts a sweet into his mouth*] I swear on my honour, on anything you like, that the estate will not be sold! [*excited*] I'll stake my happiness! Here's my hand, you can call me a good-for-nothing liar if I allow the auction to take place. I swear on my soul!

ANYA [*calmer, with an air of happiness*]. How good you are, uncle, and how sensible! [*puts her arms round him*] I feel calmer now. I feel so calm and happy.

Enter FIRS.

FIRS [*reproachfully*]. Leonid Andreyevich, aren't you ashamed of yourself? When are you going to bed?

GAYEV. Presently, presently. You go away, Firs. I don't need your help. Well, children dear, bye-bye now . . . All the news tomorrow, you must go to bed now. [*kisses* ANYA *and* VARYA] You know, I'm a man of the 'eighties. People don't think much of that period, but all the same, I can say that I've suffered quite a lot in the course of my life for my convictions. It's not for nothing that the peasants love me. You have to know the peasants! You have to know from which side . . .

ANYA. You're starting it again, uncle!

VARYA. You'd better keep quiet, uncle dear.

FIRS [*sternly*]. Leonid Andreyevich!

GAYEV. Coming, coming! Go to bed! In off the cushion! I pot the white! . . . [*goes out;* FIRS *hobbles after him*]

ANYA. My mind is at rest now. I don't really feel like going to Yaroslavl, I don't like Grandmamma; but still, I'm not worrying. I'm grateful to uncle. [*she sits down*]

VARYA. I must get some sleep. I'm going. Oh, by the way, while you were away something unpleasant happened here. You know, there are only a few old servants living in the servants' quarters: just Yefemushka, Polya, Yevstigney and Karp. Well, they let some tramps sleep there, and I didn't say anything about it. But some time afterwards I heard some gossip; people said I had ordered them to be fed on nothing but dried peas. Because I was mean, you see . . . Yevstigney was at the bottom of it all. 'Well,' I said to myself, 'if that's how the matter stands, just you wait!' So I sent for Yevstigney. [*yawns*] In he comes. 'What's all this, Yevstigney,' I said to him, 'idiot that you are.' . . . [*she walks up to* ANYA] Anichka! [*a pause*] She's asleep! . . . [*takes her arm*] Come to bed! Come! [*leads her away*] My darling's fallen asleep! Come . . .
[*they go towards the door. The sound of a shepherd's pipe is heard from far away, beyond the orchard.* TROFIMOV *crosses the stage, but, seeing* VARYA *and* ANYA, *stops*]

VARYA. Sh-sh! She's asleep . . . asleep . . . Come, my dear.

ANYA [*softly, half-asleep*]. I'm so tired . . . I can hear bells tinkling all the time . . . uncle . . . dear . . . mamma and uncle . . .

VARYA. Come, darling, come . . . [*they go into* ANYA's *room*]

TROFIMOV [*deeply moved*]. Anya . . . my one bright star! My spring flower!

CURTAIN

ACT TWO

An old wayside shrine in the open country; it leans slightly to one side and has evidently been long abandoned. Beside it there are a well, an old seat and a number of large stones which apparently served as gravestones in the past. A road leads to GAYEV's *estate. On one side and some distance away is a row of dark poplars, and it is there that the cherry orchard begins. Further away is seen a line of telegraph poles, and beyond them, on the horizon, the vague outlines of a large town, visible only in very good, clear weather.*

The sun is about to set. CHARLOTTA, YASHA *and* DUNYASHA *are sitting on the seat;* YEPIKHODOV *is standing near by, playing a guitar; all look pensive.* CHARLOTTA *is wearing a man's old peaked cap; she has taken a shotgun off her shoulder and is adjusting a buckle on the strap.*

CHARLOTTA [*thoughtfully*]. I don't know how old I am. I haven't got a proper identity card, you see . . . and I keep on imagining I'm still quite young. When I was little, father and mother used to tour the fairs and give performances – very good ones they were, too. And I used to jump the *salto-mortale* and do all sorts of other tricks. When papa and mamma died, a German lady took me into her house and began to give me lessons. So then I grew up and became a governess. But where I come from and who I am, I don't know. Who my parents were – perhaps they weren't properly married – I don't know. [*she takes a cucumber from her pocket and begins to eat it*] I don't know anything. [*pause*] I'm longing to talk to someone, but there isn't anyone. I haven't anyone . . .

YEPIKHODOV [*plays the guitar and sings*]. 'What care I for the noisy world? . . . What are friends and foes to me?' How pleasant it is to play the mandolin!

DUNYASHA. That's a guitar, not a mandolin. [*she looks at herself in a hand mirror and powders her face*]

YEPIKHODOV. To a man that's crazy with love this is a mandolin.

[*sings quietly*] 'If only my heart might be warmed by the ardour of love requited.' . . .

[YASHA *joins in*]

CHARLOTTA. How dreadful their singing is! . . . Ach! It is like the jackals.

DUNYASHA [*to* YASHA]. You are lucky to have been abroad!

YASHA. Of course I am. I'm bound to agree with you there. [*yawns, then lights a cigar*]

YEPIKHODOV. Stands to reason. Abroad everything's been in full swing . . . I mean to say, everything's been going on for ever so long.

YASHA. Obviously.

YEPIKHODOV. Personally, I'm a cultured sort of fellow, I read all sorts of extraordinary books, you know, but somehow I can't seem to make out where I'm going, what it is I really want, I mean to say – to live or to shoot myself, so to speak. All the same, I always carry a revolver on me. Here it is. [*shows the revolver*]

CHARLOTTA. I have finished. Now I'm going. [*slips the strap of the gun over her shoulder*] Yes, you are a very clever man, Yepikhodov, and rather frightening, too; the women must fall madly in love with you! Brrr! [*walks off*] All these clever people are so stupid, I have no-one to talk to. I am so lonely, always so lonely, no-one belongs to me, and   and who I am, what I exist for, nobody knows . . . [*goes out leisurely*]

YEPIKHODOV. Candidly speaking, and I do want to keep strictly to the point, by the way, but I feel I simply must explain that Fate, so to speak, treats me absolutely without mercy, just like a storm treats a small ship, as it were. I mean to say, supposing I'm wrong, for instance, then why should I wake up this morning and suddenly see a simply colossal spider sitting on my chest? Like this . . . [*makes a gesture with both hands*] Or supposing I pick up a jug to have a drink of *kvass*, there's sure to be something frightful inside it, such as a cockroach. [*pause*] Have you read Buckle? [*pause*] May I trouble you for a word, Avdotya Fyodorovna?

DUNYASHA. All right, carry on.

YEPIKHODOV. I'd very much like to speak to you alone. [*sighs*]

DUNYASHA [*embarrassed*]. Very well then . . . only will you bring me my little cape first . . . It's hanging beside the wardrobe. It's rather chilly here . . .

YEPIKHODOV. Very well, I'll bring it . . . Now I know what to do with my revolver. [*picks up his guitar and goes, twanging it*]

YASHA. Two-and-twenty misfortunes! He's a stupid fellow, between you and me. [*yawns*]

DUNYASHA. I hope to God he won't shoot himself. [*pause*] I've got sort of anxious, worrying all the time. I came to live here with the master and mistress when I was still a little girl, you see. Now I've got out of the way of living a simple life, and my hands are as white . . . as white as a young lady's. I've grown sensitive and delicate, just as if I was one of the nobility; I'm afraid of everything . . . Just afraid. If you deceive me, Yasha, I don't know what will happen to my nerves.

YASHA [*kisses her*]. Little peach! Mind you, a girl ought to keep herself in hand, you know. Personally I dislike it more than anything if a girl doesn't behave herself.

DUNYASHA. I love you so much, so much! You're educated, you can reason about everything.

[*pause*]

YASHA [*yawns*]. Y-yes . . . To my way of thinking, it's like this: if a girl loves somebody, it means she's immoral. [*pause*] It's nice to smoke a cigar in the open air . . . [*listens*] Someone's coming this way. Our ladies and gentlemen . . . [DUNYASHA *impulsively puts her arms round him*] Go home now, as if you'd been down to the river bathing; go by this path, or you'll meet them, and they might think I've been keeping company with you. I couldn't stand that.

DUNYASHA [*coughing softly*]. My head's aching from that cigar . . . [*goes out*]

YASHA *remains sitting by the shrine. Enter* LYUBOV ANDREYEVNA, GAYEV *and* LOPAKHIN.

LOPAKHIN. We must decide once and for all: time won't wait. After all, my question's quite a simple one. Do you consent to lease your land for villas, or don't you? You can answer in one word: yes or no? Just one word!

LYUBOV ANDREYEVNA. Who's been smoking such abominable cigars here? [*sits down*]

GAYEV. How very convenient it is having a railway here. [*sits down*] Here we are – we've been up to town for lunch and we're back home already. I pot the red into the middle pocket! I'd like to go indoors now and have just one game . . .

LYUBOV ANDREYEVNA. You've plenty of time.

LOPAKHIN. Just one word! [*beseechingly*] Do give me an answer!

GAYEV [*yawns*]. What do you say?

LYUBOV ANDREYEVNA [*looking into her purse*]. Yesterday I had a lot of money, but today there's hardly any left. My poor Varya is feeding everyone on milk soups to economise; the old servants in the kitchen get nothing but dried peas to eat, and here I am, spending money senselessly, I don't know why . . . [*she drops the purse, scattering gold coins*] Now I've scattered it all over the place . . . [*annoyed*]

YASHA. Allow me, madam, I'll pick them up in a minute. [*gathers up the money*]

LYUBOV ANDREYEVNA. Thank you, Yasha . . . Why did I go out to lunch? It was quite vile, that restaurant of yours, with its beastly music; and the tablecloths smelt of soap, too . . . Need one drink so much, Lyonya? Need one eat so much? And talk so much? Today at the restaurant you talked too much again, and it was all so pointless. About the seventies, about the decadents. And who to? Fancy talking about the decadents to the restaurant waiters!

LOPAKHIN. Yes, fancy.

GAYEV [*waving his hand*]. I'm hopeless, I know. [*to* YASHA, *with irritation*] Why are you always buzzing about in front of me?

YASHA [*laughs*]. I can never hear you talk without laughing.

GAYEV [*to his sister*]. Either he goes, or I do . . .

LYUBOV ANDREYEVNA. Go away, Yasha, go along.

YASHA [*hands the purse to* LYUBOV ANDREYEVNA]. I'll go now. [*he can hardly restrain his laughter*] This very minute . . . [*goes out*]

LOPAKHIN. You know, that wealthy fellow Deriganov, he's intending to buy your estate. They say he's coming to the auction himself.

LYUBOV ANDREYEVNA. Where did you hear that?

LOPAKHIN. They were saying so in town.

GAYEV. Our aunt in Yaroslavl promised to send us money but when and how much it will be we don't know.

LOPAKHIN. How much will she send you? A hundred thousand? Two hundred?

LYUBOV ANDREYEVNA. Well, hardly . . . Ten or twelve thousand, perhaps. We'll be thankful for that much.

LOPAKHIN. You must forgive me for saying it, but really I've never met such feckless, unbusinesslike, queer people as you are. You are told in plain language that your estate is up for sale, and you simply don't seem to understand it.

LYUBOV ANDREYEVNA. But what are we to do? Tell us, what?

LOPAKHIN. I keep on telling you. Every day I tell you the same thing. You must lease the cherry orchard and the land for villas, and you must do it now, as soon as possible. The auction is going to be held almost at once. Please do try to understand! Once you definitely decide to have the villas, you'll be able to borrow as much money as you like, and then you'll be out of the wood.

LYUBOV ANDREYEVNA. Villas and summer visitors! Forgive me, but it's so vulgar.

GAYEV. I absolutely agree with you.

LOPAKHIN. Honestly, I feel I shall burst into tears, or shriek, or fall down and faint. I simply can't stand it. You've literally worn me out. [to GAYEV] An old woman, that's what you are!

GAYEV. What's that?

LOPAKHIN. An old woman!

LYUBOV ANDREYEVNA [alarmed]. No, don't go, do stay, my dear. Please stay! Perhaps we could think of something.

LOPAKHIN. It hardly seems worth trying.

LYUBOV ANDREYEVNA. Don't go, please! Somehow it's more cheerful with you here. [pause] I keep expecting something dreadful to happen . . . as if the house were going to fall down on us.

GAYEV [in deep thought]. I cannon off the cushions! I pot into the middle pocket . . .

LYUBOV ANDREYEVNA. We've sinned too much . . .

LOPAKHIN. Sinned, indeed! What were your sins?

GAYEV [puts a sweet into his mouth]. They say I've eaten up my whole fortune in sweets. [laughs]

LYUBOV ANDREYEVNA. Oh, my sins! Look at the way I've always squandered money, continually. It was sheer madness. And then I got married to a man who only knew how to get into debt.

Champagne killed him – he was a terrific drinker – and then, worse luck I fell in love with someone else. We had an affair, and just at that very time – it was my first punishment, a blow straight to my heart – my little boy was drowned here, in this river . . . and then I went abroad. I went away for good, and never meant to return, I never meant to see the river again . . . I just shut my eyes and ran away in a frenzy of grief, but he . . . he followed me. It was so cruel and brutal of him! I bought a villa near Mentone because he fell ill there, you see, and for three years I never had any rest, day or night. He was a sick man, he quite wore me out; my soul seemed to dry right up. Then, last year when the villa had to be sold to pay the debts, I went to Paris, and there he robbed me and left me; he went away and lived with another woman . . . I tried to poison myself . . . It was all so foolish, so shameful! And then suddenly I felt an urge to come back to Russia, to my own country and my little girl . . . [wipes away her tears] Oh, Lord, Lord, be merciful, forgive me my sins! Don't punish me any more! [takes a telegram out of her pocket] I had this from Paris today. He's asking my forgiveness, begging me to return . . . [tears up the telegram] Sounds like music somewhere. [listens]

GAYEV. That's our famous Jewish band. Do you remember, four violins, a flute and a double-bass?

LYUBOV ANDREYEVNA. Is that still in existence? It would be nice to get them to come to the house one day, and we could have a little dance.

LOPAKHIN [listens]. I can't hear anything . . . [sings quietly] 'And the Germans, if you pay, will turn Russian into Frenchman, so they say.' . . . [laughs] I saw such a good play at the theatre yesterday. Very amusing.

LYUBOV ANDREYEVNA. I'm sure it wasn't at all amusing. Instead of going to see plays, you should take a good look at yourself. Just think what a drab kind of life you lead, what a lot of nonsense you talk!

LOPAKHIN. It's perfectly true. Yes, I admit it, we lead an idiotic existence . . . [pause] My dad was a peasant, a blockhead, he didn't understand anything, and he didn't teach me anything, but just beat me when he was drunk, and always with a stick at that. As a matter of fact, I'm just as much of a fool and a half-wit myself. No-one taught me anything, my writing is awful, I'm ashamed even to show it to people: it's just like a pig's.

LYUBOV ANDREYEVNA. You ought to get married, my friend.

LOPAKHIN. Yes . . . That's true.

LYUBOV ANDREYEVNA. You ought to marry our Varya. She's a nice girl.

LOPAKHIN. Yes.

LYUBOV ANDREYEVNA. She comes from the common folk, and she's a hard-working girl: she can work the whole day without stopping. But the main thing is that she loves you, and you've been attracted by her for a long time yourself.

LOPAKHIN. Well . . . I'm quite willing . . . She's a nice girl.

[pause]

GAYEV. I've been offered a job at the bank. Six thousand a year. Have you heard?

LYUBOV ANDREYEVNA. Indeed I have. You'd better stay where you are.

Enter FIRS *with an overcoat.*

FIRS [*to* GAYEV]. Will you please put it on, sir, it's so chilly.

GAYEV [*puts on the overcoat*]. You are a nuisance.

FIRS. Tut, tut! You went off this morning and never told me you were going. [*Looks him over*]

LYUBOV ANDREYEVNA. How you've aged, Firs!

FIRS. What can I get you, madam?

LOPAKHIN. They say, you've aged a lot.

FIRS. I've been alive a long time. They were going to marry me off before your dad was born. [*laughs*] And when freedom was granted to the people, I'd already been made a chief valet. I wouldn't take my freedom then, I stayed with the master and mistress . . . [*pause*] I remember everyone was glad at the time, but what they were glad about, no-one knew.

LOPAKHIN. Oh, yes, it was a good life all right! At least, people got flogged!

FIRS [*not having heard him*]. Rather! The peasants belonged to the gentry, and the gentry belonged to the peasants; but now everything's separate, and you can't understand anything.

GAYEV. Be quiet, Firs. Tomorrow I must go to town. I was

promised an introduction to some general or other who'll lend
us some money on a promissory note.

LOPAKHIN. Nothing will come of that. And you won't be able to
pay the interest, anyway.

LYUBOV ANDREYEVNA. He's talking through his hat. There aren't
any generals.

Enter TROFIMOV, ANYA *and* VARYA.

GAYEV. Here come the children.

ANYA. There's mamma.

LYUBOV ANDREYEVNA. Come here, my dears. My dear children . . .
[*embraces* ANYA *and* VARYA] If you both only knew how much I
love you! Sit down beside me, here.

[*all sit down*]

LOPAKHIN. Our 'eternal student' is always with the young ladies.

TROFIMOV. It's none of your business, anyway.

LOPAKHIN. He'll soon be fifty, yet he's still a student.

TROFIMOV. I wish you'd drop your idiotic jokes.

LOPAKHIN. But why are you getting annoyed? You are a queer
chap!

TROFIMOV. Why do you keep pestering me?

LOPAKHIN [*laughs*]. Just let me ask you one question: what do you
make of me?

TROFIMOV. My opinion of you, Yermolay Alexeyevich, is simply
this: you're a wealthy man, and before long you'll be a million-
aire; and in so far as a wild beast is necessary because it devours
everything in its path and so converts one kind of matter into
another, you are necessary also.

[*everybody laughs*]

VARYA. You'd better tell us about the planets, Petya.

LYUBOV ANDREYEVNA. No, let's continue what we were talking
about yesterday.

TROFIMOV. What were we talking about?

GAYEV. About pride.

TROFIMOV. We talked a lot yesterday, but we didn't agree on
anything. The proud man, in the sense you understand him, has
something mystical about him. Maybe you're right in a way, but
if we try to think it out simply, without being too far-fetched
about it, the question arises – why should he be proud? Where's

the sense in being proud when you consider that man, as a species, is not very well constructed physiologically, and in the vast majority of cases is coarse, stupid, and profoundly unhappy, too? We ought to stop all this self-admiration. We ought to – just work.

GAYEV. You'll die just the same, whatever you do.

TROFIMOV. Who knows? And anyway, what does it mean – to die? It may be that man is possessed of a hundred senses, and only the five that are known to us perish in death, while the remaining ninety-five live on afterwards.

LYUBOV ANDREYEVNA. How clever you are, Petya!

LOPAKHIN [*ironically*]. Oh, awfully clever!

TROFIMOV. Humanity is perpetually advancing, always seeking to perfect its own powers. One day all the things that are beyond our grasp at present are going to fall within our reach, only to achieve this we've got to work with all our might, to help the people who are seeking after truth. Here, in Russia, very few people have started to work, so far. Nearly all the members of the intelligentsia that I know care for nothing, do nothing and are still incapable of work. They call themselves 'intelligentsia', but they still talk contemptuously to their servants, they treat the peasants as if they were animals, they study without achieving anything, they don't read anything serious, they just do nothing. As for science, they only talk about it, and they don't understand much about art either. They all look very grave and go about with grim expressions on their faces, and they only discuss important matters and philosophise. Yet all the time anyone can see that our work-people are abominably fed and have to sleep without proper beds, thirty to forty to a room, with bed-bugs, bad smells, damp, and immorality everywhere. It's perfectly obvious that all our nice-sounding talk is intended only to mislead ourselves and others. Tell me then, where are the crèches which we're always talking about, where are the reading rooms? We only write about them in novels, but actually there just aren't any. There's nothing but dirt, bestiality, Asiatic customs . . . I'm afraid of these deadly serious faces, I don't like them; I'm afraid of serious talk. It would be better for us just to keep quiet.

LOPAKHIN. Well, let me tell you that *I'm* up soon after four every morning, and I work from morning till night. I always have money in hand, my own and other people's, and I have plenty of opportunities to learn what the people around me are like. You only have to start on a job of work to realise how few honest, decent people there are about. Sometimes, when I can't sleep, I start brooding over it. The Lord God has given us vast forests, immense fields, wide horizons; surely we ought to be giants, living in such a country as this . . .

LYUBOV ANDREYEVNA. Whatever do you want giants for? They're all right in fairy-tales, otherwise they're just terrifying.

[YEPIKHODOV *crosses the stage in the background, playing his guitar*]

LYUBOV ANDREYEVNA [*pensively*]. There goes Yepikhodov . . .

ANYA [*pensively*]. There goes Yepikhodov . . .

GAYEV. The sun's gone down, ladies and gentlemen.

TROFIMOV. Yes.

GAYEV [*in a subdued voice, as if reciting a poem*]. Oh, glorious Nature, shining with eternal light, so beautiful, yet so indifferent to our fate . . . you, whom we call Mother, uniting in yourself both life and death, you live and you destroy . . .

VARYA [*imploringly*]. Uncle, dear!

ANYA. You're starting again, uncle!

TROFIMOV. You'd better screw back off the red into the middle pocket.

GAYEV. I'll keep quiet, I'll keep quiet.

   [*they all sit deep in thought; the silence is only broken by the subdued muttering of* FIRS. *Suddenly a distant sound is heard, coming as if out of the sky, like the sound of a string snapping, slowly and sadly dying away*]

LYUBOV ANDREYEVNA. What was that?

LOPAKHIN. I don't know. Somewhere a long way off a lift cable in one of the mines must have broken. But it must be somewhere very far away.

GAYEV. Or perhaps it was some bird . . . a heron, perhaps.

TROFIMOV. Or an owl . . .

LYUBOV ANDREYEVNA [*shudders*]. It sounded unpleasant, somehow . . .
   [*a pause*]

FIRS. It was the same before the misfortune: the owl hooted and the samovar kept singing.

GAYEV. What misfortune?

FIRS. Before they gave us freedom.

[*a pause*]

LYUBOV ANDREYEVNA. Come along, my friends! Let us go home, it's getting dark. [*to* ANYA] You've got tears in your eyes. What is it, my little one? [*embraces her*]

ANYA. Never mind, mamma. It's nothing.

TROFIMOV. Someone's coming.

Enter a TRAMP *in a white battered peaked cap and an overcoat; he is slightly tipsy.*

TRAMP. Excuse me, can I get straight to the station through here?

GAYEV. You can. Follow the road.

TRAMP. I'm greatly obliged to you, sir. [*coughs*] Lovely weather today. [*recites*] 'Oh, my brother, my suffering brother! . . . Come to mother Volga, whose groans . . .' [*to* VARYA] Mademoiselle, may a starving Russian citizen trouble you for a few coppers?

[VARYA *cries out, frightened*]

LOPAKHIN [*angrily*]. Really, there's a limit to everything!

LYUBOV ANDREYEVNA [*at a loss what to do*]. Take this . . . here you are. [*searches in her purse*] I have no silver . . . Never mind, here's a gold one . . .

THE TRAMP. I'm deeply grateful to you! [*goes off*]

[*laughter*]

VARYA [*frightened*]. I'm going . . . I'm going . . . Oh, mamma dear, you know there's no food in the house, and you gave him all that!

LYUBOV ANDREYEVNA. Well, what can you do with a fool like me? I'll give you all I've got when we get home. Yermolay Alexeyevich, you'll lend me some more, won't you?

LOPAKHIN. Certainly I will.

LYUBOV ANDREYEVNA. Let's go on now, it's time. By the way, Varya, we almost fixed up your marriage just now. I congratulate you.

VARYA [*through her tears*]. It's no laughing matter, mamma!

LOPAKHIN. Go to a nunnery, Ophelia! . . .

GAYEV. Look how my hands are trembling: I haven't played billiards for a long time.

LOPAKHIN. Ophelia, oh nymph, remember me in thy orisons!

LYUBOV ANDREYEVNA. Come along, everybody. It's almost supper time.

VARYA. That man scared me so. My heart keeps thumping.

LOPAKHIN. My friends, just one word, please just one word: on the twenty-second of August the cherry orchard is going to be sold. Just consider that! Just think . . .

[*all go out, except* TROFIMOV *and* ANYA]

ANYA [*laughs*]. Thank the tramp for this! He frightened Varya, now we are alone.

TROFIMOV. Varya's afraid – afraid we might suddenly fall in love with each other – so she follows us about all day long. She's so narrow-minded, she can't grasp that we are above falling in love. To rid ourselves of all that's petty and unreal, all that prevents us from being happy and free, that's the whole aim and meaning of our life. Forward! Let's march on irresistibly towards that bright star over there, shining in the distance! Forward! Don't fall behind, friends!

ANYA [*raising her hands*]. How well you talk! [*a pause*] It's wonderful here today.

TROFIMOV. Yes, the weather's marvellous.

ANYA. What have you done to me, Petya? Why is it that I don't love the cherry orchard as I used to? I used to love it so dearly, it seemed to me that there wasn't a better place in all the world than our orchard.

TROFIMOV. The whole of Russia is our orchard. The earth is great and beautiful and there are many, many wonderful places on it. [*a pause*] Just think, Anya: your grandfather, your great grandfather and all your forefathers were serf owners – they owned living souls. Don't you see human beings gazing at you from every cherry tree in your orchard, from every leaf and every tree-trunk, don't you hear voices? . . . They owned living souls – and it has perverted you all, those who came before you, and you who are living now, so that your mother, your uncle and even you yourself no longer realise that you're living in debt, at other people's expense, at the expense of people you don't admit further than the kitchen. We are at least two hundred years behind the times; we still have no real background, no clear attitude to our past, we just philosophise and complain of depression, or drink vodka. Yet it's perfectly clear that to begin to live in the present, we must first atone for our past and be finished with it, and we can only atone for it by suffering, by extraordinary, unceasing exertion. You must understand this, Anya.

ANYA. The house we live in hasn't really been ours for a long time. I'll leave it, I give you my word.

TROFIMOV. Leave it, and if you have any keys to it, throw them down a well. Be free like the wind.

ANYA [*in rapture*]. How well you put it!

TROFIMOV. You must believe me, Anya, you must. I'm not thirty yet, I'm young, and I'm still a student, but I've suffered so much already. As soon as the winter comes, I get half-starved, and ill, and worried, poor as a beggar, and there's hardly anywhere I haven't been to, where I haven't been driven to by Fate. And yet, always, every moment of the day and night my soul has been filled with such marvellous hopes and visions. I can see happiness, Anya, I can see it coming . . .

ANYA [*pensively*]. The moon's coming up.

[YEPIKHODOV *can be heard playing his guitar, the same melancholy tune as before. The moon rises. Somewhere in the vicinity of the poplars* VARYA *is looking for* ANYA *and calling: 'Anya! Where are you?'*]

TROFIMOV. Yes, the moon is rising. [*a pause*] There it is — happiness — it's coming nearer and nearer, I seem to hear its footsteps. And if we don't see it, if we don't know when it comes, what does it matter? Other people will see it!

VARYA'S VOICE. Anya! Where are you?

TROFIMOV. That Varya again! [*angrily*] It's disgusting!

ANYA. Well? Let us go to the river. It's nice there.

TROFIMOV. Let's go.

[TROFIMOV *and* ANYA *go out*]

VARYA'S VOICE. Anya! Anya!

CURTAIN

ACT THREE

The drawing-room of the Ranevskaya's house. Adjoining the drawing-room at the back, and connected to it by an archway, is the ballroom. A Jewish band, the same that was mentioned in Act Two, is heard playing in the hall. It is evening; the candles in a chandelier are alight. In the ballroom a party is dancing the Grand-Rond. SIMEONOV–PISHCHIK *is heard to call out:* 'Promenade à une paire!', *then all come into the drawing-room.* PISHCHIK *and* CHARLOTTA IVANOVNA *form the leading couple, then come* TROFIMOV *and* LYUBOV ANDREYEVNA, ANYA *with a post-office clerk,* VARYA *with the station-master, and so on.* VARYA *cries quietly and wipes away her tears as she dances.* DUNYASHA *is in the last couple. They walk across the drawing-room.* PISHCHIK *shouts:* 'Grand rond balancez!' *and* 'Les cavaliers à genoux et remerciez vos dames!'

FIRS, *wearing a tail-coat, crosses the room with soda-water on a tray.* PISHCHIK *and* TROFIMOV *re-enter the drawing-room.*

PISHCHIK. I've got this high blood-pressure – I've had a stroke twice already, you know – and it makes dancing difficult; but if you're one of a pack, as the saying goes, you've got to wag your tail, whether you bark or not. Actually I'm as strong as a horse. My dear father – he liked his little joke, God bless him – he used to say that the ancient family of Simeonov-Pishchik was descended from the very same horse that Caligula sat in the Senate. [*sits down*] But the trouble is, we've no money. A hungry dog can only think about food . . . [*falls asleep and snores, but wakes up almost at once*] Just like myself – I can't think of anything but money . . .

TROFIMOV. It's quite true, there is something horsy about your build.

PISHCHIK. Oh, well, the horse is a good animal, you can sell a horse . . .

From the adjoining room comes the sound of someone playing billiards.
VARYA appears in the ballroom, under the arch.

TROFIMOV [*teasing her*]. Madame Lopakhin! Madame Lopakhin!

VARYA [*angrily*]. The 'moth-eaten gent'!

TROFIMOV. Yes, I am a moth-eaten gent, and I'm proud of it.

VARYA [*brooding bitterly*]. So now we've hired a band – but how are we going to pay for it? [*goes out*].

TROFIMOV [*to* PISHCHIK]. If all the energy you've wasted in the course of a lifetime looking for money to pay interest on your debts – if all that energy had been used for something else, you'd probably have turned the world upside down by now.

PISHCHIK. The philosopher Nietzsche, the greatest, the most famous – a man of the highest intellect, in fact – says it's justifiable to forge bank-notes.

TROFIMOV. Have you read Nietzsche then?

PISHCHIK. Well, no . . . Dashenka told me. But just now I'm in such a frightful position that I wouldn't mind forging a few bank-notes. The day after tomorrow I've got to pay three hundred and ten roubles. I've borrowed one hundred and thirty already . . . [*feels in his pockets with alarm*] The money's gone! I've lost the money. [*tearfully*] Where's the money? [*with an expression of joy*] Here it is, inside the lining! The shock's made me sweat! . . .

Enter LYUBOV ANDREYEVNA *and* CHARLOTTA.

LYUBOV ANDREYEVNA [*singing 'Lezghinka'* * *under her breath*]. Why is Leonid so late? What's he doing in town? [*to* DUNYASHA] Dunyasha, offer the musicians some tea.

TROFIMOV. I suppose the auction didn't take place.

LYUBOV ANDREYEVNA. The band came at the wrong time, and the party started at the wrong time . . . Well . . . never mind . . . [*sits down and sings quietly*]

CHARLOTTA [*hands a pack of cards to* PISHCHIK]. Here's a pack of cards – think of any card, now.

PISHCHIK. I've thought of one.

CHARLOTTA. Now shuffle the pack. That's right. Now give it to me, my good Monsieur Pishchik. *Ein, zwei, drei*! Now look for it. There it is, in your breast pocket.

* A popular dance tune.

PISHCHIK [*takes the card out of his breast-pocket*]. The eight of spades, absolutely right! [*in astonishment*] Fancy that!

CHARLOTTA [*holding the pack of cards on the palm of her hand, to* TROFIMOV]. Tell me quickly, which card is on top?

TROFIMOV. Well . . . Let us say, the queen of spades.

CHARLOTTA. Here it is! [*she claps her hand over the pack of cards, which disappears*] What fine weather we're having today!

[*a woman's voice, apparently coming from beneath the floor, answers her: 'Oh yes, Madam, the weather's perfectly marvellous!'*]

CHARLOTTA [*addressing the voice*]. How charming you are, quite delightful!

VOICE. And I like you very much also, madam.

STATION-MASTER [*applauding*]. Madame ventriloquist, well done!

PISHCHIK [*astonished*]. Fancy that! Charlotta Ivanovna, how fascinating you are! I'm quite in love with you!

CHARLOTTA [*shrugging her shoulders*]. In love? Do you know how to love? *Guter Mensch, aber schlechter Musikant.*

TROFIMOV [*slaps* PISHCHIK *on the shoulder*]. A regular old horse!

CHARLOTTA. Attention please! Here's just one more trick. [*she takes a rug from a chair*] Now I'm offering this very nice rug for sale . . . [*shakes it out*] Would anyone like to buy it?

PISHCHIK [*astonished*]. Just fancy!

CHARLOTTA. *Ein, zwei, drei!* [*she lifts up the rug and discloses* ANYA *standing behind it;* ANYA *drops a curtsey, runs to her mother, gives her a hug, then runs back into the ballroom. Everyone is delighted*]

LYUBOV ANDREYEVNA [*clapping*]. Bravo, bravo!

CHARLOTTA. Just once more. *Ein, zwei, drei!* [*lifts the rug; behind it stands* VARYA, *who bows*]

PISHCHIK [*astonished*]. Fancy that!

CHARLOTTA. Finished! [*she throws the rug over* PISHCHIK, *curtseys and runs off to the ballroom*]

PISHCHIK [*hurries after her*]. The little rascal! . . . Have you ever seen anything like it . . . have you ever . . . [*goes out*]

LYUBOV ANDREYEVNA. Still no Leonid. I can't understand what he's doing all this time in town. In any case, everything must be over by now, either the estate's been sold or the auction never took place. Why must he keep us in ignorance so long?

VARYA [*trying to comfort her*]. Uncle bought it, dear uncle, I'm sure he did.

TROFIMOV [*sarcastically*]. Oh yes?

VARYA. Grandmamma sent him power of attorney to buy the estate in her name, and transfer the mortgage to her. She's done it for Anya's sake . . . God will help us, I'm sure of it – uncle will buy the estate.

LYUBOV ANDREYEVNA. Grandmamma sent us fifteen thousand roubles to buy the estate in her name – she doesn't trust us, you see – but the money wouldn't even pay the interest. [*she covers her face with her hands*] Today my fate is being decided, my fate . . .

TROFIMOV [*to* VARYA, *teasingly*]. Madame Lopakhin!

VARYA [*crossly*]. The eternal student! Why, you've been thrown out of the University twice already!

LYUBOV ANDREYEVNA. Why get so cross, Varya? He does tease you about Lopakhin, but what's the harm? If you feel inclined to, why don't you marry Lopakhin: he's a nice, interesting fellow. Of course, if you don't feel like it, don't. No-one's trying to force you, darling.

VARYA. I do take it very seriously, mamma dear . . . and I want to be frank with you about it . . . he's a nice man and I like him.

LYUBOV ANDREYEVNA. Then marry him. What are you waiting for? I can't understand you.

VARYA. Mamma darling, I can't propose to him myself, can I? It's two years now since everyone started talking to me about him, and everyone is still doing it, but he either says nothing, or else he just talks in a sort of bantering way. I understand what's the matter. He's getting rich, he's occupied with his business, and he's no time for me. If only I had some money, just a little, even a hundred roubles, then I'd have left everything and gone away, the farther the better. I'd have gone into a convent.

TROFIMOV. A beautiful life!

VARYA [*to* TROFIMOV]. Of course, a student like you has to be clever! [*softly and tearfully*] How plain you've become, Petya, how much older you look! [*to* LYUBOV ANDREYEVNA, *her tearfulness gone*] The only thing I can't bear, mamma dear, is to be without work. I must be doing something all the time.

Enter YASHA.

YASHA [*with difficulty restraining his laughter*]. Yepikhodov's broken a billiard cue! . . . [*goes out*]

VARYA. But why is Yepikhodov here? Who allowed him to play billiards? I can't understand these people . . . [*goes out*]

LYUBOV ANDREYEVNA. Don't tease her, Petya. Don't you see she's upset already?

TROFIMOV. She's too much of a busybody, she will poke her nose into other people's affairs. She wouldn't leave us alone the whole summer, neither Anya nor me. She was afraid we might fall in love with each other. Why should she mind? Besides, I didn't show any sign of it. I'm too far removed from such trivialities. We are above love!

LYUBOV ANDREYEVNA. And I suppose I'm below love. [*in great agitation*] Why isn't Leonid back? I only want to know whether the estate's sold or not. Such a calamity seems so incredible that somehow I don't even know what to think, I feel quite lost. Honestly, I feel I could shriek out loud this very moment . . . I shall be doing something silly. Help me, Petya. Say something, speak!

TROFIMOV. Isn't it all the same whether the estate's sold today or not? It's finished and done with long ago, there's no turning back, the bridges are burnt. You must keep calm, my dear; you mustn't deceive yourself, for once in your life you must look the truth straight in the face.

LYUBOV ANDREYEVNA. What truth? You can see where the truth is and where it isn't, but I seem to have lost my power of vision, I don't see anything. You're able to solve all your problems in a resolute way – but, tell me, my dear boy, isn't that because you're young, because you're not old enough yet to have suffered on account of your problems. You look ahead so boldly – but isn't that because life is still hidden from your young eyes, so that you're not able to foresee anything dreadful, or expect it? You've a more courageous and honest and serious nature than we have, but do consider our position carefully, do be generous – even if only a little bit – and spare me. I was born here, you know, my father and mother lived here, and my grandfather, too, and I love this house – I can't conceive life without the cherry orchard, and if it really has to be sold, then sell me with it . . . [*embraces* TROFIMOV, *kisses him on the forehead*] You know, my son was drowned here . . . [*weeps*] Have pity on me, my dear, dear friend.

TROFIMOV. You know that I sympathise with you with all my heart.

LYUBOV ANDREYEVNA. But you must say it differently . . . differently. [*takes out a handkerchief; a telegram falls on to the floor*] There's such a weight on my mind today, you can't imagine. This place is too noisy, my very soul seems to shudder with every sound, and I'm trembling all over – yet I can't go to my room for fear of being alone and quiet . . . Don't blame me, Petya . . . I love you as if you were my own child. I would willingly let Anya marry you, honestly I would, but, my dear boy, you must study, you must finish your course. You don't do anything, Fate seems to drive you from one place to another – such a strange thing . . . Isn't it? Isn't it? And you should do something about your beard, make it grow somehow . . . [*laughs*] You are a funny boy!

TROFIMOV [*picks up the telegram*]. I don't want to be a dandy.

LYUBOV ANDREYEVNA. That telegram's from Paris. I get one every day . . . Yesterday and today. That savage is ill again, and things are going badly with him . . . He wants me to forgive him, implores me to return, and, really, I do feel I ought to go to Paris and stay near him for a bit. You're looking very stern, Petya, but what's to be done, my dear boy, what am I to do? He's ill, and lonely, and unhappy, and who's there to take care of him, to prevent him from making a fool of himself, and give him his medicine at the proper time? And anyway, why should I hide it, or keep quiet about it? I love him, of course I love him. I do, I do . . . It's a millstone round my neck, and I'm going to the bottom with it – but I love him and I can't live without him. [*she presses* TROFIMOV's *hand*] Don't think badly of me, Petya, don't speak, don't say anything . . .

TROFIMOV [*with strong emotion*]. Please – please forgive my frankness, but that man's been robbing you!

LYUBOV ANDREYEVNA. No, no, no, you mustn't talk like that . . . [*puts her hands over her ears*]

TROFIMOV. He's a cad, you're the only one who doesn't know it! He's a petty-minded cad, a worthless . . .

LYUBOV ANDREYEVNA [*angry, but in control of herself*]. You're twenty-six or twenty-seven years old, but you're still like a schoolboy in a prep school!

TROFIMOV. Never mind me!

LYUBOV ANDREYEVNA. You ought to be a man, at your age you ought to understand people who are in love. And you ought to be able to love . . . to fall in love! [*angrily*] Yes, yes! And you're not 'pure', but you just make a fad of purity, you're a ridiculous crank, a freak . . .

TROFIMOV [*horrified*]. What is she saying?

LYUBOV ANDREYEVNA. 'I'm above love!' You're not above love, you're daft, as our Firs would say. Not to have a mistress at your age! . . .

TROFIMOV [*horrified*]. This is dreadful! What's she saying? [*walks quickly towards the ballroom, his head between his hands*] This is dreadful . . . I can't, I'm going . . . [*goes out, but returns at once*] Everything's finished between us! [*goes out through the door into the hall*]

LYUBOV ANDREYEVNA [*calls after him*]. Petya, wait! You funny fellow, I was joking! Petya!

[*from the hall comes the sound of someone running quickly upstairs, then falling down with a crash; there are shrieks from ANYA and VARYA, followed by laughter*]

What's happened?

ANYA *runs in.*

ANYA [*laughing*]. Petya's fallen downstairs. [*runs out*]

LYUBOV ANDREYEVNA. What a queer fellow he is! [*the STATION-MASTER stands in the middle of the ballroom and begins to recite 'The Sinner' by Alexyei Tolstoy. The others listen, but he has hardly had time to recite more than a few lines when the sound of a waltz reaches them from the hall, and the recitation breaks off. Everyone dances*]

Enter from the hall TROFIMOV, ANYA *and* VARYA.

LYUBOV ANDREYEVNA. Now, Petya . . . there, my dear boy . . . I ask your forgiveness . . . let's dance . . . [*she dances with* PETYA]
[ANYA *and* VARYA *dance*]

Enter FIRS, *then* YASHA. FIRS *stands his walking-stick by the side door.* YASHA *looks at the dancers from the drawing-room.*

YASHA. How goes it, grandad?

FIRS. I'm not too well . . . We used to have generals, barons, and admirals dancing at our balls, but now we send for the post-office clerk and the station-master, and even they don't come

too willingly. I seem to have grown so weak somehow . . .
My old master, that's the mistress's grandfather, used to give
everyone powdered sealing wax for medicine, whatever the
illness was. I've been taking it every day for the last twenty years,
or perhaps even longer. Maybe that's why I'm still alive.

YASHA. How you weary me, grandad! [*yawns*] I wish you'd go
away and die soon.

FIRS. Eh, you! . . . You're daft . . . [*mutters*]

[TROFIMOV *and* LYUBOV ANDREYEVNA *dance in the ball-room,
then in the drawing-room*]

LYUBOV ANDREYEVNA. Thank you. I'd like to sit down for a bit.
[*sits down*] I'm tired.

Enter ANYA.

ANYA [*agitated*]. A man in the kitchen was saying just now that the
cherry orchard was sold today.

LYUBOV ANDREYEVNA. Sold? Who to?

ANYA. He didn't say. He's gone. [*she dances with* TROFIMOV; *both go
to the ballroom*]

YASHA. There was some old man there, gossiping away. A stranger.

FIRS. And Leonid Andreyevich's not back yet, he's still not back.
He's only got his light overcoat on – his 'between-seasons' coat –
and he might easily catch a cold. These youngsters!

LYUBOV ANDREYEVNA. I feel as though I'm going to die. Yasha, go
and find out who bought it.

YASHA. But the old man's been gone a long time. [*laughs*]

LYUBOV ANDREYEVNA. [*with a touch of annoyance*]. Well, what are
you laughing at? What are you so happy about?

YASHA. Yepikhodov's such a comic chap – a stupid fellow. Two-
and-twenty misfortunes!

LYUBOV ANDREYEVNA. Firs, if the estate is sold, where will you go?

FIRS. I'll go wherever you order me to.

LYUBOV ANDREYEVNA. Why are you looking like that? Are you ill?
I should go to bed, you know . . .

FIRS. Yes . . . [*with a faint smile*] If I went to bed, who'd wait on the
guests, who'd keep things going? There's no-one in the house
but me.

YASHA [*to* LYUBOV ANDREYEVNA]. Lyubov Andreyevna! I want to
ask you for something, please! If you go to Paris again, do me a

favour and take me with you. It's quite impossible for me to stay here. [*looking round, in a subdued voice*] There's no need for me to say it: you can see it for yourself – the people are uneducated, and they're immoral, too. Besides, it's so boring, and the food they give you in the kitchen is abominable. Then this Firs keeps on walking around and muttering all sorts of silly things. Take me with you, please do!

Enter PISHCHIK.

PISHCHIK. Allow me to ask you for a dance, beautiful lady . . . [LYUBOV ANDREYEVNA *gets up to dance*] I'll have that hundred and eighty roubles from you all the same, my charmer . . . Yes, I will . . . [*dances*] Just one hundred and eighty roubles, that's all . . .
[*they go into the ballroom*]
YASHA [*sings quietly*]. 'Will you understand the agitation of my soul? . . .'
[*in the ballroom a woman in check trousers and a grey top hat starts jumping in the air and throwing her arms about; there are shouts of: 'Bravo, Charlotta Ivanovna!'*]
DUNYASHA [*stops to powder her face*]. The young mistress ordered me to dance: there are so many gentlemen and only a few ladies; but I get so dizzy from dancing, and my heart beats too fast. Firs Nikolayevich, the post-office clerk told me something just now that quite took my breath away.
[*the music stops*]
FIRS. What did he tell you?
DUNYASHA. You are like a flower, he said.
YASHA [*yawns*]. What ignorance! . . . [*goes out*]
DUNYASHA. Like a flower . . . I'm so sensitive, I love it when people say nice things to me.
FIRS. You'll get your head turned all right.

Enter YEPIKHODOV.

YEPIKHODOV. Avdotya Fyodorovna, you don't seem to want to look at me . . . as if I were some sort of insect. [*sighs*] What a life!
DUNYASHA. What is it you want?
YEPIKHODOV. Perhaps you may be right, no doubt. [*sighs*] But, of course, if one looks at it from a certain point of view – if I may so express myself – forgive my frankness – you've driven me

into such a state . . . I know what my fate is; every day some misfortune's sure to happen to me, but I've been so long accustomed to it, that I look at life with a smile. You gave me your word, and though I . . .

DUNYASHA. Please, please, let's have a talk later, but now leave me alone. I feel in a kind of dream just now. [*plays with her fan*]

YEPIKHODOV. Some misfortune or other happens to me every day, and yet — if I may so express myself — I only smile, I even laugh.

VARYA *enters from the ballroom.*

VARYA. Haven't you gone yet, Semyon? What an ill-mannered fellow you are, really! [*to* DUNYASHA] You'd better go, Dunyasha. [*to* YEPIKHODOV] First you go and play billiards and break a cue, and now you're walking about the drawing-room, like a visitor.

YEPIKHODOV. Permit me to inform you that you can't start imposing penalties on me.

VARYA. I'm not imposing penalties, I'm merely telling you. All you do is to walk from one place to another, instead of getting on with your work. We keep a clerk, but what for no-one knows.

YEPIKHODOV [*offended*]. Whether I work, walk about, eat or play billiards, the only people who are entitled to judge my actions are those who are older than me and know what they're talking about.

VARYA. You dare say that to me? [*flying into a temper*] You dare to say that? You're suggesting I don't know what I'm talking about? Get out of here! This very minute!

YEPIKHODOV [*cowed*]. I wish you'd express yourself more delicately.

VARYA [*beside herself*]. Get out this minute! Out!

[*he goes to the door, she follows him*]

Two-and-twenty misfortunes! I don't want any more of you here! I don't want ever to set eyes on you again!

[YEPIKHODOV *goes out; his voice is heard from outside the door:* 'I'll complain about you.']

Ah, you're coming back, are you? [*she seizes the stick which* FIRS *left by the door*] Come along, come along . . . I'll show you! Ah, you're coming back . . . are you? There, I'll give it to you . . .

She swings the stick, and at that moment LOPAKHIN *enters.*

LOPAKHIN [*whom the stick did not, in fact, touch*]. Thank you very much!

VARYA [*angry and sarcastic*]. I beg your pardon!

LOPAKHIN. Don't mention it. Thanks for a pleasant surprise.

VARYA. It's not worth thanking me for. [*goes to the side, then looks round and says gently*] I haven't hurt you, have I?

LOPAKHIN. No, not at all . . . There's a huge bump coming up, though.

VOICES IN THE BALLROOM. Lopakhin's arrived! Yermolay Alexeyevich!

PISHCHIK. Look here, you can see him, you can hear him! . . . [*embraces* LOPAKHIN] You smell of cognac, my dear fellow, my bonny boy! We're making merry here, too.

Enter LYUBOV ANDREYEVNA.

LYUBOV ANDREYEVNA. It's you, Yermolay Alexeyevich? Why have you been so long? Where is Leonid?

LOPAKHIN. Leonid Andreyevich returned with me, he's coming along.

LYUBOV ANDREYEVNA [*agitated*]. Well, what happened? Was there an auction? Speak, tell me!

LOPAKHIN. [*embarrassed, fearing to betray his joy*]. The auction was over by four o'clock . . . We missed our train and had to wait until half-past nine. [*with a deep sigh*] Ugh! My head's going round . . .

Enter GAYEV; *he carries some parcels in his right hand and wipes away his tears with his left.*

LYUBOV ANDREYEVNA. Lyonya, what happened? Well, Lyonya? [*impatiently, with tears*] Tell me quickly, for God's sake! . . .

GAYEV [*does not reply, but waves his hand at her; to* FIRS, *weeping*]. Here, take this . . . it's some anchovies and Kerch herrings . . . I've had nothing to eat all day . . . What I've been through! [*through the open door leading to the billiard room comes the sound of billiard balls in play and* YASHA'S *voice saying: 'Seven and eighteen'.* GAYEV'S *expression changes and he stops crying*] I'm dreadfully tired. Come, Firs, I want to change. [*goes out through the ballroom,* FIRS *following*]

PISHCHIK. What happened at the auction? Come, do tell us!

LYUBOV ANDREYEVNA. Has the cherry orchard been sold?

LOPAKHIN. It has.

LYUBOV ANDREYEVNA. Who bought it?

LOPAKHIN. I did. [*a pause*]

LYUBOV ANDREYEVNA *is overcome; only the fact that she is standing beside a table and a chair prevents her from falling.* VARYA *takes a bundle of keys off her belt, throws them on the floor in the middle of the drawing-room and walks out.*

Yes, I bought it. Wait a moment, ladies and gentlemen, do, please. I don't feel quite clear in my head, I hardly know how to talk . . . [*laughs*] When we got to the auction, Deriganov was there already. Of course, Leonid Andreyevich only had fifteen thousand roubles, and Deriganov at once bid thirty over and above the mortgage. I could see how things were going, so I muscled in and offered forty. He bid forty-five, I bid fifty-five; he kept on adding five thousand each time and I added ten thousand each time. Well, it finished at last – I bid ninety thousand over and above the mortgage, and I got the property. Yes, the cherry orchard's mine now! Mine! [*laughs*] My God! the cherry orchard's mine! Come on, tell me I'm drunk, tell me I'm out of my mind, say I've imagined all this . . . [*stamps his foot*] Don't laugh at me! If only my father and grandfather could rise from their graves and see everything that's happened . . . how their Yermolay, their much-beaten, half-literate Yermolay, the lad that used to run about with bare feet in the winter . . . how he's bought this estate, the most beautiful place on God's earth! Yes, I've bought the very estate where my father and grandfather were serfs, where they weren't even admitted to the kitchen! I must be asleep, I must be dreaming, I only think it's true . . . it's all just my imagination, my imagination's been wandering . . . [*picks up the keys, smiling tenderly*] She threw these down because she wanted to show she's not mistress here any more. [*jingles the keys*] Well, never mind. [*the band is heard tuning up*] Hi! you musicians, come on now, play something, I want some music! Now then, all of you, just you wait and see Yermolay Lopakhin take an axe to the cherry orchard, just you see the trees come crashing down! We're going to build a whole lot of new villas, and our children and great-grandchildren are going to see a new living world growing up here . . . Come on there, let's have some music!

[*the band plays.* LYUBOV ANDREYEVNA *has sunk into a chair and is crying bitterly*] [*reproachfully*] Why didn't you listen to me before, why didn't you? My poor, dear lady, you can't undo it now. [*with great emotion*] Oh, if only we could be done with all this, if only we could alter this distorted unhappy life somehow!

PISHCHIK [*taking his arm, in a subdued voice*]. She's crying. Come into the ballroom, leave her alone . . . Come along . . . [*takes his arm and leads him away to the ballroom*]

LOPAKHIN. Never mind! Come on, band, play up, play up! Everything must be just as I wish it now. [*ironically*] Here comes the new landowner, here comes the owner of the cherry orchard! [*he pushes a small table accidentally and nearly knocks over some candle-sticks*] Never mind, I can pay for everything! [*goes out with* PISHCHIK]

No-one remains in the ballroom or drawing-room save LYUBOV ANDREYEVNA, *who sits hunched up in a chair, crying bitterly. The band continues playing quietly.* ANYA *and* TROFIMOV *enter quickly;* ANYA *goes up to her mother and kneels beside her,* TROFIMOV *remains standing by the entrance to the ballroom.*

ANYA. Mamma! . . . Mamma, you're crying? Dear, kind, sweet mamma, my darling precious, how I love you! God bless you, mamma! The cherry orchard's sold, it's quite true, there isn't any cherry orchard any more, it's true . . . but don't cry, mamma, you still have your life ahead of you, you still have your dear, innocent heart. You must come away with me, darling, we must get away from here! We'll plant a new orchard, even more splendid than this one – and when you see it, you'll understand everything, your heart will be filled with happiness, like the sun in the evening; and then you'll smile again, mamma! Come with me, darling, do come! . . .

CURTAIN

ACT FOUR

The same setting as for Act One. There are no pictures on the walls or curtains at the windows; only a few remaining pieces of furniture are piled up in a corner, as if for sale. There is an oppressive sense of emptiness. At the back of the stage, beside the door, suitcases and other pieces of luggage have been piled together as if ready for a journey. The voices of VARYA *and* ANYA *can be heard through the door on the left, which is open.* LOPAKHIN *stands waiting;* YASHA *is holding a tray laden with glasses of champagne. In the hall* YEPIKHODOV *is tying up a large box. From somewhere behind the scenes comes the low hum of voices: the peasants have called to say goodbye.* GAYEV's *voice is heard, saying: 'Thank you, friends, thank you.'*

YASHA. The villagers have come to say goodbye. In my view, Yermolay Alexeyevich, they're kind-hearted folk, but they haven't much understanding.

The hum subsides. LYUBOV ANDREYEVNA *and* GAYEV *enter from the hall;* LYUBOV ANDREYEVNA *is not crying but her face is pale and tremulous. She seems unable to speak.*

GAYEV. You gave them your purse, Lyuba. You shouldn't have done that. You really shouldn't.

LYUBOV ANDREYEVNA. I couldn't help myself, I couldn't help myself!
[*both go out*]

LOPAKHIN [*calls after them through the door*]. Have some champagne, please do, please! Just one little glass before you go. I didn't think of bringing any from town, and I could only get one bottle at the station. Do have some, please. [*a pause*] Won't you have any, ladies and gentlemen? [*walks away from the door*] If I'd known, I wouldn't have brought any . . . Then I won't have any either.
[YASHA *carefully puts the tray on a chair*]
You have a drink, Yasha, if nobody else will.

YASHA. Here's to the travellers! And here's to you staying behind. [*drinks*] This champagne isn't the real thing, I can tell you.

LOPAKHIN. Eight roubles a bottle. [*a pause*] It's devilishly cold here.

YASHA. The stoves weren't lit today. It doesn't matter as we're going. [*laughs*]

LOPAKHIN. Why are you laughing?

YASHA. Because I'm feeling glad.

LOPAKHIN. October's here, but it's still sunny and calm, as if it were summer. Good building weather. [*looks at his watch, then at the door*] Ladies and gentlemen, don't forget there are only forty-six minutes before the train's due to leave. That means we must start in twenty minutes. Hurry up.

TROFIMOV, *wearing an overcoat, comes in from outdoors.*

TROFIMOV. I think it's time to start. The horses are at the door. God knows where my goloshes are, they've disappeared. [*calls through the door*] Anya, my goloshes aren't here; I can't find them.

LOPAKHIN. And I must be off to Kharkov. I'll travel with you on the same train. I shall stay the whole winter in Kharkov: I've hung around here too long, and it's torture having no work to do. I can't be without work: I just don't know what to do with my hands; they feel limp and strange, as if they didn't belong to me.

TROFIMOV. We'll soon be gone, then you can start your useful labours again.

LOPAKHIN. Have a little drink, do.

TROFIMOV. No, thanks.

LOPAKHIN. You're going to Moscow, then?

TROFIMOV. Yes, I'll see them off to town, and then, tomorrow I'm off to Moscow.

LOPAKHIN. Well, well . . . I expect the professors are holding up their lectures, waiting for your arrival!

TROFIMOV. That's none of your business.

LOPAKHIN. How many years have you been studying at the university?

TROFIMOV. I wish you'd think up something new, that's old and stale. [*looks for his goloshes*] Incidentally, as we're not likely to meet again, I'd like to give you a bit of advice, by way of a farewell: stop throwing your arms about! Try to get rid of that habit of making wide, sweeping gestures. Yes, and all this talk, too, about building villas, these calculations about summer residents that are going to turn into smallholders, these forecasts – they're all sweeping gestures, too . . . When all's said and done, I like you, despite everything. You've slender, delicate fingers, like an artist's, you've a fine, sensitive soul . . .

LOPAKHIN [*embraces him*]. Goodbye, my friend. Thank you for everything. I can let you have some money for your journey, if you need it.

TROFIMOV. Whatever for? I don't want it.

LOPAKHIN. But you haven't any!

TROFIMOV. Yes, I have, thank you. I've just had some for a translation. Here it is, in my pocket. [*anxiously*] But I can't see my goloshes anywhere.

VARYA [*from the other room*]. Take your beastly things! [*she throws a pair of rubber goloshes into the room*]

TROFIMOV. But why are you angry, Varya? Hm . . . but these aren't my goloshes!

LOPAKHIN. I had a thousand acres of poppy sown last spring, and now I've just made forty thousand net profit on it. And when they were in bloom, what a picture it was! What I want to say is that I've made the forty thousand, and now I'm offering to lend you money because I'm in a position to do it. Why are you so stuck up? I'm a peasant . . . I've no manners.

TROFIMOV. Your father was a peasant, mine had a chemist's shop. But there's nothing in that.

[LOPAKHIN *takes out his wallet*]

Leave it alone, leave it alone . . . Even if you offered me two hundred thousand, I wouldn't take it. I'm a free man. And all that you value so highly and hold so dear, you rich men – and beggars, too, for that matter – none of it has the slightest power over me – it's all just so much fluff blowing about in the air. I'm strong, I'm proud, I can do without you, I can pass you by. Humanity is advancing towards the highest truth, the greatest happiness that it is possible to achieve on earth, and I am in the vanguard!

LOPAKHIN. Will you get there?

TROFIMOV. Yes. [*a pause*] I'll get there myself, or show others the way to get there.

[*the sound of an axe striking a tree is heard in the distance*]

LOPAKHIN. Well, goodbye, my friend, it's time to go. We show off in front of one another, and in the meantime life is slipping by. When I work for long hours on end, without taking any time off, I feel happier in my mind and I even imagine I know why I exist. But how many people there are in Russia, my friend, who exist to no purpose whatever! Well, never mind, perhaps it's no matter. They say Leonid Andreyevich has taken a post at the bank, at six thousand a year. I don't expect he'll stick to it: he's too lazy . . .

ANYA [*in the doorway*]. Mamma asks you not to cut the orchard down until she's left.

TROFIMOV. I should say not! Haven't you got any tact? [*goes out through the hall*]

LOPAKHIN. All right, all right . . . These people! [*follows* TROFIMOV]

ANYA. Has Firs been taken to hospital?

YASHA. I told them to take him this morning. He's gone, I think.

ANYA [*to* YEPIKHODOV, *who passes through the ballroom*]. Semyon Panteleyevich, will you please find out whether Firs has been taken to hospital?

YASHA [*offended*]. I told Yegor this morning. Need you ask ten times?

YEPIKHODOV. This superannuated Firs – candidly speaking, I mean – he's beyond repair, he ought to go and join his ancestors. As for me, I can only envy him. [*he places a suitcase on top of a cardboard hat-box and squashes it*] There you are, you see! . . . I might have known it! [*goes out*]

YASHA [*sardonically*]. Two-and-twenty misfortunes!

VARYA [*from behind the door*]. Has Firs been taken to the hospital?

ANYA. Yes.

VARYA. Why haven't they taken the letter to the doctor, then?

ANYA. I'll send someone after them with it . . . [*goes out*]

VARYA [*from adjoining room*]. Where's Yasha? Tell him, his mother is here and wants to say goodbye to him.

YASHA [*waves his hand*]. She makes me lose patience with her.
[*while the foregoing action has been taking place,* DUNYASHA *has been fussing with the luggage; now that* YASHA *is alone, she comes up to him*]

DUNYASHA. If only you'd look at me once, Yasha! You're going . . . you're leaving me behind! . . . [*she cries and throws her arms round his neck*]

YASHA. What's the point of crying? [*drinks champagne*] In a week's
time I'll be in Paris again. Tomorrow we'll get into an express
train – and off we'll go – we shall just disappear! I can hardly
believe it. *Vive la France*! This place doesn't suit me, I can't live
here – there's nothing going on. I've seen enough of all this
ignorance. I've had enough of it. [*drinks*] What are you crying
for? Behave like a respectable girl, then there won't be any
need to cry.

DUNYASHA [*looking into a hand-mirror and powdering her nose*]. Write
to me from Paris, won't you? You know that I've loved you,
Yasha. I've loved you so much! I've got a soft heart, Yasha!

YASHA. Someone's coming. [*pretends to be busy with a suitcase, singing
quietly to himself*]

Enter LYUBOV ANDREYEVNA, GAYEV, ANYA *and* CHARLOTTA
IVANOVNA.

GAYEV. We ought to be going. There isn't much time left. [*looks at*
YASHA] Who's smelling of herring here?

LYUBOV ANDREYEVNA. In ten minutes we ought to be getting into
the carriage . . . [*glances round the room*] Goodbye, dear house, old
grandfather house. Winter will pass, spring will come again, and
then you won't be here any more, you'll be pulled down. How
much these walls have seen! [*kisses her daughter ardently*] My little
treasure, you look simply radiant, your eyes are shining like
diamonds. Are you glad? Very glad?

ANYA. Yes, very. Our new life is just beginning, mamma!

GAYEV [*brightly*]. So it is indeed, everything's all right now. Before
the cherry orchard was sold everybody was worried and upset,
but as soon as it was all settled finally and once for all, everybody
calmed down, and felt quite cheerful, in fact . . . I'm an em-
ployee of a bank now, a financier . . . I pot the red . . . and you,
Lyuba, you're looking better, too, when all's said and done.
There's no doubt about it.

LYUBOV ANDREYEVNA. Yes, my nerves are better, it's true.
[*someone helps her on with her hat and coat*]
I'm sleeping better, too. Take my things out, Yasha, it's time.
[*to* ANYA] My little girl, we'll soon be seeing each other again.
I'm going to Paris – I shall live there on the money which
your Grandmamma in Yaroslavl sent us to buy the estate –

God bless Grandmamma! – and that money won't last long either.

ANYA. You'll come back soon, mamma . . . quite soon, won't you? I shall study and pass my exams at the high school and then I'll work and help you. We'll read all sorts of books together, mamma . . . won't we? [*she kisses her mother's hands*] We'll read during the long autumn evenings, we'll read lots of books, and a new, wonderful world will open up before us . . . [*dreamily*] Mamma, come back . . .

LYUBOV ANDREYEVNA. I'll come back, my precious. [*embraces her*]

Enter LOPAKHIN; CHARLOTTA *quietly sings to herself.*

GAYEV. Happy Charlotta! She's singing.

CHARLOTTA [*picks up a bundle that looks like a baby in swaddling clothes*] Bye-bye, little baby. [*a sound like a baby crying is heard*] Be quiet, my sweet, be a good little boy. [*the 'crying' continues*] My heart goes out to you, baby! [*throws the bundle down*] Are you going to find me another job, please? I can't do without one.

LOPAKHIN. We'll find you one, Charlotta Ivanovna, don't worry.

GAYEV. Everybody's leaving us, Varya's going away . . . we've suddenly become unwanted.

CHARLOTTA. I haven't got anywhere to live in town. I shall have to go. [*hums*] Oh, well, never mind.

Enter PISHCHIK.

LOPAKHIN. What a phenomenon!

PISHCHIK [*out of breath*]. Och, let me get my breath . . . I'm worn out . . . My good friends . . . Give me some water . . .

GAYEV. I suppose you've come to borrow money? I'd better go . . . Excuse me . . . [*goes out*]

PISHCHIK. I've not been to see you for a long time . . . my beautiful lady . . . [*to* LOPAKHIN] So you're here . . . I'm glad to see you . . . you're a man of great intelligence . . . here . . . take this . . . [*hands money to* LOPAKHIN] Four hundred roubles . . . I still owe you eight hundred and forty . . .

LOPAKHIN [*shrugs his shoulders, bewildered*]. It's like a dream . . . Where did you get it from?

PISHCHIK. Wait a moment . . . I'm so hot . . . A most extraordinary thing happened. Some English people came to see me and discovered a sort of white clay on my land . . . [*to* LYUBOV ANDREYEVNA] Here's four hundred for you also, my dear . . . enchantress . . . [*hands her the money*] You'll get the rest later on. [*takes a drink of water*] Just now a young fellow in the train was telling me that some great philosopher or other . . . advises people to jump off roofs. You just jump off, he says, and that settles the whole problem. [*as though astonished at what he has just said*] Fancy that! More water, please.

LOPAKHIN. Who were these Englishmen?

PISHCHIK. I let the land with the clay to them for twenty-four years . . . And now you must excuse me, I'm in a hurry. I've got to get along as quickly as I can. I'm going to Znoikov's, then to Kardamonov's . . . I owe money to all of them. [*drinks*] Good health to you all. I'll call again on Thursday . . .

LYUBOV ANDREYEVNA. We're just on the point of moving to town, and tomorrow I'm going abroad.

PISHCHIK. What's that? [*in agitation*] What are you going to town for? I see now . . . this furniture and the suitcases . . . Well, never mind. [*tearfully*] Never mind . . . These Englishmen, you know, they're men of the greatest intelligence. . . . Never mind . . . I wish you every happiness, God be with you. Never mind, everything comes to an end eventually. [*kisses* LYUBOV ANDREY-EVNA's *hand*] And when you hear that my end has come, just think of – a horse, and say: 'There used to be a fellow like that once . . . Simeonov-Pishchik his name was – God be with him!' Wonderful weather we're having. Yes . . . [*goes out, over-come with embarrassment, but returns at once and stands in the doorway*] Dashenka sent greetings to you. [*goes out*]

LYUBOV ANDREYEVNA. Well, we can go now. I'm leaving with two worries on my mind. One is Firs – he's sick, you know. [*glances at her watch*] We have another five minutes or so . . .

ANYA. Mamma, Firs has been taken to hospital already. Yasha sent him this morning.

LYUBOV ANDREYEVNA. The other is Varya. She's been accustomed to getting up early and working, and now, without work, she's like a fish out of water. She's got so thin and pale, and she cries a lot, poor thing: [*a pause*] You know very well, Yermolay Alexe-yevich, that I'd been hoping to get her married to you . . . and everything seemed to show that you meant to marry her, too.

[*whispers to* ANYA, *who nods to* CHARLOTTA, *and they both go out*] She loves you, and you must be fond of her, too . . . and I just don't know, I just don't know why you seem to keep away from each other. I don't understand it.

LOPAKHIN. Neither do I myself, I must confess. It's all so strange somehow . . . If there's still time, I'm ready even now . . . Let's settle it at once – and get it over! Without you here, I don't feel I shall ever propose to her.

LYUBOV ANDREYEVNA. That's an excellent idea! You'll hardly need more than a minute, that's all. I'll call her at once.

LOPAKHIN. There's champagne here, too, quite suitable for the occasion. [*takes a look at the glasses*] But they're empty, someone's drunk it up. [YASHA *coughs*] I should have said lapped it up.

LYUBOV ANDREYEVNA [*with animation*]. I'm so glad. We'll go outside. Yasha, *allez*! I'll call her . . . [*through the door*] Varya, come here a moment, leave what you're doing for a minute! Varya! [*goes out with* YASHA]

LOPAKHIN [*glancing at his watch*]. Yes . . . [*a pause*]

[*suppressed laughter and whispering is heard from behind the door, and finally* VARYA *comes in and starts examining the luggage. After some time she speaks*]

VARYA. It's strange, I just can't find . . .

LOPAKHIN. What are you looking for?

VARYA. I packed the things myself, yet I can't remember . . .

[*a pause*]

LOPAKHIN. Where are you going to now, Varvara Mikhaylovna?

VARYA. I? To the Rogulins. I've agreed to look after the house for them . . . to be their housekeeper, or something.

LOPAKHIN. That's at Yashnevo, isn't it? About seventy miles from here. [*a pause*] So this is the end of life in this house . . .

VARYA [*examining the luggage*]. But where could it be? Or perhaps I've packed it in the trunk? . . . Yes, life in this house has come to an end . . . there won't be any more . . .

LOPAKHIN. And I'm going to Kharkov presently . . . On the next train. I've got a lot to do there. And I'm leaving Yepikhodov here . . . I've engaged him.

VARYA. Well! . . .

LOPAKHIN. Do you remember, last year about this time it was

snowing already, but now it's quite still and sunny. It's rather cold, though . . . About three degrees of frost.

VARYA. I haven't looked. [*a pause*] Besides, our thermometer's broken . . . [*a pause*]

[*a voice is heard from outside the door: 'Yermolay Alexeyevich!'*]

LOPAKHIN [*as if he had long been expecting it*]. Coming this moment! [*goes out quickly*]

VARYA, *sitting on the floor, with her head on the bundle of clothes, sobs softly. The door opens,* LYUBOV ANDREYEVNA *enters quietly.*

LYUBOV ANDREYEVNA. Well? [*a pause*] We must go.

VARYA [*stops crying and wipes her eyes*]. Yes, it's time, mamma dear. I'll just be able to get to the Rogulins today, if only we don't miss the train.

LYUBOV ANDREYEVNA [*calls through the door*]. Anya, put your coat on.

Enter ANYA, *followed by* GAYEV *and* CHARLOTTA IVANOVNA. GAYEV *wears a heavy overcoat with a hood. Servants and coachmen come into the room.* YEPIKHODOV *fusses with the luggage.*

Now we can start on our journey!

ANYA [*joyfully*]. Yes, our journey!

GAYEV. My friends, my dear, kind friends! Now as I leave this house for ever, how can I remain silent, how can I refrain from expressing to you, as a last farewell, the feelings which now overwhelm me . . .

ANYA [*imploringly*]. Uncle!

VARYA. Uncle, dear, please don't!

GAYEV [*downcast*]. I pot the red and follow through . . . I'll keep quiet.

Enter TROFIMOV, *then* LOPAKHIN.

TROFIMOV. Well, ladies and gentlemen, it's time to go.

LOPAKHIN. Yepikhodov, my coat!

LYUBOV ANDREYEVNA. I'll just sit down for one little minute more. I feel as if I'd never seen the walls and ceilings of this house before, and now I look at them with such longing and affection . . .

GAYEV. I remember when I was six years old – it was Holy Trinity day – I was sitting on this window-sill, looking at father – he was just going to church . . .

LYUBOV ANDREYEVNA. Have they taken out all the luggage?

LOPAKHIN. It looks as if they have. [*to* YEPIKHODOV, *as he puts on his coat*] See that everything's all right, Yepikhodov.

YEPIKHODOV [*in a husky voice*]. Don't worry, Yermolay Alexeyevich!

LOPAKHIN. What are you talking like that for?

YEPIKHODOV. I've just had a drink of water, I must have swallowed something.

YASHA [*with contempt*]. What ignorance!

LYUBOV ANDREYEVNA. When we leave here there won't be a soul in the place . . .

LOPAKHIN. Until the spring.

VARYA [*pulls an umbrella from a bundle of clothes;* LOPAKHIN *pretends to be frightened that she is going to strike him*]. Now, why . . . why are you doing that? . . . I never thought of . . .

TROFIMOV. Ladies and gentlemen, come, let's get into the carriage. It's high time. The train will be in soon.

VARYA. Petya, here they are, your goloshes, beside the suitcase. [*tearfully*] And how dirty and worn-out they are! . . .

TROFIMOV [*puts them on*]. Come along, ladies and gentlemen!

GAYEV [*greatly embarrassed, afraid of breaking into tears*]. The train, the station . . . In off into the middle pocket . . .

LYUBOV ANDREYEVNA. Let us go!

LOPAKHIN. Is everyone here? No-one left behind? [*locks the door on the left*] There are some things put away there, it had better be locked up. Come along!

ANYA. Goodbye, old house! Goodbye, old life!

TROFIMOV. Greetings to the new life! . . . [*goes out with* ANYA]
    [VARYA *glances round the room and goes out slowly.* YASHA *and* CHARLOTTA, *with her little dog, follow*]

LOPAKHIN. And so, until the spring. Come along, ladies and gentlemen . . . *Au revoir!* [*goes out*]

[LYUBOV ANDREYEVNA *and* GAYEV *are left alone. They seem to have been waiting for this moment, and now they embrace each other and sob quietly, with restraint, so as not to be heard*]

GAYEV [*with despair in his voice*]. Sister, my sister . . .

LYUBOV ANDREYEVNA. Oh my darling, my precious, my beautiful orchard! My life, my youth, my happiness . . . goodbye! . . . Goodbye!

ANYA'S VOICE [*gaily*]. Mamma! . . .

TROFIMOV'S VOICE [*gaily and excitedly*]. Ah-oo! . . .

LYUBOV ANDREYEVNA. For the last time – to look at these walls, these windows . . . Mother used to love walking up and down this room . . .

GAYEV. Sister, my sister! . . .

ANYA'S VOICE. Mamma!

TROFIMOV'S VOICE. Ah-oo!

LYUBOV ANDREYEVNA. We're coming . . . [*both go out*]

[*The stage is empty. The sound of doors being locked is heard, then of carriages driving off. It grows quiet. The stillness is broken by the dull thuds of an axe on a tree. They sound forlorn and sad*]

There is a sound of footsteps and from the door on the right FIRS *appears. He is dressed, as usual, in a coat and white waistcoat, and is wearing slippers. He looks ill.*

FIRS [*walks up to the middle door and tries the handle*]. Locked. They've gone . . . [*sits down on a sofa*] They forgot about me. Never mind . . . I'll sit here for a bit. I don't suppose Leonid Andreyevich put on his fur coat, I expect he's gone in his light one . . . [*sighs, preoccupied*] I didn't see to it . . . These youngsters! . . . [*mutters something unintelligible*] My life's gone as if I'd never lived . . . [*lies down*] I'll lie down a bit. You haven't got any strength left, nothing's left, nothing . . . Oh, you . . . you're daft! . . . [*lies motionless*]

[*a distant sound is heard, coming as if out of the sky, like the sound of a string snapping, slowly and sadly dying away. Silence ensues, broken only by the sound of an axe striking a tree in the orchard far away*]

CURTAIN

THE BEAR

A Jest in One Act

Characters in the Play

POPOVA, Yelena Ivanovna, the young widow of a landowner,
  pretty, with dimpled cheeks
SMIRNOV, Grigoriy Stepanovich, a middle-aged landowner
LUKA, Madame Popova's old manservant

The action takes place in a drawing-room of Madame Popova's house in the country.

THE BEAR

POPOVA (*in deep mourning, keeping her eyes fixed on a photograph*) *and* LUKA.

LUKA. It's not right, Madam . . . You're just killing yourself. The cook and the chambermaid have gone to pick strawberries in the woods . . . every living thing's happy . . . even the cat knows how to enjoy herself – promenading in the courtyard and chasing birds . . . And you sit indoors all day, as if you were in a nunnery, taking no pleasure in anything. Yes indeed! I believe it's nearly a year since you went out of the house!

POPOVA. And I never will go out . . . Why should I? My life is over. He lies in his grave – I have buried myself in these four walls . . . We are both dead.

LUKA. There you go again! I wish I didn't have to listen to it! Nikolay Mikhailovich's dead, that's as it had to be – it was God's will, and the kingdom of heaven be his! You've done your mourning, and now that'll do – it's time to stop. Surely you can't go on weeping and wearing mourning all your life? I lost my missus too . . . Well, what of it? I grieved and cried for a month or so, and that was enough for her. Suppose I kept on wailing like Lazarus all my life – it would be more than the old woman was worth. [*sighs*] You've forgotten all your neighbours . . . You don't visit them, and you won't receive them. We live like spiders, if you'll pardon me saying so – we don't see the light of day. The mice have eaten our liveries . . . It's not as though there weren't any nice people about – the district is full of them . . . There's a regiment stationed at Ryblovo, and the officers are proper lollipops – you simply can't take your eyes off them! In the camp there's never a Friday goes by without a ball, and the military band plays music every day, they say. Ah! Madam, my dear lady! You're young, pretty, blooming with health – all you need is to live and enjoy yourself to the full . . . You know, beauty isn't given you to keep for ever! In another ten years you may be wanting to show off before the officers too – spreading your tail like a peacock – but it will be too late then!

POPOVA [*resolutely*]. I must ask you never to speak to me like this again! You know quite well that ever since Nikolay Mikhailovich died, life has lost all its value to me. It may seem to you that I'm alive, but that's only what you think! I made a vow never to take off this mourning, never to look at the light of day till I go to my grave . . . Do you hear? May his departed spirit see how I love him . . . Yes, I know, it was no secret to you that he was often mean to me, harsh, and . . . and even unfaithful. But I will be faithful to the grave, and I will let him see how well I can love. There, from the other side of the grave, he will see me just as I was before he died . . .

LUKA. Instead of talking like that, you'd do better to take a walk in the garden or maybe have Toby or Giant put into harness and go and drop in on your neighbours . . .

POPOVA. Oh! [*weeps*]

LUKA. Madam! My dear lady! . . . What is the matter? God be with you!

POPOVA. He was so fond of Toby! He always used to drive him when he went to visit the Korchagins and the Vlasovs. How wonderfully he used to drive! How graceful he looked when he pulled at the reins with all his strength! Do you remember? Toby, Toby! Tell them to give him an extra bag of oats today.

LUKA. Yes, madam.

[*a loud ring at the door*]

POPOVA [*starts*]. Who is that? Say that I'm not seeing anyone!

LUKA. Yes, madam. [*goes out*]

POPOVA [*alone, looking at the photograph*]. You shall see, *Nicolas*, how well I can love and forgive . . . My love will only fade away when I do, when my poor heart stops beating. [*laughs, half-weeping*] Aren't you ashamed of yourself? I'm such a good little woman, such a loyal wife, I've shut myself up and I'll remain faithful to you all my life, while you . . . aren't you ashamed of yourself, you fatty? How you deceived me, and made scenes, and left me on my own for weeks on end! . . .

LUKA [*enters, flustered*]. Madam, there's someone asking for you. He wants to see you . . .

POPOVA. But didn't you tell him that I'm not seeing anybody since my husband died?

LUKA. I did, but he won't listen: he says it's a very urgent matter.

POPOVA. I won't see anybody!

LUKA. I kept telling him, but . . . he's a proper devil . . . he swore and shoved past me . . . he's in the dining-room now.

POPOVA [*irritably*]. Very well, show him in . . . How rude these people are!

[LUKA *goes out*]

How difficult they are! What do they want from me? Why will they keep upsetting my peace of mind? [*sighs*] No, it looks as if I really shall have to enter a convent . . . [*ponders*] Yes, a convent . . .

Enter LUKA *with* SMIRNOV.

SMIRNOV [*as he enters, to* LUKA]. You blockhead – you're a lot too fond of talking . . . Donkey! [*seeing* POPOVA *assumes a dignified manner*] Madam, I have the honour of introducing myself: Grigoriy Stepanovich Smirnov, landowner and retired lieutenant of artillery. I'm obliged to trouble you on a very important matter . . .

POPOVA [*not offering her hand*]. What is it you want?

SMIRNOV. At the time of his death, your late husband, with whom I had the honour of being acquainted, owed me twelve hundred roubles on two bills of exchange. As I have to make a payment of interest to the Agricultural Bank tomorrow, I should be obliged to you, Madam, if you would pay the sum owing to me today.

POPOVA. Twelve hundred . . . And what did my husband owe you money for?

SMIRNOV. He used to buy oats from me.

POPOVA [*with a sigh, to* LUKA]. Don't forget, Luka, to tell them to give Toby that extra bag of oats. [LUKA *goes out; to* SMIRNOV] If Nikolay Mikhailovich owed you something, then of course I'll pay, but I must ask you to excuse me – I have no money in hand today. The day after tomorrow my bailiff will be back from town, and I'll tell him to pay you what's owing; till then I can't settle with you . . . Besides, it's exactly seven months ago today since my husband died, and just now I'm in such a state of mind that I don't feel at all disposed to occupy myself with money matters.

SMIRNOV. And I'm in such a state of pocket that, if I don't pay the interest tomorrow, I'll be completely and utterly bankrupt! My estate will be put up for auction!

POPOVA. The day after tomorrow you will receive the money.

SMIRNOV. I need the money today, not the day after tomorrow!

POPOVA. Forgive me, I can't pay you today.

SMIRNOV. And I can't wait till the day after tomorrow!

POPOVA. But how can I help it if I haven't any money?

SMIRNOV. You mean you can't pay?

POPOVA. No, I can't.

SMIRNOV. Hm . . . Is that your last word?

POPOVA. Yes, my last.

SMIRNOV. Your last? Positively?

POPOVA. Positively.

SMIRNOV. Thank you very much indeed! We'll make a note of that! [*shrugs his shoulders*] And yet they expect me to keep my temper! Just now, on the way here I met the excise officer and he asked me: 'Why are you always in such a temper, Grigoriy Stepanovich?' I wish people would be fair – how can I help being in a temper? I need money desperately . . . I left home at daybreak yesterday, and went the round of all my debtors, but – would you believe it? – not a single one of them paid me! I was dog-tired, and I spent the night in a low-down hole – a Jewish tavern, lying beside an empty barrel of vodka . . . When at last I got here, forty miles from home, and hoping to be paid my money, I'm treated to 'a state of mind'! How can I help being in a temper?

POPOVA. I think I've explained the position clearly: when my bailiff comes back from town, you'll get your money.

SMIRNOV. I've come to see you, not your bailiff! What the hell – excuse the language – do I want your bailiff for?

POPOVA. Forgive me, sir, I'm not used to such strange expressions or to such a tone. I won't listen to you any longer! [*goes out quickly*]

SMIRNOV [*alone*]. I like that! 'A state of mind'! . . . Her husband died seven months ago! . . . But have I got to pay the interest, or haven't I? I ask you: have I got to pay the interest, or haven't I? I grant you, your husband's died, you're in a state, and all that eyewash . . . your bailiff's gone off somewhere, the devil take him! . . . But what am I supposed to do? Fly away from my creditors in a balloon, or what? Or take a run and bash the wall in with my head? I arrive at Grozdiov's — he's not at home. Yaroshevich has gone into hiding, and as for Kuritsin, I had such an awful row with him that I nearly threw him out of the window. Mazutov had a bellyache, and this one is — in a state! Not one of the wretches has paid me! And all because I've been too indulgent with them — because I'm soft-hearted, a milksop, an old woman! I'm too gentle with them! Well, you wait! I'll soon show you what I'm made of! I won't let you play your tricks on me, devil take you! I'll stay here and stick around until she pays me! Brr! How mad I feel today, how furious! I'm positively shaking with rage, I can hardly breathe . . . Ugh! my God! I'm almost fainting! [*shouts*] You there!

Enter LUKA.

LUKA. What is it?

SMIRNOV. Bring me some *kvass*, or a glass of water!

[LUKA *goes out*]

SMIRNOV. And just look at the logic of it! A man needs money so desperately that it's like a noose round his neck, but she won't pay because, if you please, she's not disposed to occupy herself with money matters! . . . Proper petticoat logic! That's why I never like and never have liked talking to women. I'd rather sit on a barrel of gunpowder than talk to a woman. Brr! . . . I've got the shivers all over — that little hussy has put me in such a rage! I've only got to set eyes on a poetical creature like that even from a distance, and it makes me so angry that I get a cramp in my legs! I almost want to shout for help.

LUKA *enters and serves him with water.*

LUKA. Madam is indisposed and is seeing no-one.

SMIRNOV. Get out!

[LUKA *goes out*]

Indisposed and seeing no-one! Very well, you needn't see me . . .

I'll just sit here till you pay me back. If you're ill for a week, I'll stay here a week . . . If you're ill for a year, I'll stay a year . . . I'll get my own back, my good woman! I won't be appeased by your mourning or your dimpled cheeks . . . We know all about those dimples! [*shouts through the window*] Semyon, unharness the horses! We're not leaving for quite a time! I'm stopping here! Tell them at the stables to give the horses some oats! You lout! You've let the left-hand horse get its legs all tangled up with the reins again! [*mimics him*] It's no-othing! . . . I'll give you something for nothing! [*goes away from the window*] Disgusting! . . . The weather's unbearably hot, no-one will pay, I've had a bad night, and on top of it all there's this mourning female with her 'states'. My head's aching . . . Ought I to have some vodka, I wonder? [*shouts*] You there!

LUKA *enters*.

LUKA. What is it?

SMIRNOV. Bring me a glass of vodka!

[LUKA *goes out*]

Ugh! [*sits down and examines himself*] I cut a fine figure, I must say! All covered with dust, my boots dirty, unwashed, uncombed, bits of straw on my waistcoat . . . I dare say the little lady took me for a thug. [*yawns*] It's hardly polite to present myself in a drawing-room looking like this . . . Well, who cares? . . . I'm not a visitor here, I'm a creditor, and there's no regulation dress for creditors . . .

LUKA [*enters and serves him with vodka*]. You're taking too much of a liberty, sir . . .

SMIRNOV [*angrily*]. What's that?

LUKA. I . . . it's nothing . . . I only . . .

SMIRNOV. Who are you talking to? Keep your mouth shut!

LUKA [*aside*]. There's a brute for you! A proper infliction! The devil himself must have brought him here . . .

[LUKA *goes out*]

SMIRNOV. Oh, what a rage I'm in! So angry, I could crush the whole world to powder! I feel almost faint . . . [*shouts*] You there!

POPOVA [*enters with downcast eyes*]. Sir, for some time I've not been accustomed to hearing human voices in my solitude, and I can't bear shouting. I beg you most earnestly not to disturb my peace.

SMIRNOV. Pay me back my money and I'll go.

POPOVA. I've told you in plain language: I have no money in hand just now. Wait till the day after tomorrow.

SMIRNOV. And with the greatest respect I told you in plain language that I need money today, not the day after tomorrow. If you don't pay me today, I shall have to hang myself tomorrow.

POPOVA. But what am I to do if I haven't the money?

SMIRNOV. So you won't pay me straight away? . . . You won't? . . .

POPOVA. I can't . . .

SMIRNOV. In that case I shall stay here; I shall sit here till I get my money . . . [sits down] So you'll pay me the day after tomorrow? Very good! Then I'll sit it out till the day after tomorrow. I'll keep on sitting just like this . . . [jumps up] I ask you: have I got to pay the interest tomorrow, or haven't I? . . . Or do you think I'm joking?

POPOVA. Sir, I beg you not to shout! This isn't a stable!

SMIRNOV. I'm not asking you about a stable, I'm asking — have I got to pay the interest tomorrow, or not?

POPOVA. You don't seem to know how to behave in the company of a lady.

SMIRNOV. Yes, I do know how to behave in the company of a lady.

POPOVA. No, you don't. You're a coarse, ill-mannered fellow! Respectable people don't talk like this to a lady.

SMIRNOV. Well, this is a surprise! How would you like me to talk to you then? In French, or what? [affectedly and with exasperation] Madame, je vous prie . . . I'm so happy to know that you're not paying me my money . . . Ah, pardon me for having troubled you! What delightful weather it is today! This mourning dress you're wearing is so becoming! [bows and clicks his heels]

POPOVA. That's rude and not in the least clever!

SMIRNOV [mimics her]. Rude and not in the least clever! I don't know how to behave in the company of ladies! Madam, in my time I've seen more women than you have sparrows! I've fought three duels over women, I've jilted twelve and nine have jilted me. Yes indeed! There was a time when I used to play the fool, when I sentimentalised over women, and flattered them, when I scattered compliments, bowed and scraped . . . I loved, I suffered, I sighed at the moon, I went limp, I melted, I shivered in turn . . . I loved passionately, madly, in every way you can think of – the devil take me! – I chattered away like a magpie about the emancipation of women and I spent half my fortune on pandering to my tender emotions! But now – thank you very much! You won't take me in now! I've had enough of it! Black eyes, passionate eyes, red lips, dimpled cheeks, moonlight, whisperings, bated breath – Madam, I won't give you twopence for all the lot of it! I'm not referring to present company, but all women, young and old alike, are affected and deceitful – spiteful gossips and consummate liars. They are vain, too, petty-minded, merciless, outrageously illogical, and as for this – [*slaps his forehead*] excuse my frankness – any sparrow could give ten points to a philosopher in petticoats. You gaze at one of these poetical beings – all muslin and airs and graces – a demi-goddess . . . and you go into a million raptures! But peep inside her mind and you see – just the most ordinary crocodile! [*clutches the back of a chair; the chair creaks and breaks*] But what revolts me more than anything is that this crocodile imagines for some reason that her monopoly and privilege, in fact, her special gift is – the capacity for experiencing the tender passion! The devil take it – you can hang me head downwards on that nail there if a woman is capable of loving any living thing apart from a lap-dog! All she can do when she's in love is to moan and blubber. While the man suffers and makes sacrifices, she expresses all the love she feels for him by trailing her skirts about and trying to lead him more and more firmly by the nose. You have the misfortune to be a woman, so you must know woman's nature from your own. Very well then, tell me on your honour: have you ever in your life met a woman who was really sincere, loyal and constant? You haven't! Only the old and ugly women are faithful and constant! You'd be more likely to meet a cat with horns or a white snipe than a constant woman!

POPOVA. Excuse me – then who do you think is faithful and constant in love? Surely not the man?

SMIRNOV. Yes, the man, of course.

POPOVA. The man! [*laughs angrily*] The man is faithful and constant in love! That's news indeed! [*with feeling*] But what right have you to say that? Men are faithful and constant! If it comes to that, I may tell you that of all the men I have ever known, my late husband was the best . . . I loved him passionately, with all my being, as only a young thoughtful woman can love. I gave him my life, my youth, my happiness, my fortune. He was the breath of my life, I worshipped him as if I were a pagan and he my god, and . . . and – what do you think? That best of men deceived me at every turn in the most unscrupulous way! After his death I found a drawer full of love letters in his desk, and when he was alive – it's dreadful to remember it! – he used to leave me alone for weeks on end. He made love to other women before my very eyes and was actually unfaithful to me. He spent my money recklessly, and laughed at my feeling for him . . . Yet despite everything, I loved him and was loyal to him . . . More than that: though he is dead now, I am still faithful and loyal to him. I've buried myself within these four walls for ever, and I won't take off this mourning till my dying day . . .

SMIRNOV [*laughs scornfully*]. Mourning! I don't know what you take me for! As if I didn't know why you wear this black domino and bury yourself inside these four walls! Rather! It's so mysterious, so poetical! Suppose some youngster from a military school or some little fool of a poet happened to pass by your house – wouldn't he glance up at your windows and think: 'There lives the mysterious Tamara who has buried herself within four walls out of love for her husband.' We know all these tricks!

POPOVA [*flaring up*]. What? How dare you say this to me?

SMIRNOV. You've buried yourself alive, yet you haven't forgotten to powder your face!

POPOVA. But . . . how dare you speak to me like this?

SMIRNOV. Please don't shout, I'm not your bailiff! Allow me to call a spade a spade. I'm not a woman and I'm used to expressing my views without beating about the bush. So please don't shout.

POPOVA. It isn't I who does the shouting, it's you. Be so good as to leave me alone!

SMIRNOV. Pay me back my money and I'll go.

POPOVA. I'm not going to give you the money.

SMIRNOV. Yes, you are!

POPOVA. Just to spite you, I won't give you a farthing! Leave me alone!

SMIRNOV. As I haven't the pleasure of being either your spouse or your betrothed, there's no need to make scenes for my benefit. [*sits down*] I don't like it.

POPOVA [*breathless with anger*]. You dare to sit down?

SMIRNOV. Yes, I do.

POPOVA. I ask you to go away.

SMIRNOV. Give me back my money . . . [*aside*] Ah, how furious I am! . . . How furious!

POPOVA. I refuse to talk to insolent people! Be so good as to get out of here! [*a pause*] You're not going? Well?

SMIRNOV. No.

POPOVA. No?

SMIRNOV. No.

POPOVA. Very well then. [*rings*]

Enter LUKA.

POPOVA. Luka, put this gentleman out!

LUKA [*approaches* SMIRNOV]. Sir, be so good as to leave when you're told to . . . You mustn't . . .

SMIRNOV [*leaping up*]. Shut up! Who are you talking to? I'll make mincemeat out of you!

LUKA [*clutches at his heart*]. Holy Fathers! . . . Saints! . . . [*sinks into an armchair*] Oh, I feel ill, I feel ill! I can't get my breath!

POPOVA. Where's Dasha? Dasha! [*shouts*] Dasha, Pelageia, Dasha! [*rings*]

LUKA. Ough! They've all gone to pick strawberries. There's no one at home . . . I feel faint! Water!

POPOVA [*to* SMIRNOV]. Will you please get out of here!

SMIRNOV. Will you please be more polite?

POPOVA [*clenching her fists and stamping her feet*]. You're a boor! An ill-mannered bear! A brute! A monster!

SMIRNOV. What did you say?

POPOVA. I said that you're a bear, a monster!

SMIRNOV [*advancing towards her*]. Excuse me, what right have you to insult me?

POPOVA. Yes, I am insulting you . . . what of it? Do you imagine I'm afraid of you?

SMIRNOV. And do you imagine that because you happen to be one of those poetical beings you have the right to insult others with impunity? You do? I challenge you!

LUKA. Holy Fathers . . . Saints . . . Water!

SMIRNOV. Pistols!

POPOVA. Do you imagine that because you have huge fists and can bellow like a bull, I'm going to be afraid of you? Do you? You bully!

SMIRNOV. I challenge you! I won't allow anyone to insult me, and I don't care if you are a woman, a fragile creature!

POPOVA [*trying to shout him down*]. Bear, bear, bear!

SMIRNOV. It's high time we gave up the notion that only men have to answer for their insults! If women are to have equal rights, let them be equal, the devil take it! I challenge you!

POPOVA. You want a duel? By all means!

SMIRNOV. Now, this minute!

POPOVA. This very minute! My husband had some pistols . . . I'll go at once and get them. [*goes out hurriedly, then returns*] How I'll enjoy putting a bullet slap through your brazen head! Damnation take you! [*goes out*]

SMIRNOV. I'll pot her off like a chicken! I'm not a youngster, a sentimental puppy! . . . Delicate creatures don't exist for me.

LUKA. Good, kind sir! . . . [*kneels before him*] Do me a favour, take pity on an old man! Go away from here! You've scared me to death, and now you're going to fight a duel!

SMIRNOV [*ignoring him*]. A duel! Yes, that's equality of rights, that's emancipation! There's equality of sexes for you! I'll pop her off just as a matter of principle! But what a woman! [*mimics her*] 'Damnation take you! I'll put a bullet slap through your brazen head.' What a woman! Her face flushed, her eyes sparkled! . . . She accepted my challenge! My word! I've never seen one like her in my life! . . .

LUKA. Kind sir, do go away! I'll say prayers for you for the rest of my life!

SMIRNOV. That's a woman for you! That's the kind I appreciate! A real woman! Not one of these soft weak females, but a creature of fire, gunpowder, fireworks! I'm almost sorry to have to kill her!

LUKA [*weeps*]. My good sir . . . go away!

SMIRNOV. I positively like her! Positively! Even if she does have dimples in her cheeks, I like her! I am even ready to let her off her debt . . . and my anger's vanished . . . A wonderful woman!

POPOVA [*enters carrying pistols*]. Here they are, the pistols . . . But before we begin, be good enough to show me how to fire. I've never had a pistol in my hands before . . .

LUKA. The Lord save us, the Lord have mercy on us! I'll go and look for the gardener and the coachman . . . What can have brought this trouble upon our heads? . . . [*goes out*]

SMIRNOV [*examining the pistols*]. You see, there are several sorts of pistols . . . There are special duelling pistols, that's the Mortimer make with capsules. But these pistols of yours are Smith-Wessons, triple action with extractor . . . Beautiful pistols! . . . They're worth at least ninety roubles the brace . . . You must hold the revolver like this . . . [*aside*] What eyes, what eyes! A woman to set you on fire!

POPOVA. Like this?

SMIRNOV. Yes, that's right . . . Then you raise the cock ... . take aim like this . . . Hold your head back a little! Stretch your arm full length . . . that's it . . . Then with this finger press on that little thing – and that's all . . . But the most important rule is not to get excited and to take your aim without hurrying . . . You must try to keep your hand from shaking.

POPOVA. Very well . . . It's not very convenient to shoot indoors, let's go into the garden.

SMIRNOV. All right. Only I warn you that I shall fire into the air.

POPOVA. Whatever next? Why?

SMIRNOV. Because . . . because . . . It's my business why.

POPOVA. You're funking it, aren't you? Is that it? Ah-ah! No, sir! No wriggling! Be good enough to follow me! I won't rest a wink till I've made a hole in your forehead – that forehead I detest so much! So you're funking it?

SMIRNOV. Yes, I am.

POPOVA. That's a lie! Why won't you fight?

SMIRNOV. Because . . . because you . . . I like you.

POPOVA [*laughs angrily*]. He likes me! He dares to say that he likes me! [*points to the door*] You can go.

SMIRNOV [*puts down the revolver in silence, picks up his cap and goes to the door. He stops by the door and for about half a minute they look at each other without speaking, then he approaches her hesitantly*]. Listen . . . Are you still angry? . . . I'm devilish angry too, but, don't you see . . . How can I explain? . . . The fact is that . . . you see . . . strictly speaking . . . it's something like this . . . [*shouts*]

Anyway, is it my fault that I've taken a liking to you? [*clutches the back of a chair which creaks and breaks*] Damnation, what fragile furniture you've got! I like you! Do you understand? I . . . I'm almost in love with you.

POPOVA. Keep away from me – I hate you!

SMIRNOV. My God, what a woman! I've never seen anything like it in my life! I'm lost! I'm done for! I'm caught like a mouse in a trap!

POPOVA. Keep away, or I'll shoot!

SMIRNOV. Shoot! You can't imagine how happy I'd be to die with those wonderful eyes looking at me, to be killed by a bullet from a weapon held by that little velvet-smooth hand! . . . I've gone off my head! You must consider and decide now, because if I once leave here, we shall never see each other again. You must decide! . . . I come from a good family, I'm an honest man, I've an income of ten thousand roubles a year . . . I can put a bullet through a halfpenny tossed in the air . . . I have excellent horses . . . Will you be my wife?

POPOVA [*indignant, brandishes the revolver*]. A duel! I challenge you!

SMIRNOV. I've gone out of my mind. I don't understand anything. [*shouts*] You there! Water!

POPOVA [*shouts*]. Let us fight!

SMIRNOV. I've gone off my head, I've fallen in love like a young-ster, like a fool! [*seizes her by the hand; she shrieks with pain*] I love you! [*kneels before her*] I love you as I've never loved before! I've jilted twelve women, nine have jilted me, but I've never loved any of them as I love you! . . . I've gone all soft and soppy . . . Here I am on my knees like a fool, offering you my hand . . . It's a shame, a disgrace! I haven't fallen in love for five years. I vowed I wouldn't; and all of a sudden here I am – up to my neck in it! I'm offering my hand in marriage! Yes, or no? You don't want it? Very well, you don't have to! [*gets up and walks quickly to the door*]

POPOVA. Wait a minute . . .

SMIRNOV [*stopping*]. Well?

POPOVA. No, it's nothing . . . You can go . . . Wait though . . . No, go away, go! I hate you! However . . . No, don't go. Oh, if you only knew how furious I am, how furious! [*flings the revolver on to the table*] My fingers are quite numb from holding the horrid thing! . . . [*tears her handkerchief in a fury*] Well, why are you standing there? Get out!

SMIRNOV. Goodbye!

POPOVA. Yes, yes, go! . . . [*shouts*] Where are you going? Wait . . . you'd better go, though. Oh, how angry I feel! Don't come near me, don't come near me!

SMIRNOV [*going up to her*]. How angry I am with myself! I've fallen in love like a schoolboy, I've been on my knees . . . It positively makes my flesh creep . . . [*gruffly*] I love you! It's the last thing I wanted to do! I've got to pay the interest tomorrow, the hay-making's just started, and now you . . . [*takes her by the waist*] I'll never forgive myself for it!

POPOVA. Keep away from me! Take your hands off! I . . . I hate you. I . . . challenge you!

[*a prolonged kiss*]

LUKA *enters, carrying an axe. He is followed by a* GARDENER *with a rake, a* COACHMAN *with a pitchfork, and several* WORKMEN *with cudgels.*

LUKA [*seeing the embracing couple*]. Holy Fathers!

[*a pause*]

POPOVA [*with downcast eyes*]. Luka, tell them not to give Toby any oats at all today.

CURTAIN

THE PROPOSAL

A Jest in One Act

Characters in the Play

CHUBUKOV, Stepan Stepanovich, a landowner
NATALYA STEPANOVNA (Natasha), his daughter, aged 25
LOMOV, Ivan Vasilyevich, a landowner and neighbour of Chub-
    ukov, a healthy, well-nourished but hypochrondriacal person

The action takes place on the estate of Chubukov.

THE PROPOSAL

The drawing-room in CHUBUKOV's *house.* CHUBUKOV *and* LOMOV; *the latter enters wearing evening dress and white gloves.*

CHUBUKOV [*going to meet him*]. My dearest friend, fancy seeing you! Ivan Vasilyevich! I'm so glad! [*shakes hands*] Well, this is a real surprise, dear old boy! . . . How are you?

LOMOV. Thank you. And how are you, pray?

CHUBUKOV. We're getting on reasonably well, my cherub – thanks to your prayers and all that . . . Please do sit down . . . You know it's too bad of you to forget your neighbours, old fellow. But, my dear friend, why all this formality? Tails, gloves, and all the rest of it! Are you going visiting, or what, dear boy?

LOMOV. No, I've only come to see you, my dear Stepan Stepan-ovich.

CHUBUKOV. Then why wear tails, dear boy? As though you were making a formal call on New Year's day!

LOMOV. The fact is, you see . . . [*takes his arm*] I've come to ask a favour of you, my dear Stepan Stepanovich – if I'm not causing too much trouble. I've taken the liberty of seeking your help more than once in the past, and you've always, so to speak . . . But forgive me, I'm in such a state . . . I'll take a drink of water, my dear Stepan Stepanovich. [*drinks water*]

CHUBUKOV [*aside*]. He's come to ask for money! I shan't give him any! [*to* LOMOV] What's the matter, my dear young fellow?

LOMOV. You see, my dear Stepanich . . . Forgive me, Stepan, my dear . . . I mean I'm in such a state of nerves – as you can see . . . In short, you're the only man who can possibly help me, though, of course, I haven't done anything to deserve it, and . . . and I have no right to count on your assistance . . .

CHUBUKOV. Oh, don't spin it out, dear boy! Out with it! Well?

LOMOV. Yes, yes . . . I'll tell you straight away . . . The fact is that I've come to ask for the hand of your daughter, Natalya Stepanovna.

CHUBUKOV [*joyfully*]. Ivan Vasilyevich! My dearest friend! Say it again — I didn't quite hear you!

LOMOV. I have the honour to ask . . .

CHUBUKOV [*interrupting him*]. My dearest chap! . . . I am so very glad, and so forth . . . Yes, indeed — and all that sort of thing. [*embraces and kisses him*] I've wished it for a long time. It always has been my wish. [*sheds a tear*] I've always loved you as if you were my own son, my dearest fellow! May God grant you love and sweet concord, and all the rest of it. As for myself, I've always wished . . . But why am I standing here like an idiot? I'm stunned with joy, simply stunned! Oh, with all my heart . . . I'll go and call Natasha, and so on . . .

LOMOV [*moved*]. My dear Stepan Stepanych, what do you think she'll say? May I count on her consenting?

CHUBUKOV. She not consent to it? — and you such a good-looker, too! I bet she's up to her ears in love with you, and so forth . . . I'll tell her straight away! [*goes out*]

LOMOV [*alone*]. I'm cold . . . I'm trembling all over as if I were going in for an examination. The main thing is to make up your mind. If you think too long, keep talking and hesitating and waiting for the ideal woman or for real true love, you'll never get married. Brr! . . . I'm cold! Natalya Stepanovna is an excellent housekeeper, educated, not bad-looking . . . What more do I want? But I'm in such a state that I'm beginning to have noises in my head . . . [*drinks water*] Yet I mustn't stay single. In the first place, I'm thirty-five already — a critical age, so to speak. Secondly, I must have an ordered, regular life . . . I've got a heart disease, with continual palpitations . . . I flare up so easily, and I'm always getting terribly agitated . . . Even now my lips are trembling and my right eyelid's twitching . . . But the worst thing is my sleep. No sooner do I get into bed and start dropping off to sleep than something stabs me in my left side. Stab! and it goes right through my shoulder to my head . . . I jump up like a madman, walk about for a bit and lie down again . . . But directly I start dozing off, there it goes again in my side — stab! And the same thing happens twenty times over . . .

Enter NATALYA.

NATALYA. Oh, so it's you! And Papa said: go along, there's a customer come for the goods. How do you do, Ivan Vasilyevich?

LOMOV. How do you do, my dear Natalya Stepanovna?

NATALYA. Excuse my wearing this apron and not being properly dressed. We're shelling peas for drying. Why haven't you been to see us for so long? Do sit down . . .

[*they sit down*]

Will you have some lunch?

LOMOV. No, thank you, I've already had lunch.

NATALYA. Won't you smoke? Here are some matches . . . It's a magnificent day, but yesterday it rained so hard that the men did nothing all day. How many ricks did you manage to get in? Would you believe it, I was so set on getting it done that I had the whole meadow cut, and now I almost feel sorry – I'm afraid the hay may rot. It might have been better to wait. But what's all this? I believe you're wearing tails! This is something new! Are you going to a ball or something? By the way, you've changed – you're better looking! . . . But really, why are you dressed up like this?

LOMOV [*in agitation*]. You see, dear Natalya Stepanovna . . . The fact is that I've decided to ask you to . . . listen to me . . . Naturally, you'll be surprised, possibly even angry, but I . . . [*aside*] How dreadfully cold it is!

NATALYA. What is it then? [*a pause*] Well?

LOMOV. I'll try to be brief. You are aware, of course, my dear Natalya Stepanovna, that I've had the honour of knowing your family a long time – from my very childhood, in fact. My late aunt and her husband – from whom, as you know, I inherited the estate – always entertained a profound respect for your father and your late mother. The family of the Lomovs and the family of the Chubukovs have always been on the friendliest and, one might almost say, on intimate terms. Besides, as you are aware, my land is in close proximity to yours. Perhaps you will recollect that my Volovyi meadows lie alongside your birch wood.

NATALYA. Excuse me, but I must interrupt you there. You say 'my' Volovyi meadows . . . But are they really yours?

LOMOV. Yes, mine . . .

NATALYA. Well, what next! The Volovyi meadows are ours, not yours!

LOMOV. No, they're mine, dear Natalya Stepanovna.

NATALYA. That's news to me. How do they come to be yours?

LOMOV. What do you mean, how? I'm speaking of the Volovyi meadows that lie like a wedge between your birch wood and the Burnt Swamp.

NATALYA. But yes, of course . . . They're ours.

LOMOV. No, you're mistaken, my dear Natalya Stepanovna, they are mine.

NATALYA. Do come to your senses, Ivan Vasilyevich! How long have they been yours?

LOMOV. What do you mean by 'how long'? As long as I can remember – they've always been ours.

NATALYA. Well, there you must excuse me for disagreeing.

LOMOV. You can see it in the documents, my dear Natalya Stepanovna. It's true that the Volovyi meadows were a matter of dispute at one time, but now everyone knows that they're mine. There's really no need to argue about it. If I may explain – my aunt's grandmother handed over those meadows to your great-grandfather's peasants for their use, rent free, for an indefinite period, in return for their firing her bricks. Your great-grandfather's peasants used the meadows rent free for forty years or so and got accustomed to looking upon them as their own . . . and then when the settlement was made after the emancipation . . .

NATALYA. But it wasn't at all as you say! Both my grandfather and my great-grandfather considered that their land reached to the Burnt Swamp – so the Volovyi meadows must have been ours. So why argue about it? I can't understand you. It's really rather annoying!

LOMOV. I'll show you the documents, Natalya Stepanovna!

NATALYA. No, you must be just joking, or trying to tease me . . . What a surprise indeed! We've owned the land for something like three hundred years, and now suddenly someone declares that the land isn't ours! Forgive me, Ivan Vasilyevich, but I just can't believe my own ears . . . I set no value on those meadows. They're not more than fifteen acres, and they're only worth about three hundred roubles, but it's the injustice of it that disgusts me! You can say what you like, but I can't tolerate injustice.

LOMOV. Do hear me out, I implore you! Your father's grandfather's peasants, as I've already had the honour of telling you, fired bricks for my aunt's grandmother. My aunt's grandmother, wishing to do something for them . . .

NATALYA. Grandfather, grandmother, aunt . . . I don't understand anything about it! The meadows are ours, that's all!

LOMOV. They're mine!

NATALYA. They're ours! You can go on trying to prove it for two days, you can put on fifteen dress suits if you like, but they're still ours, ours, ours! . . . I don't want what's yours, but I have no desire to lose what's mine . . . You can please yourself!

LOMOV. I don't want the meadows, Natalya Stepanovna, but it's a matter of principle. If you wish, I'll give them to you as a present.

NATALYA. But I'm the one who could make a present of them to you — because they're mine! . . . All this is very strange, Ivan Vasilyevich, to say the least of it! Till now we've always regarded you as a good neighbour, a friend of ours. Last year we lent your our threshing machine, and because of that we had to finish threshing our own corn in November. And now you're treating us as if we were gypsies! You're making me a present of my own land! Forgive me, but this isn't neighbourly conduct! To my mind it's almost impertinent, if you want to know . . .

LOMOV. You mean to say then that I'm a usurper? I've never stolen other people's land, madam, and I won't allow anyone to accuse me of it . . . [goes rapidly to the decanter and drinks water] The Volovyi meadows are mine!

NATALYA. That's not true, they're ours!

LOMOV. They're mine!

NATALYA. It isn't true! I'll prove it to you! I'll send my men to mow those meadows today.

LOMOV. What's that?

NATALYA. My men will be working there today!

LOMOV. I'll kick them out!

NATALYA. You daren't do that!

LOMOV [clutches at his heart]. The Volovyi meadows are mine! Don't you understand that? Mine!

NATALYA. Don't shout, please! You can shout and choke with rage when you're at home, but please don't overstep the mark here!

LOMOV. If it weren't for these dreadful agonising palpitations, Madam – if it weren't for the throbbing in my temples, I should speak to you very differently! [*shouts*] The Volovyi meadows are mine!

NATALYA. Ours!

LOMOV. Mine!

NATALYA. Ours!

LOMOV. Mine!

Enter CHUBUKOV.

CHUBUKOV. What's all this? What are you shouting about?

NATALYA. Papa, please explain to this gentleman: to whom do the Volovyi meadows belong – to him or to us?

CHUBUKOV [*to* LOMOV]. The meadows are ours, dear chap.

LOMOV. But forgive me, Stepan Stepanich, how do they come to be yours? At least you might be reasonable! My aunt's grandmother gave over the meadows to your grandfather's peasants for temporary use without payment. The peasants had the use of the land for forty years and got accustomed to regarding it as their own. But when the settlement was made . . .

CHUBUKOV. Pardon me, my dear friend . . . You forget that it was just because there was a dispute and so on about these meadows that the peasants didn't pay rent to your grandmother, and all the rest of it . . . And now every dog knows that they're ours – yes, really! You can't have seen the plans!

LOMOV. But I'll prove to you that they're mine!

CHUBUKOV. You won't prove it, my dear man.

LOMOV. Yes, I will!

CHUBUKOV. But why shout, my dear boy? You won't prove anything by shouting! I don't want what is yours, but I've no intention of letting go of what's mine. Why should I? If it comes to that, my dear friend – if you're thinking of starting a dispute about the meadows and all the rest of it, I'd sooner make a present of them to the peasants than to you. So that's that!

LOMOV. I don't understand this! What right have you to give away someone else's property?

CHUBUKOV. Permit me to decide whether I have the right or not! And really, young man, I'm not used to being spoken to in that tone, and so forth . . . I'm twice your age, young man, and I beg you to speak to me without getting excited, and all that . . .

LOMOV. No, you're simply taking me for a fool and laughing at me! You call my land yours, and then you expect me to stay cool and talk to you in the ordinary way. Good neighbours don't behave in this way, Stepan Stepanich! You're not a neighbour, you're a usurper!

CHUBUKOV. What's that? What did you say?

NATALYA. Papa, send the men to mow the meadows at once!

CHUBUKOV [to LOMOV]. What was it you said, sir?

NATALYA. The Volovyi meadows are ours, and I won't give them up! I won't, I won't!

LOMOV. We shall see about that! I'll prove to you in court that they're mine.

CHUBUKOV. In court? You take it to court, sir, and all the rest of it! You do it! I know you — you've really just been waiting for a chance to go to law, and all that. It comes natural to you — this petty niggling. Your family always had a weakness for litigation. All of them!

LOMOV. Please don't insult my family! The Lomovs have all been honest men, and not one of them has ever been on trial for embezzling money like your uncle!

CHUBUKOV. Every member of the Lomov family has been mad!

NATALYA. Every one of them — every one!

CHUBUKOV. Your grandfather was a dipsomaniac, and your youngest aunt, Nastasyia Mikhailovna — yes, it's a fact — ran away with an architect, and all the rest of it . . .

LOMOV. And your mother was deformed! [clutches at his heart] This shooting pain in my side! . . . The blood's gone to my head . . . Holy Fathers! Water!

CHUBUKOV. Your father was a gambler and a glutton!

NATALYA. Your aunt was a scandal-monger — and a rare one at that!

LOMOV. My left leg's paralysed . . . And you're an intriguer . . . Oh, my heart! . . . And it's an open secret that before the

elections you . . . There are flashes in front of my eyes . . .
Where's my hat? . . .

NATALYA. It's mean! It's dishonest! It's perfectly vile!

CHUBUKOV. And you're just a malicious, double-faced, mean
fellow! Yes, you are!

LOMOV. Here it is, my hat . . . My heart . . . Which way do I go?
Where's the door? Oh! I believe I'm dying . . . I've lost the use
of my leg . . . [walks to the door]

CHUBUKOV [calling after him]. I forbid you to set foot in my house
again!

NATALYA. Take it to court! We shall see!

[LOMOV goes out staggering]

CHUBUKOV. The devil take him! [walks about in agitation]

NATALYA. Have you ever seen such a cad? Trust good neighbours
after that!

CHUBUKOV. The ridiculous scarecrow! The scoundrel!

NATALYA. The monster! Grabs other people's land, then dares to
abuse them into the bargain!

CHUBUKOV. And this ridiculous freak, this eyesore – yes, he has the
impertinence to come here and make a proposal and all the rest
of it! Would you believe it? A proposal!

NATALYA. What proposal?

CHUBUKOV. Yes, just fancy! He came to propose to you.

NATALYA. To propose? To me? But why didn't you tell me that
before?

CHUBUKOV. That's why he got himself up in his tail-coat. The
sausage! The shrimp!

NATALYA. To me? A proposal? Oh! [drops into a chair and moans]
Bring him back! Bring him back! Oh, bring him back!

CHUBUKOV. Bring whom back?

NATALYA. Be quick, be quick! I feel faint! Bring him back! [shrieks
hysterically]

CHUBUKOV. What is it? What do you want? [clutches at his head]
What misery! I'll shoot myself! I'll hang myself! They've worn
me out!

NATALYA. I'm dying! Bring him back!

CHUBUKOV. Phew! Directly. Don't howl. [runs out]

NATALYA [alone, moans]. What have we done! Bring him back!
Bring him back!

CHUBUKOV [*runs in*]. He's coming directly, and all the rest of it. Damnation take him! Ugh! You can talk to him yourself; I don't want to, and that's that!

NATALYA [*moans*]. Bring him back!

CHUBUKOV [*shouts*]. He's coming, I tell you! What a job it is, O Lord, to be a grown-up daughter's father!* I'll cut my throat! Yes, indeed, I'll cut my throat! We've abused the man, we've insulted him, we've kicked him out, and it was all your doing – your doing!

NATALYA. No, it was yours!

CHUBUKOV. So now it's my fault! What next!

Enter LOMOV.

LOMOV [*exhausted*]. These dreadful palpitations . . . My leg feels numb . . . a shooting pain in my side . . .

NATALYA. Forgive us, we were rather hasty, Ivan Vasiliyevich . . . I remember now: the Volovyi meadows really are yours.

LOMOV. My heart's going at a terrific rate . . . The meadows are mine . . . Both my eyelids are twitching . . .

NATALYA. Yes, they're yours, yours . . . Sit down . . .

[*they sit down*]

We were wrong.

LOMOV. To me it's a matter of principle . . . I don't value the land, but I value the principle . . .

NATALYA. That's it, the principle . . . Let's talk about something else.

LOMOV. Especially as I have proof. My aunt's grandmother gave over to your father's grandfather's peasants . . .

NATALYA. Enough, enough about that . . . [*aside*] I don't know how to begin . . . [*to him*] Will you soon be going shooting?

LOMOV. I expect to go grouse shooting after the harvest, dear Natalya Stepanovna . . . Oh, did you hear? Just fancy – what bad luck I've had! My Tryer – you know him – he's gone lame.

NATALYA. What a pity! What was the cause of it?

LOMOV. I don't know. . . . He may have dislocated his paw, or he

---

* A quotation from *The Misfortune of Being Clever*, by Griboyedov. It had become so much a part of ordinary speech that quotation marks were omitted by Chekhov.

may have been bitten by other dogs. . . . [*sighs*] My best dog, to say nothing of the money! You know, I paid Mironov a hundred and twenty-five roubles for him.

NATALYA. You paid too much, Ivan Vasiliyevich.

LOMOV. Well, I think it was very cheap. He's a marvellous dog!

NATALYA. Papa paid eighty-five roubles for his Flyer, and Flyer is better than your Tryer by far.

LOMOV. Flyer better than Tryer? Come, come! [*laughs*] Flyer better than Tryer!

NATALYA. Of course he's better! It's true that Flyer's young – he's hardly a full-grown dog yet – but for points and cleverness even Volchanetsky hasn't got a better one.

LOMOV. Excuse me, Natalya Stepanovna, but you forget that he's got a pug-jaw, and a dog with a pug-jaw can never grip properly.

NATALYA. A pug-jaw? That's the first I've heard of it.

LOMOV. I assure you, his lower jaw is shorter than the upper one.

NATALYA. Why, did you measure it?

LOMOV. Yes. He's all right for coursing, of course, but when it comes to gripping, he's hardly good enough.

NATALYA. In the first place our Flyer is a pedigree dog – he's the son of Harness and Chisel – whereas your Tryer's coat has got such a mixture of colours that you'd never guess what kind he is. Then he's as old and ugly as an old hack . . .

LOMOV. He's old, but I wouldn't take five of your Flyers for him . . . I wouldn't think of it! Tryer is a real dog, but Flyer . . . it's absurd to go on arguing. . . . Every sportsman has any number of dogs like your Flyer. Twenty-five roubles would be a lot to pay for him.

NATALYA. There's some demon of contradiction in you today, Ivan Vasilyevich. First you pretend that the meadows are yours, and now you're saying that Tryer is better than Flyer. I don't like it when people say what they don't really believe. After all, you know perfectly well that Flyer is a hundred times better than your . . . well, your stupid Tryer. So why say the opposite?

LOMOV. I can see, Natalya Stepanovna, that you think I'm either blind or a fool. Won't you understand that your Flyer has a pug-jaw?

NATALYA. That isn't true.

LOMOV. He has a pug-jaw.

NATALYA [*shouts*]. It's not true! . . .

LOMOV. What are you shouting for, madam?

NATALYA. Why are you talking nonsense? This is quite revolting! It's time your Tryer was shot, and you're comparing him to Flycr!

LOMOV. Excuse me, I can't continue this argument. I have palpitations.

NATALYA. I've noticed that the people who understand least about shooting are the ones who argue most about it.

LOMOV. Madam, please be silent . . . My heart's bursting . . . [*shouts*] Be quiet!

NATALYA. I won't be quiet till you admit that Flyer is a hundred times better than your Tryer.

LOMOV. He's a hundred times worse! It's time he was dead, your Flyer! Oh, my head . . . my eyes . . . my shoulder! . . .

NATALYA. As for your idiot Tryer – I don't need to wish him dead: he's half-dead already!

LOMOV [*weeping*]. Be quiet! My heart's going to burst.

NATALYA. I won't be quiet!

Enter CHUBUKOV.

CHUBUKOV. Now what is it?

NATALYA. Papa, tell us frankly, on your honour: which dog's the better – our Flyer or his Tryer?

LOMOV. Stepan Stepanich, I implore you, tell us just one thing: has your Flyer got a pug-jaw, or hasn't he? Yes or no?

CHUBUKOV. Well, what if he has? As if it mattered! Anyway, there's no better dog in the whole district, and all that.

LOMOV. But my Tryer is better, isn't he? On your honour!

CHUBUKOV. Don't get excited, my dear boy . . . Let me explain . . . Your Tryer, of course, has his good points . . . He's a good breed, he's got strong legs, he's well built and all the rest of it. But if you really want to know, my dear friend, the dog has two serious faults: he's old and he's snub-nosed.

LOMOV. Excuse me, I've got palpitations . . . Let us look at the facts . . . Perhaps you'll remember that when we hunted in the Maruskin fields my Tryer kept up with the Count's Spotter, while your Flyer was a good half-mile behind.

CHUBUKOV. He dropped behind because the Count's huntsman hit him with his whip.

LOMOV. He deserved it. All the other dogs were chasing the fox, but Flyer started worrying the sheep.

CHUBUKOV. That's not true! . . . My dear friend, I lose my temper easily, so I do beg you, let's drop this argument. The man hit him because people are always jealous of other people's dogs . . . Yes, everyone hates the other man's dog! And you, sir, are not innocent of that either! Yes! For instance, as soon as you notice that someone's dog is better than your Tryer, you immediately start something or other . . . and all the rest of it . . . You see, I remember everything!

LOMOV. So do I!

CHUBUKOV [*mimics him*]. So do I! And what is it you remember?

LOMOV. Palpitations . . . My leg's paralysed . . . I can't . . .

NATALYA [*mimics him*]. Palpitations . . . What sort of a sportsman are you? You ought to be lying on the stove in the kitchen squashing blackbeetles instead of hunting foxes! Palpitations indeed!

CHUBUKOV. Yes, honestly, hunting's not your line at all! With your palpitations and all that, you'd be better at home than sitting on horseback being jolted about. It wouldn't matter if you really hunted, but you only go out so that you can argue, or get in the way of other people's dogs, and all the rest of it . . . I get angry easily, so let's stop this conversation. You're just not a sportsman, and that's all there is to it.

LOMOV. What about you – are you a sportsman? You only go out hunting to make up to the Count, and intrigue against other people . . . Oh, my heart! You're an intriguer!

CHUBUKOV. What! I – an intriguer? [*shouts*] Be silent!

LOMOV. Intriguer!

CHUBUKOV. Milksop! Puppy!

LOMOV. You old rat! Hypocrite!

CHUBUKOV. Hold your tongue, or I'll shoot you with a dirty gun like a partridge! Windbag!

LOMOV. Everyone knows – oh, my heart! – that your wife used to beat you! . . . My leg . . . my head . . . flashes in front of my eyes . . . I'm going to fall down . . . I'm falling . . .

CHUBUKOV. And your housekeeper has got you under her thumb!

LOMOV. Oh! oh! oh! . . . My heart's burst! My shoulder's gone . . . Where's my shoulder? . . . I'm dying! [*drops into an armchair*] A doctor! [*faints*]

CHUBUKOV. Milksop! Puppy! Windbag! I'm feeling faint. [*drinks water*] Faint!

NATALYA. A sportsman indeed! You don't even know how to sit on a horse! [*to her father*] Papa! What's the matter with him? Papa! Look, Papa! [*shrieks*] Ivan Vasiliyevich! He's dead!

CHUBUKOV. I feel faint! . . . I'm suffocating! Give me air!

NATALYA. He's dead! [*shakes* LOMOV *by the sleeve*] Ivan Vasiliyich! Ivan Vasiliyich! What have we done! He's dead! [*drops into an armchair*] Doctor, doctor! [*sobs and laughs hysterically*]

CHUBUKOV. What now? What's the matter? What do you want?

NATALYA [*moans*]. He's dead! . . . Dead!

CHUBUKOV. Who's dead? [*glancing at* LOMOV] He really is dead! My God! Water! Doctor! [*holds a glass of water to* LOMOV's *lips*] Take a drink! . . . No, he won't drink . . . So he's dead and all that . . . What an unlucky man I am! Why don't I put a bullet through my brain? Why didn't I cut my throat long ago? What am I waiting for? Give me a knife! Give me a gun!

[LOMOV *makes a slight movement*]

I believe he's coming round . . . Do have a drink of water! That's right . . .

LOMOV. Flashes before my eyes . . . a sort of mist . . . Where am I?

CHUBUKOV. You'd better get married as soon as possible and – go to the devil . . . She consents. [*joins their hands*] She consents, and all the rest of it. I give you my blessing, and so forth. Only leave me alone!

LOMOV. Eh? What? [*getting up*] Who?

CHUBUKOV. She consents! Well? Kiss each other and . . . and the devil take you!

NATALYA [*moans*]. He's alive . . . Yes, yes, I consent . . .

CHUBUKOV. Come now, kiss each other!

LOMOV. Eh? Who? [*kisses* NATALYA] I am so pleased! . . . Excuse me, what's it all about? Ah! yes, I understand . . . My heart . . . flashes . . . I'm so happy, Natalya Stepanovna . . . [*kisses her hand*] My leg's numb . . .

NATALYA. I . . . I'm happy too . . .

CHUBUKOV. What a load off my back! . . . Ugh!

NATALYA. But . . . all the same, you must admit it now: Tryer is
   not as good a dog as Flyer.

LOMOV. He's better!

NATALYA. He's worse!

CHUBUKOV. There! Family happiness has begun! Bring the champagne!

LOMOV. He's better!

NATALYA. He's worse, worse, worse!

CHUBUKOV [*trying to shout them down*]. Champagne! Bring the
   champagne!

CURTAIN

A JUBILEE

A Jest in One Act

Characters in the Play

SHIPUCHIN, Andrey Andreyevich, the chairman of the Board
   of Directors of the —— Mutual Credit Society; middle-aged,
   wears a monocle
TATYANA ALEXEYEVNA, his wife, aged 25
KHIRIN, Kuzma Nikolayevich, an elderly bookkeeper at the Bank
MERCHUTKINA, Nastasya Fyodorovna, an old woman; wears an
   old-fashioned overcoat
SHAREHOLDERS
EMPLOYEES of the Bank

The action takes place at the offices of the — Mutual Credit Society.

A JUBILEE

The office of the Chairman of the Board of Directors. At left a door leading to the main office of the Bank. There are two desks. The room is furnished so as to give an impression of luxury — velvet-covered armchairs, flowers, statuary, carpets and a telephone. It is midday. KHIRIN *is alone; he is wearing felt boots.*

KHIRIN [*shouts through the door*]. Will you send to the chemist's for four pennyworth of valerian drops? And bring some fresh drinking water to the Chairman's office! Must I tell you a hundred times? [*goes over to one of the desks*] I'm quite worn out. I've been writing for three days now — I haven't slept a wink — writing the whole day here and the whole night at home. [*coughs*] And on top of all that I'm feeling feverish all over. I'm shivering, I've got a temperature and a cough — my legs ache and I keep seeing things like exclamation marks in front of my eyes! [*sits down*] That scoundrel, that buffoon of a Chairman is to read a report at our general meeting today. It's to be called: 'Our Bank, today and in the future.' He seems to fancy himself as a sort of Gambetta! [*writes*] Two . . . one . . . one . . . nought . . . one . . . six . . . He's trying to throw dust in their eyes, so I've got to sit here working for him like a galley-slave. All he did was to put into this report a lot of imaginative nonsense — that's all — the devil take him! . . . while I have to sit and click the counting beads the whole day long! [*works with the beads on the abacus*] I just hate it! . . . [*writes*] Well, it comes to . . . one . . . three . . . seven . . . two . . . one . . . nought . . . He's promised to reward me for my work. If all goes well today and he succeeds in hoodwinking the audience, he's promised to give me a gold badge and a bonus of three hundred roubles . . . We'll see. [*writes*] But if my efforts are wasted, my friend, you mustn't complain if . . .

I'm a hot-tempered man . . . When I'm roused I'm capable of committing a crime . . . Yes, indeed!

Noise and clapping off-stage. SHIPUCHIN's *voice is heard saying: 'Thank you! Thank you! I'm deeply touched!' Enter* SHIPUCHIN. *He wears evening dress and a white tie and is holding an album with which he has just been presented.*

SHIPUCHIN [*standing in the doorway and speaking into the office*]. My dear colleagues, I will cherish this gift till my dying day as a memento of the happiest occasion of my life! Yes, indeed, my dear friends! Thank you once again! [*kisses his hand to the audience and goes towards* KHIRIN] My dear, my most esteemed friend Kuzma Nikolayevich! [*while he remains on the stage employees come and go from time to time with papers for his signature*]

KHIRIN [*getting up*]. Andrey Andreyevich, may I have the honour of congratulating you on the fifteenth anniversary of our Bank and of wishing you . . .

SHIPUCHIN [*shaking his hand vigorously*]. Thank you, my dear friend. Thank you! We might even kiss to celebrate this day – this very special day – our jubilee! . . . [*they kiss*] I'm so very, very glad! Thank you for your services . . . for everything – thank you! If I've done anything useful during the time I've had the honour of being the Chairman of this Bank, I owe my success in the first place to my colleagues. [*sighs*] Yes, my friend, fifteen years! Fifteen years – that's a fact – as true as my name is Shipuchin. [*eagerly*] Well, how's my report? Getting on?

KHIRIN. Yes, I've only got five more pages to do.

SHIPUCHIN. That's fine. Then it'll be ready by three o'clock?

KHIRIN. If nothing prevents me I'll finish it by then. There's only a trifle still to be done.

SHIPUCHIN. Excellent! Excellent! That's a fact – as true as my name's Shipuchin! The general meeting is at four o'clock. My friend, give me the first half, I'll go through it . . . Give it to me quickly . . . [*takes the report*] I pin my highest hopes on this report . . . This is my *profession de foi* or, to put it more accurately, my firework display! . . . My firework display – that's a fact, as true as my name's Shipuchin! [*sits down and reads the report to himself*] I feel devilish tired though . . . I had an attack of gout last night and the whole morning I've been fussing and running around . . . Then all these ovations, and the emotion and agitation . . . I am tired!

KHIRIN [*writes*]. Two . . . nought . . . nought . . . three . . . nine . . . two . . . nought . . . Everything's going green in front of my eyes with all these figures . . . Three . . . one . . . six . . . four . . . one . . . five . . . [*clicks the beads of the abacus*]

SHIPUCHIN. Then there was an unpleasant episode . . . This morning your wife came to see me and complained about you again. She told me that last night you'd been chasing her with a knife – and your sister-in-law, too . . . That sort of thing won't do, Kuzma Nikolayich! It really won't do at all!

KHIRIN [*sternly*]. Andrey Andreyich, since this is our jubilee day, may I take the liberty of making a request? I beg you not to interfere with my family life, if only out of consideration for the incredibly hard work I'm doing here. Please don't!

SHIPUCHIN [*sighs*]. You're an impossible character, Kuzma Nikolayich. You're a good man, really, quite a respectable fellow, and yet with women you behave like Jack the Ripper, or someone of that sort. Really, I can't understand why you hate them so!

KHIRIN. And I can't understand why you love them so.

[*a pause*]

SHIPUCHIN. The employees have just presented me with an album and I hear that the shareholders are going to present me with an address and a silver tankard . . . [*plays with his monocle*] That's fine! As true as my name's Shipuchin! It won't do any harm! . . . A certain amount of ceremony is necessary for the reputation of the bank, devil take it! You're one of us, so you know all about it, of course . . . I composed the address myself, and as for the silver tankard – I bought that too. I also bought the cover for the address – that cost me forty-five roubles, but it can't be helped! They wouldn't have thought of it themselves. [*looks round*] What a fine set of furniture though! What a collection! There! They say I pay too much attention to trifles, that I only want the door handles polished, the employees to wear smart ties and a fat porter to stand at the front door. But no, my dear sirs! The door handles and the fat porter are not trifles! I can be as much of a plebeian as I like at home, I can eat and sleep like a pig, I can have my drinking bouts . . .

KHIRIN. I beg you to refrain from making insinuations! . . .

SHIPUCHIN. Oh, I'm not insinuating anything! What an impossible character you are! . . . I was just saying that at home I can be a plebeian, a parvenu if I like: I can indulge my habits – whereas here everything must be on the grand scale. This is a bank. Here every detail must impress, everything must have a solemn air, so to speak. [*picks up a scrap of paper from the floor and throws it into the fireplace*] My chief merit lies simply in this – I've raised the reputation of the Bank to a very high level! . . . It's the tone of the whole thing that matters so much! That's a fact – as true as my name's Shipuchin! [*looks* KHIRIN *up and down*] My dear fellow, the deputation from the shareholders may be here at any moment – and you're wearing felt boots and that scarf . . . and your jacket's a simply incredible colour . . . You might have put on a frock coat, or at least a black jacket . . .

KHIRIN. My health is more important to me than all your share-holders. I've got inflammation all over me . . .

SHIPUCHIN [*agitated*]. But you must agree that this is out of place! You're spoiling the whole effect!

KHIRIN. I can hide if the deputation comes. As if it mattered! [*writes*] Seven . . . one . . . seven . . . two . . . one . . . five . . . nought . . . I don't like things being out of place myself! Seven . . . two . . . nine . . . [*clicks the beads of the abacus*] I simply can't stand things being out of place! You'd have done better not to invite ladies to the jubilee dinner today . . .

SHIPUCHIN. What nonsense!

KHIRIN. I know you'd like to fill the hall with them today just to show off, but you'd better watch out! They might mess up the whole thing for you! They cause nothing but trouble and disorder.

SHIPUCHIN. On the contrary, the society of women is elevating!

KHIRIN. Indeed! . . . Take your wife for instance. She's supposed to be well educated, but last Monday she blurted something out – and it took me two days to get over it. All of a sudden she comes and asks me in the presence of strangers: 'Is it true that my husband bought a lot of Driashko-Priashko shares for our bank, and then the price fell on the Stock Exchange? My husband is so worried!' And all that in the presence of strangers! I just can't understand why you confide in women! Do you want them to land you in court?

SHIPUCHIN. That'll do, that'll do! This is all too gloomy for our jubilee day. By the way, you've just reminded me. [*looks at his watch*] My dear wife is due to arrive quite soon. In fact, I ought to have gone to the station to meet her – poor little thing! But there's no time and . . . and I feel too tired. To tell you the truth, I'm not very pleased that she's coming at all. I mean I am pleased, but it would have been better still if she'd stayed at her mother's a day or two longer. She'll insist on my spending the whole evening with her, and we'd planned a little expedition for tonight after dinner . . . [*starts*] You see, I'm beginning to tremble from sheer nervousness. My nerves are so on edge that I feel a mere trifle might make me burst into tears . . . No, no, I must be strong . . . that's a fact – as true as my name's Shipuchin!

Enter TATYANA ALEXEYEVNA. *She wears a raincoat and has a travelling handbag on a strap over her shoulder.*

SHIPUCHIN. Ah! We'd just been talking about you – and here you are!

TATYANA. Darling! [*runs to her husband; a prolonged kiss*]

SHIPUCHIN. Yes, we were just talking about you . . . [*looks at his watch*]

TATYANA [*breathlessly*]. Did you miss me? Are you well? I haven't been home yet – I've come straight here from the station. I've got such a lot to tell you, such a lot! . . . I can hardly wait . . . I won't take my things off – I'll only stay a minute. [*to* KHIRIN] How do you do, Kuzma Nikolayich? [*to her husband*] Is everything all right at home?

SHIPUCHIN. Yes, everything's all right. I believe you've got plumper and prettier during the week you've been away . . . Well, did you have a nice trip?

TATYANA. Excellent! Mamma and Katya send you their greetings. Vasiliy Andreyich told me to give you a kiss. [*kisses him*] Auntie sent you a pot of jam, and everyone's cross with you for not writing. Zina said I was to kiss you from her. [*kisses him*] Oh, if you only knew the things that have been happening! The things that have been happening! It makes me frightened even to speak of it! Such goings-on! But I see from your expression you're not really glad to have me back!

SHIPUCHIN. On the contrary! . . . Darling! [kisses her]

[KHIRIN coughs angrily]

TATYANA [sighs]. Poor dear Katya, the poor darling! I'm so sorry for her, so very sorry!

SHIPUCHIN. My dear, we're celebrating our jubilee today. A deputation from the shareholders may be here at any moment, and you're not properly dressed.

TATYANA. Of course – the jubilee! Congratulations, my friends! I wish you . . . So there's going to be a reception and a dinner! That's what I like! . . . By the way, you remember that beautiful speech you've been composing for the shareholders – it took you such a time! – are they going to read it to you today?

[KHIRIN coughs angrily]

SHIPUCHIN [embarrassed]. Darling, it isn't usual to talk about such things . . . Really, you'd better go home.

TATYANA. In a moment, in a moment! . . . It won't take me a minute to tell you, and then I'll go. I'll tell you everything from the beginning. Well . . . After you'd seen me off I sat down beside that stout lady – you remember – and began to read. I don't like talking on railway journeys. So I kept on reading until we'd passed three stations, and didn't exchange a word with anybody. Then evening came on and I began to have all sorts of depressing thoughts. A young man was sitting opposite me – a fellow with dark hair, not at all bad-looking . . . Well, we got talking . . . A naval man joined in, then a sort of student . . . [laughs] I told them I wasn't married . . . What a fuss they made of me! We chatted right on till midnight. The dark-haired fellow was telling screamingly funny stories, and the naval man kept on singing. I laughed so much that my chest began to ache. And when the navy man – oh, these sailors! – when he found out that my name was Tatyana, do you know what he started singing? [sings in a bass voice]

        'Onegin, I cannot deny,
        I'll love Tatyana till I die' . . .

[breaks into laughter. KHIRIN coughs angrily]

SHIPUCHIN. All the same, Tanyusha, we're disturbing Kuzma Nikolayich. Do go home, darling . . . You can tell me afterwards.

TATYANA. Never mind, never mind, let him hear it too. It's most interesting. I won't be long telling you. Well, Seryozha met me at the station. Another young man turned up, too – a tax-inspector, I think – quite a nice-looking fellow – especially his eyes . . . Seryozha introduced us and we all took a cab . . . The weather was wonderful . . .

Voices off-stage: 'You mustn't go in there! It's not allowed. What do you want?' Enter MERCHUTKINA.

MERCHUTKINA [*in the doorway, waving her arms at someone outside*]. You don't need to grab at me! What next! I want to see the chief . . . [*comes in, to* SHIPUCHIN] May I have the honour of introducing myself, your Excellency? I'm Nastasya Fyodorovna Merchutkina . . . a provincial secretary's wife . . .

SHIPUCHIN. What can I do for you?

MERCHUTKINA. If it please your Excellency, it's like this: my husband, provincial secretary Merchutkin, has been ill five months, and while he was at home receiving treatment, they dismissed him from his job without any reason, your Excellency. And when I went to get his pay, they'd gone and deducted twenty-four roubles thirty-six kopecks if you please! Whatever for, I ask you? They told me he'd borrowed from the Mutual Aid Fund and other people had guaranteed the loan. But how could that have happened? As if he'd borrow anything without asking my permission first! They shouldn't have done it, your Excellency. I'm a poor woman – I can only keep myself going by taking lodgers . . . I'm weak and defenceless . . . I have to put up with insults from everybody, and I never hear a kind word from anyone.

SHIPUCHIN. Excuse me . . . [*takes her application from her and reads it standing up*]

TATYANA [*to* KHIRIN]. But I must begin at the beginning . . . Last week I unexpectedly got a letter from mamma. She wrote to tell me that a certain Grendilevsky had made a proposal of marriage to my sister Katya. A very nice, modest young man, but entirely without means, or any definite position in life. And unfortun-ately – just imagine it – Katya was rather attracted by him. What was to be done? So mamma asked me to come at once and use my influence with Katya . . .

KHIRIN [*sternly*]. Excuse me, you've made me lose my place! . . . You – your mamma and Katya – and now I don't know where I am and I'm all mixed up!

TATYANA. As if it mattered! You should listen when a lady is talking to you! Why are you so cross today, anyway? Are you in love, or what? [*laughs*]

SHIPUCHIN [*to* MERCHUTKINA]. Excuse me, what's all this about? I don't understand . . .

TATYANA. Are you in love? Ah-ah! You're blushing!

SHIPUCHIN [*to his wife*]. Tanyusha, darling, please go into the office for a minute. I won't be long.

TATYANA. Very well. [*goes out*]

SHIPUCHIN. I don't understand this at all. Obviously, madam, you've come to the wrong place. In fact, your business has nothing whatever to do with us. You should apply to the department where your husband used to be employed.

MERCHUTKINA. But sir, I've been to five different places already and they wouldn't even read my application. I just couldn't think what else I could do – but my son–in–law, Boris Matveyich – I'm grateful to him – he gave me the idea of coming to you. 'Go to Mr Shipuchin, mamma,' he says, 'he's an influential gentleman, he can do anything.' . . . Please, your Excellency, do help me!

SHIPUCHIN. Madam Merchutkina, we really can't do anything for you. Do please understand: your husband, as far as I can make out, worked in the Medical Department of the War Office, whereas our institution here is a private one, a commercial concern, a bank. Can't you understand that?

MERCHUTKINA. As for my husband's illness, your Excellency, I have the doctor's certificate to prove it. Here it is, if you'd be kind enough to look at it . . .

SHIPUCHIN [*with irritation*]. That's excellent. I believe you, but I repeat – it doesn't concern us.

[TATYANA's *laughter is heard off-stage; then a man's laughter*]
[*glancing at the door*] She's interrupting the work of the clerks out there. [*to* MERCHUTKINA] It's a queer business and even rather absurd. Doesn't your husband know where you have to apply?

MERCHUTKINA. My husband doesn't know anything, your Excellency. All he keeps saying is: 'It's not your business! Get out!' That's all.

SHIPUCHIN. I must repeat, madam, your husband was employed at the Medical Department of the War Office, whereas this is a bank, a private commercial institution . . .

MERCHUTKINA. Just so, just so . . . I understand, sir . . . So would you please tell them to pay me just fifteen roubles, your Excellency? I don't mind not having all of it at once.

SHIPUCHIN [*sighs*]. Ough!

KHIRIN. Andrey Andreyich, I shall never finish the report at this rate!

SHIPUCHIN. Just a moment. [*to* MERCHUTKINA] You don't seem to be able to take it in. Please try to understand that to make a request like this from us is just as absurd as to apply for a divorce at . . . let's say at a chemist's shop or at the Assay Office . . .

[*a knock on the door;* TATYANA's *voice off-stage: 'Andrey, can I come in?'*]

SHIPUCHIN [*shouts*]. Wait a bit, darling! In a minute! [*to* MERCHUTKINA] You weren't given his full pay, but what has it got to do with us? Besides, madam, we're having a jubilee today – we're busy, and . . . someone might come in here at any moment . . . Please excuse me . . .

MERCHUTKINA. Your Excellency, do have pity on an orphan woman! I'm weak and defenceless . . . I feel so worn out, I might just as well be dead . . . The things I have to do – taking lodgers to court, running round on my husband's affairs, looking after the house – and now my son-in-law is out of a job, too.

SHIPUCHIN. Madam Merchutkina, I . . . No, forgive me, I can't talk to you! My head's going round and round . . . You're disturbing us, and you're wasting your own time too . . . [*sighs, apart*] What a dunderhead! And that's a fact – as true as my name's Shipuchin! [*to* KHIRIN] Kuzma Nikolayich, please explain to Madam Merchutkina . . . [*makes a hopeless gesture and goes out into the office*]

KHIRIN [*approaches* MERCHUTKINA, *sternly*]. What is it you want?

MERCHUTKINA. I'm a weak, defenceless woman . . . I may look strong, but if you could take me to bits and look at me properly, you'd see there isn't a single healthy bit in my body! I can hardly keep on my feet, and my appetite's all gone. I drank some coffee this morning – and I didn't enjoy it a bit . . .

KHIRIN. I'm asking you a question – what is it you want?

MERCHUTKINA. Please, sir, just tell them to pay me fifteen roubles. I can wait a month or so for the rest.

KHIRIN. But surely you've just been told in plain language that this is a bank!

MERCHUTKINA. Of course, of course . . . And if necessary, I can show you the medical certificate.

KHIRIN. Have you or have you not got a head on your shoulders?

MERCHUTKINA. Kind sir, I'm only asking for what is legally due to me. I don't want anything that isn't mine.

KHIRIN. Madam, I'm asking you a simple question: have you a head on your shoulders, or is it something else? . . . Well, devil take it, I haven't the time to talk to you! I'm busy! [*shows her the door*] Please!

MERCHUTKINA [*surprised*]. But what about the money? . . .

KHIRIN. The fact is that you haven't got a head at all, you've got this instead . . . [*taps the desk and then his forehead with his finger*].

MERCHUTKINA [*offended*]. What's that? You mind your own business! You can do that sort of thing with your own wife, not with me . . . I'm a government official's wife . . . You'd better not take any liberties with me!

KHIRIN [*flaring up, in a low voice*]. If you don't go away this minute, I'll send for the hall-porter! Out with you! [*stamps his feet*]

MERCHUTKINA. Steady, steady! I'm not scared of you! We've seen the likes of you before . . . Pen-pusher! . . .

KHIRIN. I don't believe I've ever seen anyone looking so repulsive in my life! Ough! She makes me feel quite dizzy with anger . . . [*breathes heavily*] I'll tell you once more . . . D'you hear? If you don't go away from here, I'll grind you to powder, you old fright! I've got such a temper that I'm capable of making a cripple of you for life! I'm capable of any crime!

MERCHUTKINA. Your bark's worse than your bite! I'm not afraid of you. I've seen the likes of you before.

KHIRIN [*in despair*]. I can't bear to look at her! I feel quite sick! I can't stand it! [*goes to his desk and sits down*] He's filled the bank with petticoats – how can I get on with the report – I just can't!

MERCHUTKINA. I'm not asking for anything that's not mine; I'm asking for what belongs to me by law. You shameless fellow! wearing felt boots in a place like this! You yokel!

Enter SHIPUCHIN *and* TATYANA.

TATYANA [*following her husband*]. Well, then we went to an evening party at the Berezhnitskys. Katya was wearing a little blue taffeta frock trimmed with fine lace, with a low neck . . . It suits her so to have her hair done in a pile on top of her head, and I arranged it myself. When she was dressed and had her hair done, she looked simply enchanting!

SHIPUCHIN [*he is suffering from migraine*]. Quite so, quite so . . . Enchanting . . . Someone may be coming any moment now . . .

MERCHUTKINA. Your Excellency!

SHIPUCHIN [*dispirited*]. What now? What do you want?

MERCHUTKINA. Your Excellency! [*points at* KHIRIN] That man there . . . Yes, him . . . He tapped on the desk, and then on his forehead . . . You told him to look into my case, but he's just being sarcastic and saying all sorts of things . . . I'm a weak, defenceless woman . . .

SHIPUCHIN. Very well, madam . . . I'll look into it . . . and take the appropriate measures . . . Just go away now . . . Later on! . . . [*aside*] I've got an attack of gout coming on! . . .

KHIRIN [*approaching* SHIPUCHIN, *in a low voice*]. Andrey Andreyevich, allow me to send for the hall-porter and tell him to throw her out of here. This is getting impossible!

SHIPUCHIN [*alarmed*]. No, no! She'll start screaming – there are a lot of private dwellings in this building!

MERCHUTKINA. Your Excellency!

KHIRIN [*in a tearful voice*]. But I've got to write the report! I shan't have time to finish it! [*returns to his desk*] I just can't go on!

MERCHUTKINA. Your Excellency, when am I going to be paid the money, please? I need it right now.

SHIPUCHIN [*aside, indignantly*]. What an extraordinarily repulsive woman! [*to* MERCHUTKINA, *in a gentle voice*] Madam, I have already informed you that this is a bank, a private commercial concern . . .

MERCHUTKINA. Be kind to me, your Excellency, be a father to an orphan woman! . . . If the medical certificate isn't enough, I can get a paper from the police too. Do tell them to pay me the money!

SHIPUCHIN [*sighs heavily*]. Ough!

TATYANA [*to* MERCHUTKINA]. But Granny, haven't they told you that you're in the way here? You really are a strange person!

MERCHUTKINA. Madam, my beautiful lady, I've nobody to help me with my troubles . . . Eating and drinking don't mean a thing . . . I had coffee this morning, and I didn't enjoy it the least little bit.

SHIPUCHIN [*at the end of his tether, to* MERCHUTKINA]. How much is it you want?

MERCHUTKINA. Twenty-four roubles thirty-six kopecks.

SHIPUCHIN. Very well! [*takes a 25-rouble note out of his wallet and gives it to her*] Here's twenty-five roubles for you. Take it and . . . please go away!

[KHIRIN *coughs angrily*]

MERCHUTKINA. Thank you kindly, your Excellency. [*puts the money away*]

TATYANA [*sits down beside her husband*]. I ought to be going home though . . . [*looks at her watch*] But I haven't quite finished telling you yet . . . I'll finish in a moment, then I'll go . . . The things that have been happening! Oh, the things that have been happening! Well, we went along to the party at Berezhnitsky's . . . It was so-so, quite jolly, but not specially jolly . . . Katya's admirer, Grendilevsky, was there too, of course . . . Well, I had a talk with Katya, I cried a little, I used my influence with her and she agreed to talk it over with Grendilevsky there and then at the party, and she refused him. Now, I thought, everything's straightened out as well as anyone could wish. I've made mamma happy, I've saved Katya, and now I can relax a bit too. But what do you think? Just before supper Katya and I were taking a stroll in the garden and suddenly . . . [*agitated*] And suddenly we heard a shot! No, I can't speak of it calmly! [*fans herself with her handkerchief*] I just can't! . . .

SHIPUCHIN [*sighs*]. Ough!

TATYANA [*weeping*]. We ran to the summer house and there . . . there lay poor Grendilevsky . . . with a pistol in his hand . . .

SHIPUCHIN. No, I just can't bear it! I can't bear it! [*to* MERCHUTKINA] Now what do you want?

MERCHUTKINA. Please your Excellency, could my husband have his job back?

TATYANA [*weeping*]. He'd shot straight at his heart . . . just there . . . Katya dropped down in a dead faint, poor dear . . . And he, too, was dreadfully scared . . . He just lay there and . . . and begged us to send for the doctor. The doctor came quite soon and . . . saved the unfortunate young man . . .

MERCHUTKINA. Your Excellency, could my husband have his job back?

SHIPUCHIN. No! – I can't bear this any longer! [*weeps*] I really can't! [*stretching both his arms towards* KHIRIN, *in despair*] Turn her out! Turn her out, I implore you!

KHIRIN [*coming up to* TATYANA]. Get out of here!

SHIPUCHIN. No, not her – that one . . . that horror . . . [*pointing at* MERCHUTKINA] That one!

KHIRIN [*not understanding him, to* TATYANA]. Get out of here! [*stamps his feet*] Get out, I tell you!

TATYANA. What? What are you saying? Are you mad?

SHIPUCHIN. This is dreadful! How unfortunate I am! Make her go away! Go on, turn her out!

KHIRIN [*to* TATYANA]. Out of here! I'll make a cripple of you! I'll smash you to pieces. I'll commit a crime!

TATYANA [*runs away from him while he chases her*]. How dare you? You're being extremely impertinent! Andrey! Save me! Andrey! [*screams*]

SHIPUCHIN [*running after them*]. Do stop this, I implore you! Be quiet! Spare my reputation!

KHIRIN [*chases after* MERCHUTKINA]. Get out of here! Catch her! Smash her to pulp! Make mincemeat of her!

SHIPUCHIN [*shouts*]. Stop, stop! I beg you! I implore you!

MERCHUTKINA. Holy Fathers! . . . Saints! . . . [*screams*] Holy Fathers! . . .

TATYANA [*shouts*]. Help! Save me! Oh! Oh! . . . I feel faint! I'm fainting! [*jumps on to a chair, then falls down on to a sofa and moans as if in a swoon*]

KHIRIN [*chasing* MERCHUTKINA]. Smash her! Flay her alive! Cut her to pieces!

MERCHUTKINA. Oh! oh! Holy Fathers! . . . Everything's going black in front of my eyes! Oh! [*drops senseless into* SHIPUCHIN's *arms. A knock on the door. A voice off-stage says: 'The deputation'.*]

SHIPUCHIN. Deputation . . . reputation . . . occupation . . .

KHIRIN [*stamping his feet*]. Get out! The devil take it! [*pulls up his sleeves*] Just let me get hold of her! I could commit a crime!

Enter a deputation of five men all dressed in frock-coats. One holds the address in a velvet cover, another the silver tankard. Employees of the bank look in through the open office door. TATYANA *is on the sofa,* MERCHUTKINA *in* SHIPUCHIN's *arms, both moaning softly.*

A SHAREHOLDER [*reads in a loud voice*]. Our dear and most respected friend, Andrey Andreyevich! As we cast a retrospective glance at the past of our financial institution and survey in our mind's eye the history of its gradual development, we receive an impression which is, in the highest degree, satisfactory and refreshing. It is no doubt true that in its early stages the small dimensions of its original capital, its failure to carry through any big financial operations, and the indefinite character of its aims, set before us in sharpest outline Hamlet's question: 'To be or not to be?' In fact, at one time voices were raised suggesting that the bank should be closed. But then you put yourself at the head of our concern. Your knowledge, your energy, your outstanding gift of tact – all these qualities brought about extraordinary success and exceptional prosperity . . . The reputation of the Bank . . . [*coughs*] The reputation of the Bank . . .

MERCHUTKINA [*groans*]. Oh! Oh!

TATYANA [*moans*]. Water! Water!

SHAREHOLDER [*continues*]. The reputation . . . [*coughs*] the reputation of the Bank has been raised by you to such heights that our institution can now compete with the best concerns abroad . . .

SHIPUCHIN. Deputation . . . reputation . . . occupation . . .

> 'One night two friends went out for a walk
> And as they strolled they had an earnest talk . . .'
> 'Oh, do not say your youthful life is ruined –
> That through my jealousy you suffered pains untold' . . .

SHAREHOLDER [*continues in embarrassment*]. Then, as we cast a realistic glance at the present, our dear and most respected friend, Andrey Andreyevich . . . [*dropping his voice*] In the circumstances we'd better postpone it . . . It will be better to postpone it . . .

> [*they go out in confusion*]

CURTAIN

244 Educate two worker
work two educator